The Status of Women in Jewish Law: Responsa

by

David Golinkin

The Center for Women in Jewish Law
at the Schechter Institute of Jewish Studies

Jerusalem 2012

ISBN 978-965-7105-69-6

Distribution:
Schechter Institute of Jewish Studies
POB 16080, Jerusalem 91160 Israel

Tel. 074-7800-600
Fax 02-6790840
schechter@schechter.ac.il
www.schechter.edu

Produced by Leshon Limudim Ltd., Jerusalem
leshon@netvision.net.il
Printed in Israel

In memory of my mother and teacher

Devorah Golinkin z"l (1922-2012)

Wife, mother and grandmother
Spanish professor and Hebrew teacher

and

my friend and colleague

Rabbi Monique Süsskind Goldberg z"l (1947-2012)

Rabbi and Scholar
one of the *lamed-vovniks*

This book was published thanks
to generous support from the

David Berg Foundation

and

Aharon and Tony Weber
and their family
in memory of
Rabbi Monique Süsskind Goldberg z"l

TABLE OF CONTENTS

PREFACE

Our Sages said: "*Im yomar... Yagata velo matzata, al taamein* – if he says to you... you toiled and did not find, don't believe" (*Megillah* 6b). I have been toiling on and off on this book for 25 years. Ten of the responsa were originally written for the Va'ad Halakhah of the Rabbinical Assembly of Israel between 1987 and 1999 and I thank the members of the Va'ad for their comments at the time.

Initial encouragement to translate those responsa into English came from Profs. David Ellenson and Shaye Cohen and initial financial support came from my Uncle Rabbi Baruch G. Goldstein and from Prof. Menahem Schmelzer and the Kazis Publication Fund of the Jewish Theological Seminary. Initial translations were done by Dahlia Friedman, Zippy Brody z"l and Rabbi Yosef Kleiner,

In the interim, a collection of my Hebrew responsa about women entitled *Ma'amad Ha'ishah Bahalakhah: She'eilot Uteshuvot* was published by the Center for Women in Jewish Law at the Schechter Institute in 2001.

The current translations of those ten responsa and one of the introductory essays were prepared by Rabbi Monique Susskind Goldberg z"l and *tibadel lehayyim* Rabbi Diana Villa and completed by myself.

In addition, this volume contains a second introduction about women and Jewish law from 1845–2010, which was published in *NASHIM* in 2011, as well as five new responsa which I had published in English in my "Responsa in a Moment" column at www.schechter.edu during the past few years.

In the current volume, I have added some new material to the notes and the bibliography of each chapter. I did not, however, attempt to update all of the responsa. For example, at least fifty new items regarding women and Torah study (Chapter 15, paragraph II) have appeared since 2001, but they have not been added to the bibliography.

Since the fifteen responsa in this volume were written over the course of 25 years – ten in Hebrew and five in English – it is not surprising that the style varies somewhat between the responsa. But the general approach does not. I try to examine every halakhic topic in a thorough fashion from the Bible until the most recent discussions. I have explained elsewhere my general approach to writing responsa (*Responsa in a Moment,* Jerusalem, 2000, pp. 11–21) and I have explained below my general approach towards women and Jewish law (see pp. 41 and 347).

I hope and pray that these two introductory essays and fifteen responsa will help modern Jews grapple with one of the most important halakhic topics of our time.

I would like to thank all of the people mentioned above for their assistance in preparing this volume for publication as well as Donny Finkel and Dahlia Friedman at Leshon Limudim who typeset the book and Linda Price and the staff of Stefanie and Ruti who prepared the cover. However, all opinions expressed here are my own.

My heartfelt gratitude is extended to the David Berg Foundation in New York and the Weber family in Tel Aviv for their generous financial support of this project.

This book is dedicated to two very special women who passed away this year and for whom I am now reciting *Kaddish* – my mother Devorah Golinkin z"l who would have turned 90 today and my friend and colleague Rabbi Monique Susskind Goldberg z"l. Rather than say a brief sentence about them in this preface, I have included my eulogies for them at the end of this volume. I felt that in a volume dedicated to women and Jewish law, we could do no better than to learn from these two amazing role models. *Yehi zikhran barukh*!

David Golinkin
The Schechter Institute of Jewish Studies
Jerusalem
18 Elul 5772

Introductory Essays

THE PARTICIPATION OF JEWISH WOMEN IN PUBLIC RITUALS AND TORAH STUDY 1845-2010

There is no question that Jewish women today play a much greater role in public Jewish ritual life and Torah study than they did 150 years ago. Women now participate freely and regularly in roles that were once reserved for men. Some scholars date these changes to the feminist revolution of the 1960s and 1970s.[1] Indeed, it is true that there has been an acceleration of such changes during the past forty years, but, to understand this topic, one must begin in 1845, not in the 1970s. In this article, we shall survey forty-one events which occurred in relation to our topic since 1845 and then draw seven general conclusions from this timeline of events.[2]

I. A Timeline of Change 1845-2010

In 1845, the Reform Congregation of Berlin abolished the women's gallery and the *meḥitzah*. Henceforth, men and women sat on the same floor but in separate sections, men on the left and women on the right. In the early 20th century, the Hamburg Temple, the cradle of German Reform, refused a donation of one million marks from the German-American banker Henry Budge because the donation was conditional on "men and women

1. See Anne Lapidus Lerner, *American Jewish Year Book* 77 (1977), pp. 3–38; Sylvia Barack Fishman, *ibid.* 89 (1989), pp. 7 ff.; *idem., A Breath of Life: Feminism in the American Jewish Community*, New York, 1993, pp. 6 ff.; Jonathan Sarna, *American Judaism: A History*, New York, 2004, pp. 338–344.
2. Much of the information cited below was originally discovered by other scholars. In order to save space, I have mentioned their names in the notes without repeating them in the text of the article.

sitting together". Indeed, in the Hamburg Temple, men and women sat separately until the Shoah.[3]

At the Breslau Rabbinical Conference of 1846, Rabbi David Einhorn submitted the following resolution:

> The Rabbinical Conference declares that the woman is equal to the man in all religious rights and obligations: that the woman is obligated in positive time-bound commandments, to the extent that such commandments still have relevance for us. The blessing "who has not made me a woman" shall be erased from the prayers; a woman shall be obligated from her youth to participate in religious education and in public prayer and shall be counted in the *minyan* of ten; the woman like the man is considered an adult at age thirteen.[4]

This resolution was never voted on for lack of time, but it indicates the direction of the more radical reformers such as Einhorn in the 1840s.

Around that time, an Orthodox woman named Rivka Hina, who was the granddaughter of Rabbi Ḥayyim of Volozhin (1749-1821), was given *semikhah* by her husband Rabbi Eliezer (Laizer) Halevi of Grodno (d. 1853). Rabbi Laizer was a *dayan* who studied at home. He would sequester himself in his study and his wife Rivka Hina would pass the queries of the townswomen to him through the door. She became proficient in handling questions about the *kashrut* of slaughtered fowl. Her grandson Yeḥezkel Kotik (1847-1921) reports that "her husband listened to her evaluation and tested her, and then granted her *semikhah* to decide easy questions".[5] This story is *sui generis* and had no later

3. Jonathan Sarna, "Mixed Seating in the American Synagogue" in: Jack Wertheimer, ed., *The American Synagogue: A Sanctuary Transformed,* Cambridge, 1987, p. 364.
4. *Protokolle der dritten Versammlung deutscher Rabbiner...,* Breslau, 1847, pp. 264-265 = *JQR* 18 (1906), pp. 655-656 = *Ve'idot Harabbanim B'germania Bashanim 1844-1846,* Jerusalem, 1986, p. 65. For further details, see Michael Meyer, *Bein Masoret L'kidmah,* Jerusalem, 1989, pp. 164-165 and note 148.
5. Yeḥezkel Kotik, *Meine Zikhroiness,* Vol. 1, Berlin, 1922, p. 171 = *Mah Shera'iti,*

echoes in Jewish law or life, but it may indicate that Orthodox Rabbis are more flexible about women's participation when it occurs in a natural fashion without connection to feminism or mass demand.

The first Reform temple with "family pews", i.e. mixed seating, was established in Albany, New York in October 1851. Rabbi Isaac Mayer Wise, who later founded Hebrew Union College, was fired from Beth El Congregation two days before Rosh Hashanah in 1850. He and his supporters than established a new congregation called Anshe Emeth. They purchased a former Baptist Church and they unanimously decided to retain the family pews in that building. According to this account, family pews entered Judaism for pragmatic rather than ideological reasons.[6]

Rabbi Ya'akov Ettlinger (1798-1871) was one of the leading Orthodox Rabbis in the nineteenth century. In December 1866, he officiated and spoke at the first Confirmation ceremony for girls at the great synagogue of Altona. Thirty-six years before, in 1830, he had opposed such ceremonies in Baden and allowed them only if they did not disturb the regular service and if the grown women sat separately from the men. In 1866, he was forced to allow such ceremonies because Prussia took over Altona in 1864 and obligated Confirmation as part of the laws of equality. His speech is quite apologetic, explaining the difference between Christian Confirmation and this ceremony which "includes the *mitzvah* of *Kiddush Hashem*, the sanctification of God's name, which is considered by us one of our most important *mitzvot*". After giving the girls the formal exam obligated by law, and before his speech, the synagogue's boys' choir sang the first 16 verses of Psalm 119 which deal with the observance of *mitzvot* and the love of Torah. At the end of his speech, Rabbi Ettlinger

edited by David Assaf, Jerusalem, 1998, p. 230 = David Assaf, *Journey to a Nineteenth Century Shtetl: The Memoirs of Yeḥezkel Kotik*, Detroit, 2002, p. 252. I learned about this episode from Brenda S. Bacon, *Nashim* 15 (2008), pp. 47-48.

6. Sarna (above, note 3), pp. 364-368.

turned to the girls and recited a paraphrase of "*Yesimekh Elohim*" and the Priestly Blessing (Numbers 6:24-26), normally recited on Friday nights.

Thus, it seems that Rabbi Ettlinger took a ceremony which was forced upon him by the Prussian government and turned it into a religious ceremony for Jewish girls.[7]

Rabbi Mordecai Kaplan is usually credited with inventing the *Bat Mitzvah* ceremony in 1922 (see below). But in fact, this ceremony began in different forms in Italy, France and Baghdad in the nineteenth century.

In the communities of Torino and Milano in the second half of the 19th century, the girls used to gather on a weekday in the synagogue together with their families, schoolmates, the congregation and the Chief Rabbi. The ceremony took place in front of the Holy Ark. The girls dressed in white and sometimes put wreaths of flowers in their hair. The Ark was opened and the girls took turns reciting the verses of a lengthy prayer. It is a combination of *Birkat Hagomel, Sheheḥeyanu* and various verses. It is a declaration of Jewish faith, of *Kiddush Hashem* and of the willingness to speak up against the "misleaders". This ceremony later migrated with Italian Jews to Alexandria as well as to Tunis in the 1930s. The prayer sounds like a Hebrew translation of a Confirmation prayer and some scholars say that it is similar to the Catholic ceremonies of learning the Catechism and First Communion.[8]

In his responsum about the *Bat Mitzvah*, Rabbi Yitzḥak Nissim quotes a handwritten responsum by Rabbi Avraham Musafiyah,

7. See Avraham (Rami) Reiner, "The Attitude to *Bat Mitzvah* Ceremonies" etc., *Netu'im* 10 (5763), pp. 55-64. For opposition to Confirmation for girls, see Rabbi Aharon Walkin (1865-1942), *Responsa Zekan Aharon*, Vol. 1, Pinsk, 1932, No. 6.
8. For the lengthy prayer, see Aharon Cohen, *Zeved Habat*, Jerusalem, 1990, pp. 26-27, which is reprinted in Aliza Lavi, *Tefillat Nashim*, Tel Aviv, 2007, p. 42. For a description of the ceremony, see Cohen as well as Shalom Tsabar *et al*, *Ma'agal Haḥayyim*, Jerusalem, 2006, pp. 176-177, which includes photographs from Rome (1920) and Tunis (ca. 1930). My thanks to Dr. Roni Weinstein who referred me to the latter work.

son of Rabbi Ḥayyim Yitzḥak Musafiyah (Jerusalem 1760 – Split 1837). Rabbi Avraham wrote that

> he who makes a *se'udah* [feast] on the day that his daughter reaches the age of *mitzvot,* i.e. 12 years and one day, it seems to me that it is a *se'udat mitzvah* [a *mitzvah* feast] like a boy at 13 years and one day, for what is the difference? And this is a correct custom, and so do they make a *se'udat mitzvah* and a day of joy in the cities of France and other towns for a boy and also for a girl, and the practical *halakhic* implication is that if he is invited, he must go.[9]

The third Rabbi in the 19th century who permitted a *Bat Mitzvah* celebration was Rabbi Yosef Ḥayyim of Baghdad (ca. 1833-1909), author of *Ben Ish Ḥay, Responsa Rav Pe'alim* and other *halakhic* works. His *Ben Ish Ḥay* was first printed in 1899, but it includes sermons from 1870ff. In *Parashat R'ei,* he states that a boy is obligated to perform *mitzvot* at age 13 and one day, at which time his father should recite *Barukh Shepetarani.* He should try to make a *se'udat mitzvah* for his friends and family, and the most important of the invitees should put their hands on the boy's head and bless him with the Priestly Blessing, and the boy or the father or a scholar should give a *derashah.* The boy should wear a new garment and recite *sheheḥeyanu* and if he can't afford new clothing, then he should recite it on a new fruit.

> And also a girl, on the day she is obligated to observe *mitzvot* [i.e. 12 years and one day], even though they are not accustomed to make her a *se'udah,* even so, she should be happy that day and wear Shabbat clothes, and if she can afford it, she should wear a new garment and recite

9. Rabbi Yitzḥak Nissim, *Noam* 7 (5724), pp. 4-5 = *Or Hamizraḥ* 13/3-4 (Tishrei 5724), p. 35 = *Responsa Yein Hatov,* Jerusalem, 1979, Part 2, No. 6, p. 241. For a biography of Rabbi Ḥayyim Yitzḥak Musafiyah, see Ya'akov Gellis, *Entziklopedia Letoledot Ḥakhmei Eretz Yisrael,* Vol. 1, Jerusalem, 1974, col. 387 and Vol. 3, Jerusalem, 1978, cols. 236-237.

> *sheheḥeyanu* and also intend [the blessing] to include her entry into the yoke of commandments.[10]

Thus, Rabbi Yosef Ḥayyim seems to have invented a *Bat Mitzvah* celebration in Baghdad in the late nineteenth century. Even though it did not include a *se'udat mitzvah,* it did include some of the *Bar Mitzvah* customs: joy, Shabbat clothing, and *sheheḥeyanu* on a new garment.

In 1893, the President of the Israelite Community of Vienna, Wilhelm Ritter von Guttman, wanted to introduce some reforms in the religious service which would attract young women. He addressed his question to Dr. David Kaufmann (1852-1899) in Budapest and to Lector Meir Friedmann (Ish Shalom; 1831-1908) in Vienna. Both were members of the "positive historical school", which many view as the European precursor of the Conservative movement. Kaufmann taught at the Rabbinical Seminary of Budapest, while Friedmann taught at the Bet Midrash of Vienna where Solomon Schechter was one of his students.[11]

Kaufmann's reply dealt mainly with the need to teach women Hebrew, prayer and Jewish Studies.[12] Friedman's responsum in German, entitled "Participation of Women in Worship", is devoted mostly to the permissibility of women singing in public *(kol b'ishah erva)* and *aliyot* for Women. After discussing the *halakhic* sources on these topics, he expresses his opposition to Confirmation for girls.

> Wouldn't it be better to call our girls as *Bar Mitzvah* [*sic!*] to the Torah exactly like the boys? The impression and the

10. Rabbi Yosef Ḥayyim of Baghdad, *Ben Ish Ḥay* to *Parashat R'ei,* first year, paragraph 17, Jerusalem, 1985, p. 348. Cf. below, p. 148.
11. Regarding the latter connection, see Norman Bentwich, *Solomon Schechter: A Biography,* Philadelphia, 1938 pp. 35-38 and see Schechter's *semiḥah* certificates from Rabbi Meir Friedmann and Rabbi Isaac Hirsch Weiss which were published in the *JTS Students' Annual* 3 (1916), pp. 13, 15.
12. David Kaufmann, "Wie heben wir den religiosen Sinn unserer Madchen und Frauen?", *Oestereichische Wochenschrift,* February 3 and 10, 1893 = Marcus Brann, editor, *Gesammelte Schriften von David Kaufmann,* Vol. 1, Frankfurt am Main, 1908, pp. 104-120 = *Bameh narim et ruaḥ hadat bekerev nasheinu uvnoteinu?* (Hebrew), Zhitomir, 1909.

> effect will definitely be greater than by the imitative Confirmation.
> As far as I'm concerned, calling women to the Torah today will not offend *kevod hatzibbur* [the honor of the congregation]. On the contrary, Jewish domestic and community life will gain extraordinarily if the women will be deemed worthy of this religious practice. It goes without saying that one must erect a covered staircase directly from the women's gallery to the *bimah,* so that those called up can ascend and descend without being seen.[13]

Thus, Rabbi Meir Ish Shalom allowed *aliyot* for *Bat Mitzvah* girls in 1893, provided that a covered staircase be built from the women's gallery to the *bimah.*

Less than a decade later, in 1902, Dr. Yeḥezkel Caro, the Reform Rabbi in Lvov, held a *Bat Mitzvah* celebration at his Temple. It is not clear exactly what transpired at the ceremony, but the Zionists in town, whom Rabbi Caro opposed at every opportunity, held a protest demonstration outside the Temple during the *Bat Mitzvah* celebration. Afterwards, two reactions to the event appeared in *Voschod* (East), the Russian-language Zionist newspaper. Rabbi Dr. Mordechai Ehrenpreiss, a Zionist, who held pulpits in Djakovo (Croatia), Sofia and Stockholm, defended the new practice. Shlomo Schiller, a Zionist thinker and activist who lived in Lvov, was opposed to the new practice. He admitted that Jewish girls needed to absorb the Jewish spirit, but not by adopting foreign customs. He says that eventually the *Bat Mitzvah* custom "will find the appropriate/proper form".[14]

Five years later, in 1907, Rabbi Ya'akov Ze'ev Kahana of

13. Meir Friedmann, "Mitwirkung von Frauen beim Gottesdienste", *HUCA* 8-9 (1931-1932), pp. 511-523. The quotations were translated from pp. 520-521. This suggestion seems bizarre to us because he is mixing a talmudic approach which allows women to have *aliyot* (see below, note 28) with a medieval custom which requires a *meḥitzah* (see below, note 27). Re. Friedman, cf. below. p. 323 about the supposed women's gallery in Alexandria.
14. Dov Sadan, "*Bat Mitzvah*" in *Dat Umedinah,* Tel Aviv, 1949, which was reprinted in *Dat Yisrael Umedinat Yisrael,* New York, 1951, pp. 136-139.

Pasval north of Kovno, published a responsum in Vilna: "I am in doubt if women may be counted in a *minyan* for prayer". He then writes a lengthy and learned dissertation in which he weighs all of the opinions and finally concludes that this is not allowed. Furthermore, in that same volume of responsa, he suggested with some hesitation due to fear of his friends and teachers, that women may be counted in a *minyan* for the *Sheva Berakhot* recited under the *huppah.*[15] This was certainly a liberal approach in his time and place.

Ten years later, in 1917, Sara Schnirer (1883-1935) founded the first Bais Ya'akov school in Cracow with the approval of the *Ḥafetz Ḥayyim* (Rabbi Israel Meir Hacohen) and other prominent Rabbis. Her motive was the fact that many girls in Eastern Europe were receiving a secular education instead of a Jewish education, since they were not usually part of the *ḥeder* system. Her idea caught on quickly and by 1939 there were 40,000 girls in Bais Ya'akov schools across Europe and elsewhere.[16]

The next few events, which occurred between 1918 and 1922, were probably influenced by women's suffrage, since women achieved the right to vote in Soviet Russia, Canada, Germany, Austria, Poland, the United States, Hungary and Great Britain between 1917 and 1920.

In 1918, there was a huge controversy in Palestine about whether women could vote or be elected to public office in the governing bodies of the *Yishuv*. Responsa were written by many of the prominent Rabbis at that time, including Rabbi Abraham Isaac Kuk, Rabbi Ben-Zion Meir Ḥai Uziel and Rabbi David Tzvi

15. For the first responsum, see Rabbi Ya'akov Ze'ev Kahana, *Sefer Toledot Ya'akov,* Vilna, 1907, *Oraḥ Ḥayyim,* No. 5. My thanks to Professor David Halivni and Dr. Efraim Halivni who referred me to this *teshuvah* and cf. below, Chapter 3 for a thorough discussion of the same sources. For the second responsum, see Rabbi Kahana, *Even Ha'ezer*, No. 5 and cf. below, pp. 264 ff.

16. See *Encyclopaedia Judaica*, second edition, 2007, Vol. 18, p. 121 with Bibliography and Vol. 19, p. 274; Deborah Weissman in Elizabeth Koltun, editor, *The Jewish Woman: New Perspectives*, New York, 1976, pp. 139-148.

Hoffmann. Some forbade both, some allowed both, and some allowed women to vote but not to be elected to public office.[17]

In 1921-1923, also in Palestine, Henrietta Szold and her American friends ran what would today be called an egalitarian *minyan*. Szold made *aliyah* in 1920 and, at first, tried to attend an Orthodox synagogue. It had a small and dusty women's section and, in general, it made her feel very uncomfortable. She then went to shul to recite *kaddish* on a *yahrzeit*, but there was so much noise she could not hear when *kaddish* was recited. Finally, in frustration, she and some of her expatriate friends founded an egalitarian *minyan* in the home of one of the group. An article published in July 1923 described the service:

> We formed a Congregation, meeting in the home of one of the group. Men, women and children pray together and each person takes part in the service, even in the reading of the law...

They used a prayer book compiled by Szold and Sophia Berger, which included non-liturgical readings in which women fully participated and men and women sang songs in unison.[18]

The year 1922 was a momentous year vis-a-vis our topic in the United States.

On March 18, 1922, Judith Kaplan celebrated her *Bat Mitzvah* at SAJ (Society for the Advancement of Judaism) in Manhattan when she was twelve-and-a-half years old. Interestingly enough, both of her grandmothers were opposed to the celebration. As Judith recalls, her father Rabbi Mordecai Kaplan, did not decide exactly what to do until the night before. On Friday night, after Shabbat dinner, he took her into his study and they practiced the blessings before and after the Torah reading. He then selected a passage from the weekly portion which she practiced reading in

17. For a summary of their responsa and arguments, see below, pp. 352-358, 377-380 and Zvi Zohar in Harvey Goldberg, editor, *Sephardi and Middle Eastern Jewries*, New York, 1996, pp. 119-133.
18. Baila Round Shargel, *Lost Love: The Untold Story of Henrietta Szold*, Philadelphia, 1997, pp. 332-333. Cf. below, p. 253 for Henrietta Szold's attitude to the mourner's *kaddish*.

Hebrew and English. At SAJ, men sat up front and women behind, so Judith sat with the men. Judith was called up to the Torah, recited the blessings and read a portion from the weekly portion. Rabbi Kaplan himself read the *haftorah* blessings and *haftorah*. But this did not mean full equality for women at SAJ. It took more than twenty years for women to be called regularly to the Torah.[19]

In 1922, the CCAR (Central Conference of American Rabbis) of the Reform movement voted on whether to ordain women as rabbis. Rabbi J. Z. Lauterbach, the leading Talmudist at HUC (Hebrew Union College), wrote a detailed responsum opposing the ordination of women. The CCAR held a thorough discussion of his *teshuvah* and, not surprisingly, took the liberal position,[20] but the first woman Rabbi was only ordained by HUC in 1972, as we shall see below.

Ten years after Judith Kaplan's *Bat Mitzvah,* in 1932, Rabbi Morris Silverman, a prominent Conservative Rabbi in Hartford, Connecticut, did a "Survey on Ritual" for the Rabbinical Assembly. This is what he reported to the Rabbinical Assembly Convention at that time:

> In regard to the question of the *Bas Mitzvah* [*sic!*] ceremony, the ceremony should have been explained in view of the fact that some know nothing of its existence and have confused it with the confirmation ceremony. The *Bas Mitzvah* is an individual ceremony for the girl and corresponds to the *Bar Mitzvah* ceremony of the boy. After a year of training and study of Hebrew, the girl, upon reaching the age of 12 or 13, is called up to the pulpit after the *Haftara*, reads in Hebrew and English the prayer "Make pleasant we therefore beseech Thee, etc.", then reads a

19. There are various accounts as to what Judith Kaplan actually did at her *Bat Mitzvah*. Our description is based on Mel Scult, *Judaism Faces the Twentieth Century: A Biography of Mordecai M. Kaplan,* Detroit, 1993, pp. 301-302 and cf. Mel Scult, editor, *Communings of the Spirit: The Journals of Mordecai M. Kaplan, Vol. 1, 1913-1934,* Detroit, 2001, p. 159.
20. Walter Jacob, editor, *American Reform Responsa,* New York, 1983, pp. 24-43.

> portion of the Bible in Hebrew and English, which in some congregations is followed by a brief original address which the *Bas Mitzvah* has written herself. Then she is welcomed by the rabbi. In some cases, a certificate is given the *Bas Mitzvah* or the *Bas Mitzvah* signs a pledge in advance. The benediction by the rabbi concludes the ceremony. Professor Kaplan has originated this ceremony and it is now followed in 6 congregations according to the replies. Three plan to introduce it in the near future, and 2 others intend to use it at the Friday Night Services.[21]

The most interesting thing about this report is not that six congregations do the ceremony and five plan to, but the fact that ten years after the first American *Bat Mitzvah*, Rabbi Silverman still needed to explain what it was!

Rabbi Regina Jonas (1902-1944), studied at the Reform Hochschule in Berlin from ca. 1924 and completed her thesis "Can a woman hold rabbinical office?" in 1930. Professor Eduard Baneth, a distinguished Talmudic scholar, accepted her thesis, but passed away before he could give her the oral exam obligated of rabbinical candidates. At the Hochschule, only a Talmud Professor could ordain. Prof. Hanokh Albeck was opposed and other faculty members concurred. Finally, Regina Jonas was given private ordination by Rabbi Max Dienemann, a leading Reform Rabbi in Germany, in 1935. He wrote in her *Hatarat Hora'ah* [ordination document]:

> Since I have recognized that her heart is with God and Israel and that she gives her soul to the purpose which she intends for herself and that she is God-fearing; and since she passed the exam which I gave her in *halakhic* matters, I attest that she is capable of answering questions of *halakhah* and that she deserves to be appointed to the rabbinical

21. Rabbi Morris Silverman, "Report of Survey on Ritual", *Proceedings of the Rabbinical Assembly* 4 (1930-1932), p. 331.

> office. And may God support her and stand by her and accompany her on all her ways.[22]

This was a truly a historic event, but unfortunately Rabbi Regina Jonas and most German Jews were murdered in the Holocaust so we have no way of knowing how this momentous event would have played out in Europe or elsewhere.

In 1937, Rabbi J. B. Soloveitchik founded the Maimonides day school in Boston, Massachusetts, in which boys and girls studied Talmud together. In 1972, he delivered the inaugural lecture in Talmud at Stern College in order to show that it is permissible to teach Talmud to women. There is no question that this approach had a huge impact on modern Orthodoxy in ensuing decades. Indeed, the women in Stern College requested and were granted their own Beit Midrash in 1992 and a new expanded Beit Midrash in 2007.[23]

After a hiatus due, perhaps, to the Holocaust, there were two events which occurred vis-à-vis our topic in 1947:

As part of the controversy regarding the abolition of the *meḥitzah* at Chizuk Amuno Congregation in Baltimore, which involved a lengthy *halakhic* correspondence with Prof. Louis Ginzberg, we find the following resolution from December 1947:

> Whereas, out of the total membership of three hundred and seventy six (376) congregations in the United Synagogue of America, of which organization, founded thirty-four (34)

22. Pamela S. Nadell, *Women Who Would be Rabbis: A History of Women's Ordination 1889-1985*, Boston, 1998, p. 87 and cf. pp. 85-87 and Elisa Klapheck, *Fraulein Rabbiner Jonas: The Story of the First Woman Rabbi*, San Francisco, 2004, which includes a lot of new information about Rabbi Regina Jonas.
23. See below, p. 360, note 27; Rabbi Beni Brama in Amnon Shapira, *Teshuvah Laḥaverim Hasho'alim B'inyan Ḥevra Me'urevet*, Tel Aviv, 1982, pp. 57-59; Joel Wolowelsky in *Tradition* 22/1 (Spring 1986), pp. 78-79 and *idem., Women, Jewish Law and Modernity*, Hoboken, NJ, 1997, pp. 113-118; Seth Farber, *An American Orthodox Dreamer: Rabbi Joseph B. Soloveitchik and Boston's Maimonides School*, Hanover and London, 2004, Chapter 4; *The Jerusalem Post Magazine*, March 18, 2005, p. 27; Fran Tanner, *Kol Hamevaser* 3/6 (March 24, 2010), pp. 24-25.

> years ago, our Congregation is a charter member, three-hundred-and-seventy-two (372) of the members, or practically ninety-nine percent (99%), worship in family pews...[24]

We learn from this resolution that by 1947, 99% of the Conservative congregations in the United Synagogue had abolished the *meḥitzah.*

In that same year, Rabbi Yosef Elia Henkin (1880-1973) wrote his first *teshuvah* allowing women to recite mourners' *kaddish,* as long as they remain in the women's section. This was certainly not the first responsum on this topic and Rabbi Henkin's approach followed the standard custom in his native Lithuania.[25] However, I believe that this question was asked in the United States in 1947 as part of the gradual process of allowing women greater roles in the synagogue.

Two years later, in December 1949, Rabbi David Aronson, President of the Rabbinical Assembly and Rabbi of Beth El in Minneapolis, reported the following in the President's Column of the Bulletin of the Rabbinical Assembly:

> It happened! A woman chanted the *Kiddush* in the presence of a large congregation at the late Friday night service. Not only that, but on the Sabbath morning following at 11:00 o'clock, women conducted a second *Minyan*. The women took charge of the service, while the men who had the courage remained to watch the *Ḥiddush,* the new experience in the history of the Synagogue. There was an abridged *Shaḥarit* conducted by women dressed in white robes and skull caps. They chanted the prayer before the Ark, read out of the Scroll with the traditional chant, called

24. David Golinkin, editor, *The Responsa of Professor Louis Ginzberg,* New York and Jerusalem, 1996, p. 95 and cf. *ibid.,* pp. 90-100 and see more recently Jan Bernhardt Schein, *On Three Pilars: The History of Chizuk Amuno Congregation 1871-1996,* Baltimore, 2000, pp. 198-214.
25. Rabbi Yosef Elia Henkin, *Kitvei Hagria Henken,* Vol. 2, New York, 1989, p. 6; the *teshuvah* is dated 5707 (1946-1947). Cf. below, Chapter 11, where I survey the responsa and explain the Lithuanian custom.

> up for *Aliyot* a *Bat-Kohen* [daughter of a *Kohen*], *Bat-Levi* [daughter of a *Levi*], etc., chanted the *Maftir* better than most men could, blessed the new month, and let two members of the *Bat Mitzvah* class lead in the chanting of the *Mussaf* service. O yes, there was a short sermon on the *sidra* of the week given by a woman too.
>
> What was the reaction of the men? Said one of the venerable members, a former president of the congregation: "It was a service done so beautifully, with dignity, knowledge and understanding. It was a profound religious experience. I am all for it." Said an old *Ḥassid*, the father of the woman who read the *Torah:* "When a congregation can produce those who can participate in that kind of service so sincerely and devotedly, then we, too, can see that it is good." Said a mere man: "It is a revolutionary act. Now women will want the *Aliyot*." He then added: "Perhaps this will spur the men to guard their honors and to attend the synagogues more regularly".
>
> It happened in Minneapolis in connection with the 25th anniversary observance of the Beth El Women's League. It is the sign of the times. Some day it will reach your congregation. Are you ready to resist it, welcome it, encourage it? Whatever your position, you better begin thinking seriously about it. The role of women in the synagogue presents a growing challenge which Rabbis will not be able to ignore much longer.[26]

Rabbi Aronson is describing here the first women's *minyan* or prayer group, 22 years before such groups were founded by women in 1971 (see below). He prophetically predicted that "the role of women in the synagogue presents a growing challenge which Rabbis will not be able to ignore much longer".

Indeed, the "war of the *meḥitzah*" transpired in the United

26. Rabbi David Aronson, *Bulletin of the Rabbinical Assembly*, December 1949, p. 11, which I quoted in *American Jewish Archives* 47/2 (Fall-Winter 1995), pp. 248-249.

States from 1953-1957, when members of synagogues sued their fellow members in secular courts in Cincinnatti; Mt. Clemens, Michigan; and New Orleans for having removed the *meḥitzah* or women's gallery. Various Orthodox and Conservative Rabbis were called to testify in court and Baruch Litvin of Mt. Clemens published a 670 page book in English, Hebrew and Yiddish – *The Sanctity of the Synagogue* – in which he collected the Orthodox letters opposed to removing the *meḥitzah*. In 1959, Rabbi Norman Lamm stated that the *meḥitzah* issue had created a *meḥitzah* between Orthodox and Conservative Jews, and in subsequent years the Union of Orthodox Congregations (OU) made every effort to convince congregations to put up a *meḥitzah* or be expelled from the OU.[27]

While this "war" was going on, in 1955, the Committee on Jewish Law and Standards of the Conservative Movement issued two *teshuvot* about *aliyot* for women: Rabbi Sanders Tofield allowed *aliyot* for women at a *Bat Mitzvah* and other special occasions, while Rabbi Aaron Blumenthal allowed *aliyot* for women without any conditions.[28] Ironically, Rabbi Blumenthal did not succeed in allowing this in his own synagogue.[29] This practice slowly spread in the Conservative movement and by 1995, 88% of Conservative synagogues allowed *aliyot* for women.[30]

One year later, in Tel Aviv, Rabbi Hillel Posek, a well-known Orthodox *posek*, published a responsum entitled "Good Advice or

27. See *Conservative Judaism* 11/1 (Fall 1956), the entire issue; Baruch Litvin, *The Sanctity of the Synagogue,* New York, 1959 and Rabbi Norman Lamm, *ibid.*, English Section, pp. 311-312 and a letter from the OU in the third edition, 1987, pp. 513-514; Sarna (above, note 3), pp. 363-394; Douglas Aronin, *Cornerstone* 2 (1997), p. 83; below, Chapter 14; Shira Wolosky, *Nashim* 17 (2009), pp. 9-32.
28. *Proceedings of the Rabbinical Assembly* 19 (1955), pp. 33-41, 168-190 = David Golinkin, editor, *Proceedings of the Committee on Jewish Law and Standards of the Conservative Movement 1927-1970,* Jerusalem and New York, 1997, Vol. 1, pp. 382-390 and Vol. 3 pp. 1086-1108 and cf. below, Chapter 6.
29. Personal communication from his son Rabbi Prof. David Blumenthal, January 11, 2006.
30. See below, p. 184, note 18.

a Surprising Ruling". He was asked how to help elderly Jews in settlements of the Histadrut. Each settlement contained 7-8 elderly men who could not constitute a *minyan*. Rabbi Posek suggested that they invite two young men to stay with them every Shabbat, "and if that too is impossible, then a surprising ruling, that it is also permissible to count women for the Torah reading, for they even are counted among the seven and do not read in public because of *kevod hatzibbur*, but to count them in the *minyan* for the reading is certainly permissible (OH 282) ....".[31]

Rabbi Posek did not allow women to have *aliyot* because of *kevod hatzibbur*, but he did allow them to be counted in the *minyan* for the Torah reading *bish'at had'ḥak*, in an emergency, in order to allow elderly men to read from the Torah.

It is ironic that not much occurred vis-à-vis Jewish women in public life during the turbulent decade of women's liberation in the 1960s. On the other hand, the 1970s was an important decade with regard to our topic.

In the fall of 1971, Jewish feminists began to organize women's *minyanim* on college campuses. A number of years later, the first Orthodox women's *tefillah* or prayer group was founded. Today there are many such groups all over the world, despite the opposition of five *Rashey Yeshivah* [heads of a *yeshivah*] at Yeshiva University in 1985 and other Rabbis. In some, the women recite the regular blessings before and after the Torah reading. In others, they recite the blessing "*la'asok b'divrei torah*" [to occupy oneself with words of Torah] in order to emphasize that their Torah reading is not a real or regular Torah reading.[32]

31. Rabbi Hillel Posek, *Hillel Omer*, Tel Aviv, 1956, No. 187. My thanks to his grandson Hillel Posek, an M.A. student at the Schechter Institute in Jerusalem, who gave me a copy of the book and referred me to this *teshuvah*.
32. For feminist *minyanim*, see Alan Silverstein, *Conservative Judaism* 30/1 (Fall 1975), p. 46, note 8 and p. 49; Anne Lerner (above, note 1), pp. 7-8. For Orthodox women's prayer groups, see *The Forward*, January 31, 1997, p. 2; Avi Weiss, *Women at Prayer*, Hoboken, New Jersey, 1990, pp. xv-xvi; Sylvia Barack Fishman, *A Breath of Life* (above, note 1), pp. 158 ff; *Hadarom* 54 (Sivan 5745), pp. 49-50; *In Jerusalem*, June 8, 2000, pp. 4-5; and the literature

In 1971-1972, a group of young women, many of them Conservative, founded an organization called Ezrat Nashim. They advocated that women be granted membership in synagogues, be counted in the *minyan*, be recognized as witnesses in Jewish Law, and be permitted to attend Rabbinical and cantorial schools. Among other things, they "stormed" the Rabbinical Assembly Convention in March 1972 and Rabbi David M. Feldman wrote a *halakhic* reaction to their manifesto.[33]

That same year, the Reform movement ordained Rabbi Sally Preisand at HUC-JIR, fifty years after the CCAR decision in 1922. By the year 2000, HUC-JIR had ordained 335 women Rabbis.[34]

In 1973, the Committee on Jewish Law and Standards (CJLS) of the Conservative movement debated whether women could be counted in the *minyan*. Rabbi Philip Sigal and Rabbi Aaron Blumenthal wrote responsa in favor, while Rabbi David M. Feldman wrote a responsum opposed. In the end, the CJLS approved a *takkanah* to count women in the *minyan* and by 1988, 64% of Conservative synagogues did so.[35]

In 1976, Rabbi Chaim Brovender and Malka Bina founded the first Orthodox women's yeshivah called Michlelet Bruria in Jerusalem. There are now forty such institutions in Israel in which 3,000 women learn every year. Some are full-time for post high school students, some are built on the *Kolel* model in which married women students are paid to sit and learn every day, and

cited by Rabbi Daniel Sperber, *Darkah Shel Halakhah*, Jerusalem, 2007, p. 17, note 15.

33. Alan Silverstein (above, note 32), pp. 41-51; Anne Lerner (above, note 1), p. 6; David M. Feldman in: Seymour Siegel and Elliot Gertel, editors, *Conservative Judaism and Jewish Law*, New York, 1977, p. 294; Sarna, (above, note 1), p. 339 and note 127.
34. See Gary P. Zola, *Women Rabbis: Exploration and Celebration*, Cincinnati etc., 1996, p. ix and Sarna (above, note 1), p. 341.
35. See Rabbi Philip Sigal in Siegel and Gertel (above, note 33), pp. 282-292; Rabbis Sigal, Blumenthal, and Feldman in a summary sent out by Rabbi Seymour Siegel on October 5, 1973 (unpublished); Rabbi David M. Feldman in *Conservative Judaism* 48/1 (Fall 1995), p. 39; Edya Arzt, *Women's League Outlook*, Fall 1988, pp. 17-18.

some are part-time for married women who want to continue learning.[36]

Beginning in 1972, various groups tried to convince JTS and/or the Rabbinical Assembly to ordain women Rabbis. In May 1977, the Rabbinical Assembly passed a resolution encouraging JTS to admit women into Rabbinical School and to set up a Commission to study the question. The Commission convened in December 1977 and published its report in December 1978. In January 1979, the JTS faculty decided not to ordain women. Chancellor Gerson Cohen then tried to set up a parallel course for women and men with a different title, but that effort did not bear fruit. By 1983, three senior Talmud professors who were opposed to women's ordination had left JTS and Professor Saul Lieberman had passed away in April 1983. As a result, JTS decided to ordain women in October 1983 and Rabbi Amy Eilberg was ordained in May 1985.[37]

Leah Shakdiel, a modern Orthodox woman, was a member of the city council in Yeruḥam in the Negev. In January 1986, the City Council nominated her as one of four new members of the *Mo'etzah Datit* [Religious Council], but the powers-that-be refused to seat her on the Council. New responsa were written echoing the above-mentioned battle from 1918 on the same issue. In the end, the Supreme Court of Israel ruled in December 1987 that the Religious Council of Yeruḥam must seat Leah Shakdiel on the Council. Even so, the issue has resurfaced in other Religious Councils in Israel.[38]

36. This is based on Esti Barel's unpublished Ph.D. dissertation, Bar Ilan University, 2009. I heard her summarize her research at the World Congress of Jewish Studies in Jerusalem on August 2, 2009. Also see Ruti Feuchtwanger in *Nashim* 18 (2009), pp. 166-186. There are also some women's *yeshivot* in the U.S., such as the Drisha Institute founded in New York in 1979.
37. See the literature which I cite below, p. 31, note 4; an unpublished letter from Prof. Gerson Cohen to the members of the Rabbinical Assembly, March 26, 1980, announcing a new program towards a professional degree in divinity for men and women; *Women's League Outlook* 76/2 (Winter 2005), pp. 14-29; *Rabbinical Assembly Newsletter* 70/2 (February 2010), pp. 1, 8.
38. See above, note 17.

In 1988, a group of Orthodox, Conservative and Reform women founded the Women of the Wall. They wanted to hold a women's *Tefillah* at the *Kotel* every Rosh Ḥodesh, including a Torah reading. They were opposed by the "Rabbi of the *Kotel*" and various government ministries and were physically attacked by men and women at the *Kotel*. After a lengthy legal battle, they were given a permanent place to pray on Rosh Ḥodesh in the Davidson Archaeological Park at Robinson's Arch. Beginning in November 2009, they tried once again to pray at the *Kotel* and a number of the women were arrested.[39]

In 1987, the Seminary of Judaic Studies (later renamed the Schechter Rabbinical Seminary) affiliated with the Conservative/ Masorti Movement in Israel began to discuss the ordination of women. It was decided at that time that the institution and the movement were too small and too young to deal with this divisive issue. The issue was reopened in 1992 and the *Va'ad Halakhah* [Law Committee] of the Rabbinical Assembly of Israel wrote three responsa on the subject – one opposed, one in favor with certain conditions, and one in favor. In the end, the Board of Directors of the Seminary voted to ordain women without any conditions in December 1992 and Rabbi Valery Stessin was ordained in Jerusalem in November 1993.[40]

39. For the history of the Women of the Wall, see Sylvia Barack Fishman, *A Breath of Life* (above, note 1), pp. 167-171; Phyllis Chesler and Rivka Haut, eds., *Women of the Wall: Claiming Sacred Ground at Judaism's Holy Site*, Woodstock, Vermont, 2002; Shmuel Shilo, *Tehumin* 17 (5757), pp. 160-174; *The Jerusalem Post* 25/9/1998, pp. 1, 18; 26/5/2000, p. B6; 11/4/2003, p. B7; 31/10/2003, p. 4; *In Jerusalem*, 3/9/2004, pp. 10-11; Matthew Wagner, *The Jerusalem Post*, November 18, 2009; Peretz Rodman, *ynet*, November 22, 2009; Nofrat Frenkel, *Forward.com*, November 24, 2009; Gil Troy, *Jpost.com*, November 26, 2009; Isabel Kershner, *The New York Times*, December 21, 2009; Ron Kampeas, *JTA*, December 28, 2009; Editorial, *Forward*, January 15, 2010; Ben Harris, *The Jerusalem Post*, January 15, 2010, p. 8; Josh Nathan-Kazis, *Forward*, February 5, 2010; Elana Sztokman, *In Jerusalem*, August 20, 2010, pp. 14-15.
40. See David Golinkin, *Responsa of the Va'ad Halakhah of the Rabbinical Assembly of Israel* 5 (5752-5754), pp. 7-8 and the responsa on pp. 13-83 and cf. an expanded version of my responsum below, Chapter 15.

In 1987, Margaret Niger of Ra'anana wrote to Chief Rabbis Shapira and Eliyahu and to the Ministry of Religion and requested permission to become a *To'enet Rabbanit,* a Rabbinic Court Pleader, a role which until then had been filled only by men. The Chief Rabbis agreed, but the Ministry of Religion refused because a regulation from 1968 said that a *To'ein Rabbani* had to have learned in a *yeshivah* for at least four years. Therefore, it became necessary to change the regulations and to set up an appropriate study framework for women.

In 1989, Nurit Fried, the Director of Midreshet Lindenbaum for women, heard that there was a plan to change the regulations regarding this issue. She and Rabbi Shlomo Riskin, who was the head of Midreshet Lindenbaum, opened a course for *To'anot Rabbaniyot* in September 1990. 120 women applied and 30 were accepted into an intensive two-and-a-half year program which met two days a week for 16 hours every week. 19 women completed the course and the first 9 were certified by Chief Rabbi Eliyahu Bakshi-Doron in February 1994. There are now 70 *To'anot Rabbaniyot* in Israel. Even so, the Midreshet Lindenbaum program closed in 2009 for lack of enrollment. This is because a *To'enet Rabbanit* can only appear before an Israeli Rabbinic Court, while a lawyer can appear before a Rabbinic Court and a secular Family Court.[41]

In 1997, Rabbanit Chana Henkin started the first course to train *Yo'atzot Halakhah, halakhic* advisors for matters related to the laws of *Niddah,* at Nishmat in Jerusalem. Since then, 61 women have completed this course and they have addressed over

41. *The Jerusalem Post Magazine,* August 9, 1991, p. 13; *ibid.,* February 5, 1993, p. 12; *ibid.,* May 20, 1999, p. 15; Yair Sheleg, *Hadatiyim Haḥadashim,* Jerusalem, 2000, p. 66; Yoram Kirsh, *Mahapeikhot Bahalakhah,* Or Yehuda, 2002, Chapter 1; www.rbc.gov.il. My thanks to Rachel Levmore, a veteran *To'enet Rabbanit,* who referred me to the last two sources and explained why the Midreshet Lindenbaum program had recently closed. This latter point was confirmed to me by Dr. Hadass Cohen, the last graduate of the program, in August 2010.

100,000 questions from women via the Internet and a telephone hot line.[42]

In 1997, Blu Greenberg founded JOFA, The Jewish Orthodox Feminist Alliance, in New York, whose mission is "to expand the spiritual, ritual, intellectual and political opportunities for women within the framework of *halakhah*". JOFA publishes a periodical entitled *JOFA Journal* and runs an annual conference in New York. In 1998, Dr. Chana Kehat founded Kolech in Israel, which has similar goals. Kolech publishes a weekly *parashat shavua* sheet (60,000 copies) which is distributed at 4,700 synagogues throughout Israel, runs a bi-annual conference and has published four volumes of the proceedings of those conferences, and advocates on behalf of Agunot and pre-nuptial agreements.[43]

In 1999, the Schechter Institute of Jewish Studies in Jerusalem founded the Center for Women in Jewish Law, which has published a periodical and a major book on the subject of modern-day *agunot*, a periodical and a major book on the subject of women in Jewish law, and a website and a book entitled *Ask the Rabbi* in which two women Rabbis write responsa.[44]

In 2001, the CJLS of the Conservative Movement approved two responsa allowing women to serve as witnesses for all

42. See Tova Genzel, *De'ot* 8 (Tammuz 5760), pp. 15-17; Joel Wolowelsky, *Tradition* 36/4 (Winter 2002), pp. 54-63 and reactions *ibid*. 37/2 (Summer 2003), pp. 93-100; *The Jerusalem Post Magazine,* May 20, 1999, p. 16; *ibid.*, October 23, 2009, pp. 26-27 and *In Jerusalem*, November 6, 2009, pp. 10-13. Regarding the history of Nishmat, see also *In Jerusalem*, July 18, 1997, p. 4.
43. See the websites of JOFA and Kolech.
44. *The Jewish Law Watch,* Nos. 1-7 (Hebrew and English); *Za'akat Dalot: Solutions to the Agunah Dilemma in the Twentieth Century* (Hebrew); *To Learn and to Teach,* Nos. 1-5 (in five languages); David Golinkin, *Ma'amad Ha'ishah Bahalakhah*, Jerusalem, 2001, which is now appearing in expanded form in ths volume; *Ask the Rabbis* (English). Most of this material was written by Rabbi Monique Susskind Goldberg z"l and Rabbi Diana Villa and edited by me. For other organizations which fight for the rights of *agunot*, see www.icar.org.il.

matters in Jewish law. They also published two concurring opinions and one dissent.[45]

In 2002, Shira Ḥadasha was founded in Jerusalem by Dr. Eli Holtzer and Dr. Tova Hartman. This was self-defined as an Orthodox *minyan* which had a *meḥitzah* but allowed women to serve as Cantor for non-statutory parts of the service such as *Kabbalat Shabbat* and *Psukei D'zimra,* read from the Torah and have *aliyot* and read the *Haftarah.* Reading from the Torah was bolstered by responsa by Rabbis Daniel Sperber and Mendel Shapiro. This idea caught on and there are now similar "partnership *minyanim*" in Baka, Jerusalem, New York and Australia.[46]

Finally, in recent years, Orthodox women have begun to be ordained as Rabbis or to be given similar titles. Rabbi Mimi Feigelson studied with Rabbi Shlomo Carlebach and was ordained in Israel in 1994. Rabbi Eveline Goodman-Thau was ordained by Rabbi Jonathan Chipman in 2000. Rabbi Haviva Ner-David was ordained by Rabbi Aryeh Strikovsky in 2006. Sara Hurwitz was ordained by Rabbi Avi Weiss in New York on March 22, 2009; Rabbi Daniel Sperber also signed the ordination certificate. Rabbi Weiss initially gave Hurwitz the title *Maharat: Manhigah Hilkhatit Ruḥanit Toranit* and he opened a school headed by her to train other women as Maharat. Rabbi Weiss bolstered his decision by soliciting responsa from Rabbis Daniel Sperber, Yoel Bin-Nun and Joshua Maroof. He later gave her the title Rabba in January 2010, but was forced to promise not to use

45. See the five responsa at www.Rabbinicalassembly.org under Contemporary Halakhah, Ḥoshen Mishpat, Testimony.

46. Barbara Sofer, *The Jerusalem* Post, 31/1/2003, p. B8 and *The Jerusalem Post Magazine,* 2/2/2007, p. 4; Tamar Weiss, *De'ot* 15 (February 2003), pp. 15-18, 39; Rabbi Mendel Shapiro, *The Edah Journal* 1/2 (Sivan 5761); Rabbi Daniel Sperber, *ibid.,* 3/2 (Elul 5763), which he then expanded into a Hebrew volume *Darkah Shel Halakhah,* Jerusalem, 2007 and cf. the English volume *Women and Men in Communal Prayer: Halakhic Perspectives,* New York, 2010; Hadass Porat-Roash, *De'ot* 38 (August 2008), pp. 25-29; *The Jewish Week,* July 30, 2010.

that title again due to heavy pressure from the RCA (Rabbinical Council of America). [47]

Dina Najman has served as Rosh Kehillah and Mara D'atra at Congregation Orach Eliezer in New York since 2006, while Lynn Kaye serves as Assistant Congregational Leader at Congregation Shearith Israel in New York.[48] Midreshet Lindenbaum in Jerusalem runs the Manhigot program, while Bet Morasha runs the Halakhah program for women. Both were founded in 2005 and train women in *pesikat halakhah*, how to make halakhic decisions.[49] Finally, the Star-K Kashrus agency in Baltimore is planning its first training event for women as *mashgiḥot*.[50]

II. General Conclusions

After surveying forty-one events which transpired over the course of 155 years, we would now like to draw some general conclusions about our topic.

First of all, it is commonly assumed that changes in Judaism move from Reform to Conservative to Orthodox. As can be seen from the survey above, that is not entirely true regarding women in Judaism. For example, the *Bat Mitzvah* celebration began in

47. Haviva Ner-David, *Life on the Fringes*, Needham, Massachusetts, 2000; *The Jerusalem Post Magazine*, March 18, 2005, pp. 27-29; *In Jerusalem*, May 5, 2006, p. 9-11; Mimi Feigelson, *Eretz Aḥeret* 31 (Tevet 5766), pp. 12-17; unpublished responsa by Rabbis Daniel Sperber, Yoel Bin-Nun, and Joshua Maroof, March 22, 2009; Elicia Brown, *The Jewish Week*, April 8, 2009; Anthony Weiss, *The Forward*, May 29, 2009; Jonathan Mark, *The Jewish Week*, Feb. 23, 2010; *JTA*, February 25, 2010; Editorial, *The Jerusalem Post*, March 1, 2010; Ben Harris, *JTA*, March 9, 2010; JOFA Statement, March 9, 2010; Josh Nathan-Kazis, *The Forward*, March 19, 2010; JOFA letters to the Members of the RCA, April 12, 2010; Ilana Hostyk, *Yeshiva University Observer*, April 19, 2010; Ben Harris, *JTA*, April 19, 2010; Gary Rosenblatt, *The Jewish Week*, April 20, 2010; JOFA statement in Response to the RCA Resolution, April 30, 2010; Abigail Pogrebin, *New York Magazine*, July 11, 2010; www.yeshivat-maharat.org.
48. See Michael Luo, *The New York Times*, August 21, 2006; Ben Harris, *JTA*, December 11, 2007; JOFA announcement of a program "Beyond the Glass Ceiling", held at the Manhattan JCC, October 15, 2009.
49. See *In Jerusalem*, November 6, 2009, pp. 10-13.
50. *Kosher Today*, May 4, 2009.

Italy, France and Baghdad **before** Reform Rabbi Yeḥezkel Karo innovated his ceremony in 1902 and before Conservative Rabbi Mordecai Kaplan innovated his ceremony in 1922. Sara Schnirer founded the Bais Yaakov schools not as a reaction to **Reform** but as a reaction to **modernity**, since Eastern European Jewish girls studied more about French and German culture than about Judaism. Finally, Rabbi Meir Ish Shalom and Henrietta Szold, both "Conservative" Jews, allowed *aliyot* for women **before** the Reform movement.[51]

It is also assumed by many that "Jewish Feminism" is an American Jewish phenomenon. However, it is clear from our survey that that is a simplification. It appears that the increasing participation of Jewish women in public ritual life and Torah study in modern times is an international phenomenon reflecting Jewish migration and shifting Jewish population centers from Europe to the United States to Israel.

From 1845 until the Holocaust, most of the events described took place in Germany (6), Eastern Europe (3), Italy (1), France (1) and even Baghdad (1). I believe that we can learn from the ordination of Rabbi Regina Jonas in 1935 that this trend would have continued had European Jewry not been decimated by the Holocaust.

From 1922 until today, seventeen of the events described took place in the United States. This was probably the result of women's suffrage; the growing role of women in American life, occupations and higher education; and "women's liberation" in the 1960s.

From 1976 until today, nine of the events described transpired in Israel. Many of them were **initiated** by American immigrants, but some are primarily Israeli phenomena e.g. forty yeshivot for women, the struggle to be seated on *Mo'etzot Datiyot, To'anot Rabbaniyot,* and the Center for Women in Jewish Law and other organizations which fight for *agunot.*

51. It seems that *aliyot* for women in the Reform movement began in the United States sometime before 1944. See Solomon Freehof, *Reform Jewish Practice,* augmented edition, 1976, Volume I, pp. 49-52 and Volume II, pp. 67-69; *idem, Reform Responsa,* 1960, pp. 40-42.

We can also learn from our survey that major changes regarding women in Judaism transpired over long periods of time in **all** of the movements, including Reform.

In the Reform movement, Rabbi Isaac Mayer Wise innovated family pews in 1851, but German Reform temples maintained separate seating without a *meḥitzah* until the Shoah.

Rabbi David Einhorn wanted to declare women equal to men in 1846 and the CCAR decided to ordain women in 1922, yet the Hochschule would not ordain Regina Jonas in 1930 and HUC-JIR only ordained its first woman rabbi in 1972.

B'nai Jeshurun, which later became a Conservative synagogue, abolished its *meḥitzah* in 1874,[52] but it took until 1947 for 99% of Conservative synagogues to do so. Rabbi Meir Ish Shalom allowed *aliyot* for women in 1893, while Henrietta Szold and Rabbi Mordechai Kaplan did so in 1921 and 1922. Yet at SAJ, Rabbi Kaplan's synagogue, it took more than twenty years for women to be called regularly to the Torah. Similarly, Rabbi Aaron Blumenthal allowed women to have *aliyot* in 1955, but he was not able to implement this innovation in his own synagogue until he retired. It took until 1995 for 88% of Conservative synagogues to allow *aliyot* for women. Rabbi Mordecai Kaplan introduced the *Bat Mitzvah* ceremony in 1922, yet in 1932 some Conservative Rabbis still knew nothing of its existence.

In the Orthodox world, not surprisingly, innovations regarding women in Judaism also took many years. Rabbi Ya'akov Ettlinger opposed confirmation for girls in 1830, but reluctantly allowed it when forced by the government in 1866. The *Bat Mitzvah* ceremony was innovated by Orthodox Rabbis in the 19th century, but it is still being debated and discussed by Orthodox Rabbis until today.[53] The topic of women in public office was debated thoroughly in 1918 and yet it had to be re-debated in 1986. Women's *tefillah* groups started in the late 1970s, but

52. Sarna (above, note 3), pp. 372-378.
53. See Rami Reiner (above, note 7), the literature which he cites in note 1, and Erica Brown in Michah Halpern and Chana Safrai, editors, *Jewish Legal Writings by Women*, Jerusalem, 1998, pp. 232-258.

women only began to play a public role in a regular *minyan* in 2002. Women began to study as Rabbinic Court Pleaders in 1990 and as *niddah* advisors in 1997, but most Orthodox Jews are still opposed to ordaining women as "Rabbis".

A fourth lesson to be learned is that Orthodox Rabbis and congregations, as a rule, ignore non-Orthodox rulings on women in Judaism in two ways:

They usually do not cite non-Orthodox responsa. For example, Rabbi Mendel Shapiro in his lengthy *teshuvah* regarding *aliyot* for women written for Shira Ḥadasha in 2001, cites my brief article in *Tarbitz* about *aliyot* for women, but does **not** cite my much more detailed responsum which was the basis for my article.[54]

More interestingly, Orthodox Rabbis seem to go out of their way to find a **different** way to allow the same or a similar thing. Thus, beginning in the 1970s, some Orthodox Rabbis allowed separate women's prayer groups. However, had they known that Rabbi David Aronson had done the same thing at his Conservative synagogue in 1949, chances are they would have forbidden the practice. Instead of allowing women to have *aliyot* by dealing directly with the issue of *kevod tzibbur* [the honor of the congregation] as in the Conservative responsa, Rabbi Daniel Sperber skirted the issue by dealing primarily with *kevod habriyot* [the honor of God's creatures], which is not directly related to the topic and is much more problematic.[55] Similarly, instead of ordaining women as Rabbis, they trained *To'anot Rabbaniyot, Yo'atzot Halakhah* and *Maharat*. Finally, at Shira Ḥadasha they do not start *shaharit* until ten men and ten women are present. Again, it is good that they did not know that this practice was first suggested by a Conservative Rabbi many years ago.[56]

54. See Rabbi Mendel Shapiro (above, note 46), note 166; David Golinkin, *Tarbitz* 68 (5759), pp. 429-433; below, Chapter 6. A notable exception is Rabbi Daniel Sperber who does refer to Conservative responsa – see his Hebrew volume (above, note 46), p. 18, note 15 and p. 109, note 158.
55. Rabbi Daniel Sperber (above, note 46).
56. I do not recall which Rabbi made this suggestion.

In my opinion, this approach is a shame. Maimonides already stated "accept the truth from he who says it" and this idea was echoed by many famous Rabbis.[57] Ignoring non-Orthodox responsa or looking for alternative approaches entails a lot of wasted effort and leads to unnecessary or even mistaken *halakhic* results.

On the other hand, when it comes to expanding the participation of Jewish women in public ritual life, Jewish **women** tend to ignore and cross denominational lines:

Henrietta Szold's *minyan* in Jerusalem in 1921-1923 included Reform Jews such as Rabbi Judah Magnes.

"Women of the Wall" was founded in 1988 by a coalition of Orthodox, Conservative, and Reform women and that pluralism has been maintained until today.

The Center for Women in Jewish Law at the Schechter Institute is Conservative, but it is an active member of ICAR, the International Coalition of Agunah Rights, which includes Orthodox, Conservative, Reform and secular women's organizations.

Finally, when Orthodox feminist Blu Greenberg convened two meetings at her home in Riverdale, New York, in 2009, in order to discuss what title should be bestowed upon Sara Hurwitz who was to be ordained by Orthodox Rabbi Avi Weiss, she invited about two dozen prominent Jewish women and men. One of them was Rabbi Jacqeuline Koch Ellenson, a Reform Rabbi, who is married to Rabbi Prof. David Ellenson, the president of HUC-JIR, the Reform rabbinical seminary.[58]

57. *Berakhot* 5b; *Shabbat* 55a; *Massekhet Sofrim* 13:6, ed. Higger p. 244; *Bemidbar Rabbah* 12:3; *Yoma* 69b; *Yerushalmi Berakhot* 7:3, fol. 11c; *Ḥullin* 124a; Rav Sa'adia Gaon, *Emunot V'deot*, ed. Kafiḥ, Jerusalem, 1970, pp. 6-7; Rambam in *HUCA* 3 (1926), p. 351 and in *Shmoneh Perakim*, Chapter 4 (which we quoted in the text) and in *Moreh Nevukhim*, Part II, Chapter 47, ed. Kafiḥ, p. 443; Rabbi Avraham ben Harambam, *Kovetz Teshuvot Harambam V'igrotav*, Leipzig, 1859, Part 2, p. 41ff. ; Shadal in his introduction to his commentary to Isaiah, Padua, 1855; Harav Kuk, *Igrot Re'iyah*, Vol. 2, p. 20.

58. *New York Magazine*, July 11, 2010 at www.nymag.com. Cf. Tamar Ross, *Expanding the Palace of Torah: Orthodoxy and Feminism*, Hanover and London,

A sixth lesson has to do with the timespan involved in changing the roles of women in modern Jewish movements. Reform efforts to give women greater roles in Judaism lasted for approximately 125 years (1846-1972) as did Conservative efforts (1874-2001). Most Orthodox efforts, however, have been concentrated in the past thirty years (1978-2010). The latter is the result of the "Women's Liberation Movement" in general and of the decision to teach women Talmud in particular. Once Orthodox women received the same Jewish education as Orthodox men, many of the changes described above were predictable or even inevitable.

Finally, we would like to relate to a prediction made by Samuel Freedman in his book *Jew vs Jew* in 2000, in which he predicts a re-division of Jews into three movements. He calls the second movement "Conservadox":

> Conservadox: There is a truism among the most iconoclastic of the Modern Orthodox that goes, "I'd rather be the baddest boy of Orthodoxy than the *tzaddik* ('righteous man') of Conservativism." It is a comment I have never heard, though, from an Orthodox woman, and that silence is revealing. The feminist revolution within Judaism will create a crisis of definition for the Modern Orthodox movement. The lesson of feminism in Reform and particularly Conservative Judaism is that once you start a revolution of rising expectations, you can't stop it wherever you'd like. It seems impossible to me that Modern Orthodoxy – having given women full religious education, *tefillah* groups, even some pastoral and legal duties – can dodge the ultimate decision to ordain women as Rabbis and give them full roles in worship. Whenever that happens, Modern Orthodoxy will give up its already tenuous partnership with the *ḥaredim* and find more logical partners on the right wing of the Conservative movement.

2004, p. 241, who calls this phenomenon "diminished emphasis on denominational politics".

> That faction of Conservative clergy and laity already follows much of *halakhah* and espouses a good deal of the social conservatism of Modern Orthodoxy. It could easily share with the Modern Orthodox a synagogue with mixed seating, women reading Torah and in all other ways a deeply traditional praxis, not unlike the Library Minyan's in Los Angeles.[59]

This prediction seems to be borne out by events in July 2009. As part of a speech attacking modern Orthodox religious Zionist Rabbis as "*neo-Reformim*", Rabbi Yehoshua Shapira, a leading *Ḥardal* (*Ḥaredi Leumi,* ultra-Zionists who also tend to behave more like *Ḥaredim*) Rabbi, attacked the Kolech organization. He also attacked Shira Ḥadasha as "outside the border" and said that the women who pray there are "not Orthodox".[60] Only time will tell if Freedman's prediction comes true, but there is no question that the conflicting attitudes towards the topics we have discussed will continue to have a huge impact on Jewish society and practice for decades to come.

59. Samuel G. Freedman, *Jew vs. Jew: The Struggle for the Soul of American Jewry*, New York, 2000, pp. 355-356. The Library Minyan is a traditional minyan founded at Temple Beth Am, a Conservative Synagogue in Los Angeles, in 1971 – see Freedman, pp. 124-161 and www.libraryminyan.org.
60. See Kobi Nahshoni, *ynet*, July 5, 2009, and the many reactions *ibid.*, July 5-12, 2009.

NINE APPROACHES TO THE STATUS OF WOMEN IN JEWISH LAW IN THE TWENTIETH CENTURY

Introduction

This topic expresses, perhaps more than any other, the tension which exists between *halakhah* and modernity. It is, therefore, not surprising that it has been discussed extensively specifically within the Conservative/Masorti movement, which strives to bridge the gap between tradition and change. In in an index of Conservative responsa published between 1917-1990, one tenth are devoted to this subject.[1] As a *posek* for the Conservative Movement, I am asked about this topic more than any other and have already published many responsa on the subject.[2] In addition, because of the considerable interest in this subject, I have been teaching it for over thirty years, including many academic courses at the Schechter Institute of Jewish Studies in Jerusalem. Finally, the importance of this topic led to the creation of an M.A. track in Jewish Women's and Gender Studies at the same institution.

The tension between *halakhah* and modernity has caused, is causing and will continue to cause division and disagreement

* This article is largely based on a lecture delivered at the Twelfth World Congress of Jewish Studies in Jerusalem on August 5, 1997. The bibliographical references – with a few exceptions – are updated until that time.

1. David Golinkin, *An Index of Conservative Responsa and Practical Halakhic Studies 1917-1990*, New York, 1992, pp. 71-78. For a survey of Conservative responsa on this topic, see Mayer Rabinowitz, *Conservative Judaism* 39/1 (Fall 1986), pp. 7-33; Ellen Wolintz, *ibid.*, 51/3 (Spring 1999), pp. 59-78.
2. All of my published responsa on this topic are now included in this book.

within the Jewish people. In the 1950s, the *meḥitzah* in the synagogue created a real and permanent separation between Orthodoxy and the Conservative movement in North America.[3] From 1979-1983, the ordination of women as rabbis caused a split within the faculty of Jewish Theological Seminary of America, and led to the creation of a new movement called the Union for Traditional Judaism, which today has its own rabbinic organization and seminary.[4] Furthermore, this subject continues to divide Conservative congregations abroad and Masorti congregations in Israel. In recent years, starting from "women's prayer groups" in the late 1970s to the "Women of the Wall" in the present, the status of women in *halakhah* has begun to cause division between modern Orthodoxy and the *Ḥaredi* [ultra-Orthodox] camp in Israel and abroad.[5]

Therefore, after decades of debates and discussions about the status of women in *halakhah*, the time has come to categorize the different approaches existing among *poskim*, rabbis and women

3. See *Conservative Judaism* 11/1 (Fall 1956) (the entire issue); Baruch Litvin, ed., *The Sanctity of the Synagogue*, New York, 1959 (in Hebrew, Yiddish and English) and Rabbi Norman Lamm, *ibid.*, English section, pp. 311-312; Jonathan Sarna, "The Debate Over Mixed Seating in the American Synagogue" in: Jack Wertheimer, ed., *The American Synagogue: A Sanctuary Transformed*, Cambridge, 1987, pp. 363-394; Douglas Aronin, *Cornerstone* 2 (1997), p. 83.
4. For the history of the debate over the ordination of women at the Jewish Theological Seminary of America, see Robert Gordis, *Judaism* 33/1 (Winter 1984), pp. 6-12; Arnon Bruckstein, *Semikhat Nashim Lerabanut Veḥazanut Batenu'ah Hakonservativit*, M.A. thesis, Hebrew University of Jerusalem, 1990; Ezra Kopelowitz, *Nashim* 1 (Winter 1998), pp. 136-153; Pamela Nadell, *Women Who Would Be Rabbis*, Boston, 1990, pp. 170-214; and above, p. 18, note 37. Regarding the "Union for Traditional Judaism", see *American Jewish Year Book* 92 (1992), pp. 257-258.
5. See, for example, *Hadarom* 54 (Sivan 5745), pp. 49-50 (against women's *hakafot* and prayer groups); Yeḥezkel Cohen, *Nashim Behanhagat Hatzibbur*, Jerusalem 1991 (about the Shakdiel case); *Teḥumin* 17 (5757), pp. 160-174 (on women's prayers at the Western Wall). Mention should also be made of the attacks by hundreds of *Ḥaredim* against a Masorti *minyan* at the Western Wall plaza on the holiday of *Shavu'ot* in the years 1997-1999 – I was an eyewitness to those attacks.

regarding this important topic. Due to space constraints, we will illustrate each approach with one or two examples. It should be stressed that there are approaches which are not limited to one stream in contemporary Judaism; some of them are supported by representatives of different streams.

I. Opposition to *any* change in Judaism, including this one

This approach justifies the *status quo* and states that even if something is **halakhically** permitted, it should be prohibited for **other** reasons:

1. Rabbi Yair Ḥayyim Bachrach (1638-1701) ruled as follows in his responsum on the recitation of the Mourner's *Kaddish* by women:

> **And even though there is no proof to contradict the fact** that a woman is also commanded to sanctify God's name [*Sanhedrin* 74b], even if there is a *minyan* of males constituting "the children of Israel" [*Megillah* 23b], and even though the action of Rabbi Akiva, which is the source for orphans to recite the Mourner's *Kaddish*, involved a male child, in any case, there is an opinion that there is also benefit and satisfaction to the soul [of the departed] from a daughter['s recitation] because she is his offspring. **In any case, one should fear** that doing so **will weaken the power of the customs** of the Jewish people, which are also Torah, and then **everyone will build an altar for himself** [*Ḥagigah* 22a] according to his interpretation, and the **words of the Sages will be seen as an object of derision and jest** and this will lead to their being disrespected.[6]

2. A similar approach is expressed in the responsum of Rabbi Moshe Feinstein (1895-1986) from 1976 "on the matter of the new

6. *Responsa Ḥavot Ya'ir*, No. 222. Cf. below, pp. 231-235.

movement of important and carefree women known as women's liberation."[7] Rabbi Feinstein prefaces his words by stating that

> the entire Torah, be it the written Torah, or the Oral Torah, was given by the Holy-One-Blessed-Be-He at Mount Sinai through Moses our teacher of blessed memory, and it is impossible to change even one iota, not to be lenient and not to be stringent.

The exemption of women from PTBC, such as *tzitzit,* is from the Torah and the reason for it is unknown, even to great scholars. In any case, there are

> also reasons that are apparent to all, that women... are the ones assigned the task of raising the boys and girls and so it is that the Lord created in the nature of every species that the females raise the offspring.

The women who are adamant and want to fight and change are deemed deniers of the Torah by Maimonides, *Hilkhot Teshuvah,* 3, 5: "There are three who are called deniers of the Torah.... and the one who says that one thing has been replaced" and even though Maimonides says that "the **Creator** replaced this commandment," it is all the more so when he says that **people** have permission to replace, as in doing so he is saying that the Torah is not eternal.[8]

> Clearly, every woman is allowed to observe even the *mitzvot* which the Torah did not require and they have a *mitzvah* and a reward for observing these commandments. And, according to the approach of *Tosafot,* they are even allowed to recite the blessings on these *mitzvot* as is our custom that they observe the commandments of *shofar* and *lulav* and they also pronounce the blessing, [on condition that the garment with *tzitzit*] will be different from male

7. *Igrot Moshe, Oraḥ Ḥayyim,* Part 4, No. 49. For a recent analysis of that responsum, see Norma Joseph Baumel, *Nashim* 21 (Spring 2011), pp. 67-87.
8. This is a paraphrase of Rabbi Feinstein's words.

> clothing... But it is simple that this only applies if her soul desires to observe *mitzvot*, even though she wasn't commanded, **but since it is not for this motive but out of her grievance against God, Blessed be He, and His Torah, it is not a *mitzvah* at all, but, on the contrary, a forbidden act**; because the prohibition of heresy – that she thinks that it is possible for something to change in the laws of the Torah – she also does in practice, which is more serious.

In other words, a woman who wants to wear a *tallit* does so by definition out of her grievance against God and His Torah and out of a desire to change Judaism, and therefore there is no *mitzvah* in doing so, but rather it is a forbidden act of heresy.[9]

II. Opposition specifically to changes in the synagogue, which is the last bastion against the negative influences of modern Western society

1. Rabbi Menachem Mendel Kasher (1895-1983), the author of *Torah Sheleimah*, addressed our subject in his responsum on the *meḥitzah* in the synagogue, which was written in the 1950s. At the end of his letter, he stated:

> The Holy One, blessed be He, had a precious gift in his treasure-house, and "holiness" was its name... Unfortunately, for part of Jewry this spiritual world has been destroyed; all these sanctities have been profaned; and some observe these *mitzvot* in a secular form and manner – they expelled the sacred character inherent in the *mitzvot*. What is yet left us? Only the synagogue, the "holy place",

9. Rabbi Joel Wolowelsky, *Women, Jewish Law and Modernity – New Opportunities in a Post-Feminist Age*, Hoboken, 1997, pp. 7-8, thinks that Rabbi Feinstein would have permitted women "whose soul desires to observe *mitzvot*" to wear a *tallit* and the like, but according to the simple meaning, it appears that Rabbi Feinstein **annuls** the permission granted at the beginning of his remarks with the prohibition at the end of them.

> the "House of God" and to our sorrow, even this saving remnant they are destroying before our eyes and changing it into a "community center"... They expelled the *Shekhinah* from the synagogues...

Therefore, in his opinion, the sanctity of the synagogue must be safeguarded by preserving the *meḥitzah*.[10]

2. Rabbi Samuel Schafler (1929-1990) was a Conservative Rabbi who also ran educational institutions, such as Hebrew College in Boston. In an article he published in 1980, he objected to calling women up to read from the Torah, the inclusion of women in a *minyan*, and the ordination of women as Rabbis by the Jewish Theological Seminary of America:

> But if you are willing to consider the possibility that the synagogue need not necessarily reflect or mirror or echo contemporary American society, then let us together go on a journey of exploration.
>
> The crucial point here is our view of Judaism. Is Judaism a distinct religion – or to use Kaplan's phrase – a religious civilization with its own value system and its own distinct categories, and not simply a pale and pliable echo of Western practice? I submit that it is. I submit that Judaism is a culture, a civilization of its own that must be understood in its own categories and not judged by alien categories...
>
> If that is so, there is no reason to believe that the definition of the woman's role in American civilization must be transferred bodily into Jewish civilization...
>
> I am increasingly convinced that, if the Conservative Movement is to survive, it needs to preserve the synagogue as an island of sanctity and traditional Jewish modes and values, not to change the synagogue into a palid echo of the values or the fads of the larger American culture.
>
> It is the pre-eminent task of the synagogue to preserve classical Jewish practices, not to provide a legitimizing

10. Rabbi M. M. Kasher in: Litvin (above, note 3), Hebrew section, p. 32.

hekhsher for practices that are not indigenous to Jewish civilization.[11]

III. Women and men have equal status, but their equality must be expressed through different roles and *mitzvot*.

1. This approach is clearly expressed in two articles by Dr. Miriam Klein Shapiro (1938-2005), who was a well-known educator in the Conservative movement in the United States. She opposes the trend of Jewish women striving to fill male roles in Judaism, such as inclusion in a *minyan*. There is an assumption that the male role grants honor and status and most of the feminists accepted this argument. She even compares the situation to that of blacks in the U.S. In the 1960s, they argued that blacks and whites are **identical**; afterward, they argued that blacks are different and "black is beautiful!" Slavery means accepting the definition others use to define you. She is unwilling to accept this definition:

> ...but precisely as a feminist that I am opposed to the push of women into those ritual roles which have been men's within Judaism. We should be militant – militant in seeking those roles which are our heritage but which not only have been denied to us, but **even the knowledge that they exist** has been denied to us. It is for us now to say, "Jewish womanhood is beautiful."[12]

2. A similar approach is expressed in two articles by Rabbi Elliot Dorff, a well-known philosopher and *posek* in the Conservative movement in the United States.[13] Despite his advocating equality

11. Rabbi Samuel Schafler, *Beineinu* 10/7 (May 1980), pp. 36, 38.
12. Miriam Klein Shapiro, *Cornerstone* 1/1 (1986), pp. 48-50; the emphasis is in the original. Cf. her previous article in *Conservative Judaism* 32/1 (Fall 1978), pp. 63-66. Also cf. Carol Gilligan, *In a Different Voice*, Cambridge, Mass., 1982.
13. Rabbi Elliot Dorff, "Equality with Distinction" in: *Male and Female God*

among men and women based on factual, ethical and religious considerations, he also advocates differentiating between men and women on the basis of cognitive, psychological and religious considerations. As a compromise between these two principles, he favors "equality with distinction." For example, he seeks to hold a *Bat Mitzvah* ceremony **that differs** from a *Bar Mitzvah* ceremony. The ceremonies of *simḥat bat* and *zeved habat* (celebrating the birth of a daughter) that have developed in recent years are inherently different from the circumcision ceremony and he welcomes this. Just as it is customary to bury a Jewish man in his *tallit*, a Jewish woman should be buried in a feminine symbol, such as the shawl worn when lighting candles. According to Jewish law, both men and women are obligated to light Shabbat candles and to recite the *kiddush* on Shabbat,[14] but, according to custom, women light candles and men recite the *kiddush*. Prof. Dorff sees these customs as a prototype for the "equality with distinction" approach.

IV. Willingness to accept certain changes due to "It is time to act for the Lord, they have made Your Torah void," in order not to drive women away from Judaism

This approach appears three times in the responsa of Rabbi Yeḥiel Ya'akov Weinberg (1885-1966), the author of *Seridei Eish* and the last Rector of the Orthodox Rabbinical Seminary in Berlin.[15] Here, for example, is his responsum to Paris from 1961 in which he was asked about the height of the *meḥitzah* in the

Created Them, University Papers, The University of Judaism, Los Angeles, March 1984, pp. 13-23. He reiterated this more recently in *Conservative Judaism* 49/3 (Spring 1997), pp. 3-21 and see *ibid.*, 51/1 (Fall 1998), pp. 63-73 for various reactions to that article.

14. See OH 263:2-3; 271:2.
15. *Seridei Eish*, Part 2, No. 8 – on a co-ed youth organization for boys and girls; *ibid.*, No. 14 – on the height of the *meḥitzah* in the synagogue; *ibid.*, Part 3, No. 93 – on the *Bat Mitzvah* ceremony. The quote below is taken from the second responsum.

synagogue. He responded that the *meḥitzah* is necessary but it is possible to be lenient and require a height of just 18 *tefaḥim* [handsbreadths] and in accordance with Rabbi Moshe Feinstein's approach. The Rabbis of Hungary ruled

> that if the synagogue does not have such a *meḥitzah*, [which is taller than the women] it is forbidden to pray there and it is forbidden for the women to come and pray and it is preferable that they stay home... **but in our time, the situation has changed and the nature of things has changed** [*nishtanu hatva'im*], **and if the women stay home and do not come to the synagogue, Judaism shall be forgotten by them entirely**, and surely it is prohibited to push them away and distance them due to an excessive stringency that has no solid basis in the Talmud and among the *poskim*... **and in our time women mind stongly if they are kept away from the synagogue; and going to pray in the synagogue is, in our day, the survival of Judaism for women and mothers.**

Indeed, Rabbi Weinberg took a lenient approach when it came to a co-ed organization and co-ed singing for boys and girls, the height of the *meḥitzah*, and *Bat Mitzvah* celebrations. All of this was in order not to offend women and girls and not to drive them away from the synagogue and from Judaism.[16]

V. "Liberal Feminism" – One must find leniencies within the framework of existing Jewish Law and, slowly but surely, change the status of women in Jewish Law.

This camp has representatives from all streams of contemporary Judaism, with each one having a different red line or pace of change, **but the common denominator is the desire for change within the framework of traditional *halakhah***. This is

16. However, he also makes some strict rulings regarding our subject – see *ibid.*, Part 2, No. 52 and Part 3, No. 105 – on a woman's right to vote and to be elected.

the approach of Orthodox scholars such as Rabbi Saul Berman, Blu Greenberg, Rabbi Eliezer Berkovits, Rabbi Joel Wolowelsky and Rabbi Avi Weiss;[17] of Conservative Rabbis such as Rabbi David Feldman, Rabbi Joel Roth and myself;[18] and of Reform Rabbis such as Rabbi Moshe Zemer.[19]

1. Blu Greenberg is an Orthodox representative of this approach. She supports a long series of changes or innovations, including: women's prayer, women's *zimmun* [before reciting the grace after meals], women reciting *kiddush*, women's *hakafot* on *Simḥat Torah*, *aliyot* for women in women's prayer groups, *Bat Mitzvah*, women reading the *Megillah* even in front of a mixed congregation, greater participation by women in the marriage ceremony, recitation of the Mourner's *Kaddish* by women, and Torah study by women.

She calls these changes a "revolution of small signs". This trend is positive, in her opinion, because the Orthodox world lives according to precedents and they have more influence than conversations and discussions. If small steps are taken, as opposed to large ones, there is a greater sense of connection to the tradition and there is still an attachment to the Revelation on Mount Sinai. Continuity is not merely a *halakhic* matter, but also a psychological one. When there is an organic change, it is not

17. Rabbi Saul Berman, *Tradition* 14/2 (Fall 1973), pp. 5-28; *idem*, in *Response* 40 (Spring 1981), pp. 5-17; Blu Greenberg, *On Women and Judaism – a View from Tradition*, Philadelphia, 1981; *idem.*, in *Lilith* (Summer 1992), p. 11-17; Rabbi Eliezer Berkovits in: *Ha'ishah Bimekorot Ha'yahadut*, Jerusalem 1987, pp. 27-34; and in an expanded version in his book, *Jewish Women in Time and Torah*, Hoboken, 1990; Rabbi Joel Wolowelsky, cited above, note 9; and cf. his articles in *Judaism* 47/4 (Fall 1998), pp. 499-507; *ibid.*, 48/1 (Winter 1999), pp. 124-125; *De'ot* 5 (Elul 5759), pp. 6-11; Rabbi Avraham Weiss, *Women at Prayer: A Halakhic Analysis of Women's Prayer Groups*, Hoboken, 1990.
18. Rabbi David Feldman, *Conservative Judaism* 26/4 (Summer 1972), pp. 29-39; Rabbi Joel Roth in: Simon Greenberg, ed., *The Ordination of Women as Rabbis – Studies and Responsa*, New York, 1988, pp. 127-187. For my responsa, see below in this volume.
19. Rabbi Moshe Zemer, *Halakhah Shefuyah*, Tel Aviv, 1994, pp. 207-237 = *Evolving Halakhah*, Woodstock, Vermont, 1999, pp. 239-280.

perceived as a new approach but rather as a smooth progression in time, in history and in society.[20]

2. Rabbi Joel Wolowelsky – an Orthodox Rabbi and educator – also belongs to this school of thought. In his book on the subject, he argues that it is possible to accept specific proposals of feminism without accepting the feminist ideology. Perhaps the motive of women a few years ago was feminism, but now, due to the increase in Torah study by women, the motive is a desire to develop from a religious perspective.[21]

> Thus we take for granted that when halakhah allows for it, and the motivations are religious in nature, we should encourage increased involvement for women in all areas of Jewish life – in our homes, at our life-cycle celebrations, in our synagogues, and in our yeshivot – to enable women to enrich their spiritual lives. We should not be embarrassed about our position, nor should we allow ourselves to be dismissed or marginalized as proponents of either anti-halakhic feminism or the equally antinomian egalitarianism taking hold in the Conservative movement. The possibilities should be explored in classical halakhic terms with reference to classic texts and recognized authorities – not as skirmishes in a battle against the feminist bogey-person. As we shall see, these discussions are part and parcel of legitimate halakhic discourse.[22]

Indeed, later on in the book, he tries to justify women's *zimmun, simḥat-bat, birkat hagomel, Bat Mitzvah, sheva berakhot,* reciting "*shelo asani isha*" in an undertone, the Mourner's *Kaddish,* reading of the *Megillah,* women's prayer groups, women's yeshivas, and even the ordination of women.

3. Rabbi David Feldman, a Conservative Rabbi in New Jersey and an expert on Jewish law, is ready for changes in the status of

20. Greenberg, *Lilith* (above, note 17), pp. 16-17.
21. Wolowelsky (above, note 9), pp. x-xi.
22. *Ibid.*, pp. xi-xii.

women within the framework of *halakhah*: "There is a need for a more in-depth look at the *halakhic* structure and the *halakhic* criteria in light of the modern ideas on equality, in order to **assess what can be done within this structure** to enable greater participation of women".[23]

4. And so I wrote in 1992 in my responsum on the ordination of women as Rabbis:

> I do not think that gender equality is an absolute value neither in society nor in Judaism. This phenomenon is too new to be judged. For the time being, it can only be stated that equality is an aspiration in the Western world, and *halakhah* and Judaism must struggle with this aspiration. Similarly, I do not think there is an ethical imperative to ordain women because ethics continually change with changes in time and place. For the time being, it can only be stated that, in the eyes of the majority of Jews in the Western world, this is a fair, logical and desirable step. **If so, it remains for us to determine if this step, which appears to us to be fair, logical and desirable, is also in keeping with the demands of Jewish law.**[24]

VI. The discriminatory *halakhot* were enacted according to the sociological conditions of their time. We need to adjust them to our time, even if there is no basis for this in the sources or even if the sources are merely a support.

Rabbi Aaron Blumenthal (1907-1982) was one of the first Conservative Rabbis to call for change in the status of women in Jewish law. In 1955 he published a responsum that permitted women to be called up to the Torah, and in 1977 he published an article dealing with twelve additional issues related to women in

23. Feldman (above, note 18), p. 29.
24. Cf. my responsum on the ordination of women, below, p. 347.

Jewish law.[25] That article opens with a brief discussion of the *halakhic* sources. He determines that "there is no *halakhic* problem" with a woman reciting "Behold you are consecrated unto me" as part of a wedding ceremony. He goes on to rule that "we declare on behalf of the Conservative Movement, that the *mitzvah* of studying Torah applies to women just as it does to men"; "we declare that women are permitted to testify in every matter, the same as men"; women may perform *sheḥitah*, circumcision and judge – and **therefore**, they may serve in the role of Rabbi and cantor.[26] But his real approach is expressed only at the end of the article:

> Texts are important. We cherish them. They are part of the glory of our heritage. But we should not become prisoners of the past. The time has come for modern *halakhists* to admit that, reflecting an evolution which covers almost 4,000 years, the vehicle of the *halakhah* occasionally has paused to take on unnecessary baggage at various stations along its difficult and often tragic journey into the present. Today it is overloaded and therefore finds itself almost incapable of movement.
>
> Jewish men must recognize the fact that the *halakhah* often has been unfair, ungracious and discriminatory towards our women. We cannot undo the past, **but we can measure up to the needs of the present by granting full equality to Jewish women under the *halakhah*.**[27]

In other words, we must, in his opinion, realize the principle of full equality. The texts just provide a support in order to reach that goal.

25. For the responsum, see below p. 185. The article appeared in *Conservative Judaism* 31/3 (Spring 1977), pp. 24-40.
26. *Ibid.*, pp. 30, 33, 34, 37-38.
27. *Ibid.*, p. 40. For a similar approach, see Robert Gordis, *The Dynamics of Judaism: A Study in Jewish Law*, Bloomington and Indianapolis, 1990, pp. 164-185; Rabbi Mayer Rabinowitz in: *Ordination* (above, note 18), pp. 107-123; Judith Hauptman in: Susan Grossman and Rivkah Haut, eds., *Daughters of the King: Women and the Synagogue*, Philadelphia, 1993, pp. 159-181.

VII. The equality of women is a lofty ethical imperative and we must change the *halakhah* via *takkanot* even if there is no basis for this in the sources.

This approach is expressed by several Conservative Rabbis in Israel and abroad:

1. Rabbi David Aronson (1894-1988), who discussed our topic over the course of many decades,[28] expressed this approach in his 1983 article on the ordination of women:

> The challenge of the radical change that has occurred in the moral standards of our times – a change that recognizes the just demand of women for equal rights – makes the discussion of the traditional details that restrict women's rights irrelevant. It is absurd to argue that contemporary women are less able than men to serve as witnesses. The old laws simply have no basis in the reality of the Jewish or general society in our time. Instead of engaging in a lengthy process of interpreting or reinterpreting the ancient limitations that were imposed on women, let us present the ordination of women as an enactment necessitated by the ethical standards of our times...[29]

2. Rabbi Gilah Dror – who has served for many years as a congregational rabbi in Be'er Sheva and in Hampton, Virginia and was also President of the Rabbinical Assembly – was one of the first Israeli women to be ordained as a Conservative rabbi. She took a similar approach in her 1992 responsum on the ordination of women:

> ... even if we had not seen the change in the attitude to the status of women in society in modern times, **the principles of justice themselves demand of us that we establish the status of Jewish women as full partners in every aspect of**

28. For a survey of his articles on the subject over the course of sixty years, see my article in *American Jewish Archives* 47/2 (Fall-Winter 1995), pp. 243-260.
29. Rabbi David Aronson, *Judaism* 33/1 (Winter 1984), p. 18.

> **the Jewish tradition and as of equal spiritual value to Jewish men and to give halakhic expression to this principle.** In order to illustrate this principle, we must establish and stress unequivocally that not only is it **permissible** to ordain women as rabbis, but that we are **obligated** to ordain women as rabbis...[30]

VIII. The *Halakhah* is not binding; women and men are equal in Judaism; yet it is still worthwhile to look for precedents to justify specific actions.

1. This approach is the prevailing one in the Reform movement.[31] At the Breslau Conference in 1846, Rabbi David Einhorn proposed the following resolution:

> The Rabbinical Conference declares that the woman is equal to the man in all religious rights and obligations: that the woman is obligated in positive time-bound commandments, to the extent that such commandments still have relevance for us. The blessing "who has not made me a woman" shall be erased from the prayers; a woman shall be obligated from her youth to participate in religious education and in public prayer and shall be counted in the *minyan* of ten; the woman like the man is considered an adult at age thirteen.[32]

This resolution was not discussed due to lack of time,[33] but it

30. Rabbi Gilah Dror, *Responsa of the Va'ad Halakhah of the Rabbinical Assembly of Israel* 5 (5752-5754) p. 32, which is also available at responsafortoday.com. For similar opinions, see Rabbi Reuven Hammer, *ibid.*, p. 15; and Rabbi Michael Graetz, *ibid.*, pp. 19, 20, 23.
31. For a general survey see Riv-Ellen Prell, *Judaism* 30/4 (Fall 1981), pp. 418-426. For additional material on the Reform approach, see my above-mentioned article on Rabbi Aronson (above, note 28), note 6.
32. See above, p. 2, note 4.
33. Prell (above, note 31), p. 422.

expresses clearly the non-halakhic, egalitarian approach which characterizes the Reform movement until today.[34]

2. Rabbi Solomon Freehof (1892-1990) was the leading *posek* of the Reform movement for fifty years. In one of his books, after he lists several lenient opinions on the subject, he adds:

> Inequality is a remnant of the past. It does not constitute lack of respect for women in *halakhah*... the Reform movement is **completing** the process of extending the rights to women and declares that women are equal to men in all matters pertaining to *halakhah*. And therefore they are included in a *minyan* and receive the same education as the boys.[35]

3. In his responsum on *aliyot* for women, Rabbi Freehof quotes the source which allows this in a city that is made up entirely of *Kohanim*.[36] And he adds:

> ...it is clear that the subject has bearing upon our actual Reform practice. It is, of course, our principle that women have complete religious equality with men. Yet we are strengthened by these precedents, for they help us realize that our principle in the matter is not "out of thin air," but is a development of a tendency toward equality, which is inherent in Jewish tradition...[37]

In other words, there is a basic premise of equality and the precedents are cited in order to anchor that basic premise in Jewish tradition.

34. There is a similar approach in the discussion of the ordination of women as rabbis conducted at Hebrew Union College in 1922 – see Walter Jacob, ed., *American Reform Responsa*, New York, 1983, pp. 31, 34, 36.
35. Rabbi Solomon Freehof, *Reform Jewish Practice*, Vol. I, 1963, p. 52.
36. *Beit Yosef* to *Tur* OH, end of paragraph 135, *s.v. katav hakolbo*, in the name of Rabbeinu Yeruḥam and the latter quotes the Maharam of Rothenburg [=*Teshuvot Pesakim Uminhagim*, Part 1, Y. Z. Kahana edition, Jerusalem, 5717, p. 159, No. 100].
37. Rabbi Solomon Freehof, *Reform Responsa*, 1960, p. 42.

IX. A Halakhic Revolution – 'Radical Feminism'

This last approach is clearly expressed in Judith Plaskow's book, *Standing Again at Sinai.*[38] In her opinion, it is not enough to add women to the tradition which remains as it is; rather it is necessary to transform Judaism into a religion shaped by women and men together. Most of the civil and religious restrictions were removed in recent years, but these changes did not turn Judaism into a feminist tradition. In the meantime, women are teaching and preserving a male religion. They appear to be equals, but they leave the history, the structure and the texts that exclude them from the collective unchanged.[39] Later on in her book, she states:

> Any *halakhah* that is part of a feminist Judaism would have to look very different from *halakhah* as it has been. It would be different not just in its specifics but in its fundamentals. It would begin with the assumption of women's equality and humanity and legislate only on that basis. Laws governing the formation and dissolution of relationships, for example, would acknowledge women's full agency, so that the present laws of marriage and divorce would be ruled unjust and unacceptable. It would be different not only in its content but in its practitioners. Women would shape *halakhah* along with men, codetermining the questions raised and the answers given. The boundaries of the legal system would be both contracted and expanded as certain questions would become unthinkable, others imperative. It would be different also in method, for it would know that law is human and be aware of and humble before its own potential ideological abuse and captivity. It would be open to continual transformation in the light of deeper understandings of justice.[40]

38. Judith Plaskow, *Standing Again at Sinai,* San Francisco, 1990.
39. *Ibid.,* p. xvi.
40. *Ibid.,* pp. 72-73.

We have surveyed nine approaches to the status of women in Jewish law in the twentieth century and there are, undoubtedly, other approaches to the subject. Our objective was not to determine who is "right" in this important debate. But one way or another, one thing is clear: this subject will continue to occupy the Jewish world in the coming years and, undoubtedly, every Jew in Israel and abroad who is concerned about the future of Judaism will have to take a stand on the matter.

Responsa

1. WOMEN AND *TEFILLIN*

Oraḥ Ḥayyim 38:3

Question: *Is it permissible for women to put on tefillin?*[1]

Responsum: A discussion of our question concludes as follows:

> In conclusion, women are not permitted under any circumstances to wear *tefillin*. In view of the fact that the Rema, the authoritative codifier of law for Ashkenazic Jewry and virtually all other *poskim*, forbid the wearing of *tefillin* by women, there is very little basis for a contemporary to permit the wearing of *tefillin* by women. The Rema... views the prohibition as Rabbinic in origin. The optional wearing of *tefillin* is prohibited lest it lead to the desecration of their sanctity. This is a typical Rabbinic enactment, and its purpose is the establishment of "a fence around the Torah"; i.e., to ensure the proper performance of Torah-based laws... As is the case with all such Rabbinic enactments, the law is binding on everyone, whether or not he feels that he needs the fence.[2]

1. For the convenience of the English reader, I frequently refer to *EJ* in addition to secondary literature in Hebrew, though the Hebrew references are usually more thorough. All translations in this responsum are my own. See the Bibliography at the end of the responsum.
2. Rabbi Meiselman, pp. 150-151 and see all of Chapter 21 in his book entitled "*Tefillin*". Unfortunately, that entire chapter is one-sided, apologetic, and contains at least ten factual errors. Here is one glaring example: After quoting the opinion of the Maharam of Rothenburg, the author writes on p. 150: "He is followed in this view by Tashbetz (d. 1444) and the *Kol Bo* (14th century)." This sentence contains three errors of fact. Neither the Tashbetz nor the *Kol Bo* **follow** the Maharam's view; they both **transmit** his words

In the following responsum, we shall disprove every one of these assertions. We shall show that the Talmud and "virtually all other *poskim*" **before** the Rema permit women to wear *tefillin*; that there is ample halakhic basis to permit women to wear *tefillin*; and that no such "Rabbinic enactment" was ever enacted by the Sages. Rather, almost all opposition to women wearing *tefillin* stems from one thirteenth-century Ashkenazic Rabbi – the Maharam of Rothenburg.

From a halakhic point of view, our topic can be divided into four categories: the Talmudic period, the *Geonim* and *Rishonim*, Rabbi Meir of Rothenburg and those who followed his ruling, and those who viewed *tefillin* as a *keli gever*, male apparel.

I. The Talmudic Period

In the tannaitic period there may have been some *Tannaim* who thought that women are **obligated** to wear *tefillin*. We read in a *beraita* (*Eruvin* 96b and cf. *Tosefta Eruvin* 8:15, ed. Lieberman, pp. 136-137):

> He who finds *tefillin* [on Shabbat in the street] brings them indoors by wearing them one pair at a time – **this applies to both men and women**, to new and old *tefillin* – these are the words of Rabbi Meir. Rabbi Yehudah forbids it in the case of new *tefillin*, but permits it in the case of old ones.

The Talmud continues:

without commenting at all. Indeed, both of these books are primarily anthologies and not codes of Jewish law. Furthermore, the Tashbetz who quotes the Maharam is Rabbi Shimshon bar **Tzadok**, his pupil (late 13th century), and not Rabbi Shimon bar **Tzemaḥ** Duran, who died in North Africa in 1444. Thus, Meiselman has mistakenly presented **one** statement made by the Maharam as if it were the opinion of **three** separate *poskim*! For a thorough analysis of these three sources, see below, paragraph III.
For some of the sources concerning women and *tefillin* see Rabbi Ellinson, though he too is very one-sided in his choice of sources. See Yalon for an important analysis of the early sources; Berger for an important analysis of the Maharam and the *Aḥaronim*; and Rabbi Berkovits for a liberal Orthodox approach.

> Rabbi Meir and Rabbi Yehudah disagree only regarding new and old, but they agree regarding women. Thus, *tefillin* must be a positive commandment **without** a fixed time and women are **obligated** to perform all such commandments.

Thus, according to the Babylonian Talmud, Rabbi Meir and Rabbi Yehudah **obligate** women to wear *tefillin*.[3] This opinion had no echo in later *halakhah* because most *Tannaim* felt that *tefillin* **is** a PTBC [positive time-bound commandment] since they are not worn on Shabbat or festivals,[4] and thus women are exempt from wearing them.

Nevertheless, the majority view of the *Tannaim* is expressed by the Mishnah in the tractate of *Berakhot* (3:3; Bavli fol. 20a-b): "**Women**, slaves, and minors are **exempt** from reciting the *Shema* and from ***tefillin***...". The Mishnah offers no explanation for this exemption, but other Rabbinic texts attempt to fill in the gap. The *Mekhilta*[5] and the Yerushalmi[6] (which is the source of *Pesikta Rabbati*[7]) explain through different *derashot* that since women are exempt from Torah study, they are also exempt from *tefillin*. The *Tosefta* (*Kiddushin* 1:10, ed. Lieberman, p. 279) and the Bavli (*Kiddushin* 34a, 35a, and cf. *Berakhot* 20b), on the other hand, derive this exemption from the fact that *tefillin* is a PTBC from which women are generally exempt (cf. Mishnah *Kiddushin* 1:7).

3. But see Rabbi Yosef Dinner, *Ḥiddushei Haritzad*, Vol. I, Jerusalem, 1981[2], pp. 149-150 and Rabbi David Weiss Halivni, *Mekorot Umesorot: Masekhtot Eruvin Upesaḥim*, Jerusalem, 1982, p. 247 for a completely different explanation of this section in the Bavli.
4. According to Rabbi Akiva (*Eruvin* 96a and parallels), *tefillin* are not worn on Shabbat and festivals.
5. *Mekhilta de-Rabbi Yishmael, Massekhta Depasḥa*, ed. Horowitz–Rabin, Jerusalem, 1970[2], p. 68 which is the source for *Midrash Tanḥuma, Bo*, end of section 14 and for *Massekhet Tefillin, Halakhah* 3, ed. M. Higger in: *Sheva Massekhtot Ketanot*, New York, 1930, pp. 42-43. For traditions regarding Tabi (see below), cf. Yerushalmi *Eruvin* 10:1, fol. 26a; Yerushalmi *Sukkah* 2:1, fol. 52d; *Semaḥot* 1:10, ed. Zlotnick, New Haven and London, 1966, p. 2.
6. Yerushalmi *Berakhot*, Chapter 2, fol. 4c = Yerushalmi *Eruvin* 10:1, fol. 26a (and cf. Yerushalmi *Berakhot* 3:3, fol. 6b).
7. Meir Ish-Shalom edition, Vienna, 1880, *Parashah* 22, fol. 112b.

However, the *Mekhilta*, Yerushalmi and Bavli add some important information. The *Mekhilta* adds:

> Mikhal bat Kushi[8] used to wear *tefillin*. Jonah's wife used to ascend to Jerusalem on the three pilgrim festivals. Tabi the slave of Rabban Gamliel used to wear *tefillin*.[9]

The Yerushalmi quotes that same *beraita* with two contradictory additions:

> But we have learned in a *beraita*: Mikhal bat Kushi used to wear *tefillin* and Jonah's wife used to ascend to Jerusalem on the three pilgrim festivals **and the Sages did not protest**. Rabbi Ḥizkiah said in the name of Rabbi Abbahu: Jonah's wife was forced to return home and as for Mikhal bat Kushi – **the Sages did protest.**[10]

The Bavli's version of the *beraita* (*Eruvin* 96a) concurs with the first version in the Yerushalmi:

> Mikhal bat Kushi used to wear *tefillin* **and the Sages did not protest**; Jonah's wife used to ascend to Jerusalem on the three pilgrim festivals **and the Sages did not protest**.

Various speculations have been made concerning the origins of these anecdotes about Mikhal[11] and Jonah's

8. *Kushi* = King Saul. See Psalms 7:1 and *Sifrei Bemidbar, Piska* 99, ed. Horowitz, Jerusalem, 1966^2, p. 99; the sources in the notes there; as well as the sources cited by Prof. Louis Ginzberg, *Legends of the Jews*, Vol. VI, Philadelphia, 1928, p. 274, note 134.
9. See above, note 5.
10. See above, note 6.
11. Prof. Louis Ginzberg, *Legends* (above, note 8), and in a much clearer fashion in Ginzberg, p. 289. Despite the brilliance of his hypothesis, it has no textual support whatsoever and assumes that the *Mekhilta* knew *midrashim* similar to those found in such late *midrashim* as *Midrash Hagadol*, *Midrash Eishet Ḥayil*, and *Yalkut Shimoni*. Alternatively, Ginzberg (pp. 286 and 288, note 44) hints that Mikhal and Jonah's wife may have been references to women who actually lived during the early tannaitic period, but he does not develop this suggestion. Solomon Schechter, *Studies in Judaism*, First Series, Philadelphia, 1911, p. 320, suggested that since the Sages could only imagine such behavior in "the remotest past", they therefore attributed the acts described

wife.[12] There can be no doubt, however, that the story about Tabi, Rabban Gamliel's slave, is a historical fact about that famous slave which concurs with other episodes in Tabi's life.[13] Furthermore, the line about Tabi indicates that the *Mekhilta* looked favorably on the behavior of Mikhal and Jonah's wife, since Tabi's observance of *mitzvot* was generally admired by Rabban Gamliel and the *Tannaim*.[14] This assumption is supported by the fact that in the two parallel sources in the Yerushalmi we are told that Tabi put on *tefillin* "and the Sages did not protest". This is also the case in tractate *Semaḥot* (1:10, ed. Zlotnick, p. 2):

> Even he [Rabban Gamliel] allowed him to wear *tefillin*. They [his students] said to him: "Rabbi, did you not teach us that slaves are exempt from *tefillin*?" He answered them: "My slave, Tabi, is not like other slaves, he is a worthy man".[15]

The question remains: Where did the additions to the ancient *beraita* in the *Mekhilta* come from? Why do the Bavli and the *beraita* in the Yerushalmi add "**and the Sages did not protest**", whereas Rabbi Abbahu adds "**and the Sages did protest**"? Prof. Louis Ginzberg suggests very plausibly that:

> ...according to the simple meaning, in the *Mekhilta* they wanted to say that even though women are exempt from *tefillin*, Mikhal used to wear them, and Jonah's wife used to ascend to Jerusalem even though it is a PTBC because they

to Mikhal the Daughter of King Saul and to the wife of Jonah. Yalon, p. 36, made the same suggestion without mentioning Schechter. For an entire monograph regarding Mikhal bat Shaul wearing *tefillin*, see Mirsky.

12. A. Büchler, *JQR*, Old Series X (1898), p. 705; Ginzberg, pp. 286-287; S. Safrai, *Ha'aliyah Laregel Biyemei Bayit Sheini*, Jerusalem, 1985², p. 91; and M. Z. Fuchs, "*Simḥat Beit Hasho'eva*", *Tarbitz* 55 (1986), p. 196, note 147.
13. See, for example, Aharon Hyman, *Toledot Tannaim Ve'amoraim*, London, 1910, pp. 521-522 and *EJ*, s.v. *Tabi*.
14. See *ibid*.
15. See above, end of note 5.

> were pious and dealt strictly with themselves. But since the words of the *Mekhilta* can be construed in different fashions, the memorizers of the *beraitot*[16] inserted their own interpretations into the *beraitot*. Thus some had the version: "**And the Sages did not protest**" and some had the version: "**And the Sages did protest**".[17]

Regardless of the precise development of these traditions, we can summarize the different approaches from the Mishnaic and Talmudic periods as follows: According to the Bavli, Rabbi Meir and Rabbi Yehudah **obligated** woman to wear *tefillin*, while according to the Mishnah, women are **exempt** from *tefillin*. According to the *Mekhilta* and the Bavli, women are **exempt** from *tefillin*, but may wear them like Mikhal bat Kushi. The Bavli adds (*Eruvin* 96b) that this concurs with the opinion of Rabbi Yossi in his argument with Rabbi Yehudah. Rabbi Yossi maintained that even though women are **exempt** from PTBC, they are **allowed** to perform them, just as women used to place their hands on the *ḥagigah* sacrifice on *Yom Tov*.[18] Only Rabbi Abbahu in the Yerushalmi and the *Pesikta* feels that women are exempt from *tefillin* and **may not** put them on since, in his opinion, the Sages did indeed protest against the actions of Mikhal bat Kushi.

Thus, if we were going to rule on the basis of talmudic sources alone, our ruling would have to be that women may wear *tefillin*. This is in accordance with the well-established principle that when the Bavli contradicts the Yerushalmi, we follow the Bavli.[19]

16. The "*Tannaim*" – see Y. N. Epstein, *Mavo Lenusaḥ Hamishnah*, Jerusalem, 1948, pp. 673ff. and *EJ*, Vol. 15, col. 800 at the bottom.
17. Ginzberg, p. 290. For an analysis of the term "protest", see Berger, note 18.
18. *Sifra, Dibura Denedavah, Parsheta* 2, *Halakhah* 2, ed. Weiss, Vienna, 1862, fols. 4b-4c = Bavli *Ḥagigah* 16b and parallels. And see now Rabbi Louis Finkelstein, *Sifra Devei Rav*, II, New York, 1983, p. 20 and III, pp. 59-60.
19. See, for example, the responsum of Rav Hai Gaon in *Teshuvot Hage'onim*, ed. S. Assaf, Jerusalem, 1929, pp. 125-126 and the parallels cited there; Rif at the end of tractate *Eruvin*, ed. Vilna, fol. 35b; and other sources cited by Menaḥem Elon, *Hamishpat Ha'ivri*, Jerusalem, 1988[3], p. 902, note 68 and Y.N. Epstein, *Mevo'ot Lesifrut Ha'amora'im*, Jerusalem-Tel Aviv, 1962, pp. 290-291.

Before we move on to the geonic period, we must mention one more Rabbinic source of a non-halakhic nature – *Targum Pseudo-Yonatan* to Deut. 22:5.[20] The verse "A women must not put on a man's apparel" is translated there as: "A cloak with *tzitzit* and *tefillin* shall not be worn by a woman because they are a man's apparel". This particular translation has no talmudic basis, as we have seen above, but we shall see that it was used by some of the *Aḥaronim*.

II. The Period of the *Geonim* and the *Rishonim*

In the geonic period, there is scarcely any mention of our topic. The *She'iltot* (written 748 C.E.) mention the fact that women and slaves are exempt from reciting the *Shema* and *tefillin*,[21] while the author of *Halakhot Gedolot* quotes the Mishnah and *Gemara* from *Berakhot* without any further comment.[22]

20. Scholars today refer to it as *Targum Yerushalmi* I – see *EJ*, vol. 4, col. 845 and Zunz–Albeck, *Haderashot Beyisrael*, Jerusalem, 1947, pp. 36ff. On the contradictions between some of the *halakhot* in the Palestinian *Targumim* and normative Rabbinic *halakhah*, see the following: A. Geiger, *Hamikra Vetargumav*, Jerusalem, 1949, pp. 103-109 and 290-315; H. Albeck, *B.M. Lewin Jubilee Volume*, Jerusalem, 1940, pp. 93-104; Y.Y. Weinberg, *The Abraham Weiss Jubilee Volume*, New York, 1964, Hebrew section, pp. 367-368; M. Ohana, *Vetus Testamentum* 23 (1973), pp. 385-399; J. Heinemann, *Journal of Jewish Studies* 25 (1974), pp. 114-122; J. Faur, *JQR* 66 (1975), pp. 19-26; Bernard Bamberger, *ibid.*, pp. 27-28; Yishayahu Ma'ori, *Te'udah* 3 (1983), pp. 235-250; S.Z. Havlin, *Sidra* 2 (1986), pp. 25-36 and the literature *ibid.*, note 1; Dov Herman, *Sinai* 103 (1989), pp. 45-52 and the literature *ibid.*, note 1; E.E. Urbach in: S. Friedman, ed., *Saul Lieberman Memorial Volume*, New York and Jerusalem, 1993, pp. 53-63; and the literature listed by Avigdor Shinan in: *Targum Va'aggadah Bo*, Jerusalem, 1993, p. 44, note 155.
21. *She'iltot*, ed. Mirsky, No. 47, Vol. III, Jerusalem, 1964, p. 72 and No. 164, Vol. V, Jerusalem, 1977, p. 20.
22. *Halakhot Gedolot*, ed. Warsaw, 1875, p. 4. Regarding his reading in the *Gemara*, see R.N.N. Rabinowitz, *Dikdukei Soferim* to *Berakhot*, Munich, 1868, p. 97, note 2. This Talmudic passage is missing in the parallel section of *Halakhot Gedolot*, ed. Jerusalem, Vol. I, 1971, p. 12. There were men in Geonic times who wanted to prevent menstruating women from touching *tefillin* – *Teshuvot Hage'onim Haḥadashot*, Jerusalem, 1995, No. 161, p. 235 – but that custom undoubtedly derived from the foreign custom that forbade women from touching Torah scrolls. See *ibid.*, note 22, and the articles listed below in note 64.

In the period of the *Rishonim* (1000-1500), many of the major *poskim* such as the Rif[23], the Rambam[24], the Rosh[25], the *Tur*[26] and Rabbi Yosef Karo in the *Shulḥan Arukh*[27], simply repeat or paraphrase the Mishnah that women are **exempt** from *tefillin* without dealing with the question of whether they are **permitted** to wear *tefillin* if they wish to do so. This is particularly noticeable in the Rosh, who quotes the *Mekhilta* and the second passage in the Yerushalmi (*Berakhot* 3:3, fol. 6b), yet refrains from mentioning Mikhal bat Shaul at all, either to agree or disagree.

Nonetheless, many *Rishonim* do deal with our issue both directly and indirectly. As Rabbi Joel Roth has pointed out,[28] three basic attitudes can be discerned among the *Rishonim* vis-à-vis women performing PTBC:

1. The Ra'avad of Posquieres (1120-1198) is generally **opposed** to women performing such *mitzvot*:

> ...because all the *mitzvot* from which women are exempt [and] if they do them it is possible that they will be treat them lightly or perform them incorrectly – the Sages protested, like Mikhal bat Shaul who used to put on *tefillin* and the Sages protested... since women are not careful to observe them properly...[29]

Furthermore, the Ra'avad goes on to rule like Rabbi Yehudah and Rabbi Meir (in the Mishnah and in Bavli *Rosh Hashanah* 32b-33a) – and against Rabbi Yossi – that women are not allowed to

23. Rif to *Berakhot*, Chapter 3, ed. Vilna, fols. 11b-12a.
24. Rambam, *Hilkhot Tefillin* 4:13.
25. *Hilkhot Tefillin* at the end of Bavli *Menaḥot*, paragraph 29, ed. Vilna, fol. 122b.
26. *Tur* OH 38.
27. *Shulḥan Arukh* OH 38:3.
28. In his responsum "On the Ordination of Women as Rabbis" in: Simon Greenberg, ed., *The Ordination of Women as Rabbis: Studies and Responsa*, New York, 1988, pp. 129-133, and briefly in his article "Ordination of Women: An *Halakhic* Analysis", *Judaism* 33/1 (Winter 1984), pp. 70-71.
29. Ra'avad, Commentary to *Sifra* (above, note 18), ed. Weiss, Vienna, 1862, fol. 4b.

perform PTBC. The only exceptions he mentions are sitting in the *sukkah* and waving the *lulav* which women may perform without a blessing "because there is no possibility that they will be treat them lightly or perform them incorrectly".[30] The Ra'avad is apparently the only *Rishon* to hold this opinion.[31]

2. A large group of *Rishonim* led by Rashi[32] and the Rambam rule that women may perform PTBC, but **without a blessing**. As the Rambam states:

> Women, slaves, and minors are exempt from *tzitzit* from the Torah... Women and slaves who want to wrap themselves in *tzitzit* may do so without a blessing and so too other positive commandments from which women are exempt – if they want to perform them without a blessing **one does not protest**.[33]

The final phrase, "one does not protest", may imply that the Rambam learned this general principle from the story about Mikhal in *Eruvin* 96a: "And the Sages **did not protest**". The Rambam gives no inkling as to **why** women may not recite the blessing over PTBC, but a number of *Rishonim* are clearly worried about a blessing being recited in vain (*berakhah levatalah*) and therefore ask: how can they recite "Who has sanctified us with His commandments and commanded us" if they were not commanded to do so?[34] This general approach was accepted by a

30. *Ibid.*, fol. 4c.
31. For a similar opinion, see the "*gadol*" quoted by *Hagahot Maimoniot* to *Hilkhot Tzitzit*, Chapter 3, note 30. The same sage is wary of "a woman's hair is a sexual distraction" (*Berakhot* 24a). See Berger, pp. 102-103, for an analysis of this issue.
32. Quoted by *Hagahot Maimoniot, ibid.*, note 40 and in *Or Zaru'a, Hilkhot Rosh Hashanah*, paragraph 266, Vol. 2, Zhitomir, 1862, fol. 62a (twice) and again in *Hilkhot Sukkah*, paragraph 314, fol. 68d and see "*Rabbeinu Shaḥ*" quoted in *Maḥzor Vitry*, Berlin, 1889, p. 414. Regarding the latter Rabbi, see my article "*Rabbeinu Shaḥ*" in *Sinai* 98 (1986), pp. 201-214 and especially the appendix on pp. 213-214.
33. *Hilkhot Tzitzit* 3:9.
34. See *Or Zaru'a, Hilkhot Rosh Hashanah*, fol. 62a, at the top and fol. 62b towards

number of *Rishonim*[35] and codified by Rabbi Yosef Karo in the *Shulḥan Arukh*.[36]

3. A much larger group of *Rishonim* led by one of Rashi's teachers (11th century) in Germany,[37] Rabbeinu Tam (ca.1100-1171) in France,[38] Rabbi Zeraḥia Halevi (12th century) in Provence,[39] and the Rashba (1235-1310) in Spain[40] rule that women may perform PTBC **and recite the blessing as well**. Rabbeinu Tam specifically rules according to Rabbi Yossi, following the well-known talmudic principle (*Gittin* 67a) that the *halakhah* follows Rabbi Yossi because "he has deep reasons for whatever he says" (*nimuko imo*). Furthermore, Rabbi Zeraḥia, Rabbeinu Tam, and the

the middle; "*Rabbeinu Shaḥ*" in *Maḥzor Vitry* (above, note 32); *Semag*, Positive Commandments, paragraph 42, ed. Venice, 1547, fol. 119b; *Piskei Harosh* to *Kiddushin*, Chapter 1, paragraph 49, ed. Vilna, fol. 87c; and *Maggid Mishneh* to Rambam, *Hilkhot Sukkah* 6:13, at the end.

35. Rabbi Isaac of Vienna in *Or Zaru'a* quoted above; Rabbi Isaiah Detrani in *Sefer Hamakhria*, paragraph 78, Munkacs, 1900, fol. 54c = Jerusalem, 1998, columns 481-492 and more briefly in *Piskei Harid* to *Rosh Hashanah* 33a, Jerusalem, 1971, cols. 159-160; the Meiri in *Beit Habeḥira* to *Eruvin* 96a, ed. Hirshler, Jerusalem, 1962, pp. 392-393; *Tur* OH 17; and cf. *Tosafot* to *Eruvin* 96b at end of s.v. *dilma* and to *Rosh Hashanah* 33a s.v. *ha* and *Piskei Harosh* (above, note 34).
36. OH 589:6 and see his explanation in the *Beit Yosef* to *Tur* OH 17 s.v. *aval*.
37. Rabbi Yitzḥak **Halevi** according to *Teshuvot Rashi*, ed. Elfenbein, New York, 1943, No. 68, pp. 80-81 and the sources cited there. But Rabbi Yitzḥak **ben Yehudah** according to *Or Zaru'a, Hilkhot Rosh Hashanah*, fol. 62a; *Tosafot* to *Rosh Hashanah* 33a s.v. *ha*; *Piskei Harosh, loc. cit.*; and Rabbeinu Yeruḥam, *Toledot Adam Veḥavah, Netiv* 27, Vol. 1, ed. Venice, 1553, fol. 227d. In *Abudraham Hashalem*, Jerusalem, 1963, p. 28, he is called Rabbi Yitzḥak **ben Giya[t]** which is clearly a scribal error, but Rabbi Ovadia Yosef, was misled by this error in *Yehaveh Da'at*, Vol. 4, p. 130 in the note. For Ibn Giyyat's actual opinion, see below, note 46. For further discussion of this responsum, see below, p. 159, note 6.
38. Quoted by more than fifteen *Rishonim*. See, for example, *Tosafot* to *Eruvin* 96a s.v. *dilma* and to *Rosh Hashanah* 33 s.v. *ha*.
39. In his *Ma'or Hakatan* to the Rif, *Rosh Hashanah*, Chapter 4, ed. Vilna, fol. 9b. His opinion is also quoted by *Shibbolei Haleket*, paragraph 295, ed. Buber, Vilna, 1887, p. 278.
40. *Responsa Rashba*, Vol. I, No. 123.

Rashba all base their permission to recite the blessing on the precedent of Mikhal bat Shaul!

Rabbi Zeraḥia Halevi deals with our issue in his commentary *Hama'or Hakatan* to the Rif on Bavli *Rosh Hashanah* 33a. The Mishnah (fol. 32b) states that "we do not prevent minors from blowing the *shofar*" on *Rosh Hashanah*. The *Gemara* explains:

> This would imply that women **are prevented**. But we have learned in a *beraita*: "**We do not prevent** neither women nor children from blowing the shofar on *Yom Tov*"? Abaye replied: There is no contradiction: one is the opinion of Rabbi Yehudah [who is opposed to the observance of PTBC by women]; the other is the opinion of Rabbi Yossi and Rabbi Shimon [who are in favor of women observing PTBC].

Upon this, Rabbi Zeraḥia Halevi comments:

> Since we established that the Mishnah follows Rabbi Yehudah, while Rabbi Yossi and Rabbi Shimon disagree with it – we reject the Mishnah in favor of the *beraita*. And all PTBC, even though they are not obligated [for women], they are a permissible *mitzvah*, and even if they bless on them "who has sanctified us with His commandments and commanded us" to blow the *shofar* or to hear [the *shofar*] or to sit in the *sukkah* or to wave the *lulav*, **we do not protest**, like Mikhal bat Shaul who used to put on *tefillin* and like Jonah's wife who used to ascend to Jerusalem on the three pilgrim festivals and the Sages did not protest, as it is written in Chapter *Hamotzei Tefillin* (*Eruvin* 96a). **And thus the ruling has gone forth from before the Sages of this place** [= Provence] may their memory be blessed, **and from before the Sages of France** and they brought proofs for their words at length and they are written in their books and responsa.[41]

Rabbeinu Tam's opinion is quoted in many places. He says:

41. See above, note 39.

> ...And they may recite the blessings over a PTBC, even though they are exempt from that *mitzvah* and they may occupy themselves with that *mitzvah* like Mikhal bat Kushi who, it can be assumed, also recited the blessing.[42]

And the Rashba replies in one of his responsa :

> You already know the disagreement of the *Rishonim* and their proofs and I agree with he who says that if they desire they can do all positive commandments and recite the blessings [which we learn] from Mikhal bat Shaul who used to wear *tefillin* and they did not protest; rather she did so with the approval of the Sages and it is obvious that since she puts on *tefillin*, she pronounces the blessing.[43]

This opinion of the Rashba is quoted by Rabbi Aharon Hacohen of Lunel in his *Orḥot Ḥayyim* without taking a stand.[44] Hassar Micoucy (Rabbi Shimson ben Shimson of Coucy), on the other hand, explicitly allows women to put on *tefillin* with a blessing.[45] This general approach to PTBC is accepted and codified by **many** *Rishonim*[46] and also by the Rema in the *Shulḥan*

42. This quotation is from *Tosafot* to *Rosh Hashanah* 33a, s.v. *ha*. The bracketed phrase was added from *Tosafot Harosh ibid.*, ed. Ravitz, Benei Berak, 1968.
43. See above, note 40.
44. Vol. I, Florence, 1750, *Hilkhot Tefillin*, paragraph 3, fol. 7b.
45. Quoted by *Hagahot Maimoniot* (above, note 32); *idem*, to Rambam, *Hilkhot Ḥanukah* 3, paragraph 5; and *Tosafot* to *Berakhot* 14a, s. v. *yamim*. My thanks to Yisrael Ḥazzani for the second reference which we shall discuss again below in note 75.
46. Other *Rishonim* who rule thus are: Rabbi Yitzḥak ibn Giyyat, *Sha'arei Simḥah*, ed. Bamberger, Furth, 1861, p. 38 (according to the version quoted in *Sefer Ha'ittur*, ed. Meir Yonah, Vol. 2, Vilna, 1874, fol. 99d; *Shibbolei Haleket*, above, note 39; and *Piskei Harosh* to *Rosh Hashanah*, Chapter 4, paragraph 7); *Ḥiddushei Haramban* to *Kiddushin* 31a s.v. *man de'amar*; *Ḥiddushei Haritva* to *Kiddushin* 31a, s.v. *veyesh doḥim*; Rabbi Aharon Halevi of Barcelona quoted in the Ritva, *ibid.*; Rabbeinu Yeruḥam, above, note 37; *Ḥiddushei Haran* to *Rosh Hashanah* 33a, s.v. *ve'ein elu re'ayot*; Rabbi Eliezer ben Yoel Halevi, *Sefer Ra'aviyah*, ed. Aptowitzer, Vol. 2, New York, 1983^2, *Massekhet Megillah*, paragraph 597, pp. 336-340; Rabbi Ya'akov of Marvege, *She'elot Uteshuvot Min Hashamayim*, ed. Margaliot, Tel Aviv, 1957, No. 1;

Arukh.[47] Thus, once again, if we were to rule on the basis of these *Rishonim*, our ruling would be: women are exempt from *tefillin* but may perform this *mitzvah* as well as other PTBC with a blessing (Rabbi Zeraḥia, Rabbeinu Tam, Rashba and others) or without a blessing (Rashi, Rambam and others).

III. Rabbi Meir of Rothenburg

Almost all opposition to women wearing *tefillin* stems from one sentence uttered by Rabbi Meir of Rothenburg, the Maharam (Germany, d. 1293),[48] and unfortunately even this sentence has come down to us in two different versions.

Rabbeinu Simḥah quoted by *Hagahot Maimoniot*, above, note 32, who allowed women to recite the blessing for blowing the shofar; Rabbi Meir of Rothenburg in relation to ***tzitzit*** quoted by *Tashbetz*, paragraph 270 (but see below, p. 62, for his view on women and ***tefillin***!). The author of the *Aggudah* simply quoted Rabbeinu Tam and seems to have concurred – see *Sefer Ha'aggudah* to Shabbat, Chapter 2, paragraph 46 and to *Eruvin*, Chapter 10, paragraphs 97-98.

47. OH 589:6. We should add that *Sefer Haḥinukh* (ed. Chavel, Jerusalem, 1986, paragraph 420, p. 537) explicitly allows women to wear *tefillin* but does not deal with the issue of the blessings. *Sefer Ha'ittur* (see beginning of previous note), fol. 61b apparently allows women to wear *tefillin* since he quotes from Yerushalmi *Berakhot* 3:3, Bavli *Eruvin* 96a, and the *Mekhilta*, yet leaves out Yerushalmi *Berakhot* Chapter 2 which is opposed. However, he too does not discuss the blessings.
48. There were two other *Rishonim* opposed to women wearing *tefillin*, but neither had any effect on later *poskim*. *Sefer Ha'eshkol*, ed. Auerbach, Part 2, Halberstadt, 1868, p. 90 explicitly rules like Rabbi Abbahu in the Yerushalmi that we do protest, the reason being that *tefillin* require "a clean body" like Elisha Ba'al Kenafayim (Bavli *Shabbat* 49a). In other words, he says explicitly what many tried to read into the Maharam (see below) but, as we shall see, there is no reason to rule like the Yerushalmi against the Bavli and no reason to assume that women cannot maintain "a clean body". Moroever, there are doubts regarding the reliability of *Sefer Ha'eshkol*, ed. Auerbach – see EJ, Vol. 2, cols. 146-147, and Berger, note 45.
    The second opponent was *Piskei Ri'az* to *Rosh Hashanah* 33a (Jerusalem, 1971, col. 84) also quoted by *Shiltei Hagiborim* (to Rif, *Rosh Hashanah*, ed. Vilna, fol. 9b). He says that women "may not wear *tefillin* even without a blessing because it appears like the way of the heretics who transgress the words of the Sages and do not want to explain the verses as they do". This statement

However, before quoting the Maharam, we must mention an explanation offered two generations earlier[49] in the *Tosafot* to *Eruvin* 96a which **may** have served as the basis for the Maharam's statement. The authors of the *Tosafot* there are trying to explain why Rabbi Abbahu in *Pesikta Rabbati* said that the Sages protested against Mikhal bat Shaul. They suggest:

> And it seems that the reason behind those who say that [women] do not have permission [to wear *tefillin*] is because ***tefillin* require a clean body and women are not scrupulous to be careful...**

It must be emphasized that *Tosafot* in *Eruvin* did not rule thus as a matter of law, but simply suggested this as a means of explaining Rabbi Abbahu in *Pesikta Rabbati*.

The Maharam, on the other hand, makes a similar statement as a matter of law. His pupil Rabbi Shimshon bar Tzadok, the *Tashbetz*, quotes him as follows:

> And women are exempt from *tefillin* and *tzitzit* because both are PTBC, since *tefillin* are not worn on Shabbat and *tzitzit* are not worn at night. But, in any case, one should not protest against their wrapping themselves in *tzitzit* and reciting the blessing because they can accept upon themselves an obligation as is evident from *Kiddushin* [fol. 31a – "Greater is he who is commanded and performs *mitzvot* than he who is not commanded.] **However, they should not wear *tefillin* because they do not know how to keep themselves in purity.**[50]

Rabbi Aharon Hacohen of Lunel in *Orḥot Ḥayyim*, as well as

is difficult to fathom, since *Eruvin* 96a clearly states that the Sages did **not** protest against Mikhal bat Shaul. Furthermore, the verses adduced in the Yerushalmi and *Mekhilta* do not say that women are **forbidden** to wear *tefillin* but only that they are **exempt** from doing so.

49. See E.E. Urbach, *Ba'alei Hatosafot*, Jerusalem, 1980^4, pp. 605-607.

50. *Sefer Tashbetz*, Lemberg, 1858, paragraph 270.

the related work *Kol Bo,* quote the Maharam more briefly as follows:[51]

> Rabbi Meir, may he rest in peace, wrote that women are exempt from *tefillin* and **if they want to wear them, we do not listen to them, because they do not know how to keep themselves in cleanliness.**

This passage is quoted from the *Kol Bo* by the Rema[52] as the *halakhah* and from then on was widely accepted as the *halakhah.*[53] However, this statement by the Maharam is extremely problematic:

1. First of all, Rabbi Aharon Hacohen of Lunel himself asks:

> And this is difficult for me to understand from that which we say in *Eruvin,* Chapter *Hamotzei,* that Mikhal bat Shaul used to wear *tefillin* and the Sages did not protest.[54]

In other words, how could the Maharam rule against the plain meaning of the *Gemara* in *Eruvin*? This question led to a series of attempts to defend the Maharam:

A. Rabbi Yosef Karo does not quote the Maharam in the *Shulḥan Arukh* because he apparently does not accept his view. Nevertheless, in his *Beit Yosef* he tries to justify the Maharam:

51. *Orḥot Ḥayyim,* above, note 44 and *Sefer Kol Bo,* Lvov, 1860, *Hilkhot Tefillin,* paragraph 21, fol. 13c. The quotation here is from *Orḥot Ḥayyim.* On the relationship between these two books, see Hayyim Tchernowitz, *Toledot Haposkim,* II, New York, 1947, pp. 182-186, 251-254; Elon, above, note 19, pp. 1040-1042; *EJ,* Vol. 2, cols. 12-13 and Vol. 10, cols. 1159-1160.
52. OH 38:3. In *Darkei Moshe Ha'arokh,* Fiorda, 1760, *ibid.,* the Rema simply quotes the *Beit Yosef* who quotes the *Kol Bo.*
53. Rabbi Mordekhai Yaffe in the *Levush Hatekhelet* to OH 38:3 and see *ibid.,* 17:2; Rabbi Shlomo Luria in *Yam Shel Shlomo* to *Kiddushin,* Chapter 1, paragraph 64; Rabbi Ḥayyim Yosef David Azulai in *Birkei Yosef* to OH 38:1; *Responsa Maharam Schick* to OH, No. 15; *Arukh Hashulḥan* OH 38:6; and *Mishnah Berurah* to OH 38, subparagraph 13 (but cf. OH 39, *Bei'ur Halakhah,* s.v. *kasher*). For *Aḥaronim* who nevertheless allowed women to put on *tefillin,* see *Responsa Mass'at Binyamin,* No. 62 (quoted by Berger, p. 99) and *Responsa Rabaz,* No. 73 (quoted *ibid.,* pp. 112-113).
54. See above, note 44.

> I believe that Rabbi Meir's reason is as the Tosafot wrote, that it is written in the Pesikta that the Sages protested, and they explained that the reason behind this was that *tefillin* **require a clean body** and women are not scrupulous to be careful, and Rabbi Meir wanted to take the Pesikta's opinion into account.[55]

Despite our great respect for Rabbi Yosef Karo, it is difficult to accept this answer, because "a clean body" and "purity" are not necessarily identical concepts; because the Maharam makes no mention of the *Pesikta;* and if there is a disagreement between the Bavli and the Pesikta, one should always rule according to the Bavli.[56]

B. Rabbi Shlomo Luria (Maharshal, 1510-1579) in his *Yam Shel Shelomo* to *Kiddushin* quotes the *Beit Yosef*'s justification for the Maharam and continues:

> And I say that we don't need all of this. Rather, the reason they did not protest against Mikhal was because she was an extremely righteous woman,[57] and the king's wife and had no children and could thus keep herself in cleanliness, which is not the case with other women.[58]

Once again, this explanation is problematic. The Maharshal reads into the Bavli and the Maharam a number of points that are not mentioned at all. Furthermore, it hinges on the reading

55. *Beit Yosef* to OH 38, s.v. *katav hakolbo.*
56. See Yerushalmi *Pe'ah* 2:6, fol. 17a = Yerushalmi *Ḥagigah* 1:8, fol. 76d and the discussion by *Yad Malakhi, Kelalei Hagemara,* paragraph 72; *Sedei Ḥemed, Ma'arekhet Ha'alef,* paragraph 95; Z. H. Ḥayyot, *Kol Sifrei Maharatz Ḥayyot,* Vol. I, Jerusalem, 1958, pp. 243-253; and ET, Vol. 9, cols. 252-253.
57. *Arukh Hashulḥan,* above, note 53, also makes this point without referring to Rabbi Shlomo Luria. I was unable to find any rabbinic source which refers to Mikhal as an "extremely righteous woman".
58. *Yam Shel Shlomo,* above, note 53. This explanation was accepted by the Ḥida in *Birkei Yosef, ibid.* For a lengthy analysis of the Maharshal's words, see Berger, pp. 95-98.

"*benekiut*" meaning physical cleanliness, whereas the Maharam probably said "*betohorah*" which means ritual purity.

C. The Gaon of Vilna (1720-1797) also tried to justify the Maharam and the Rema. He quotes the Beit Yosef and Yerushalmi *Berakhot* and adds that the Bavli was aware of **both** opinions found in the Yerushalmi and agreed with Rabbi Abbahu that the Sages protested against Mikhal bat Kushi. The Bavli only quoted the first opinion in order to search for the *Tannaim* who said that *tefillin* are worn on Shabbat, but it rejected this suggestion and decided that this *beraita* follows Rabbi Yosi who said that women may lay their hands on the *ḥagigah* sacrifice. Rabbi Abbahu, however, thought that even though they may lay their hands on the sacrifice, they may not wear *tefillin*. Thus, according to the Gaon of Vilna, the Bavli also agrees with Rabbi Abbahu.[59] A similar suggestion was made 500 years earlier by Rabbi Yitzḥak *Or Zaru'a*,[60] but there is no textual support for their hypothesis. The Bavli clearly only knew **one** version of the *beraita* about Mikhal, and that version said that the Sages **did not** protest.[61]

Therefore the riddle remains: even if the Maharam was aware of the Yerushalmi or the *Pesikta* – neither of which has been proven[62] – how could he rule on the basis of these sources and against the Bavli?

2. The second riddle is just as difficult to unravel:[63] According to the Tashbetz, the Maharam thought that women "do not know how to keep themselves in purity". However, there is no

59. *Bei'ur Hagra* to OH 38:3.
60. In *Hilkhot Rosh Hashanah* (above, note 32).
61. The Gaon of Vilna and Rabbi Isaac of Vienna may have assumed that the Bavli knew the Yerushalmi. Today, this is no longer the assumption. See, for example, Y.N. Epstein, above, note 19, pp. 291-292.
62. Since the Maharam often relied on the Yerushalmi (see Irving Agus, *Rabbi Meir of Rothenburg*, I, New York, 1970^2, p. 32), it stands to reason that he did not mention the Yerushalmi here because he did not rely on it in this case.
63. Cf. this analysis to that of Berger, pp. 89-93, 104-108.

Talmudic basis for this assertion. Furthermore, even if this were so, how would it prevent women from wearing *tefillin*? After all, the Rambam ruled (*Hilkhot Tefillin* 4:13) on the basis of Bavli *Sukkah* 26b that "all of the impure are obligated to wear *tefillin* like the pure". Furthermore, "words of Torah are not susceptible to impurity" (*Berakhot* 22a) and this principle was accepted by the major *poskim*.[64] Thus, even a menstruant woman would be allowed to put on *tefillin*. Therefore, there is no textual basis for excluding women because of impurity.

On the other hand, we could prefer the reading "*benekiut*" (in cleanliness) as found in *Orḥot Ḥayyim* and *Kol Bo*[65] and, following Rabbi Yosef Karo, connect the Maharam to *Tosafot* who spoke of "a clean body" as found in Bavli *Shabbat* 49a.[66] Once again, however, this would not exclude women from wearing *tefillin*. The Talmud in *Shabbat* says that:

64. See Yedidya Dinari, *Te'udah* 3 (1983), pp. 17-37 and Shaye Cohen in: Susan Grossman and Rivkah Haut, eds., *Daughters of the King: Women and the Synagogue*, Philadelphia, 1992, pp. 103-115. Despite the clear ruling in the Talmud, many Ashkenazic *poskim* followed *Beraita Demasekhet Niddah* and *Ḥasidei Ashkenaz* and **prevented** women from entering the synagogue or touching a *Sefer Torah* during *niddah*. Perhaps **this** is the source of the Maharam's opposition to women wearing *tefillin*, but I was unable to find any Ashkenazic *posek* who **links** the two restrictions. For a new theory about the origin of distancing menstruants from the synagogue, see Elisheva Baumgarten in: Avraham Reiner *et al*, eds., *Ta Shema*, Alon Shevut, 2012, pp. 85-104.
65. Indeed, Y. Z. Kahana (*Rabi Meir b"r Barukh [Maharam] Merothenburg: Teshuvot Pesakim Uminhagim*, Vol. I, Jerusalem, 1957, p. 143, No. 34) prints the *Kol Bo's* version and merely refers to *Tashbetz* and *Orḥot Ḥayim*. This is surprising since the *Tashbetz* was the Maharam's student and since the quotation in the *Tashbetz* is clearly more complete than the one in the *Kol Bo*. Regarding the *Tashbetz*, see Urbach, above, note 49, p. 561 and regarding the *Kol Bo*'s dependence on the *Tashbetz* for traditions of the Maharam, see Agus, above, note 62, p. 27 and note 64.
66. Indeed, *Aḥaronim* such as the *Magen Avraham* to OH 38, subparagraph 3 and *Arukh Hashulḥan* 38:6 were so influenced by the *Beit Yosef* that they based their rulings on *Tosafot* in *Eruvin* and totally ignored the Maharam! We should add that the Ritba to *Kiddushin* 31a had a reading in *Tosafot* which connects "cleanliness" to "a clean body": "And women are not clean, neither cleanliness of the body nor cleanliness of the mind."

> *Tefillin* require a clean body like Elisha Ba'al Kenafayim [Elisha who had wings]. What is a a clean body? Abaye said: that he should not pass wind while wearing them. Rava said: that he should not sleep in them.

The *Rishonim* interpreted "a clean body" in various ways.[67] Some, like the Rambam, simply quoted Abaye and Rava. Others, like the Ritba, Rashba and Meiri, said: clean of sins and evil thoughts. Thus, none of the known definitions of "a clean body" would exclude women! Therefore, we see that not only do the Maharam's words contradict the Bavli in *Eruvin*;[68] but there is no textual basis for his assertion that women lack "purity" or "a clean body".[69]

3. Lastly, we should add that the Rema's ruling on women and *tefillin* in the *Shulḥan Arukh* is self-contradictory as the Ḥida has already pointed out (*Birkei Yosef* to OH 38:1). On the one hand, in *Hilkhot Tefillin* 38:3, the Rema **prohibits** women from wearing *tefillin,* following the Maharam. On the other hand, in *Hilkhot Tzitzit* 17:2 and *Hilkhot Rosh Hashanah* 589:6 the Rema **allows** women to recite the blessing over PTBC, following Rabbeinu Tam. Yet Rabbeinu Tam learned this principle from the fact that Mikhal bat Shaul wore *tefillin* and must have recited the blessing![70]

67. For a good summary and discussion, see Ginzberg, pp. 257-260. He himself suggested "cleanliness" means free of excrement and of semen.
68. Cf. Rabbi Eliezer Berkovits in both of his articles.
69. It is worth noting that Rabbi Elijah Shapira in his *Elyah Rabbah* to OH 38:2 came to a similar conclusion. He writes: "And *Orḥot Ḥayyim* asked based on Mikhal bat Shaul, and that the Sages did not protest. The *Beit Yosef* and the *Aḥaronim* gave forced answers. **And it seems to me that later generations were stricter about this, because they saw that the women in our time are not too diligent. Therefore, they were strict to protest against all women to avoid any mishap".** In other words, the Maharam's objection was not really based on any Talmudic source but rather on his perception of the sociological realities of his day. This would imply that if the sociological realities have changed, so could the *halakhic* ruling.
70. Cf. Berkovits (above, note 68), who also emphasized the fact that the Rema contradicts himself. For the same contradiction on the very same page, see *Yam Shel Shlomo*, above, note 53.

IV. *Tefillin* as a Man's Garment

Beginning with Rabbi Hillel ben Naftali Hertz (Lithuania, 1615-1690) in his *Beit Hillel,* a number of *Aḥaronim* suggested that **the Torah itself** forbids women from wearing *tefillin* since *Targum Pseudo-Yonatan* quoted above translates "male apparel" as "a cloak of *tzitzit* and *tefillin*".[71] However, the author of *Beit Hillel* himself adds: "And seemingly this is difficult because we have not found any *Tanna* who thinks that we lash a woman who wears *tefillin*".[72] Furthermore, as the author of *Sedei Ḥemed* points out, if **the Torah** prohibits women from wearing *tefillin,* why does the Talmud tell us that the **Sages did not protest** against Mikhal bat Shaul? Were the Sages unaware of a **Biblical** prohibition!?[73] Lastly, we may add that this "prohibition" is not mentioned by any of the *Geonim* or *Rishonim* and, in any case, a statement made by *Targum Pseudo-Yonatan* cannot overrule the Bavli and most *poskim.*[74]

V. Did Jewish Women Ever Wear *Tefillin*?

Since we are dealing with practical *halakhah,* it is worth investigating whether Jewish women, beyond the act attributed to Mikhal bat Shaul, ever actually wore *tefillin*.

71. Above, note 20. See Rabbi Hillel ben Naftali Hertz, *Beit Hillel* to *Yoreh De'ah* 182, Durenfurth, 1691; Rabbi Ḥayyim Binyamin Pontremoli, *Petaḥ Hadvir* to OH, Izmir, 1862, OH 38, paragraph 2; Rabbi Ḥayyim Ḥizkiya Medini, *Sedei Ḥemed, Kuntress Hakelalim, Lamed, Kelal* 116, Schneyerson edition, Vol. II, p. 725; Rabbi Ya'akov Ḥayyim Sofer, *Kaf Haḥayyim* to OH 38:9; and Rabbi Gedalia Felder, *Yesodei Yeshurun,* Vol. I, Toronto, 1954, p. 92 (he seems to have misunderstood *Sedei Ḥemed* because he did not actually see *Beit Hillel* and *Petaḥ Hadevir*).
72. Lashes are frequently the punishment for a person who transgresses a negative commandment – see Rambam, *Hilkhot Sanhedrin* 18:1.
73. See above, note 71, and see the discussion *ibid*. and in his *Kuntress Hakelalim, Marekhet Tet, Kelal* 15.
74. See the literature cited above, note 56. For *Aḥaronim* who opposed the argument that *tefillin* are male apparel, see Berger, p. 100. For some other arguments by *Aḥaronim* against women putting on *tefillin,* see *ibid*., pp. 100-101.

1. There is a widespread story that Rashi's daughters wore *tefillin*, but we have been unable to find any written proof of this assertion.[74a]

2. Hassar Micoucy (Rabbi Shimson ben Shimson of Coucy) seems to indicate that women in thirteenth-century France wore *tefillin*. He mentions the issue matter-of-factly while discussing the Hallel blessing on Rosh Ḥodesh. He rules that the blessing must be pronounced even though such a recitation is only a custom:

> And it is not a blessing in vain since a person wants to obligate himself to do it, like the cases of *lulav* and *tefillin* **that these women bless even though they are not obligated and we do not protest**.[75]

Since Hassar Micoucy uses the present tense and since he mentions the *lulav* — which women clearly **did** bless in his day – it could very well be that women in his day actually wore *tefillin*. If so, they undoubtedly relied on Rabbeinu Tam or on some of the other *Rishonim* cited above.

3. Rabbi Avigdor Tzorfati was a student of Rabbi Samuel of Falaise and Rabbi Yehudah of Metz (France, second half of the 13th century). In his recently printed comments and rulings on the Torah he ruled

> that even in any case in which they are exempt, such as *tzitzit* and *tefillin* and appearing [in the Temple Courtyard], if the women were accustomed to observe them, they recite the blessings. And there is proof from Mikhal bat Shaul who used to put on *tefillin* and wear them, and Jonah's wife used to go on pilgrimage. **For this reason some saintly**

74a. It could be that the legend arose because his daughters were very learned. For an interesting modern parallel, see Yael Unterman, *Neḥama Leibowitz: Teacher and Bible Scholar*, Jerusalem and New York, 2009, p. 16 who dismisses "the notion that she [Neḥama Leibowitz] put on *tefillin*".

75. See the three references in note 45 above. I have translated the second source.

> **women used to put on *tefillin*** and pronounce the blessing and wrap themselves in *tzizit*. He also ruled that if a woman eats in the *sukkah* she pronounces the blessing "to sit in the *sukkah*", even though she is exempt.[76]

4. Rabbi Joseph Ish Arli was the head of the *yeshivah* in Sienna, Italy beginning in 1546. One of his students left the *yeshivah* and when his trunk arrived at his destination he discovered that all his letters were missing. He suspected his teacher. Rabbi Joseph denied the charges and said that **"two women who put on *tefillin* like Mikhal"** could testify that he had not been at the yeshivah at the time in question.[77] We learn from this testimony in an indirect fashion that two Italian women used to wear *tefillin* in the middle of the sixteenth century.

5. There is a widespread story about Fatzonia, Rabbi Ḥayyim ben Attar's first wife, who "used to wrap herself in a *tallit* and **wear *tefillin* like Mikhal, the first king of Israel's daughter**".[78] Rabbi Ya'akov Moshe Toledano, one of those who transmitted this story, even raises the *halakhic* question: "If so, how could a great Rabbi like the author of *Or Haḥayyim* not have protested to his wife about this?"[79] One late source even expanded the story to **both** of Rabbi Ḥayyim ben Attar's wives![80] However, in truth, this story is nothing more than a legend. It appears in print for

76. *Sefer Peirushim Upesakim Al Hatorah L'rabbeinu Avigdor Tzorfati*, Jerusalem, 1996, pp. 171-172. My thanks to my teacher Prof. David Halivni and my friend Prof. Menahem Schmeltzer who referred me to this important paragraph after this responsum appeared in *Asufot* 11 (1998).
77. Alexander Marx in: *Sefer Hayovel Likhvod Levi Ginzberg*, Hebrew section, New York, 1946, p. 294.
78. Abraham Halevi ibn Susan, *Ma'aseh Hatzadikim*, Jerusalem, 1889, fol. 1b; Ya'akov Moshe Toledano, *Sefer Ner Hama'arav*, Jerusalem, 1911, p. 155; Reuven Margaliot, *Toledot Rabbeinu Ḥayyim ibn Attar*, Lwow, 1925, p. 45 and note 16; Frumkin–Rivlin, *Toledot Ḥakhmei Yerushalayim*, Vol. III, Jerusalem, 1929, p. 12 in an addendum by Rivlin; Mordechai Margaliot, *Entziklopedia Ligdolei Yisrael*, Vol. II, Tel Aviv, 1973^2, col 525; Ya'akov Gellis, *Entziklopedia Letoledot Ḥakhmei Eretz Yisrael*, Vol. I, Jerusalem, 1974, col. 390.
79. *Sefer Yam Hagadol*, Cairo, 1931, No. 40.
80. *Sefer Mas'ot Yerushalayim*, Jerusalem, 1963^2, p. 92, note 7.

the first time in 1889, over 145 years after Rabbi Ḥayyim's death, in *Ma'ase Tzadikim,* but that book contains quite a few fanciful stories about Rabbi Ḥayyim ben Attar which have no factual basis whatsoever.[81]

6. The most famous case of a woman wearing *tefillin* before our time, is the case of Hannah Rochel Verbermacher, a *Tzadekket* [a female *Tzaddik* or Hassidic Rebbe] of the nineteenth century who became famous as the "Maiden of Ludmir". During a serious illness, she awoke and told her father: "Father, I was just in the heavenly court and they gave me a new soul, a great and exalted soul." After recovering, she began to act like a man. She put on *tefillin*, wrapped herself in a *tallit*, and spent all day praying and studying Torah.[82] However, it is difficult to consider her an example for Jewish women today. She wore *tallit* and *tefillin*

81. See, for example, *Ma'aseh Hatzadikim* (above, note 78), fols. 2b-3a, for a story about Rabbi Ḥayyim ben Attar's alleged meeting with a tribe of giants who were descendants of the Ten Lost Tribes.
82. My thanks to my father and teacher, Rabbi Noah Golinkin z"l, who first told me about the Maiden of Ludmir. The quotation is taken from S.A. Horodetzky, *Haḥassidut Vehaḥassidim*, Part 4, Tel Aviv, 19513, p. 70. There is a vast literature about her. See Michael Rodkinson, *Tefilah Lemoshe*: *Toledot Hatefillin Vekoroteihen*, Pressburg, 1883, p. 48, note 1; Tz. L. Mekler, *Fun Rebbens Hoif*, Vol. I, New York, 1931, pp. 235-236; Moshe Feinkind, *Froien Rebei'im un Barimte Perzenlichkeiten in Poilin*, Warsaw, 1937, pp. 31-36; Mordechai Biber, *Reshumot*, New Series, 2 (1946), pp. 69-76; Yoḥanan Twersky, *Habetulah Miludmir*, Jerusalem, 1949 (an entire novel about her!); Efraim Tubenhoiz, *Binetiv Hayaḥid, Ḥayei Ḥolem Veloḥem Be'ir Hamekubalim*, Haifa, 1959, pp. 37-41; *EJ*, Vol. 11, cols. 553-554; Shlomo Ashkenazi, *Dor Dor Uminhagav*, Tel Aviv, 1977, pp. 248-252; Yosef Hagelili, *Hashomerim Laboker*, Meiron, 1992, pp. 157-160; Ada Rapoport-Albert, "The Maid of Ludmir", *Kabbalah: A Newsletter of Current Research in Jewish Mysticism* 2/2 (Spring/ Summer 1987), pp. 1-3; *idem*, "On Women in Ḥasidism, S.A. Horodecky and the Maid of Ludmir Tradition" in: Ada Rapoport-Albert and Steve Zipperstein, eds., *Jewish History*: *Essays in Honor of Chimen Abramsky*, London, 1988, pp. 495-525 = Ada Rapoport-Albert, "*Al Hanashim Baḥassidut: S.A. Horodecky Umasoret Habetulah Miludmir"*, in David Assaf, ed., *"Tzadik Ve'edah: Hebetim Historiim Vetrabutiim Beḥeker Haḥassidut,* Jerusalem, 2001, pp. 496-527 (and see additional bibliography there in note 2); Gershon Winkler, "They Called Her Rebbe", *Moment* 18/6 (December 1993), pp. 56-

because she viewed herself as a **man**.[83] But today many Jewish women want to wear *tefillin* specifically **as women**, just as women have performed PTBC such as *lulav* and *sukkah* for many centuries.[84]

7. Finally, Rebbetzin Shlomtza was the granddaughter of the Admor Rabbi Isaac'l of Zidichov. She was an Admorit who travelled around the *shtetls* of Eastern Europe and preached to the masses about *Ḥassidism* and *Mussar*. Yosef Haglili relates about her as follows:

> When I had the privilege of going to the Holy Land at the beginning of the thirties [of the twentieth century], I already found her here in the Land of Israel... **During her prayers she would wrap herself in *a tallit* with *tziztiot* and would adorn herself with *tefillin*.** She would wear a "large" *tallit katan* daily and the fringes would drag on the ground. She lived in Meah She'arim...[85]

VI. Practical *Halakhah*

In light of the above survey, there is ample *halakhic* justification for allowing women to wear *tefillin*. The Mishnah exempts women from wearing *tefillin*. The *beraitot,* however, report that Mikhal bat Shaul wore *tefillin* and the *Mekhilta* and the

57, 98-100. In 1998, the Khan Theater in Jerusalem put on a play called "The Virgin of Ludmir" – see Eli Weisbert's critique in *De'ot* 1 (Nissan 1998), pp. 18-19. Finally, see a very thorough monograph devoted entirely to this topic – Nathaniel Deutsch, *The Maiden of Ludmir,* Berkeley and Los Angeles, 2003, who discusses her wearing of tefillin on pp. 127-130 where he also refers to the Hebrew version of this responsum.

83. And cf. the views of the mystics collected in *Kaf Haḥayyim,* above, note 71.
84. For interesting testimonies by women who wear *tefillin* today, see Susan Grossman in: Ellen Umansky and Dianne Ashton, eds. *Four Centuries of Jewish Women's Spirituality*, Boston, 1992, pp. 279-282; Dvorah Weisberg in: *Daughters of the King* (above, note 64), pp. 282-284; and *Women's League Outlook* 64/2 (Winter 1993), pp. 13-17.
85. Yosef Hagelili, *Hashomerim Laboker* (above, note 82), pp. 156-157.

Bavli viewed her act approvingly. Only Rabbi Abbahu in the Yerushalmi disapproved.

In medieval times, almost all *Rishonim* approved of women performing PTBC either without a blessing (Rashi, Rambam etc.) or with one (Rabbeinu Tam, Rashba etc.). Five *Rishonim* explicitly permitted women to put on *tefillin* with a blessing (Rabbeinu Tam, Hassar Micoucy, Rabbi Avigdor Tzorfati, Rabbi Zeraḥia Halevi and the Rashba).

Only a few *Rishonim* forbade this practice. The Ra'avad ruled like Rabbi Yehudah that women may not perform PTBC, ignoring the principle that the *halakhah* normally follows Rabbi Yossi. The Ra'avad's view was not followed by later *poskim*. The Maharam, on the other hand, allowed women to perform PTBC, but ruled that women may not put on *tefillin* "because they do not know how to keep themselves "in purity" or "in cleanliness". This view was adopted by the Rema and his successors. However, we have seen that the Maharam's opinion contradicts the Bavli and most of the *Rishonim* and has no textual basis whatsoever. Furthermore, if the Maharam was indeed talking about physical cleanliness, his statement is no longer valid because women in our day are **more** careful about keeping their bodies clean than men![86] Lastly, as we have seen, the Rema contradicts himself on this issue.

Thus, the overwhelming *halakhic* evidence teaches us that women may wear *tefillin* like Mikhal bat Shaul and some righteous women in France, Italy, Eastern Europe and Israel and we do not protest. Of course, they must wear them with the same devotion and halakhic requirements which apply to men.

David Golinkin
Jerusalem
3 Adar 5754

86. This point was stressed by Rabbi Berkovits, *Sinai*, p. 194.

BIBLIOGRAPHY

Benovitz	Moshe Benovitz, *Nashim* 2 (Spring 1999), pp. 155-156
Berger	Aliza Berger in: Micah Halpern and Chana Safrai, eds. *Jewish Legal Writings by Women*, Jerusalem, 1998, pp. 75-118; cf. the review in *Tradition* 33/2 (Winter 1999), pp. 70-73 and the debate, *ibid.* 34/1 (Spring 2000), pp. 105-106, 111-119
Berkovits	Rabbi Eliezer Berkovits, *Sinai* 100 (1987), pp. 192-194; *Idem*, *Jewish Women in Time and Torah*, Hoboken, 1990, pp. 72-74
Ellinson	Elyakim Ellinson, *Ha'ishah V'hamitzvot, Sefer Rishon: Bein Ha'ishah Leyotzrah*, Jerusalem, 1977^2, pp. 23-26, 59-62
Ginzberg	Levi Ginzberg, *Peirushim Veḥidushim Bayerushalmi*, Vol. I, New York, 1941
Halevi	Rabbi Ḥayyim David Halevi, *Sefer Mekor Ḥayyim Livnot Yisrael*, Tel Aviv, 1977, Chapter 3, pp. 22-24
Meiselman	Moshe Meiselman, *Jewish Woman in Jewish Law*, New York, 1978, pp. 147-151, 197-199
Mirsky	Y. Mirsky, *Kerem* 5 (1997),pp. 36-45
Yalon	Shevaḥ Yalon, "*Kol Mitzvot Aseh Shehazeman Geraman Nashim Peturot*": *Iyun Bamekorot Hatanna'iyim Uvasugyot Ha'amoraiyot*, M.A. Thesis, Bar Ilan University, Ramat Gan, 1990, pp. 33-40

2. WOMEN AND SINGING: "KOL B'ISHAH ERVAH"

Oraḥ Ḥayyim 75:3 & *Even Ha'ezer* 21:1,6

In memory of
Rabbi Moshe Zemer z"l
(1932-2011)
Rabbi, scholar and mentsch

Question: *On September 5, 2011, an IDF entertainment troupe performed at an official military event focusing on Operation Cast Lead at Bahad Eḥad, the officers' training base in the Negev. When a female soldier began to sing solo, nine observant Israeli officer cadets got up and left; they said that it was forbidden for them to listen to women singing. Their Regiment Commander Uzi Kliegler ran after them and ordered them to return to the ceremony. "Anyone refusing [this] order will be dismissed from the course." In the end, four cadets refused to return to the hall and were dismissed from the officers' training course, while five were allowed to continue the course, after convincing the committee that the move had not been preplanned. It should be noted that a considerable number of the officers' course cadets are observant and most of them did not walk out.*

Subsequently, various Orthodox rabbis were quoted in the media as being for or against their action. The Ashkenazic Chief Rabbi of Israel Yonah Metzger issued a formal responsum on September 25, 2011, justifying their actions and urging the army to arrange that only men should sing at military events where many observant men are present. Is it really forbidden for Jewish men to listen to women singing? Was there any halakhic justification for the soldiers to walk out?

Responsum:

I. The Three Talmudic Sources

All halakhic discussions of this topic are based primarily on one sentence uttered by the Amora Samuel in Babylon ca. 220 c.e. Some rabbis have claimed that his intent is clear; we shall see below that that is very far from the case. The sentence appears in three places in rabbinic literature, twice in the Bavli and once in the Yerushalmi.

1. *Berakhot* 24a contains a lengthy *sugya* [Talmudic section] about whether one may recite the *Shema* in immodest situations such as two men sharing a bed or a family sharing a bed or when the man's clothes are torn and do not cover his privates. The Talmud continues:

> Rabbi Yitzḥak said: a handsbreadth in a woman is *ervah* [nakedness, unchastity, impropriety]. [The Talmud discusses this and concludes: "rather he is talking about his wife and when reciting *Keriyat Shema*."]
>
> Rav Ḥisda said: a thigh in a woman is *ervah,* as it is written (Isaiah 47:2) "Bare your thigh, wade through the rivers" and it is written (*ibid.*, v. 3) "your *ervah* shall be uncovered and your shame shall be exposed".
>
> **Samuel said: *kol b'ishah ervah,*** a woman's voice is *ervah,* as it is written (Song of Songs 2:14) "for your voice is sweet and your appearance is comely".
>
> Rav Sheshet said: Hair in a woman is *ervah,* as it is written (*ibid.* 4:1) "your hair is like a flock of goats".

There are at least three major problems with this *sugya*:

a. None of these four *Amoraim* mention the *Shema* at all and it appears that this unit was copied here in its entirety from some other context.

b. Jastrow in his Talmudic dictionary (s.v. *ervah*, p. 1114) and many others think that Samuel is referring to a woman **singing.** But it is not at all clear whether Samuel means the **speaking** voice of a woman or the **singing** voice of a woman. On the one hand, he may mean the **speaking** voice of a woman (see Psalm 104:34; *midrashim* on the verse in Song of Songs 2:14 in the Bar Ilan Responsa Project; *Metzudat David* to Song of Songs *ad loc.*). On the other hand, he may mean the **singing** voice of a woman (see the beginning of the verse in Song of Songs; *Ta'anit* 16a; and six *midrashim* on Song of Songs 2:14).

c. It is also not clear if this is *halakhah* or *aggadah*. If they were making halakhic statements, they would have said: "it is forbidden to look at a woman's thigh or to hear her voice or look at her hair"; therefore they seem to be making aggadic statements followed by verses.

At the most, we can say that the editor of the *sugya* who copied this unit here was trying to say that when one recites the *Shema* he should avoid a woman's handsbreadth or thigh or voice or hair.

2. *Kiddushin* 70a-b contains a lengthy story about a man from Nehardea who insults Rav Yehudah while visiting Pumbedita. Rav Yehudah then excommunicates him and declares him a "slave". The man then summons Rav Yehudah to a *din torah* [Jewish court hearing] in front of Rav Naḥman in Nehardea. Rav Yehudah asks his friend Rav Huna whether he should go and Rav Huna advises him to go. Rav Yehudah then goes to Nehardea to the house of Rav Naḥman but, since he resents going, he challenges everything that Rav Naḥman does and says, frequently using the words of Samuel to do so. The story continues:

> [Rav Naḥman:] May my daughter Dunag come and give us drink?
>
> [Rav Yehudah] said to him: So said Samuel: one does not use a woman.
>
> [Rav Naḥman:] But she is a minor!
>
> [Rav Yehudah:] Samuel said explicitly one does not use a woman at all, whether she is an adult or a minor!
>
> [Rav Naḥman:] would my Lord like to send *shalom* to my wife Yalta?
>
> [Rav Yehudah] said to him: **So said Samuel: *kol b'ishah ervah,*** a voice of a woman is ***ervah*** [i.e., I am not allowed to talk to her].
>
> [Rav Naḥman:] it is possible to talk to her via a messenger.
>
> [Rav Yehudah] said to him: So said Samuel: one does not ask after the welfare of a woman.
>
> [Rav Naḥman:] Via her husband!
>
> [Rav Yehudah] said to him: So said Samuel: one does not ask after the welfare of a woman at all.
>
> [Yalta then tells her husband Naḥman to get to the point so that Rav Yehudah should stop insulting him.]

Once again, this *sugya* is making secondary use of Samuel's words "*kol b'isha ervah*", but in this case it is not the later anonymous editors of the Talmud who have quoted Samuel but Rav Yehudah, one of his main disciples, who quotes him almost 500 times in the Babylonian Talmud. Rav Yehudah understood Samuel to say: a voice of a woman is *ervah* **i.e., do not talk to women**. This is in keeping with other Talmudic dicta about avoiding conversations with women (*Avot* 1:5; *Eruvin* 53b; *Nedarim* 20a; *Ḥagigah* 5b; *Sanhedrin* 75a; *Berakhot* 43b at bottom; and cf. the brief discussion by Tal Ilan).

3. *Yerushalmi Ḥallah* Chapter 2:4, ed. Vilna, fol. 12b = ed. Venice, fol. 58c

According to the Torah (Numbers 15:17-21), when Jews bake a

loaf of bread or a cake, they are supposed to give a small portion of the dough called *ḥallah* to a Kohen. Today this small portion is burned after reciting a blessing. The Mishnah in *Ḥallah* (2:3) says that a woman can sit and separate her *ḥallah* [and make the blessing] while naked because she can cover herself. The *Talmud Yerushalmi* comments:

> From this we learn that her rear end is not forbidden because of *ervah*.
>
> This is true regarding her reciting the blessing for *ḥallah*, but to look at her, anything is forbidden. As we have learned: a person who looks at her heel is like one who looks at the house of her womb [=vagina], and a person who looks at the house of her womb is as if he slept with her.
>
> **Samuel said: a voice of a woman is *ervah*.** What is the reason? "*vehaya mikol znutah*, "the land was defiled from the sound of her harlotry" (Jeremiah 3:9; the new JPS *tanakh* translates following Radak: "the land was defiled by her casual immorality").

For the third time, Samuel's words are quoted in a secondary fashion in a Talmudic discussion. He was not part of this discussion and his words are not connected to the main topic which is **looking** at a scantily clad woman who is sitting and separating dough for *ḥallah*. Once again, it is not clear what Samuel meant to say, but there is no hint whatsoever that he is referring to the singing voice of woman; it is more likely that he is referring to her speaking voice.

Thus, if we were to rule on the basis of the three Talmudic passages, we could say that Samuel and his fellow Amoraim quoted in *Berakhot* were making aggadic statements about the dangers of looking at and listening to women. On the other hand, we could say on the basis of *Kiddushin* (and probably *Yerushalmi Ḥallah*) that Samuel made a halakhic ruling that it is forbidden to speak to women or, on the basis of the context in *Berakhot*, that it is forbidden to speak to or look at women while reciting *Keriyat Shema*. **It is pretty clear from the careful analysis above that none of these three passages say anything about a woman singing.**

II. The Rif Ignored Samuel's Statement in Both Passages in the Bavli

The Rif, Rabbi Yitzḥak Alfasi (1013-1103), was one of the most influential *poskim* in Jewish history. Maimonides states that he relied on the Rif in his Mishneh Torah in all but thirty places (*Responsa of the Rambam*, ed. Blau, No. 251, p. 459 and the literature cited there in note 7). *Hilkhot Harif*, also known as *Talmud Kattan*, the little Talmud, codified Jewish law by abbreviating each *sugya* in the Talmud. He omitted the aggadic passages and most of the give and take of the Talmudic sugya, leaving only the opinions which he considered Jewish law. In the *sugya* in *Berakhot* quoted above, the Rif (ed. Vilna, fol. 15a) **omitted** the opinion of all four Amoraim quoted by the Talmud, as emphasized by Rabbi Zeraḥia Halevi (*Hama'or Hakattan, ibid.*, fol. 15b) and by the Ra'avad of Posquieres (quoted by the Rashba to the *sugya* in *Berakhot*). In his code on *Kiddushin* (ed. Vilna, fol. 30b), the Rif quotes a few of the dicta of Samuel quoted by Rav Yehudah but **omits** the dictum *"kol b'ishah ervah"*. This means that the Rif considered Samuel's statement in both *Berakhot* and *Kiddushin* to be *aggadah* and not *halakhah*!

III. It is Forbidden to Talk to Women or to Certain Women

In the Rambam's (Egypt, 1135-1204) summary of the *sugya* in *Berakhot* (*Hilkhot Keriyat Shema* 3:16), he rules that one may not recite *Keriyat Shema* while looking at a woman, even his wife, as per the Talmud's explanation of Rabbi Yitzḥak quoted above in *Berakhot*, but he omits Samuel's opinion entirely. But in his Laws of Forbidden Sexual Relationships (*Hilkhot Issurei Biah* 21:2, 5) he rules that one should not wink at or laugh with or look at the little finger of one of the *arayot,* i.e. one of the forbidden sexual relationships listed in Leviticus 18, "and even to hear the voice of the *ervah* or to see her hair is forbidden". The Rambam seems to understand Samuel to mean "*kol b'ishah-ervah*" *[assur],* "the voice of a woman who is an *ervah*" is forbidden. This is a rather novel interpretation since that is not what Samuel said. In any case, the Rambam is clearly referring to her **speaking** voice and not to her **singing** voice.

This is proven by his famous reponsum about listening to secular Arabic girdle poems sung to music (*Responsa of the Rambam,* ed. Blau, No. 224, pp. 398-400). After giving four reasons to forbid this music he writes: "And if the singer is a woman, there is a fifth prohibition, as they of blessed memory said *kol b'ishah ervah,* **and how much the moreso if she is singing**". In other words, Samuel was referring to women **speaking** and the Rambam adds that it is even more forbidden if she is **singing**.

Rabbi Ya'akov ben Asher (Toledo, 1270-1343) followed the Rambam in his *Tur,* one of the major codes of Jewish law (*Tur* Even Haezer 21) as did the Maharshal (Cracow, 1510-1573, quoted by the *Perishah* to *Even Haezer* 21, subparagraph 2).

A similar opinion is found in *Sefer Ḥassidim,* which is attributed to Rabbi Yehudah Heḥassid, a contemporary of the Rambam (Regensburg, ca. 1150-1217; ed. Margaliot, paragraph 313). He says that "a young man should not teach girls practical Jewish law even if her father is standing there, lest he or the girl be overcome by their *yetzer* [evil inclination] and *kol b'ishah ervah,* rather a father should teach his daughter and wife". Thus, Rabbi Yehudah thinks that Samuel was opposed to listening to the speaking voice of a woman or girl.

This also seems to be the opinion of Rabbi Yitzḥak ben Isaac of Vienna (1180-1250; *Or Zarua,* Part I, fol. 24a, paragraph 133) and the Rosh (1250-1320; *Piskey Harosh* to *Berakhot,* Chapter 3, paragraph 37).

IV. It is Forbidden to Listen to Women Singing While Reciting the Shema

The halakhic *poskim* in this camp ruled according to their understanding of the *sugya* in *Berakhot,* which is connected to *Keriyat Shema,* and ignored the *sugya* in *Kiddushin.*

Rav Hai Gaon (Pumbedita, 939-1038) ruled (*Otzar Hageonim* to *Berakhot, Perushim,* p. 30, paragraph 102) that a man "should not recite the *Shema* when a woman is singing because *kol b'ishah ervah*... but when she is just talking normally it is permitted; and even if she is singing, if he can concentrate in his heart on his prayer so that he does not hear her or pay attention to her – it is permissible...". In other words, he understood from the context in *Berakhot* that Samuel only says *kol b'isha ervah* when one is reciting the *Shema* and he further understood that Samuel is referring to a woman singing. Even so, Rav Hai allowed a man to recite *Keriyat Shema* when a woman is singing if he is able to ignore her voice.

This general approach was followed by a number of classic Ashkenazic *poskim* such as Rabbi Eliezer of Metz (1115-1198; *Sefer Yerei'im Hashalem,* paragraph 392); the Ra'aviah (Cologne, 1140-1225; ed. Aptowitzer, Vol. 1, pp. 52-53, *Berakhot,* paragraph 76); and the Mordechai (Nuremberg, 1240-1298; to *Berakhot,* paragraph 80). Rabbi Eliezer of Metz, on the one hand, adds a stringency that one may not recite the Shema "or *dvar kedushah*" [anything holy] when a woman is singing; but also a leniency – that because of our sins we live among the Gentiles and therefore we are not careful not to learn while Gentile women are singing. The Ra'aviah adds a leniency that one may recite *Keriyat Shema* when a woman is singing if he is used to it (or: to her voice).

This general approach was also followed by *Aḥaronim* such as the *Beit Shmuel* to *Shulḥan Arukh Even Haezer* 21, subparagraph 4 who expands the prohibition to *tefillah* [prayer] as opposed to only the *Shema*.

V. A Combination of the Previous Two Approaches

A number of prominent *poskim* combined the previous two approaches. They ruled that a man should not **talk** to a woman on the basis of Samuel in *Kiddushin* as in paragraph III above and that a man should not recite the *Shema* while a woman is **singing** on the basis of *Berakhot* as understood in paragraph IV above.

This camp includes the Ra'avad of Posquieres (1120-1198; quoted in *Ḥiddushei Harashba* to Berakhot 24a [mislabeled 25 in the printed editions]); the Meiri (Provence, d. 1315; in *Bet Habeḥirah* to *Berakhot* 24a, pp. 84-85); and Rabbi Yosef Karo in his *Shulḥan Arukh* (*Oraḥ Ḥayyim* 75:3 and *Even Haezer* 21:1, 6).

VI. It is Forbidden to Listen to Women Singing at any Time

This approach was first suggested as a possible interpretation by Rabbi Joshua Falk (Poland, 1555-1614) in his *Perishah* to *Tur* Even Haezer 21, subparagraph 2, but he himself rejected it. The first to actually rule this way in practice was Rabbi Moshe Sofer (Pressburg, d. 1839; *Responsa Ḥatam Sofer, Ḥoshen Mishpat*, No. 190).

Aside from the fact that this very strict approach contradicts all of the halakhic sources we have seen above, we also know from the research of Emily Teitz that this approach contradicts the actual **practice** of Jewish women, who sang in the home, on festive occasions, as singers and in the synagogue throughout the Middle Ages.

Unfortunately, the Ḥatam Sofer's strict ruling was adopted by many later *poskim*. Some tried to find "leniencies" such as allowing girls and boys to sing at the same time (Rabbi Y.Y. Weinberg, *Seridei Eish*) or allowing men to listen to women who cannot be seen, such as on a record or on the radio.

VII. *Kevod Haberiyot* Sets Aside Various Prohibitions

In any case, even if one were to rule entirely according to the Ḥatam Sofer, it would be forbidden to get up and leave a concert where women are singing. Even if Samuel meant to give a halakhic ruling (which is not at all clear) and even if he meant to prohibit listening to all women singing (which we have disproved above), there is a well-known halakhic principle that *kevod haberiyot* [the honor of human beings] sets aside various prohibitions.[1] There is no question that leaving a concert is insulting to the women performing as well as to most of the soldiers at the concert and to the commanding officers – indeed that is why the commanding officer removed those soldiers from the officers' training course.

VIII. Summary and Conclusions

We have seen above that there is no general prohibition against women singing in classic Jewish law based on the Talmud and subsequent codes and commentaries until the early nineteenth century. The current blanket prohibition accepted by Ḥaredi and some modern Orthodox rabbis was first suggested and rejected by Rabbi Joshua Falk (d. 1614) and was only given as a halakhic ruling by Rabbi Moshe Sofer, the *Ḥatam Sofer*, in the early nineteenth century. However, this opinion is not in agreement with the simple meaning of the dictum by Samuel and with all of the opinions of the Rishonim. The Rif **ignored** Samuel's dictum in both *Berakhot* and *Kiddushin*. Some *Rishonim* ruled according to the *sugya* in *Kiddushin* that Samuel was referring **to the speaking voice of women** to the extent that such conversation would lead to forbidden sexual relations. This interpretation also seems to be the intent of the parallel in

1. See below, pp. 227-228 and *ibid.*, note 23; Daniel Sperber, *Darkah Shel Halakhah*, Jerusalem, 2007, pp. 34 ff. and in a reworked form in *Women and Men in Communal Prayer: Halakhic Perspectives*, New York, 2010, pp. 74 ff.; Rabbis Elliot Dorff, Daniel Nevins and Avrum Reisner, "Homosexuality, Human Dignity and Halakhah", 2006 at www.rabbinical.org.

Yerushalmi Hallah. On the other hand, Rav Hai Gaon and most of the *Rishonim* in Ashkenaz interpreted the words of Samuel according to the *sugya* in *Berakhot* and therefore ruled **that it is forbidden to recite *Keriyat Shema*** where a woman is singing because of *kol b'isha ervah*. Finally, some of the rabbis of Provence and Rabbi Joseph Karo ruled according to both of these interpretations. Furthermore, Emily Teitz has shown that in practice Jewish women sang at home, at *semaḥot*, as singers and in the synagogue throughout the Middle Ages. Thus, there is no halakhic justification for anyone walking out when women sing. But even if one accepts the very strict ruling of the Ḥatam Sofer, it is forbidden to walk out in order not to insult the female performers.

David Golinkin
Jerusalem
4 Kislev 5772

BIBLIOGRAPHY

I. ARTICLES

Rabbi Sol Berman, "*Kol Isha*", *Joseph Lookstein Memorial Volume*, New York, 1980, pp. 45-66 (the most thorough study of this topic; summarized in Hebrew by Kaddish Goldberg in *Amudim* 614 [Tishrei 5758], pp. 26-27)

Rabbi Ben Cherney, "*Kol Isha*", *Journal of Halacha and Contemporary Society* 10 (Fall 1985), pp. 57-75

Rabbi Boaz Cohen, *Law and Tradition in Judaism*, New York, 1959, p. 174, note 28

Orah Cohen, *On Both Sides of the Divide: Gender Separation in Jewish Law* (Hebrew), Bet El, 2007, pp. 189-196

Elyakim Getzel Ellenson, *Ha'ishah Vehamitzvot* (Hebrew), Vol. 2, Jerusalem, 1987, pp. 81-91

Rabbi Louis Epstein, *Sex Laws and Customs in Judaism*, New York, 1948, pp. 93-100

M. Sh. Geshuri, "The Woman and Her Singing in the Biblical Period", (Hebrew), *Maḥanayim* 98 (5725), pp. 92-103

Karla Goldman, *Beyond the Synagogue Gallery*, Cambridge, Mass. and London, 2000, pp. 83-92 and notes 31-38

Rabbi M. Harari, *Mikraei Kodesh*, p. 233 quoted by Aviad Hacohen, *Alon Shevut* 11 (Nissan 5758), p. 64, note 3

Tal Ilan, *Jewish Women in Greco-Roman Palestine*, Tubingen, 1995, pp. 126-127

Admiel Kosman, " 'And Miriam chanted for them' – Kol Isha?", www.biu.ac.il/JH/Parasha/eng, February 7, 2004

Ḥannah Pinḥassi, *Deot* 44 (October 2009), pp. 14-17

Rabbi Moshe Halevi Steinberg, *Hilkhot Nashim*, Jerusalem, 1983, p. 45 and the literature in note 23

Emily Taitz, "Kol Isha – The Voice of Women: Where was it heard in medieval Europe?", *Conservative Judaism* 38/3 (Spring 1986), pp. 46-61

Rabbi Moshe Zemer, *Halakhah Shefuyah*, Tel Aviv, 1993, pp. 234-237, 347 = *Evolving Halakhah*, Woodstock, Vermont, 1999, pp. 278-279

Rabbi Yonatan Rosenzweig, *Teḥumin* 29 (5769), pp. 138-143; Reaction: Rabbi Ya'akov Ariel, *Teḥumin* 30 (5770), pp. 212-215

II. RESPONSA

Rabbi Moshe Alashkar, *Responsa Maharam Alashkar*, No. 35

Rabbi Yisachar Baer Eilenburg, *Responsa Be'er Sheva, Be'er Mayyim Ḥayyim*, No. 3

Rabbi David Bigman, "A New Analysis of *'Kol B'isha Erva'* ", www.jewishideas.org, February 4, 2009

Rabbi Yuval Cherlow, *Reshut Harabbim*, Petaḥ Tikvah, 2002, pp. 130-131

Rabbi J. Simcha Cohen, *Intermarriage and Conversion: A Halakhic Solution*, Hoboken, New Jersey, 1987, Chapter 19

Rabbi Moshe Feinstein, *Igrot Moshe, Oraḥ Ḥayyim*, Part I, No. 26; Part 4, No. 15, paragraph 2

Rabbi Meir Friedmann, "Mitwurkung von Frauen beim Gottesdienste" (German), *Hebrew Union College Annual* 8-9 (1931-1932), pp. 511-523

Rabbi David Golinkin, *Ma'amad Ha'ishah Bahalakhah: She'elot Uteshuvot*, Jerusalem, 2001, pp. 102-103 = below, pp. 182-183

Rabbi Ya'akov Ḥagiz, *Responsa Halakhot Ketanot*, Vol. 2, No. 93

Rabbi Ḥayyim David Halevi, *Aseh Lekhah Rav*, Vol. I, No. 28; Vol. 3, No. 6

Rabbi Yonah Metzger, "*Kol B'ishah Ervah*" (Hebrew), 25.9.11

Rabbi Meir Ben-Tziyon Ḥai Ouziel, *Mishpitei Ouziel*, Vol. 4, *Ḥoshen Mishpat*, No. 6

Rabbi Eliezer Waldenberg, *Tzitz Eliezer*, Vol. 5, No. 2; Vol. 7, No. 28

Rabbi Yeḥiel Ya'akov Weinberg, *Seridei Eish*, Vol. 2, No. 8

Rabbi Yitzḥak Ya'akov Weiss, *Minḥat Yitzḥak*, Vol. 8, No. 126

Rabbi Ovadiah Yosef, *Yabia Omer*, Vol. 1, *Oraḥ Ḥayyim*, No. 6

III. NEWS ARTICLES (IN CHRONOLOGICAL ORDER)

The Jerusalem Post International Edition, August 19-25, 1979, p. 15 (the Rabbi of the Wall ordered a mixed group singing with Rabbi Shlomo Carlebach to leave the Kotel Plaza)

Ha'aretz, June 24, 2008 (IDF forbids observant soldiers from walking out of military assemblies)

The Jerusalem Post, Nov. 21, 2008, p. 7; *The Jerusalem Post Magazine*, December 11, 2009, pp. 28-30 (on a film intended for women only)

The Jewish Press, February 20, 2009, p. 30 (on a women's concert in Brooklyn)

Ynet, September 9, 2011 (news report about the latest incident)

Yizhar Hess, *Yisrael Hayom*, September 13, 2011, p. 35 (a Masorti reaction to the latest incident)

The Jerusalem Post, September 16, 2011 (Orthodox rabbinic reactions to the latest incident)

Shmuel Rosner, *The New York Times*, November 18, 2011

Ya'akov Katz, *The Jerusalem Post*, November 25, 2011, pp. 14-15

3. WOMEN IN THE *MINYAN* AND AS *SHELIḤOT TZIBBUR*

Oraḥ Ḥayyim 106:1

Question: *Are women obligated to recite the Amidah three times a day? Are they obligated to recite Mussaf and Ne'ilah? Is it permissible to count them in the minyan for Barekhu, Kaddish, the repetition of the Amidah and Kedushah? Is it permissible for them to serve as sheliḥot tzibbur for Shaḥarit, Minḥah, Ma'ariv, Mussaf and Ne'ilah?*

Responsum: Despite the voluminous literature on this subject in recent years,[1] most writers have relied on the opinions of the *Aḥaronim* who lived after Rabbi Yosef Karo (d. 1575). But an in-depth reading of the Talmud and the *Rishonim* teaches us that we can answer all of these questions in the affirmative. We shall now explain this ruling, point-by-point.

I. Are women obligated to recite the *Amidah* three times a day?

The primary source regarding a woman's requirement to recite the *Amidah* is Mishnah *Berakhot* 3:3:

> **Women**, slaves and minors are exempt from reciting the *Shema* and from *tefillin*, but are **obligated in [=to perform] *Tefillah***, *Mezuzah* and the Grace after Meals.

"*Tefillah*" in the Mishnah does not mean "prayer" in general, as some have mistakenly translated in our times,[2] but rather the

1. The abbreviations in the notes refer to the Bibliography at the end of the responsum.
2. See for example, Rabbi Meiselman, p. 130.

Amidah.[3] In other words, according to the Mishnah in *Berakhot,* women are obligated to pray the *Amidah.*

The section in Bavli *Berakhot* 22b dealing with that Mishnah has reached us in many versions, and the Me'iri *ad loc.* (p. 69) already pointed out that every *posek* ruled on this issue on the basis of the version he had in front of him. An examination of the four complete manuscripts of Bavli *Berakhot* reveals that there are three basic versions of this section and that each manuscript includes more than one version. The following are the three basic versions[4] together with a list of manuscripts which contain that version:

Version 1:

> "reciting the *Shema* and *Tefillin*" which are positive time-bound commandments, and all positive time-bound commandments – women are exempt.
>
> "*Tefillah, Mezuzah* and the Grace after Meals" which are positive commandments not bound by time, and all positive commandments not bound by time – women are obligated.

This is the version in the margin of Ms. Florence which was copied in Ashkenaz in 1176; in Ms. Munich 95, copied in Ashkenaz in 1342 (twice!); in Ms. Oxford 366, copied in a Sephardic area in the 14th-15th century; and in Ms. Paris 671, copied circa 1450.

Version 2:

> What might you say? Since it says about *Tefillah* "Evening, morning and afternoon will I pour out my heart and moan"

3. See *Mishnah Berakhot* 2:4; 3:1, 5; 4:1, 7; 5:4; *Shabbat* 1:2; *Ta'anit* 2:2; *Megillah* 2:5; *Sotah* 7:1; *Avot* 2:13 and especially *Berakhot* 4:1 and 5:4 and *Ta'anit* 2:2.
4. We will not list here all of the variant readings. The main point for our purpose is to present the three major versions in a general fashion. I was aided by the variant readings copied by Rabbi Steve Wald and by photocopies of the manuscripts.

> (Psalms 55:18) it is like a positive time-bound commandment – [the Mishnah] comes to teach us [that women are obligated to pray].

This is the version in Ms. Florence; in Ms. Munich (partly in the margin); in Ms. Oxford; in Ms. Paris; and in the Vilna edition.

Version 3:

> "but are obligated in *Tefillah*" – because it is [supplication for Divine] mercy.

This is the version between the lines in Ms. Florence; in the margin of Ms. Munich in the name of Rashi; in Ms. Paris; and in the Vilna edition.

An examination of a representative sample of Geonim and *Rishonim* reveals that they apparently had the following versions of our talmudic passage:

> **Version 1:** The Rif to *Berakhot ad loc.* (ed. Vilna, fols. 11b–12a); Maimonides, *Hilkhot Tefillah* 1:2; *Sefer Ha'eshkol*, ed. Auerbach, Vol. 1, pp. 13-14; "Some books have the reading" in *Tosfot Rabbi Yehudah Sirlion*, ed. Sacks, Jerusalem, 5729, p. 255; *Semag*, Positive Commandment 19, Venice, 1547, fol. 100c, *Orḥot Ḥayyim, Hilkhot Tefillah*, paragraph 64 = *Kol Bo*, fol. 8c.
>
> **Version 2:** *Tosfot Harosh ad loc.*; Rabbi Yisrael Alnakawa, *Menorat Hama'or*, Chapter 20, Gate 4, p. 436.
>
> **Version 3:** *Halakhot Gedolot*, ed. Warsaw, fol. 2c; Naḥmanides's critique to Maimonides' *Sefer Hamitzvot*, Positive Commandments, No. 5, ed. Chavel, pp. 154-157 (without an explicit quote); *Ḥiddushei Haritva ad loc.* It is worth noting that this is the explanation that appears in Yerushalmi *Berakhot* 3:3, fol. 6b.
>
> **Versions 1 and 3:** Rabbi Jonah's pupils on the Rif, *ad loc.*
>
> **Versions 2 and 3:** Rashi *ad loc.* (but he rejects Version 2);

Tosafot ad loc.; Tosfot Rabbi Yehudah Sirlion ibid.; Tosfot Hakhmei Angliah to *Berakhot*, ed. Blau, Jerusalem, 5740, pp. 28-29; and the Me'iri *ad loc.*, p. 69.

Versions 1, 2 and 3: *Piskei Harosh ad loc.*, Chapter 3, paragraph 13.

Now that we have seen the different versions of the *sugya*, we can understand the two main approaches of the *Rishonim*:

A. Maimonides dealt with our subject in four places:

1. *Hilkhot Tefillah* 1:1-7:

1) **To pray daily is a positive commandment,** as it is said: "You shall serve the Lord, your God" (Exodus 23:25). According to tradition they learned that this service is *Tefillah,* as it says "and to serve Him with all your heart" (Deut. 11:13), [on which] the Sages commented "What is service of the heart? It is *Tefillah*". From the Torah, there is no fixed number of prayers and no fixed form of prayer **and no fixed time for prayer.**

2) **Therefore, women and slaves are obligated to pray, since this is a positive commandment *not*** bound by time. Rather the obligation of this *mitzvah* is as follows, that each person should supplicate and pray every day and utter praise of God and then ask for his needs...

3) ...So was the matter always from Moses our Teacher until Ezra.

4) When Israel went into Exile in the days of the wicked Nebuchadnezar, they mingled with the Persians, Greeks and other nations... As a result, when one of them prayed, his tongue was not adequate to request his desires or to utter praise to the Holy One, blessed be He, in the Holy tongue, unless other languages were mixed with it. When Ezra and his court saw this, **they arose and enacted the Eighteen Benedictions** in sequence ... so that they would be set **in the mouths of everyone**... For the same reason,

they enacted all the blessings and *tefillot* arranged **in the mouths of all Israel**.

5) **And they also enacted** that the number of *tefillot* should be equal to the number of sacrifices – two *tefillot* every day... And every day when there was a *Mussaf* sacrifice, **they enacted** a third *tefillah* corresponding to the *Mussaf* sacrifice...

6) **And they also enacted that a person** should recite one *tefillah* at night... And the *Arvit* Service is not obligatory like the *Shaharit* and *Minhah* Services. Nevertheless, **all Israel have been accustomed** in all the places of their habitation to pray *Arvit* and they have accepted it upon themselves as an obligation.

7) **And they also enacted** a *tefillah* after the *Minhah* service, close to sunset, only on fast days... and this is the *tefillah* known as *Ne'ilah*...

2. *Hilkhot Tefillah* 6:10

   Women, slaves and minors are obligated in *Tefillah*.

   Any man who is exempt from reciting the *Shema* is exempt from the *Tefillah*.

3. Commentary to *Mishnah Kiddushin* 1:7, according to the Hebrew translation of Rabbi Yosef Kafih:

   ...but positive commandments which women are obligated or not entirely obligated to do – there is no general principle, rather they are transmitted orally and they are accepted. You know that eating *matzah* on the night of *Pesah* and rejoicing on the [three pilgrim] festivals and *Hakhel* and ***Tefillah***, and reading the *Megillah* and *Hanukkah* lights and the Sabbath lights and saying *Kiddush* – **all of these are positive time-bound commandments, and every one of them the obligation for women is the same as the obligation for men...**

4. *Hilkhot Avodah Zarah* 12:3:

   All negative commandments in the Torah, both men and women are obligated, except for [not destroying the beard

> and sideburns] and the Kohen's prohibition of defiling himself to the dead [that apply only to men]. And every positive commandment that is occasional and not constant, women are exempt, except for *Kiddush*, eating *matzah* on the night of *Pesaḥ*, slaughtering and eating the *Pesaḥ* sacrifice, *Hakhel*, and rejoicing [on Festivals] which women are obligated to do.

At first glance, there are contradictions between these four passages. But it is not so; they actually complement each other. The explanation is as follows: Maimonides' version in the Talmud was version 1 above, and so he **quotes** in *Hilkhot Tefillah* 1:2 – "**since this is a positive commandment *not*** bound by time". Indeed, this was the Rif's version in *Berakhot* cited above, and there is no doubt that Maimonides relied on him since Maimonides, as is well-known, relied on the Rif everywhere in the Mishneh Torah with the exception of thirty places.[5] In *Hilkhot Tefillah,* Chapter 1, Maimonides explained that originally *Tefillah* was a positive commandment without a fixed time that women were obligated by the Torah to observe. When Ezra and his court came and enacted a fixed formula and fixed times for *Tefillah*, **the enactment also included women who were biblically obligated to pray**. There are four proofs of this interpretation:

1. Many of Maimonides' commentators explained it this way, from Rabbi Yosef Karo to Rabbi Ḥayyim David Halevi.[6]

5. *Responsa of the Rambam*, ed. Blau, No. 251, p. 459, and the bibliography *ibid.*, note 7.
6. Rabbi Yosef Karo, *Shulḥan Arukh Oraḥ Ḥayyim* 106:1; Rabbi Naftali Tzvi Yehudah Berlin, *Ha'amek She'elah* to *She'ilta* 26, ed. Jerusalem, 1975, fol. 175a, s.v. *mi amrinan* (this is how he interprets the Rif); Rabbi Ḥayyim David Halevi, *Aseh Lekha Rav*, Vol. 1, Tel Aviv, 1976, No. 30 and Vol. 5, Tel Aviv, 1983, p. 333 and cf. his book *Sefer Mekor Ḥayyim Livnot Yisrael*, Tel Aviv, 1977, Chapter 4, pp. 24-28; Rabbi Michael Chernick; Dr. Steven Wald. Cf. the three *poskim* quoted by Rabbi Ovadia Yosef, *Responsa Yeḥaveh Da'at*, Vol. 3, Jerusalem, 1980, No. 7, pp. 26-27 – it requires further study to determine whether they obligate women to pray three times a day on the basis of Maimonides or Rashi. Also see Ya'akov Blidstein, *Sinai* 128 (5761), p. 66 and the literature cited there.

2. Maimonides writes: "in the mouths of everyone", "in the mouths of all Israel", "a person", and "all Israel have been accustomed". These expressions were meant to include women, who were explicitly mentioned by Maimonides at the beginning of Chapter 1.

3. This is proven from the language in *Hilkhot Tefillah*, Chapter 6 (source 2), where men's "*tefillah*" is also mentioned, meaning, of course, the *Amidah*.

4. It is also proven from the last two passages in Maimonides. In *Hilkhot Avodah Zarah* (source 4), he lists **biblical** positive time-bound commandments that women are obligated to observe, and *tefillah* is **not** included, because biblically it does not have a fixed time. But in his commentary to the Mishnah (source 3) he counts positive time-bound commandments that women are obligated to do **either biblically or rabbinically** and *tefillah is* included there, since after Ezra'a enactment it is a positive time-bound commandment that women are obligated to observe rabbinically just like men.

B. Other *Rishonim* were of the opinion that *tefillah* was **originally** a rabbinic *mitzvah* and that the Sages obligated men and women to recite the *Amidah* three times a day right from the start. This was, apparently, the opinion of the author of *Halakhot Gedolot*, Rashi and Naḥmanides on the basis of version 3 above "because *tefillah* is [supplication for Divine] mercy". Rashi explained this in his commentary to *Berakhot* 20b, s.v. *veḥayavin bitfillah*: "because *tefillah* is [supplication for Divine] mercy **and it is rabbinic and they also enacted it for women and for the education of children".**[7]

In any case, according to the Mishnah, the Bavli in all its versions and all the above-mentioned *Rishonim*, women are obligated to recite the *Amidah* three times a day just like men.

7. Rabbi Ḥizkiya da Silva agreed with Naḥmanides (*Peri Ḥadash* to *Oraḥ Ḥayyim* 89, subparagraph 1) and therefore ruled that women are obligated to pray (*Ibid.*, OH 88, at the end).

Evidence about daily prayer by women throughout the generations

Furthermore, there are many testimonies from the Talmudic period through the eighteenth century that, in practice, women used to pray at home or in the synagogue every day, and even three times a day, just like men.[8] We must stress that most of these sources inform us about women's prayer matter-of-factly, in ignorance of its legal bearing, and in Jewish law such evidence is considered reliable. The sources which follow are presented chronologically and then geographically:

THE TALMUDIC PERIOD

1. Yerushalmi *Berakhot*, end of Chapter 5, fol. 9d = Yerushalmi *Gittin*, Chapter 5, fol. 47b:

> Rabbi Aḥa [in the name of] Rabbi Tanḥuma son of Rabbi Ḥiyya in the name of Rabbi Simlai: A city in which everyone is a Kohen, they raise their hands [to bless the people]... and who responds "Amen" to them? **The women** and the children.

Since in Talmudic times the Kohanim used to bless the people at *Shaḥarit* every day of the year,[9] we learn from here that women were present in the synagogue for *Shaḥarit* on a regular basis.

8. Some of these passages have been quoted by various scholars, including: L. Löw, *Gesammelte Schriften*, Vol. IV, Szegedin, 1898, pp. 62 ff.; S. Safrai, *Tarbitz* 32 (5723), pp. 329-330 and 336 = *Biyemei Habayit Uviyemei Hamishnah: Meḥkarim Betoledot Yisrael*, Jerusalem, 1996, pp. 159-160, 166; Bernadette Brooten, *Women Leaders in the Ancient Synagogue*, Chico, California, 1982, pp. 139-141. For a source on women's daily (?) prayers in the Temple, see Yerushalmi *Ma'aser Sheini* 5:2, fol. 56a = *Eikhah Rabbah* 3:3, ed. Vilna, fol. 25a = *ibid.*, ed. Buber, p. 125. For sources which prove that women came to the synagogue or the house of study to hear the public sermons, see *Luke* 13:10 ff.; Acts 17:1-4; Yerushalmi *Sotah* 1:4, fol. 16d and parallels; and Targum Jonathan to Judges 5:24.
9. Yitzḥak Zimmer, *Olam Keminhago Noheig*, Jerusalem, 1996, pp. 132-133.

2. Yerushalmi *Sotah* 1:2, fol. 16c

> Rabbi Yossi the son of Rabbi Bun said: [A husband who was suspicious of his wife] who said to her "**do not enter the synagogue**", she may enter with him...

3. Bavli *Megillah* 23a (cf. the parallel in *Tosefta Megillah* 3:11-12, ed. Lieberman, p. 356; and cf. below, Chapter 6):

> Our rabbis taught: All go up among the seven [who read from the Torah], even a minor **and even a woman**; but the Sages said: a woman should not read from the Torah because of the honor of the congregation.

According to the first sentence, women go up to the Torah and read from it. This proves that they were present in the synagogue for public worship.

4. *Sotah* 22a

> A certain widow had a synagogue in her neighbourhood; **[yet] she used to come every day to pray in the *Beit Midrash* of Rabbi Yoḥanan**. He said to her: "My daughter, is there not a synagogue in your neighborhood?" She said to him: "Rabbi, am I not rewarded for the [extra] steps?"

It should be stressed that Rabbi Yoḥanan did not ask her: "My daughter, why did you come to the synagogue?" but rather "Why did you come to **my** synagogue?"

5. *Avodah Zarah* 38a-b:

> We have also learned in a *beraita*: A [Jewish] woman places a pot on the stove and a Gentile woman comes and stirs the pot until the Jewish woman returns from the bathhouse **or the synagogue** and she need not worry [that the food is considered as having been cooked by the Gentile woman].

THE TALMUDIC PERIOD, ACCORDING TO MEDIEVAL SOURCES

6. *Soferim* 18:5-6, ed. Higger, pp. 316-317:[10]

> And he translates [the scroll of Lamentations on the evening of the Ninth of Av] so that the rest of the people, **the women** and children may understand it; **for women are obligated to listen to the reading of the Book like men**... And they are also obligated in *Keriyat Shema, Tefillah*, the Grace after Meals and *Mezuzah*... [One should also] translate for the people, **women** and children every *Seder* [weekly portion] and the prophet for Shabbat [*Haftarah*] after the reading of the Torah...

7a. *Soferim* 18:8, p. 320:

> On the day they seated Rabbi Elazar ben Azariah [as head of the] academy, he started preaching by saying: "You stand this day, all of you... your children, **your wives**" (Deut. 29:9-10): men come to listen, **women to be rewarded for the steps** [for the distance they walked to attend services], why do the children come? To reward those who bring them. **This is the reason young Jewish girls were accustomed to come to the synagogues**, in order to reward those who bring them and in order to receive reward.

7b. *Midrash Hagadol* to Deuteronomy 29:10, ed. Fisch, p. 639:

> "You stand this day... your children, **your wives**" – "**your wives**" even if they do not understand, **they come to listen and to receive [a reward].**

8. *Yalkut Shimoni*, Ekev, paragraph 871 and parallels:

10. For an analysis of this interesting passage in tractate *Soferim* which also requires women to recite the *Shema*, as opposed to our Mishnah, see Debra Reed Blank, *Conservative Judaism* 48/1 (Fall 1995), pp. 7-10.

An old woman came before Rabbi Yossi ben Ḥalafta (ca. 150 c.e.) and wanted to die. He said to her: "what *mitzvah* are you accustomed to do every day?" She said to him: "I am accustomed that, even if I am supposed to do something nice, I leave it **and rise early every day to go to the synagogue". He said to her: "stop going to the synagogue for three days in a row".** She did so and on the third day she became ill and died...

MEDIEVAL SOURCES

Ashkenaz ca. 1200:

9. A. M. Haberman, ed., *Sefer Gezeirot Ashkenaz Vetzarefat*, Jerusalem, 1946, p. 165:

Dulche, the wife of Rabbi Elazar of Worms, and their two daughters were martyred in the year 1196. He testifies in an elegy in their memory:

She sings hymns and prayer, and she recites supplications.
[She recites] *Nishmat kol ḥai* and *Vekhol ma'aminim.*
She recites *Pitum haketoret* and the Ten Commandments...
She arranges the order of the prayers in the morning and the evening,
and she comes early to synagogue and stays late...
I will tell the story of my older daughter Bellet,
She was thirteen years old, as chaste as a bride.
She had learned all the prayers and hymns from her mother...
I will tell the story of my younger daughter,
She read *Keriyat Shema* every day, the first portion,
She was six years old, she knew how to weave and sew...

In other words, Dulche used to pray in the synagogue every morning and every evening, and her daughters aged 13 and 6 would also recite the *Shema* and learned "**all the prayers**".[11]

10. *Sefer Ḥassidim*, ed. Wistinetzki, paragraph 464, pp. 132-133:

We are informed there about an old woman who used to recite *Shaḥarit* every weekday in the synagogue:

> It is told of an old woman who used to come to the synagogue early [and she was punished severely after her death]. And she said [in a dream]: "When I was alive, I used to leave the synagogue during *seder kedushah* [=*uva letziyon*] and did not wait until the congregation left the synagogue.

11. *Ibid.*, paragraph 465, p. 133:

It is told there about another woman who used to recite *Shaḥarit* every weekday in the synagogue: "A woman left the synagogue before the congregation finished praying" and her husband got angry at the fact that she left early: "You have sinned by leaving the synagogue!"

Ashkenaz between 1690 and 1719:

12. Gluckel of Hameln relates on many occasions in her autobiography that she and her daughters used to pray in the synagogue on a regular basis both on Shabbat as well as on weekdays, and she explicitly mentions their attendance at both the *shaḥarit* and *minḥah* services.[12]

11. For an annotated translation of this elegy, see Ivan Marcus, *Conservative Judaism* 38/3 (Spring 1986), pp. 40-42.
12. The *Memoirs of Gluckel of Hameln*, translated by Marvin Lowenthal, New York, 1932, pp. 130, 136-137, 239-240, 265-266. It is worth noting that Leah Horowitz of Bolechow, Galicia (ca. 1720-1800), complained that women in her time did not attend synagogue every morning and evening, but she herself recommended it. See Chava Weissler, *Voices of the Matriarchs*, Boston, 1998, p. 111.

Rome, 1524:

13. *Sippur David Hareuveni,* ed. A.Z. Eshkoli, second edition, Jerusalem, 1993, p. 39:

> David Hareuveni stayed in Rabbi Moshe Abudrahin's house in Rome: "And he has a daughter who reads the twenty four [the Bible] **and she prays *Shaḥarit*** and ***Arvit every day***".

Pisa, 1524:

14. *Ibid.*, p. 57:

> David Hareuveni stayed in Pisa and met Marat Sara from Pisa: "And she had a virgin niece... and that young woman is wise and learned, and she reads the twenty four and **prays".**

Jerusalem, 18th century

15. The Jerusalem Enactments of 1730, ed. A. H. Freimann, in *Sefer Dinaburg*, Jerusalem, 1949, pp. 208, 210:

> "An agreement that no woman may wait to hear the last *Kaddish,* neither in *Shaḥarit, Minḥah* or *Arvit*." This enactment teaches us that women attended synagogue during all the services, and the Jerusalem rabbis decreed that they should not remain until the last *Kaddish* so that the men should not look at them when they left the synagogue.

16. An enactment from Jerusalem in 1754, *Kovetz Hayerushalmi* 3 (1931), fol. 52b:

They decreed that a woman under forty could not go to the synagogue **for *minḥah*** and ***arvit*** except for Rosh Hashanah, Yom Kippur and *Simḥat Torah*. It can be deduced from here that young women in Jerusalem used to go to the synagogue for *minḥah* and *arvit* all year long and the Rabbis tried to limit this attendance to certain holidays for reasons of modesty.

We have therefore seen that according to the Mishnah, the Bavli and the *Rishonim,* women are obligated to pray the *Amidah* three times a day and there is much evidence that they actually did so in different periods of time and in many different places. If someone were to claim that this evidence reflects exceptions to the rule, we would reply that it is difficult to see so many examples from different periods and places as exceptions to the rule.

If so, why do many *Aḥaronim* and contemporary rabbis assume that women are only obligated to pray **once a day** and that they are not obligated to recite the fixed formula of the *Amidah,* but rather any prayer? The main source of this opinion is apparently a misunderstanding of the words of Rabbi Abraham Gumbiner (Poland, 1637-1683) in his commentary, *Magen Avraham,* to *Shulḥan Arukh* OH 106:1.

Rabbi Yosef Karo ruled *ibid.,* following the Rif and Maimonides:

> Women and slaves, although exempt from reciting the *Shema,* are obligated to pray the *Amidah,* because it is a positive commandment **not** bound by time.

Rabbi Abraham Gumbiner comments (subparagraph 2):

> So wrote Maimonides because he considered *Tefillah* a biblical positive commandment... yet, according to the Bible, once a day with any wording is sufficient. **Therefore, most women are accustomed that they do not pray regularly,** since they say a petitionary prayer in the morning immediately after the ritual of washing their hands and biblically this is sufficient, **and it is possible that the Sages did not obligate them to do more than that**, but Naḥmanides thinks that prayer is rabbinic and this is the opinion of most *poskim*.

In this passage, which influenced so many *Aḥaronim*, the *Magen Avraham* is not trying to explain the Mishnah, the Bavli or the *Rishonim*. He is simply trying **to justify** the practice of "most women" in Poland in his time who prayed a short petition every morning and no more. Rabbi Gumbiner is apparently following here the Ashkenazic method, as explained by Haym Soloveitchik, of viewing the practice of the people as a source of authority no less important than the Talmud and the codes and therefore requiring justification.[13] However, it is very difficult to rely on his words from the perspective of practical *halakhah*, and this for two reasons. First of all, Maimonides, as we have seen, thought that originally men and women were biblically obligated to pray once a day, but Ezra and his court made an enactment obligating men and women to pray **three** times a day.[14] Furthermore, the author of the *Magen Avraham* himself **disagrees** at the end of his commentary with the interpretation he himself had offered at the beginning! He writes at the end: "and it is possible that the Sages did not obligate them to do more than that, **but Naḥmanides [*v'haramban*]** thinks that prayer is rabbinic and this is the opinion of most *poskim*". The letter ***vav*** in "*v'haramban*" is the *vav* of opposition, meaning "**but** Naḥmanides thinks", and that is precisely how the *Mishnah Berurah* **quotes** this phrase at the end of subparagraph 4! In other words, the author of the *Magen Avraham* is saying: but **Naḥmanides** thinks like most *poskim* that reciting the *Amidah* three times a day was a rabbinic enactment from the start which obligated women and men in an equal fashion, since prayer is a supplication of mercy from God. Thus, the first clause in the *Magen Avraham* is not the plain meaning of Maimonides, and the last clause in any case annuls the first! Even so, many *Aḥaronim* followed the *Magen Avraham's* suggestion in

13. Haym Soloveitchik, *AJS Review* 12/2 (Fall 1987), pp. 205-221, especially pp. 211ff.
14. Compare our opinion to Rabbi Ḥayyim of Brisk's astonishment regarding this passage in the *Magen Avraham* – see Rabbi Tzvi Schachter, *Nefesh Harav*, Jerusalem, 1995, p. 103.

the first clause and attempted to read his explanation back into the words of the Mishnah or Maimonides.[15]

Finally, a number of *poskim* and recent writers tried to claim that women are indeed **obligated** to pray but are **exempt** from **public** prayer.[16] However, this is a surprising suggestion considering the fact that many *Rishonim* ruled that **even men are not obligated to pray in public!**[17]

Thus, according to the ***halakhah*** presented in the Mishnah, Talmud, and the *Rishonim*, and according to the **actual practice** of women in many places over the course of 1500 years or more, women are obligated to recite the *Amidah* three times a day exactly like men.

II. Are women obligated to recite *Mussaf* and *Ne'ilah*?

The *Aḥaronim* disagree regarding women's obligation to recite *Mussaf*. Those who exempt them say, for example, that the *Mussaf* prayer is a reminder of the *Mussaf* sacrifice and women did not bring *shekalim* and therefore had no part in communal sacrifices. Those who require them to do so respond that if so, Kohanim, Levites and minors under the age of twenty, who were exempt from bringing *shekalim*, should also be exempt from the *Mussaf* prayer![18] In a case such as this, of a disagreement among

15. Rabbi Yisrael Lifshitz, *Tiferet Yisrael* to *Berakhot* 3:3, note 17; *Arukh Hashulḥan, Oraḥ Ḥayyim* 106:7; Rabbi Ovadiah Yosef, *Yabi'a Omer*, Vol. 6, *Oraḥ Ḥayyim*, No. 17 and *Yeḥaveh Da'at*, Vol. 3, No. 7, as well as part of the Bibliography listed at the end of this responsum.
16. Rabbi Aryeh Frimer, *Or Hamizraḥ* pp. 75-76 = his English article, pp. 56-57 and the many responsa cited there; Rabbi Yitzḥak Ya'akov Fuchs, pp. 252-253; Rabbi Meiselman, pp. 133-136; Rabbi David Feldman, p. 300.
17. See Rabbi Fuchs himself, pp. 22-26 and 30-37 and Rabbi Meiselman himself, *ibid*.
18. **Women are exempt from *Mussaf*** according to Rabbi Yeḥezkel Landau, *Tziyun Lenefesh Ḥayah* to *Berakhot* 26a, s.v. *veshel mussafin*; Rabbi Akiva Eiger in his glosses to OH 106; Rabbi Shaul Berlin, *Responsa Besamim Rosh*, No. 89 (and many *Aḥaronim* based themselves specifically on this source because its eighteenth-century author attributed it to the Rosh!); and others. **They are obligated to recite *Mussaf*** according to Rabbi Joseph Shaul Nathanson in *Magen Giborim* to OH 106, subparagraph 4 and again in *Responsa Sho'el*

Aḥaronim, we should follow Rabbi Louis Ginzberg who said that we should not engage in involved debates regarding the words of the *Aḥaronim*. "My method has always been to base my words on the Talmud and the *Rishonim*."[19] Indeed, there **is** no discussion in the Talmud regarding women's obligation to recite *Mussaf*, but we have already learned in *Mishnah Berakhot* 3:3: "Women... are obligated in *tefillah*", and there is no reason to distinguish between *Shaḥarit, Minḥah* and *Ma'ariv* on the one hand and *Mussaf* and *Ne'ilah* on the other.

Indeed, we have already seen that Maimonides **does not** distinguish between them. He ruled in *Hilkhot Tefillah* 6:10: "Women, slaves and minors are obligated in *Tefillah*". And in chapter 1:1-7, when he describes Ezra's enactment, there is no difference in his style when he refers to different prayers: "**And they also enacted**... two *tefillot* every day... And every day when there was a *Mussaf* sacrifice, **they enacted** a third *tefillah* corresponding to the *Mussaf* sacrifice... **And they also enacted that a person** should recite one *tefillah* at night... **And they also enacted...** and this is the *tefillah* known as *Ne'ilah*...". This is also evident from his above-mentioned commentary to *Mishnah Kiddushin*: "and ***Tefillah*... – all of these are positive time-bound commandments, and every one of them the obligation for women is the same as the obligation for men...".**

Consequently, according to the Mishnah in *Berakhot* and according to Maimonides, women are obligated to recite the

Umeishiv, second edition, Part 2, No. 55; Rabbi Isaac Elḥanan Spector, *Responsa Be'er Yitzḥak*, end of No. 20; and others. For a summary of the *Aḥaronim's* opinions, see Rabbi Ovadiah Yosef, *Responsa Yabi'a Omer*, Vol. 2, No. 6, paragraphs 4-7, abbreviated by his son Rabbi Yitzḥak Yosef in *Yalkut Yosef*, Vol. 1, Jerusalem, 1985, p. 187. Also see Rabbi Ḥayyim David Halevi, *Mekor Ḥayyim Livnot Yisrael*, Tel Aviv, 1977, Chapter 11, pp. 57-59. **However, the arguments on both sides can be refuted.** For example, the author of *Tziyun Lenefesh Ḥayah* exempts women from *Mussaf* on the basis of one word which is lacking in *Tossafot* (*Berakhot* 26a, at the end of s.v. *tefilat hashaḥar*); however, that word is found in the Vilna edition!

19. Rabbi Louis Ginzberg, *The Responsa of Professor Louis Ginzberg*, edited by David Golinkin, New York and Jerusalem, 1996, Hebrew section, p. 85; and see below, notes 37 ff.

Amidah of *Mussaf* and *Ne'ilah* just as they are obligated to recite the *Amidah* of *Shaḥarit, Minḥah* and *Ma'ariv*.

III. May women be counted in the *minyan* for *Barekhu, Kaddish, Ḥazzarat Hashatz* and *Kedushah*?

The main source requiring a *minyan* for certain liturgical functions is Mishnah *Megillah* 4:3:

> One does not recite *Shema* responsively in public, nor does one pass before the Ark [as *sheliaḥ tzibbur* for the *Amidah*], nor do [the Kohanim] lift their hands [in blessing], nor is the Torah read [publicly], nor the Haftorah read from the prophet, nor are halts made [at funerals], nor is the blessing for mourners said, nor the comfort of mourners, nor the blessing of the bridegrooms, nor is the name [of God] mentioned in the invitation to say Grace, save in the presence of ten...

The recitation of *barekhu, kaddish* and the *ḥazzarat hashatz* including *kedushah* are usually called "*devarim shebikedushah*" or "matters of holiness"[20] and many *poskim* forbid women from being counted in the *minyan* for these sections of the liturgy.[21] Nonetheless, **such a prohibition is nowhere mentioned in the Talmud or in Maimonides.** On the contrary, a careful reading of the Talmud and Maimonides by Rabbi Michael Chernick has shown that it is permissible to count women in a *minyan* for "matters of holiness".[22]

It is clear that, from a historical point of view, the *minyan* as a minimal *edah* or congregation predates this Mishnah by a thousand years or more. This is evident from the Torah, the

20. See, in general, ET, s.v. *devarim shebikdushah,* Vol. 6, cols. 714-727.
21. *Siddur Rav Sa'adia Gaon*, Jerusalem, 1941, p. 34; *Tosafot* to *Berakhot* 45b, s.v. *veha* and parallels; Rabbi Menaḥem Hameiri, *Beit Habeḥirah* to *Berakhot*, ed. Dickman, p. 179; Rabbi Aharon Hakohen of Lunel, *Orḥot Ḥayyim, Hilkhot Tefillah,* paragraph 75; *Shulḥan Arukh* OH 55:1,4; *Levush, ibid.*, 55:4; *Shulḥan Arukh Harav* 55:2; as well as the *poskim* cited by Frimer, *Or Hamizraḥ*, pp. 80-81 = his English article, pp. 61-62.
22. This paragraph is based on Rabbi Michael Chernick's informative article.

Book of Ruth, the Dead Sea Scrolls and Josephus.[23] Nonetheless, the Talmud Bavli, which constitutes the highest authority for any *halakhic* issue,[24] derives the requirement of ten for a *minyan* from a double *gezeirah shavah*:

> [What is the biblical basis for this mishnah?] Rabbi Ḥiyya bar Abba said in the name of Rabbi Yoḥanan: Because Scripture says, "that I may be sanctified **among** the Israelite people" [Leviticus 22:32], every act of holiness requires not less than ten. How does the verse denote this? As [Rabbanai, the brother of Rabbi Ḥiyya bar Abba] taught: We explain the word "**among**" here by reference to its use in another place. It is written here [in Leviticus], "that I may be sanctified **among** the Israelite people" and it is written elsewhere "Separate yourselves from **among this congregation**" [Numbers 16:21]. And we further explain the word "**congregation**" here by reference to what is written in another place: It is written there: "How long shall I bear with this evil **congregation**" [*ibid.* 14:27]. Just as there ten are indicated, so here.[25]

Some *poskim* have tried to exclude women from the *minyan* by emphasizing the words "***benei** Yisrael*" = "the **sons** of Israel", as opposed to the **daughters** of Israel, in Leviticus 22:32.[26] However, it is difficult to accept this approach since "The entire Torah was also given in male language".[27] Furthermore, we cannot invent our own *midrashim*. Finally, according to this logic, only **wicked** people can be counted in a *minyan* since the ten

23. See the sources which I have cited below, p. 269.
24. Regarding the Bavli's authority, see below, note 37 ff.
25. *Megillah* 23b and cf. the parallel source in *Berakhot* 21b. The name in brackets is based on the printed editions of *Berakhot* and *Dikdukei Soferim* to *Megillah, ad loc.*, note *reish*.
26. See *Orḥot Ḥayyim*, the *Levush* and *Shulḥan Arukh Harav* (above, note 21) and what I wrote in my above-mentioned responsum (above, note 23). They were apparently influenced by the two *derashot* in *Kiddushin* 36a and parallels.
27. *Tosafot* to *Arakhin* 2b, s.v. *lerabot*.

spies mentioned in this midrashic interpretation were wicked! It is therefore clear that this complicated midrash is simply an *asmakhta*[28] which aims to give scriptural support after the fact for an existing law or custom, and one should not attempt to engage in precise readings of additional words in the verse quoted.

On the other hand, this midrash opens up the door to counting women in the *minyan* because the very same midrash appears in *Sanhedrin* 74b as an *asmakhta* to support the sanctification of God's name – *kiddush hashem* – before a *minyan* of ten. The Talmud there assumes that Esther and other women are obligated to sanctify God's name in the presence of a *minyan* of ten Jews, and this was codified by the major *poskim*.[29] In addition, a group of *poskim* went one step further and ruled that women may be counted in the *minyan* of ten for *kiddush hashem*.[30]

It is therefore clear from these two identical midrashim that *devarim shebikdushah* and *kiddush hashem* are two sides of the same coin, since both stem from the desire to sanctify God's name in public. Therefore, if it is permissible to count women in a *minyan* for *kiddush hashem*, then it is permissible to count them in a *minyan* for *devarim shebikedushah* such as *kaddish* and *kedushah*.[31] Indeed, Rabbi Moshe Feinstein determined that in connection to laws which belong to two realms of *halakhah* which are learned from one verse "...one should not diferentiate in matters learned from one verse".[32]

28. See ET (above, note 20), note 11 for *Rishonim* who thought so. For other *asmakhtaot* supporting the *minyan* of ten, see Yerushalmi *Berakhot* 7:3, fol. 11c = Yerushalmi *Megillah* 4;4, fol. 75b. For similar exact readings and their refutations see below, pp. 267-268.
29. See the sources which I cite below, pp. 233 and additional *poskim* listed by Rabbi Frimer, *Or Hamizraḥ*, pp. 79-80.
30. Rabbi Yosef Engel, *Gilyonei Hashass* to *Sanhedrin* 74b s.v. *mah lehalan;* Rabbi Reuven Margaliot, *Margaliot Hayam: Massekhet Sanhedrin*, Part II, Jerusalem, 1977[2], p. 86, paragraph 27; and additional *poskim* listed by Rabbi Frimer, *Or Hamizraḥ*, p. 80, note 71.
31. Rabbi Frimer, *ibid.*, p. 80 admits that this is "a strange situation", but he did his best to avoid the ineluctable conclusion.
32. *Iggrot Moshe, Ḥoshen Mishpat*, Part 2, No. 66, p. 290, s.v. *aval harambam.*

Maimonides' words also open up a door to permit counting women in a *minyan*. When he discusses *ḥazzarat hashatz*, he requires "ten free **adults** (*gedolim*)".[33] As is well-known, Maimonides chose his words very carefully. Therefore, the word "adults" appears to include women, because when Maimonides wanted to exclude women from the *minyan* for *zimmun* and the Priestly Blessing, he did so explicitly.[34]

If so, even though we did not find evidence that Maimonides actually included women in the *minyan*, he did not forbid it either, and thus we have further support for allowing this. Therefore, via a careful reading of the Bavli and Maimonides, we learn that it is permissible to count women in a *minyan* for *barekhu, kaddish, ḥazzarat hashatz* and *kedushah*.

IV. May women serve as *sheliḥot tzibbur*?

The basic principle allowing someone to fulfill another's obligation is found in Mishnah *Rosh Hashanah* 3:8:

> A deaf-mute, a lunatic and a minor cannot fulfill a religious duty on behalf of a congregation. This is the general principle: one who is not obligated to perform a religious duty cannot fulfill it on behalf of a congregation.

We have shown above that women are obligated to recite the *Amidah* in every service, including *Mussaf* and *Ne'ilah*, and to sanctify God's name. Therefore, according to the general

33. *Hilkhot Tefillah* 8:4. See, however, *ibid*. 12:3: "The Torah should not be read in public if there are less than ten ***anashim*** *gedolim benei ḥorin*" (literally: ten **men** adults free). This is also the reading in Ms. Oxford (see *Sefer Ahavah*, ed. Hyamson, Jerusalem 1965, fol. 112a) and in the first printed edition, Rome 1480 (reprinted in Jerusalem, 1955). Even so, the language is redundant and *Kesef Mishneh ad loc.* and *Tur* OH 143 read *gedolim benei ḥorin* (literally: adults free) without the word *anashim* (men) and this seems to be the correct reading. Cf. Rabbi Chernik's analysis, pp. 8-9.
34. *Hilkhot Berakhot* 5:7 and *Hilkhot Nessiat Kapayim* 15:9, and cf. below, p. 268. Regarding women and *zimmun*, see below, p. 367, note 41.

principle above, it is permissible for them to serve as *sheliḥot tzibbur* for *barekhu, kaddish, ḥazzarat hashatz* and *kedushah.*

The only objection that could be raised would be with regard to reciting *Shema* because we have learned in Mishnah *Berakhot* 3:3 cited above that women are **exempt** from reciting the *Shema.* If so, how can they they fulfill the congregation's obligation to hear the *Shema*? Our reply is that this would indeed be an obstacle if we still recited *Shema* in public responsively (***porsim al shema***), i.e. that the *ḥazzan* would read the *Shema* aloud to the congregation responsively.[35] But that ancient practice disappeared 1,500 years ago and our reciting the *Shema* (***Keriyat Shema***) requires neither a *minyan* nor a *sheliaḥ tzibbur.* If so, it makes no difference whether the *sheliaḥ tzibbur* for *keriyat shema* is obligated or not. Therefore, it is permissible for a woman to be the *sheliḥat tzibbur* for all of the above services, as explained above.[36]

General considerations

A devil's advocate could present three major objections to all of the above:

1. Some might say: granted that the positions outlined above have support in the sources, yet how can we rule against the *Aḥaronim* regarding the obligation of women to pray and against the *Shulḥan Arukh* regarding counting women in the *minyan*? To this I would reply that the Geonim and Maimonides already established the principle that the Talmud Bavli is the highest authority on *halakhic* issues.[37] On this basis, many important

35. This is the conclusion of Prof. Ezra Fleischer, *Tarbitz* 41 (5732), pp. 133-144 who surveyed all extant explanations of the term "*porsin et shema*". For the exact nature of the responsive reading, see *ibid.*, pp. 140 ff.
36. And if someone were to object to a woman singing on the basis of *kol b'ishah ervah,* that it is supposedly forbidden for women to sing, see above, Chapter 2.
37. For the Geonim, see Levi Ginzberg, *Peirushim V'ḥidushim Bayerushalmi,* Vol. I, New York, 1941, Hebrew Introduction, pp. 84-90; Robert Brody, *The Geonim of Babylonia and the Shaping of Medieval Jewish Culture,* New Haven

poskim established that it is possible to rule according to the Bavli even if the ruling is against the Geonim or the major *poskim* such as the Rif, Maimonides and the *Shulḥan Arukh.* The Rosh (1250–1327) asserted in *Piskei Harosh*:

> "Yiftaḥ in his generation was like Samuel in his generation" [Rosh Hashanah 25b]; you have only "the judge who will be at the time" [Deuteronomy 17:9]. And one can contradict the words [of the Geonim], because all of the things that are not explicitly in the Talmud arranged by Rav Ashi and Ravina, a person can contradict or build up, even to contradict the words of the Geonim.[38]

Rabbi Shlomo Luria established in 16th century Poland:

> Since the days of Ravina and Rav Ashi there is no tradition to only rule like one the Geonim or one of the later *poskim;* rather only one whose words are validated by being based with clear proofs on the Talmud, or on the Yerushalmi and the *Toseftot* in a place where there is no clear decision in the Talmud.[39]

Rabbi Ḥayyim of Volozhin transmitted in the name of his teacher, the Vilna Ga'on (18th century):

> I was already warned about this by my teacher and Rabbi, the saintly Gaon of Israel, our great and pious Rabbi, not to

and London, 1998, pp. 161-166. For Maimonides, see his introductions to his *Commentary on the Mishnah* and to the *Mishneh Torah*. For Rabbi Abraham, Maimonides' son, see his responsa, ed. Freiman, Jerusalem, 1938, pp. 21, 111, 115. For the Bavli's authority in general, see Menaḥem Elon, *Hamishpat Ha'ivri,* third edition, Jerusalem, 1988, pp. 902-904 and Boaz Cohen, *Kuntress Hateshuvot*, Budapest, 1930, pp. 17-20.

38. *Piskei Harosh* to *Sanhedrin,* Chapter 4, paragraph 6 and cf. *Piskei Harosh* to *Kiddushin* Chapter 1, paragraph 41 = *Bekhorot* Chapter 9, paragraph 1; *Responsa Rosh, Kelal* 31:9; 43:12; 55:9; 100:2.
39. The Maharshal's introduction to *Yam Shel Shlomo, Ḥullin*, ed. Stetin, 1861 (before fol. 1); and cf. see Boaz Cohen (above, note 37), p. 20, note 4 for additional references.

> play favorites in halakhic rulings, even for the decisions of our teachers, the authors of the *Shulḥan Arukh*.[40]

Important *poskim* in our day, such as Rabbi Abraham Isaac Kook, Rabbi Louis Ginzberg, Rabbi Moshe Feinstein and Rabbi Ḥayyim David Halevi have followed a similar approach.[41]

Furthermore, we should always remember the warning penned by Solomon Schechter over a century ago:

> But however great the literary value of a code may be, it does not invest it with the attribute of infallibility, nor does it exempt the student or the Rabbi who makes use of it from the duty of examining each paragraph on its own merits, and subjecting it to the same rules of interpretation that were always applied to tradition.[42]

The *Shulḥan Arukh* and its commentaries are **important** guides to Jewish law, but they are not the **only** guides to Jewish law. As many *poskim* have stressed, complicated *halakhic* questions must be solved by carefully studying the Talmud, the codes and the

40. This is the version quoted by Ḥayyim Tchernowitz, *Toledot Haposkim*, Vol. 3, New York, 1947, p. 218, note 1 and by Rabbi Shlomo Yosef Zevin, *Ishim Ve'shitot*, Jerusalem, 1957, p. 18 and cf. Louis Ginzberg, *Students, Scholars and Saints*, Philadelphia, 1928, p. 141 and p. 277, note 40. In *Responsa Ḥut Hameshulash*, Vilna, 1882, No. 9, the end of the sentence about the authors of the *Shulḥan Arukh* was censored by someone, but the complete version can be found in *Sefer Aliyot Eliyahu*, Jerusalem, 5723, fol. 28b and in *Responsa Kedushat Yom Tov*, No. 34. I am indebted to Rabbi Monique Susskind Goldberg z"l for helping me correct what I wrote in the Hebrew version of this volume, pp. 63-64.
41. Rabbi Abraham Isaac Hakohen Kook, *Responsa Da'at Kohen*, No. 154 ruled on the basis of *Bekhorot* 30b regarding the acceptance of *mitzvot* by a convert, even though it explicitly contradicts the major *poskim*. Also see Rabbi Louis Ginzberg (above, note 19), Hebrew introduction, pp. 8-9; Rabbi Moshe Feinstein, *Iggrot Moshe, Yoreh Deah*, Part 1, No. 101, p. 186, s.v. *umah shekatav yedidi*; Rabbi Ḥayyim David Halevi, *Asei Lekha Rav*, Vol. 2, pp. 146-147.
42. Solomon Schechter, *Studies in Judaism*, First Series, London, 1896, p. 211. See other sources reflecting this point of view in my introduction to *Responsa of the Va'ad Halakhah of the Rabbinical Assembly of Israel* 6 (5755-5758), notes 34-36.

responsa literature, not by opening up one code and relying exclusively on whatever it says.[43]

2. Others might say: granted there is textual support for these positions, but we know that in the past women were **not** counted in a *minyan* and did **not** serve as *sheliḥot tzibbur*. Are we allowed to act against the custom of our ancestors and thereby imply that they were mistaken? To this I would reply by quoting two classic sources:

a. We read in the Torah:

> If a case is too baffling for you to decide... you shall come to the levitical priests or the magistrate in charge **at the time** and present your problem. When they have announced to you the verdict in the case, you shall carry out the verdict that is announced to you... (Deut. 17:8-11)

The Torah is emphasizing that in every generation, Jews must come before the judges serving **at that time**. Moses and Rabbi Akiva and Maimonides and Rabbi Yosef Karo cannot solve the problems of **our day** because **our** problems were not **their** problems. In every generation, we must grapple with *halakhic* problems according to the circumstances and conditions of that generation, or, to use the Talmudic idiom: "Every generation and its expositors, every generation and its Sages, every generation and its scribes" (*Avodah Zarah* 5a). The basic sources remain the same, but every generation of judges or rabbis must interpret them according to the conditions of his time and place. If we arrive at a different answer, it doesn't mean that our ancestors made a **mistake**, but that they and we arrived at different conclusions according to the conditions "at that time".

b. A similar idea was expressed by Rashi as quoted by his grandson the Rashbam in his commentary to Genesis 37:2:

43. For *poskim* who stressed this point, see Boaz Cohen (above, note 37), pp. 20-22.

> Even I, Samuel, the son of Rabbi Meir his son-in-law, may he rest in peace, argued with him and he [Rashi] admitted that, if he had the time, he would have to write different commentaries **according to the plain meanings (*peshatot*)** which renew themselves every day.

The expression in bold is very surprising. If a certain interpretation is the ***peshat***, the plain meaning of the text, how can it **renew** itself every day?! Indeed, the beauty of the Torah is that the *peshat* changes from generation to generation, as each commentator looks at the sources through the filter of his time and place. One can understand why the *Shulḥan Arukh* ruled that women may not be counted in a *minyan*; had he done otherwise the ruling would have been considered strange in his time and place. So too, Rabbi Abraham Gumbiner, the author of *Magen Avraham,* came to justify the practice of women in his day. It is our duty as *poskim* to reexamine the sources in light of the reality of our day. Of course, this does not mean that we can allow everything. But counting women in the *minyan* today is as **natural** today as it was **unnatural** in Safed in the sixteenth century. The sources are the same, but the sociological realities are incredibly different.

3. Finally, some might say that we should not declare that women are obligated to pray three times a day because we will thereby turn most women who did not pray regularly in the past and in the present into sinners.[44] To this I would reply as follows:

   a. I see no other way of reading the above sources. I believe that according to the Mishnah, Talmud and *Rishonim* women are indeed **obligated** to recite the *Amidah* at every prayer service just like men.

44. Rabbi Joel Roth, *Ordination,* 166 says that we should not make a *takkanah* (enactment) obligating all women to observe all *mitzvot* because it "would result in the creation of a large class of sinners where none now exists". I agree with that statement, but he includes **prayer** in that category, while I believe that women are **already** obligated to recite the *amidah* in every prayer service.

b. The fact that a Rabbi or a group of Rabbis rules in a certain way does not mean that **all** Jews will do or must do what they say. Throughout Jewish history, cotradictory *halakhic* rulings coexisted side by side. In the Talmud we find expressions such as "In Sura they followed Mareimar, but Rav Shisha the son of Rav Idi followed Abaye".[45] In the Geonic period, we find a series of *halakhic* disagreements between the *yeshivot* of Sura and Pumbedita.[46] According to an important work from the Geonic period, there were at least 55 *halakhic* differences between the Jews of Babylonia and the Jews of Eretz Yisrael in the Geonic period.[47] In medieval times, there were hundreds of differences between *Ashkenazim* and *Sefaradim*. For example, the *Sefaradim* practiced *yibum* while the *Ashkenazim* practiced *ḥalitzah*; the *Sefaradim* allowed bigamy while the *Ashkenazim* forbade it on the basis of Rabbeinu Gershom's decree.[48] In modern times, there were many *halakhic* disagreements between *ḥassidim* and *mitnagdim*, between the various ḥassidic dynasties and between various Sefardic ethnic groups. A Sefardic Jew who disobeyed an Ashkenazic Rabbi was not a "sinner", he was simply relying on a different custom or Rabbi. So too in the case under discussion. A woman who reads this *pesak* and continues to pray a private petition once a day instead of reciting the *Amidah* three times a day is not "a sinner"; she can rely on the author of the *Arukh Hashulḥan* and other *poskim* who so

45. *Sukkah* 46b and *Pesaḥim* 115a (according to all of the manuscripts; the printed editions read "Surya"). Cf. *Gittin* 89a for Sura vs. Nehardea and *Bava Metzia* 73a for Sura vs. Kafri. On the conflicting traditions between Sura and Pumbedita, see David Goodblatt, *HUCA* 48 (1977), pp. 210-216 and *Assufot* 8 (5754), pp. 99-129 (two articles).
46. They were collected by Simḥa Assaf in *Tekufat Hage'onim Vesifruta*, Jerusalem, 1957, pp. 261-278 and cf. the articles in *Assufot* cited in the previous note.
47. Mordechai Margaliot, ed., *Haḥillukim Shebein Anshei Mizraḥ Uvenei Eretz Yisrael*, Jerusalem, 1938.
48. See H.J. Zimmels, *Ashkenazim and Sephardim*, London, 1958, especially Parts II and III.

ruled. I would try to convince her that their interpretation is incorrect, but she is not a "sinner"; she is simply relying on another valid *halakhic* opinion.

VI. Practical *Halakhah*

In conclusion, an in-depth reading of the Talmud and *poskim* indicates that women are obligated to recite the *Amidah* in the *Shaḥarit, Minḥah, Ma'ariv, Mussaf* and *Ne'ilah* services, exactly like men. Women may be counted in the *minyan* for *Barekhu, Kaddish, Ḥazzarat Hashatz* and *Kedushah,* and women may serve as *shliḥot tzibbur* at all the above-mentioned services.

David Golinkin
Jerusalem
Isru Hag Hapesaḥ, 5757

BIBLIOGRAPHY

Adler — Rachel Adler, "Innovation and Authority : A Feminist Reading of the Women's Minyan Responsum", in: Walter Jacob and Moshe Zemer, eds, *Gender Issues in Jewish Law: Essays and Responsa*, New York, 2001, pp. 3-32

Allen — Rabbi Wayne Allen, "Women's Prayer Groups", *Tomeikh Kehalakhah,* Mt. Vernon, New York, 1986, pp. 32-40

Berkovits — Rabbi Eliezer Berkovits, *Jewish Women in Time and Torah*, Hoboken, 1990, pp. 70-99

Berman — Rabbi Saul Berman, "The Status of Women in *Halakhic* Judaism", *Tradition* 14/2 (Fall 1973), pp. 5-28

Biale — Rachel Biale, *Women and Jewish Law*, New York, 1984, pp 17-24

Bleich — Rabbi David Bleich, *Tradition* 14/2 (Fall 1973), pp. 113-117 = *Contemporary Halakhic Problems*, Vol. I, Hoboken, 1977, pp. 78-83

Bleich — Rabbi David Bleich, "Women's *Minyanim*", *Contemporary Halakhic Problems*, Vol. III, Hoboken, 1989, pp. 115-121

Brayer — Rabbi Menachem Brayer, *The Jewish Woman in Rabbinic Literature*, Vol. 2, Hoboken, 1986, pp.198-206

Chernick — Rabbi Michael Chernik, "*Hakhel Me'ish Ve'ad Ishah*" (unpublished)

CJLS — CJLS responsa of Rabbis Aaron Blumenthal, Phillip Segal, and David Feldman sent to the Rabbinical Assembly on October 5, 1973 (unpublished)

Cohen — Rabbi Alfred Cohen and others, *Journal of Halacha and Contemporary Society* XXXIV (Fall 1997), pp. 115-118 and XXXV (Spring 1998), pp. 112-114

Cohen — Rabbi J. Simcha Cohen, "Women's *Minyanim*", in: *Intermarriage and Conversion: a Halakhic Solution,* Hoboken, 1987, Chapter 16

Cohen Nusbacher
Ailene Cohen Nusbacher, "The Case of Orthodox Women's Prayer Groups", *Nashim* 2 (Spring 1999), pp. 95-113

Ellinson — Rabbi Elyakim Ellinson, *Ha'ishah Vehamitzvot Sefer Rishon: Bein Ha'ishah Leyotzrah,* Jerusalem, 1977^2, pp. 66-82

Feldman — Rabbi David Feldman in Seymour Siegel and Elliot Gertel, eds., *Conservative Judaism and Jewish Law,* New York, 1977, pp. 294-305

Francus — Rabbi Israel Francus in: Simon Greenberg, ed. *The Ordination of Women Rabbis: Study and Responsa,* New York, 1988, pp. 35-45

Freehof — Rabbi Solomon Freehof, *Reform Jewish Practice,* Vol. I, New York, 1963 , pp. 50-52

Friedman — Rabbi Tuvia Friedman, *"Teshuvah Be'inyan Nashim Beminyan",* December 1990 (unpublished)

Frimer — Rabbi Aryeh Avraham Frimer, "*Ma'amad Ha'ishah Bahalakhah – Nashim Beminyan*", *Or Hamizraḥ* 34 (5746), pp. 69-86 = *Tradition* 23/4 (Summer 1988), pp. 54-77

Frimer — Rabbis Aryeh and Dov Frimer, "Women's Prayer Services", *Tradition* 32/3 (Winter 1998), pp. 5-118; 33/2 (Winter 1999), pp. 80-90; and 33/3 (Spring 1999), pp. 110-114

Fuks — Rabbi Yitzḥak Ya'akov Fuks, *Hatefillah Betzibbur,* Jerusalem, 5738, pp. 168-169, 252-253

Ginzberg — Rabbi Levi Ginzberg, *Peirushim Veḥidushim Bayerushalmi,* Vol. 2, New York, 1941, pp. 149-152

Hadani — Ya'akov Hadani, "*Mitpalelet*", in: Shmuel Glick, ed., *Zekhor Davar L'avdekha: Sefer Zikaron L'dov Rappel,* Jerusalem, 5767, pp. 103-120

Halevi — Rabbi Ḥayyim David Halevi, *Aseh Lekha Rav,* Vol. 1, Tel Aviv, 1976, No. 30 and Vol. 5, Tel Aviv, 1983, p. 333

Halivni — Rabbi David Weiss Halivni in: *On the Ordination of Women as Rabbis,* [New York, 1979], pp. 9-8 of his responsum

Hauptman — Judith Hauptman, "Women as Cantors", *Journal of Synagogue Music* 17/1 (1987), pp. 4-8

Hauptman — Judith Hauptman, *JUDAISM* 42/1 (Winter 1993), pp. 94-103 and reactions *ibid*. 42/4 (Fall 1993), pp. 387-413

Haut I. — Irwin Haut, "Are Women Obligated to Pray?" in: Rivka Haut and Susan Grossman, eds., *Daughters of the King: Women and the Synagogue,* Philadelphia, New York and Jerusalem, 1992, pp. 89-101

Haut R. — Rivka Haut, "Women's Prayer Groups and the Orthodox Synagogue", *ibid*., pp. 135-157

Helfgott — Esther Helfgott, *Conservative Judaism* 38/3 (Spring 1986), pp. 68-69

Kahana — Rabbi Yitzḥak Ze'ev Kahana, *Responsa Toledot Ya'akov,* Vilna, 1907, *Oraḥ Ḥayyim,* No. 5

Kasdan — Rabbi Menachem Kasdan, "Are Women Obligated to Pray Daily?", *Journal of Halacha and Contemporary Society* I/2 (1981), pp. 86-106

Lubitch — Rivka Lubitch, *"Al Tefillat Nashim"*, *Teḥumin* 17 (5757), pp. 165-167 (a reaction to Schochetman)

Meiselman — Rabbi Moshe Meiselman, *Jewish Woman in Jewish Law,* New York, 1978, Chapter 20; and more recently: "The Rav, Feminism and Public Policy", *Tradition* 33/1 (Fall 1998), pp. 5-30 and 33/2 (Winter 1999), pp. 90-107

Nissel — Rabbi Menachem Nissel, *Rigshei Lev – Women and Tefillah,* Jerusalem, 2001

Novak — Rabbi David Novak, *Law and Theology in Judaism,* Vol. II, New York, 1976, pp. 145-146

Novak — Rabbi David Novak, *JUDAISM* 33/1 (Winter 1984), p. 41

Novak Rabbi David Novak, *Tomeikh Kahalakhah*, Vol. 2, 1994, pp. 6-11 and 22-23

Rabinowitz
Rabbi Mayer Rabinowitz, in: Simon Greenberg, ed. *The Ordination of Women Rabbis: Study and Responsa*, New York, 1988, pp. 112-117 = *JUDAISM* 33/1 (Winter 1984), pp. 58-64

Roth Rabbi Joel Roth, in: Greenberg, *ibid.*, pp. 127-148 and in abbreviated form in *JUDAISM, ibid.*, pp. 70-78

Sacks Rabbi Jonathan Sacks in: Moshe Sokol, ed., *Rabbinic Authority and Personal Autonomy*, Northvale, New Jersey, 1992, pp. 155-168 (an attack against Rabbi Roth's responsum)

Safrai Chana Safrai, "*Minyan, Migdar Vedemokratia*", *Ravgoni* 3 (Elul 5760), pp. 41-43

Schochetman
Eliav Schochetman, "*Minyan Nashim Bakotel*", *Teḥumin* 15 (5755), pp. 161–184; "*Od Leshe'elat Minyan Nashim Bakotel*", *ibid.* 17 (5757), pp. 168-174

Shiloh Shmuel Shiloh, "*Tefilat Nashim Betzavta Bereḥavat Hakotel*", *Teḥumin* 17 (5757), pp. 160-164

Sigal Rabbi Phillip Sigal in: Seymour Siegel and Elliot Gertel, eds. *Conservative Judaism and Jewish Law*, New York, 1977, pp. 282-292

Slay Rabbi Menachem Slay, "*Ḥiyuv Ha'ishah Betefillatt Shemoneh Esrei Al Pi Sifrut Hashut*", *Areshet: Kovetz Mukdash Le'inyinei Tefillah Ubeit Haknesset*, Jerusalem, 5744, pp. 87-91

Steinberg Rabbi Moshe Halevi Steinberg, *Hilkhot Nashim*, Jerusalem, 1983, pp. 49-50

Twersky Rabbi Mayer Twersky, "Rav Soloveitchik's Pesak Regarding Women's Prayer Groups", *Tradition* 32/3 (Spring 1998), pp. 5-18

Wald Steve Wald, "*Teshuvah Al Nashim Beminyan Ukesheliḥot Tzibbur*", Marḥeshvan 5752 (unpublished)

Weiner — Rabbi Chaim Weiner, "*Teguva Leteshuvato Shel Harav Tuvia Friedman*" (unpublished)

Weiss — Rabbi Avraham Weiss, *Women at Prayer*, Hoboken, 1990

Yalon — Shevaḥ Yalon, *Kol Mitzvot Aseh Shehazman Geraman Nashim Peturot: Iyun Bamekorot Hatanna'iyim Uvasugyot Ha'amoraiyot*, M.A. Thesis, Bar Ilan University, Ramat Gan, 1990

Yosef — Rabbi Ovadiah Yosef, *Responsa Yabi'a Omer*, Part 6, *Oraḥ Ḥayyim*, No. 17 and *Responsa Yeḥaveh Da'at*, Part 3, No. 7

4. ADDING THE *IMAHOT* TO THE *AMIDAH*[1]

Oraḥ Ḥayyim 167:10 & 187:1

Question: *There is a custom today to add the Imahot [=Matriarchs] to the first blessing of the Amidah. Is this permissible according to Jewish law?*

Responsum: Before we reply, let us present two of the versions of the *Imahot* currently in use:

a. *Sim Shalom for Shabbat and Festivals,* New York, 1998, p. 3b:

Barukh attah hashem eloheinu velohei avoteinu,
Elohei Avraham elohei Yitzḥak velohei Ya'akov,
Elohei Sarah elohei Rivkah elohei Rachel velohei Leah,
Ha'el hagadol....
Melekh ozer ***upoked*** umoshee'a umagen
Barukh atah hashem magen Avraham ***upoked Sarah.***

b. *Siddur Va'ani Tefilati,* Jerusalem, 1998, p. 68:

Barukh attah hashem eloheinu velohei avoteinu ***ve'imoteinu,***
Elohei Avraham elohei Yitzḥak velohei Ya'akov,
Elohei Sarah elohei Rivkah elohei Rachel velohei Leah,
Ha'el hagadol....
Vezokher ḥasdei avot ***ve'imahot***
Umeivee ***ge'ulah le'amo yisrael*** lema'an shemo be'ahavah.
Melekh ozer umoshee'a umagen
Barukh attah hashem magen Avraham ***veSarah.***

1. This responsum was originally written in Hebrew for the *Va'ad Halakhah* of the Rabbinical Assembly of Israel on the 19th of Tevet, 5761. This English translation has been thoroughly revised and updated. All brief citations below refer to the Bibliography at the end of the responsum.

I. Introduction

One of the slogans of the Conservative movement is "Tradition and Change".[2] There is no doubt that some Conservative Jews feel that there is something missing in the *Avot* blessing (the first blessing of the *Amidah*) and want to change it by adding mention of the *Imahot*. This is legitimate, for many changes in Judaism have resulted from the way that people feel.

However, in order to actually change the *Amidah*, which is **the** central prayer of the prayer book and of the Jewish people, it is not enough to **want** to change the wording. It is essential to prove that this is permissible from a halakhic point of view and appropriate from a liturgical and theological point of view. The applicable principle is *"hamotzi meiḥavero alav hari'ayah"* – "one who demands something from another bears the burden of proof". Authentic liturgical and halakhic changes are made on the basis of halakhic sources and historical precedents. Indeed, we have proven elsewhere that it is permissible for women to be counted in the *minyan*, serve as *sheliḥot tzibbur*, receive *aliyot*, decide halakhic issues, put on *tefillin*, and more – all on the basis of halakhic sources and historical precedents.[3] A change made on the basis of desire alone is not an authentic halakhic change that is based on tradition and which develops that tradition.

II. The Proponents of the *Imahot* Versions Presented Above[4]

The proponents of this change make three central claims with which we would like to respectfully disagree:

1. They claim that some versions of some blessings of the *Amidah* from the post-talmudic era differ from our version which was accepted at the conclusion of the Geonic Period (ca. 1000 c.e.).

2. See David Golinkin, *Halakhah for Our Time: A Conservative Approach to Jewish Law*, New York, 1991, pp. 3-4.
3. See the other chapters in this volume.
4. "The proponents" below refers to the responsum of Rabbi Joel Rembaum.

This is true, but it is not really relevant to our topic. Our question is not "Is it permissible to change a word or an expression in the *Amidah*?" but rather "Is it permissible to change the opening and closing formulae of the *Avot* blessing?"

2. They further assert that the Rabbinical Assembly has already changed certain expressions in the *siddur* such as the omission of the words *"ve'ishei yisrael"* ("and the fire offerings of Israel") in the *Amidah*; the change of "we will make and offer [sacrifices]" to "they made and offered [sacrifices]" in the *Mussaf Amidah*; and the change of the early morning blessings referring to Gentiles, slaves, and women from the negative to the positive. Therefore, it is permissible to change the opening and closing formulae of the *Avot* blessing. However, as I have written elsewhere, "the question is not **whether** we may change the *siddur*, but whether specific changes are permissible, necessary or desirable".[5] Indeed, it **is** permissible to change "we will make and offer [sacrifices]" and the early morning blessings on the basis of halakhic and liturgical precedents, as we shall see below. But such changes do not teach us anything about changing the *Avot* blessing which must be examined on its own merits.

3. There remains, therefore, only the third claim of the proponents – the halakhic claim. They argue that the proposed change is permitted by Maimonides. This claim will be examined in the next section.

III. Maimonides' Approach to Changes in the Wording of the Prayers

The proponents rely on Maimonides (*Hilkhot Berakhot* 1:6):

> "And if one altered the wording [of any blessing], as long as he mentioned God's name and sovereignty and the theme of the blessing, even if not in Hebrew, **he has fulfilled his obligation** [=*yatza*]".

5. Golinkin, p. 43 and cf. *ibid.*, pp. 41-43.

On the other hand, the proponents admit that in the previous paragraph (1:5), Maimonides ruled that "the wording of all the blessings, Ezra and his court enacted them, **and it is not appropriate to change them nor to add to one of them nor to detract from one of them, and anyone who changes the wording coined by the Sages in the blessings is simply erring**". Moreover, the proponents acknowledge that in *Hilkhot Keri'at Shema* (1:7) Maimonides expresses even more adamant opposition to changes in the wording: "The basic principle is: **anyone who changes the wording coined by the Sages in the blessings is mistaken and he must go back and bless [the blessing] as coined**".

Indeed, the leniency quoted from *Hilkhot Berakhot* 1:6 proves nothing with regard to our topic. It is clear from the language used by Rabbi Meir and Rav in the Talmud (*Berakhot* 40b), by Rav Hai Gaon (*Otzar Hageonim to Berakhot, Peirushim,* p. 56), by Maimonides himself, and by the *Shulḥan Arukh* (OH 167:10 and 187:1) that one who changes the wording fulfills his obligation [=*yatza*] **only after the fact.**[6] But those who wish to add the *Imahot* to the *Amidah* wish to do so three times daily *ab initio* [=before the fact], not after the fact, and there is no doubt that Maimonides would have strenuously objected to such a practice.

Furthermore, the proponents did not cite Maimonides' *Hilkhot Tefillah* 1:9:

> **And the three initial [blessings of the Amidah] and the three concluding [blessings of the Amidah], one may not add to them nor detract from them, nor make any change in them at all.**

Many important commentators have already discussed the internal contradiction between Maimonides' *Hilkhot Berakhot* 1:6

6. The *Mishnah Berurah* emphasized this in both places in *Oraḥ Ḥayyim*. For the use of *yatza* as meaning "after the fact", see Golinkin, *Rosh Hashanah*, p. 300 and Ḥayyim Yehoshua Kossovsky, *Otzar Leshon Hamishnah*, Volume 2, Jerusalem, 1957, pp. 869-870.

and 1:5 quoted above.[7] The Vilna Gaon was of the opinion that Maimonides actually changed his mind (*Bei'ur Hagra* to OH 68:1).

Rabbi Joseph Karo, on the other hand (*Kesef Mishneh* to Maimonides *ad loc.*), says that there is no contradiction between 1:5 and 1:6. In 1:6 which says that one has fulfilled one's obligation after the fact "he says the wording of the blessing enacted by the Sages, but he adds or subtracts something, or he uses a paraphrase of their wording... [In such a case], there is no error, but it is not appropriate to do it".

In 1:5 where Maimonides rules that he "is simply erring", he is changing the intent of the blessing, as for example, saying "blessed be the Place [=God] who created this" instead of *Hamotzi* ["Who brings forth bread from the earth"], "and since he errs, he has not fulfilled his obligation".

In *Hilkhot Keri'at Shema,* which states that he "is mistaken and he must go back and bless [the blessing] as coined", Maimonides is dealing with one who ended with *Barukh,* or began in a place where the Sages enacted not to end or not to begin and the like. But in *Hilkhot Berakhot* 1:6, which says that one has fulfilled one's obligation after the fact, we are dealing with a case of a change in the blessing in which "he did not use the exact language, **but still said the theme of the blessing in different words**, and did not change the beginning or the ending".

The proponents claim that the inclusion of the *Imahot* in the *Avot* blessing "does not change the theme of the blessing". We shall argue below that it **does** change the theme of the blessing. But even if one were to argue that it does not, this would only prove that it is permitted to change the wording **after the fact** and not *ab initio*.

In summary, the proponents have not quoted a single halakhic authority or a single liturgical precedent which proves that it is permissible to change the opening and closing formulae of the *Avot* blessing. Moreover, the proposed changes in the

7. See, for example, Ya'akov Blidstein, *Tefillah Bemishnato Hahilkhatit Shel Harambam*, Jerusalem, 1994, Chapter 6.

beginning and ending of the *Avot* blessing constitute "a change in the theme" since it attempts to change and rewrite biblical theology.

IV. Changes in the Conclusion of the *Avot* Blessing

The proposed change in the conclusion of the *Avot* blessing is unprecedented in the last 2,000 years since the time of the composition of the *Amidah*.

1. In general, the conclusions of the blessings of the *Amidah* have not changed in 2,000 years, aside from a few exceptions made in the Talmudic Period.[8]

2. The conclusion of the *Avot* blessing has never changed in any prayer rite in 2,000 years. The formula *Magen Avraham* appears in the prayer rites of all Jewish communities and in all manuscripts and *genizah* fragments examined thus far.[9]

3. The formula *Magen Avraham* is based on the verse "Do not fear Avram, I am a *magen* [=shield] for you; your reward is very great" (Genesis 15:1).

4. The *Amora* Resh Lakish who lived in *Eretz Yisrael* in the middle of the third century already knew and expounded on the traditional beginning and conclusion of this blessing (*Pesaḥim* 117b).

5. The wording "*magen Avraham* ***upoked*** Sarah" found in *Siddur Sim Shalom* is quite surprising, as Rabbi Harlow has already emphasized (p. 23). The word "*poked*" appears in the Bible ten

8. For a summary, see Yitzḥak Moshe Elbogen, *Hatefillah Beyisrael Behitpat'hu-tah Hahistorit*, Tel Aviv, 1972, pp. 32-47. For the *Bonei Yerushalayim* blessing, see *ibid.*, pp. 41-42 and for *Birkat Kohanim/Sim Shalom* see Golinkin, *Rosh Hashanah*, pp. 69-76.
9. Golinkin, *Rosh Hashanah*, p. 61, note 1b; Yeḥezkel Luger, *Tefillat Ha'amidah Leḥol Al Pee Hagenizah Hakaheereet*, Jerusalem, 2001, pp. 40-53; and cf. the discussion by Menaḥem Katz in Ze'ev Griss *et al*, eds., *Shefa Tal*, Be'er Sheva, 2004, pp. 28-30.

times and in every case it means "visits the sins" or "visits the guilt" as in the verses "who visits the sins of the parents on the children" (Exodus 20:5; 34:7; Numbers 14:18; Deuteronomy 5:9).[10]

V. Changes in the Beginning of the *Avot* Blessing

The proposed change in the beginning of the blessing is also without precedent in the last 2,000 years, Moreover, the proposed change contradicts biblical theology as well as biblical Hebrew, which is the basis of most of the phrases in *Avot,* and it also attempts to rewrite biblical history.

1. The first blessing of the *Amidah* is called *Avot* in five different places in Rabbinic literature (*Mishnah Rosh Hashanah* 4:5; *Yerushalmi Berakhot,* Chapter 4, fol. 8c = *Yerushalmi Rosh Hashanah,* Chapter 4, fol. 59d; *Rosh Hashanah* 32a; *Megillah* 17b). Indeed, the name of this blessing reflects the content and purpose of this blessing, as we shall presently see.

2. The first sentence of *Avot* is not simply Biblical **Hebrew**; it is a biblical **verse** (Exodus 3:15) "Our Lord, the God of your forefathers, the God of Abraham, the God of Isaac, and the God of Jacob" (and cf. Exodus 3:6, 16 for similar phrases). Indeed, the *Mekhilta,* the tannaitic midrash to Exodus, emphasizes this fact (*Depisḥa, Parashah* 16, ed. Horowitz–Rabin, p. 60):

> And what is the source for saying [in the *Amidah*] "Blessed are You our Lord, our God and God of our forefathers, God of Abraham, God of Isaac, and God of Jacob"? As it is written: "And God further said to Moses: Thus say to the Children of Israel: Our Lord, the God of your forefathers, the God of Abraham, the God of Isaac, and the God of Jacob" (Exodus 3:15).

3. This opening verse of the *Amidah* reflects a fundamental belief of the entire Bible – that God made a covenant with the

10. Also see Jeremiah 11:22; 23:2; 29:32; 44:29; 46:25; 50:18.

Patriarchs, Abraham, Isaac and Jacob. God made a covenant with Abraham in Genesis 15:18 and with Isaac in Genesis 26:3-4. God then said to Jacob in his dream at Beit El (Genesis 28:13-14): "I am the Lord, God of Abraham your father and God of Isaac, the land upon which you are lying, I shall give it to you and your descendants". And so we declare every morning in the *Hodu* prayer taken from I Chronicles 16:16-17: "Who made a covenant with Abraham and an oath with Isaac; and He established it for Jacob as a statute, for Israel as an eternal covenant". The Sages who wrote the *Amidah* innovated nothing here. They chose the opening for *Avot* from Exodus 3:15 and the conclusion from Genesis 15:1 in order to declare the founding fathers of our nation and their covenant with God at the beginning of **The Prayer** *par excellence*.

4. On the other hand, the phrase "God of Sarah, God of Rebecca, God of Rachel, and God of Leah" is **not** Biblical Hebrew because God did **not** make a covenant with the Matriarchs. Indeed, the expression "*Imahot*", which appears 76 times in Rabbinic literature, and the expression "Sarah, Rebecca, Rachel and Leah" which appears 15 times in Rabbinic literature (mostly in late *midrashim*) do not appear in the Bible at all.[11] There are those who say that we ought to include the *Imahot* in the *Amidah* in the wake of the Sages who created the concept of the Matriarchs but who were unable to include them because of their patriarchal ideology.[12] However, there is a simpler explanation. The Sages did not include the Matriarchs – **a concept which they themselves had created** – because *Avot* deals with the plain meaning of the biblical text and they did not want to rewrite history.

5. Indeed, it is surprising that Conservative Jews, who belong to "the Historical School" as Professors Schechter and Ginzberg called it, are interested in this case in rewriting history. To what

11. See Kaunfer, p. 95.
12. This is the opinion of Rabbi Ramon, 2001, p. 4 and 2005, pp. 160-161.

can this be compared? To rewriting the Gettysburg Address to read:

> Fourscore and seven years ago our fathers [and mothers] brought forth on this continent a new nation, conceived in Liberty, and dedicated to the proposition that all men [and women] are created equal.[13]

The United States was founded by **men** and Lincoln meant the **fathers** of the nation and not the mothers. Anyone who would add the bracketed phrases to his speech would be distorting history and distorting Lincoln's own intent. If this is true of a text written in 1863, how much the more so is it true of the *Amidah* written by our Sages 2,000 years ago and reflecting the theology of the Torah written over 3,000 years ago.

6. If we add Sarah, Rebecca, Rachel and Leah to *Avot*, why not add "Joseph, Moses, Aaron and David" as we do in the *Ushpizin* in the Sukkah, or "Moses, Aaron, David and Solomon" as we do in the *Mee Sheberakh* for the sick? Indeed, according to Rav in *Sanhedrin* 107a, King David asked God why we say "God of Abraham, God of Isaac and God of Jacob" and not "God of David"? The Talmud replies with a complicated *Aggadah*, but the simple reason is that these other fathers were **not** the founding fathers of our nation. And if we add Sarah, Rebecca, Rachel and Leah, why not add Bilhah and Zilpah, for there are midrashim which state that there were **six** Matriarchs![14] The answer is simple: *Avot* does not deal with midrash but rather with the plain meaning of the biblical text according to which there were three and only three founding fathers of the Jewish people.

7. Finally, the proponents also relied on an egalitarian *Mee Sheberakh* as a precedent. Rabbi Harlow has already responded

13. Roy Basler, ed., *Abraham Lincoln: His Speeches and Writings*, Cleveland and New York, 1946, p. 734.

14. *Shir Hashirim Rabbah* 6, 4, 2, ed. Vilna, fols. 33c-d and parallels; *Esther Rabbah* 1:12, ed. Vilna, fol. 4a and parallels; and cf. Kaunfer, p. 99.

(p. 24) that the *Mee Sheberakh* is a late custom with no fixed text,[15] and this does not prove that one may change the text of the *Amidah*. I would add that traditionally *Mee Sheberakh* prayers are also not egalitarian – some use the father's name and some use the mother's name.[16]

VI. When May One Change the Formulation of the Statutory Prayers?

In our opinion, it is permissible to change the formulation of the statutory prayers for two reasons, and only if one also has halakhic sources and liturgical precedents to support such a change:

1. In order not to recite something which is patently false: this idea is already found in a well-known *Aggadah* (*Yoma* 69b and parallels). Indeed, this is why Conservative prayer books beginning in 1927 changed the wording of *Mussaf*. They began to say "they made and offered [sacrifices]" in place of "we shall make and offer [sacrifices]", since they did not wish to ask for something contrary to their worldview. Indeed, from a halakhic point of view, this is also permissible, since the halakhic requirement regarding *Mussaf* is that it should include something new which was not already said in *Shaḥarit* (*Yerushalmi Berakhot* Chapter 4, fol. 8c), and this requirement is also met by the Conservative formulation of *Mussaf*.[17] Similarly, Professor Ephraim Elimelekh Urbach and Rabbi Ḥayyim David Halevi changed the wording of *Naḥem* for *Tisha B'av* after the Six Day

15. For 140 different versions of *Mee Sheberakh*, see a series of five articles which appeared in *Kiryat Sefer*, Vols. 33, 36, 37, 40.
16. See David Golinkin, "The Use of the Matronymic in Prayers for the Sick" in: Aaron Demsky, ed., *These Are the Names* 3 (2002), pp. 59-72.
17. Golinkin, pp. 45-46; David Golinkin, ed., *The Responsa of Professor Louis Ginzberg*, New York and Jerusalem, 1996, pp. 52-53; David Golinkin, "Is it permissible to change the wording about sacrifices in the middle blessing of the Mussaf service?", www.schechter.edu/responsa.aspx?ID=56.

War in order to avoid saying something patently false about "the city [of Jerusalem] that is ruined, despised and desolate".[18]

2. In order not to actively offend: this was the motivation of Rabbi Morris Silverman in 1946 to change the blessings which thank God "who has not made me a Gentile... a slave... a woman" to thanking God for making us "Israelites... free... in God's image". This change was made on the basis of *poskim* who were lenient in the matter, and on the basis of changes made in these blessings in the past.[19]

VII. Is an Egalitarian Liturgical Style the Ideal?

Champions of the *Imahot* wish to convert the language of our tradition into egalitarian language. But this type of language impoverishes our tradition. According to this logic, we will have to change the "Sabbath Queen" found in *Shabbat* 119a and elsewhere to the "Sabbath King"; "Come O Bride, Come O Bride" found in *Lekha Dodi* and also based on *Shabbat* 119a to "Come O Groom, Come O Groom"; "*Ḥatan Torah*" to "*Kallat Torah*" on *Simḥat Torah;*[20] "*Avinu Malkeinu*" found in *Ta'anit* 25b to "*Imeinu Malkateinu*";[21] and the *Mee Sheberakh* for the sick to "so-and-so the child of the father" instead of "the child of the mother".[22] Such changes water down the tradition and make everything in Judaism homogenous and *parve*. On the contrary, there are expressions in the masculine and expressions in the feminine and this diversity **enriches** the Jewish tradition.

18. Golinkin, pp. 44-45 and cf. Rabbi Ḥayyim David Halevi, *Aseh Lekha Rav*, Part 2, Nos. 36-39 vs. Rabbi Ovadiah Yosef, *Yeḥaveh Da'at*, Part 1, No. 43 who opposes any change in the *Naḥem* prayer. For Prof. Urbach's version, see *Ha'avodah Shebalev*, Jerusalem, 1982, p. 233 and see now Yael Levine Katz, *Teḥumin* 21 (5761), pp. 71-90.
19. Golinkin, pp. 42-43 and cf. the English article by Joseph Tabory, *Kenishta* 1 (2001), pp. 107-138.
20. Golinkin., p. 47.
21. See the article by Rabbi Dalia Marx.
22. See above, note 16.

VIII. The Difference between Liturgy and Prayer

Rabbis Debra Reed Blank and Harlan Wechsler – both of whom oppose this proposed change – have already explained that there is an enormous difference between liturgy and prayer. **Liturgy** is a more or less uniform text that expresses the classical ideas of the nation/religion. It is intended to connect us to the past rather than to be relevant and up-to-date. **Prayer**, on the other hand, is the personal expression of the worshipper which is supposed to change, and the Sages set down fixed places for such prayers: in the middle of the *Shome'a Tefillah* blessing on weekdays, just prior to the conclusion of each of the middle blessings of the *Amidah*, at the end of the *Amidah*, and in *Taḥanun*.[23]

Therefore, most of the important national events of the last 2,000 years were **not** added to the daily *Amidah*. There is no hint in the *Amidah* of the Crusades, the Expulsion from Spain, the Chmielnicki massacres of 1648-49, and the *Shoah*. These things found their way into **other** parts of the liturgy, but **not** into the *Amidah* that is recited three times a day. The Crusades are recalled in *Av Haraḥamim* and in *piyyutim*, other tragedies were memorialized in their own *piyyutim*, the Babylonian *Yeshivot* were immortalized in *Yekum Purkan*, and the State of Israel in the Prayer for the State and in the *Mee Shebeirakh* for IDF soldiers. Could one claim that these are not central events in our people's history? They are not found in the daily *Amidah* because the *Amidah* is **liturgy** that expresses biblical and rabbinic theology and not **prayer** that expresses the personal needs of every individual worshipper.

23. Rabbi Blank, pp. 62-63; Rabbi Wechsler, p. 80. For the places in the *Amidah* where an individual may add private prayers, see David Golinkin, *Rediscovering the Art of Jewish Prayer*, New York, 1996, pp. 20-21 and the literature cited there in notes 45-47.

IX. *Piyyut* as an Authentic Solution

I have been impressed by the sincere desire to include the *Imahot* in the *Amidah* and to make the *Amidah* more relevant. The problem is not the **goal** but rather the **method**. The method of changing the beginning and ending of the *Avot* is contrary to *halakhah*, contrary to our liturgy, and contrary to classic Jewish theology as explained above, and stems from the fact that the idea apparently originated with Jews who are not well-versed in Jewish law nor in Hebrew.[24]

But there is an **authentic** way to insert changes and innovations into the *Amidah* and that is through the use of *piyyutim*. From the Talmudic period onward, liturgical poets continually composed *piyyutim* in which they expounded the weekly portion and even related to contemporary events.[25] This approach was especially popular in the Land of Israel until the end of the Geonic Period. The authentic and traditional way to add the *Imahot* to the *Amidah* is to compose a short *piyyut* or several short *piyyutim* which will be recited in the **middle** of *Avot* or in the middle of other blessings of the *Amidah*.[26] In this way, the *Imahot* can be added without changing the ancient wording of the *Amidah* itself.

Rabbi Dr. Einat Ramon, the Dean of the Schechter Rabbinical Seminary in Jerusalem, has composed such a *piyyut* and it is

24. See, for example, the *Kol Haneshamah* prayerbook of the Reconstructionist Movement, Pennsylvania, 1995, p. 91. The *Avot* blessing is called there "*Avot Ve'imot*" instead of *Ve'imahot*!

25. For a survey of the important forms of *piyyut*, see Hayyim Herman Kieval, *The High Holy Days*, second edition, edited by David Golinkin and Monique Susskind Goldberg, Jerusalem, 2004, pp. 22-37 and Ezra Fleischer, *Shirat Hakodesh Ha'ivrit Beyemei Habei'nayim*, Jerusalem, 1975, pp. 137 ff. It is true that there were *poskim* who opposed *piyyutim*, but many others allowed them – see Kieval, p. 34; Blidstein (above, note 7); and Ruth Langer, *To Worship God Properly*, Cincinnati, 1998, Chapter 3.

26. A *Kerovah* is a *piyyut* which adds a line or lines of poetry to every blessing of the *Amidah*. See an explanation in Kieval (above, note 25), pp. 32-33, 185-188 and see examples in *Ginzei Kaufman*, Budapest, 1949, pp. 81-92. If one wanted to compose a *Kerovah* including the *Imahot*, one could mention Sarah

found in an Appendix to this *teshuvah*.[27] I hope that such *piyyutim* will be adopted by synagogues who wish to incorporate the *Imahot* into the *Amidah* in a halakhic and authentic fashion.

David Golinkin
Jerusalem
Rosh Ḥodesh Adar 5767

APPENDIX

A *Piyyut* about the *Imahot* for Inclusion in the *Avot* Blessing

By Rabbi Dr. Einat Ramon
(to be inserted after the words "*lema'an shemo be'ahavah*")

Navo'ah oholey Sarah, Rivka, Rachel veLeah.
Utehi gemilut ḥasdeihen lefaneinu bekhol eit uvekhol sha'ah.

Translation:

Let us enter the tents of Sarah, Rebecca, Rachel and Leah. May their acts of lovingkindness be an example to us at all times.

in the "*Al Hatzaddikim*" blessing because, according to the midrash, Sarah converted the women (*Bereishit Rabbah* 39:1); Rachel in the "*Teka Beshofar Gadol*" blessing because she is the Matriarch associated with the Ingathering of the Exiles (Jeremiah 31); Hannah in the "*Shome'a Tefillah*" blessing because she was the one who prayed to God with great feeling (I Samuel 2:1-10); and so on.

27. Rabbi Ramon's *piyyut* is used according to the *ḥazzan*'s prerogative at Schechter and in every *Amidah* at the Morristown Jewish Center in Morristown, New Jersey. For a detailed explanation of Rabbi Ramon's approach to this topic, see Ramon, 2005.

BIBLIOGRAPHY

Allen — Rabbi Wayne Allen, *Perspectives on Jewish Law and Contemporary Issues*, Jerusalem, 2009, No. 12

Blank — Rabbi Debra Reed Blank, *Conservative Judaism* 47/2 (Winter 1995), pp. 53-63

Cooper — Rabbi Levi Cooper, *Jerusalem Post: Up Front Magazine*, April 7, 2006, p. 33

Freedman — Samuel Freedman, *Jew vs. Jew*, New York, 2000, Chapter 3

Goldberg — Rabbi Hillel Goldberg, *Tradition* 38/2 (Summer 2004), pp. 86-103

Golinkin — Rabbi David Golinkin, *Conservative Judaism* 41/1 (Fall 1988), pp. 38-55

Golinkin, *Rosh Hashanah* — Rabbi David Golinkin, *Perek Yom Tov Shel Rosh Hashanah* etc., Ph.D. dissertation, The Jewish Theological Seminary, 1988

Halevi — Rabbi Ḥayyim David Halevi, *Aseh Lekha Rav*, Part 8, pp. 31–33

Harlow — Rabbi Jules Harlow, *Conservative Judaism* 49/2 (Winter 1997), pp. 3-25

Kaunfer — Rabbi Alvin Kaunfer, *JUDAISM* 44/1 (Winter 1995), pp. 94-103

Marx — Rabbi Dalia Marx, *Kescher* 3/4 (Winter 2005-2006), p. 19

Ramon, 2001 — Rabbi Einat Ramon, "Regarding Mentioning the *Imahot* in the *Avot* Blessing of the *Amidah*" (Hebrew), unpublished, 8 Tevet 5761, 6 pp.

Ramon, 2005 — Rabbi Einat Ramon, *Nashim* 10 (2005), pp. 154-177

Rembaum — Rabbi Joel Rembaum in: *Proceedings of the Committee on Jewish Law and Standards of the Conservative Movement 1986-1990*, New York, 2001, pp. 485-490 = David Fine, ed., *Responsa 1980-1990*, The Committee on Jewish Law and Standards of the

	Conservative Movement, New York, 2005, pp. 43-48 (also online at www.rabbinicalassembly.org)
Ross	Tamar Ross in: Naḥem Ilan, ed., *Ayin Tovah*, 1999, pp. 264-277
Wechsler	Rabbi Harlan Wechsler, *Conservative Judaism* 50/1 (Fall 1997), pp. 80-81

5. RECITING THE *BARUKH SHEPETARANI* BLESSING AT A *BAT MITZVAH*

Oraḥ Ḥayyim 225:2

Question from Dr. David Brody: *What is the source of the blessing Barukh Shepetarani [Blessed be He who has absolved me]? What is the original reason for reciting this blessing and is there a point in reciting it today? If so, is the blessing recited at a Bat Mitzvah and may a mother recite the blessing?*[1]

Responsum:

I. The Sources for the Blessing

This blessing is based on a midrash in *Bereishit Rabbah* 63:10 (ed. Theodor–Albeck, pp. 692-693) about the upbringing of Jacob and Esau:

> "And the boys grew up" (Genesis 25:27) – Rabbi Pinḥass in the name of Rabbi Levi: This can be compared to a *hadass* [myrtle] and an *etzbonit* [a type of thorn] which grew one atop another. When they matured, they flowered – one with its fragrance and the other with its thorns. So it was for thirteen years both of them would go to school and return. After thirteen years, one went to *batei midrash* and the other went to houses of idolatry. Said Rabbi Eleazar b"r Shimon: **A person must take care of his son for thirteen**

1. The original question was: Is a widow permitted to recite *Barukh Shepetarani* for her daughter? For the sake of completeness, we decided to discuss the other questions as well. All references are to the Bibliography at the end of the responsum.

years; henceforth he should say: "Blessed is He who has absolved me of the punishment of this one".[2]

It is not clear from the language of the *midrash* whether Rabbi Eleazar b"r Shimon actually intended to give a *halakhic* ruling. It is possible that he was merely employing a rhetorical flourish, as we say today: "Thank God that I have finished this task". In any event, six important medieval *poskim* understood it as practical *halakhah*:

1. Rabbi Aaron Hacohen of Lunel (Provence, fourteenth century) cites the above *midrash* in *Orḥot Ḥayyim* (*Hilkhot Berakhot*, paragraph 58, fol. 40c), adding:

> Some say it the first time that the son goes up to read from the Torah. And the **Gaon Rabbi Yehudai, of blessed memory**, stood up in the synagogue and recited this blessing the first time his son read from the Torah.

Some rabbis thought he meant Rav Yehudai, the Gaon of Sura, who died in 761; if so, this is a custom from the geonic period.[3] This, however, is incorrect. This story is not appropriate for the Geonic period, for at that time the custom was that a minor reads from the Torah, in accordance with the plain meaning of Mishnah *Megillah* 3:6.[4] It therefore makes no sense that Rav Yehudai Gaon recited a blessing associated with a son who reaches age thirteen for his minor son who was called up to the Torah.

2. It is worth noting that there was another midrash according to which this blessing is recited for a son who reaches the age of **twenty** – see Rabbeinu Efraim's Commentary on the Torah and the *Derashot* of Ibn Shu'ib, cited by Rabbi Menaḥem Mendel Kasher, *Torah Sheleimah,* Vol. 6, p. 1438, end of note 202. This opinion was not absorbed into *halakhic* literature and it is, apparently, based on *Shabbat* 89b and Numbers 14:29 – see Prof. Gilat, p. 182 and Rabbi Epstein, p. 189.
3. So thought Isaac Rifkind, Rabbi Yitzḥak Nissim and Rabbi Ovadiah Yosef.
4. See the solid proofs presented by Yosef Faur, "*Aliyat Katan Likro Batorah*", *Sefer Zikaron L'harav Yitzḥak Nissim,* Vol. I, Jerusalem, 5745, pp. 116-117.

2. Indeed, there is no doubt that a scribal error has crept into *Orḥot Ḥayyim*, for the original tradition is preserved in several manuscripts of *Hora'ot Rabbanei Tzarfat* [Rulings of the Rabbis of France], which were first published in 1973. Paragraph 23 states:

> He who has a son and he reached the age of thirteen years, the first time that he stands up in public to read from the Torah, the father must recite, "Blessed are You Lord who has **redeemed** me from the punishment of this one". And the Gaon **Rabbi Yehudah b"r Barukh** stood up in the synagogue and recited this blessing when his son stood up and read the Torah for the first time, **and this blessing is obligatory**.[5]

Rabbi Yehudah b"r Barukh – a disciple of Rabbeinu Gershom Me'or Hagolah and a colleague of Rabbi Yitzḥak Halevi, Rashi's teacher – was active in Mainz and Worms in the eleventh century.[6] Therefore, this custom apparently arose in Ashkenaz in the eleventh century.

3. The third authority to rule in this manner was Rabbi Shimshon bar Tzadok, a disciple of the Maharam of Rothenburg (late thirteenth century), in his *Tashbetz* (paragraph 390):

> *Bereishit Rabbah* states: Rabbi Shimon b"r Tzadok [i.e., Rabbi Eleazar b"r Shimon] said: a person must take care of his son until the age of thirteen; after that he must say: "Blessed are You Lord our God, King of the universe, who has absolved me of the punishment of this one".

The author of the *Tashbetz* does not state that one must do so,

5. *Piskei Rabbeinu Yeḥiel Miparis Vehora'ot Mirabbanei Tzarfat*, ed. Pines, Jerusalem, 5733, p. 82, paragraph 23. Yisrael Ḥazani later informed me that Naḥman Danzig had mentioned this as the source for *Orḥot Ḥayyim* in his book, *Mavo Lesefer Halakhot Pesukot*, New York and Jerusalem, 1993, pp. 458-459.

6. Regarding Rabbi Yehudah b"r Barukh, see Pines, *ibid.*, note 3 and Avraham Grossman, *Ḥakhmei Ashkenaz Harishonim*, second edition, Jerusalem, 1989, pp. 117, 277, 287.

but since his work is devoted to practical *halakhah*, it may be assumed that he intended this to be a practical ruling.

4. The fourth source to mention this custom is *Minhagei Maharil* (ed. Spitzer, Jerusalem, 5749, p. 453) which transmits the customs of Rabbi Ya'akov Moellin (Ashkenaz, died 1427):

> When his son became *bar mitzvah* and read from the Torah, he would recite the blessing over him: "Blessed are You Lord our God, King of the universe, who has absolved me of the punishment of this one", and so it is in the Great Mordechai[7] this blessing, including God's name ["Blessed are You Lord our God"] and Kingship ["King of the universe"].

5. The fifth to mention this custom is Rabbi Yosef b"r Moshe of Hochstadt. In his work *Leket Yosher* (OH, p. 40), he describes the customs of his teacher, Rabbi Yisrael Isserlein (Ashkenaz, d. 1460):

> When his son first read from a Torah, when he [the son] began to recite *Barekhu* [the blessing prior to reading the Torah portion], [Rabbi Yisrael] said [in Aramaic and Hebrew]: "Blessed be the Merciful One, King of the universe, who has absolved me of the punishment of this one". And so he said all the blessings without Kingship, since it was not explicitly mentioned in the Talmud [with] Kingship.[8]

7. This may refer to the "Mordechai of Austria", which included many additions – see Ya'akov (Joel) Roth and Mayer Rabinowitz, *Meḥkarim Umekorot* 2 (5750), pp. 3, 14-16. Cf. Rabbi Avraham Halprin, *Mavo Lesefer Mordechai Hashalem,* Jerusalem, 5752, pp. 17-19, 22-24 and Rabbi Avraham Ḥavatzelet in *Sefer Mordechai Hashalem* on tractates *Rosh Hashanah, Yoma* and *Sukkah,* Jerusalem, 5749, pp. 19-21.
8. Perhaps he means that Rabbi Isserlein used to recite **any** blessing not explicitly mentioned in the Talmud without God's name and Kingship. See the continuation there for more important details. This question deserves further study.

In other words, Rabbi Yisrael Isserlein knew the custom of reciting *Barukh Shepetarani,* but he apparently changed the beginning of the blessing to Aramaic since the blessing is not mentioned in the Talmud, and he was afraid to recite a blessing in vain.

6. Finally, this blessing is mentioned by Rabbi Moshe Isserles, the Rema, in his commentary on the *Tur, Darkhei Moshe* (OH 225). He cites from the aforementioned *Minhagei Maharil* and adds:

> And I did not find this blessing in the Gemara, and it is difficult for me that they should recite a blessing which is not mentioned in the Gemara. And in *Bereishit Rabbah,* at the beginning of the portion *Toledot,* the law is mentioned in the name of Rabbi Eliezer [=Eleazar].

Despite his hesitation, the Rema mentions the custom in his Glosses on the *Shulḥan Arukh* (OH 225:2):

> Some say that one whose son becomes *bar mitzvah* should recite, 'Blessed are You Lord our God, King of the universe, who has absolved me of the punishment of this one'. It is preferable to say the blessing without saying God's name and Kingship.

In other words, he upheld the custom for, as is well known, the Rema liked ancient customs,[9] but he opposed using God's name and Kingship, since this blessing is not mentioned in the Talmud. The controversy over whether to mention God's name and Kingship continued after the Rema,[10] but most *poskim* agreed

9. "And no custom should be abolished or scoffed at, because not for naught were they established" (OH 690:17). But see the *Ba'er Heiteiv, ibid.,* subparagraph 15, who cites the opposite opinion of the Rema himself in *Responsa HaRema,* No. 21 [=ed. Ziv, No. 19] and see the discussion by Asher Ziv, *Harema,* Jerusalem, 1957, pp. 100-106. And cf. below, p. 331 and note 22a *ibid.* My thanks to Rabbi Monique Süsskind Goldberg z"l who helped me clarify these references.
10. See the various opinions cited by Rabbis Ovadiah Yosef, J. Simḥah Cohen and Binyamin Adler and by Prof. Yitzḥak Gilat.

that one should recite the blessing *Barukh Shepetarani* after the *bar mitzvah* boy is called to the Torah.[11]

II. The Original Reason for Reciting the Blessing and its Significance Today

Rabbi Byron Sherwin suggested that Rabbi Eleazar b"r Shimon's opinion in *Bereishit Rabbah*, and the blessing created in its wake, are part of an ancient dispute within Judaism over the extent to which a person is punished for the sins of others. The Decalogue states (Exodus 20:5): "visiting the sin of the fathers on the sons" (cf. *ibid*. 34:7 and Joshua 7:24-25), while in Deuteronomy (24:16) it is said that "Fathers shall not be put to death for sons, nor shall sons be put to death for fathers; a man shall be put to death for his own sin". Although the Talmud attempted to reconcile the contradiction (*Berakhot* 7a), there is no doubt that we have here two opposing world views. This controversy continued throughout the Talmudic period. On the one hand, it is emphasized in *Sifrei Devarim* on the afore-mentioned verse (paragraph 280, ed. Finkelstein, p. 297): "A man shall be put to death for his own sin" – fathers die for their own sins and sons die for their own sins". Similarly, Bavli *Berakhot* 5a states:

> Said Rava, and some say, Rav Ḥisda: If a person sees that suffering comes upon him, let him examine his **own actions**, as it is said (Eikhah 3:40) "Let us examine **our path**... and return to God".

In other words, suffering is attributed to the actions of the sufferer.

On the other hand, it says in Bavli *Shabbat* 54b:

> Anyone who can admonish the members of his household but does not admonish, is caught for the sins of the

11. See all the *poskim* cited by Rabbi Ovadiah Yosef and all the *poskim* listed below at the end of this responsum.

> members of his household [Rashi: he is punished for their sins]; [one who can admonish] the members of his city, is punished for the members of his city; [one who can admonish] the entire world is punished for the entire world.

In other words, a person is punished for the sins of others if he did not admonish them.[12] Rabbi Sherwin suggests that Rabbi Eleazar b"r Shimon attempts in the aforementioned midrash to reconcile these two opposing positions: the father is punished for his sons' sins until age thirteen; from then on, " a man shall be put to death for his own sin".[13]

It is therefore no wonder that many Jews in our day do not say this blessing during the *bar mitzvah* ceremony, for they do not accept the approach that the father is punished for his son's sins. However, most of the *Aḥaronim* from the seventeenth century onward, emphasized another reason for saying this blessing which is very appropriate in our day.[14] The main proponent of this view is Rabbi Abraham Gumbiner, author of *Magen Avraham* on the *Shulḥan Arukh*. He states (in OH 225, subparagraph 5): " 'of the punishment of this one' means that until now the father was punished when the son sinned, **because he did not educate him properly**...". There is no doubt that he explained the blessing in this way according to *Bereishit Rabbah*, which stated: **"A person must take care of his son for thirteen years;** henceforth he should say: 'Blessed is He who has absolved me of the punishment of this one' ". Indeed, Rabbi Tuviah b"r Eliezer had already commented on the same verse in Genesis in his *Lekaḥ Tov* (ed. Buber, p. 122): "To take care of his son – **to keep him occupied with Torah and *mitzvot* until age thirteen**". In other words, the father announces at the *bar mitzvah* ceremony: Until

12. Cf. *Shabbat* 32b and *Ketubot* 8b, which state that for certain transgressions "the sons and daughters of a person die when they are young".
13. Rabbi Sherwin, p. 161, but he cites no source for his opinion.
14. See, for example, Rabbis Yehudah Leib Tzirelson, Yitzḥak Nissim and Nattan Neta Leiter. For additional explanations, see Prof. Gilat, pp. 179-181.

now I have done my best to educate my son in the way of Torah and *mitzvot*, from now on he is responsible for his actions on the basis of the education I have given him. Thus, the emphasis moves away from the issue of punishment to the importance of education, and this is an emphasis with which all modern Jews can identify.

III. Reciting the Blessing *Barukh Shepetarani* for a Daughter

Most of the *Aḥaronim* forbid this practice, basing themselves on the *Magen Avraham's* explanation. Since the blessing derives from the obligation to educate, and since the father is not obligated to educate his daughter, there is no reason for him to recite this blessing for his daughter. Here, for example, are the words of Rabbi Yosef Te'omim who lived in Ashkenaz in the 18th century (*Peri Megadim, Eshel Avraham,* OH 225:5):

> ... It should be stated that he is not obligated to educate his minor daughter – see *Magen Avraham* to OH 343, subparagraph 1 [based on *Nazir* 29b]. Even for he who says that he is obligated [to educate her], she does not have so many commandments that he is obligated to educate her when she is a minor...

On the other hand, Rabbi David Luria (Lithuania, 19th century) emphasizes the **obligation of Torah study**. In *Ḥidushei Haradal* on *Bereishit Rabbah,* he interprets the words "a person must take care of his son" thus: "This means specifically his son but not his daughter... but the main intention is that he must teach his son Torah...".[15]

However, Rabbis Yitzḥak Nissim, Amram Aburbia and Ovadiah Yosef have already permitted reciting *Barukh Shepetarani* for a daughter. Rabbi Nissim rules simply:

> And when a daughter reaches maturity, should one make the blessing? From the reasons for the blessing explained

15. And see Rabbi Ḥayyim David Halevi for a similar interpretation.

> above, it seems that **one should make the blessing for a daughter as well, for a daughter too requires education**... I say briefly that there is reason to recite the blessing for a daughter, and it should be said without God's name or Kingship.

Rabbi Amram Aburbia also rules simply:

> And in our day when the custom has spread that one also makes a *bat mitzvah* celebration for girls, and the *Ben Ish Ḥai* [Rabbi Yosef Ḥayyim of Baghdad] and the Rav Hagaon *Yaskil Avdi* [Rabbi Ovadiah Hadaya] confirmed this good custom,[15a] it is worthwhile that here too the father should bless "who has absolved me from the punishment of this one"...

Furthermore, Rabbi Ovadiah Yosef refutes at length those who oppose reciting this blessing for a daughter. He bases himself on *Tosafot Yeshanim* to *Yoma* 82a who explained that the above-mentioned passage in *Nazir* (the basis of the *Peri Megadim's* ruling) deals only with education related to the laws of the Nazirite, "**but he certainly must educate her [the daughter] with regard to other *mitzvot***". And so ruled the Meiri to *Nazir* 29a (ed. Liss, p. 91): "Just as a man is obligated to educate his son in the *mitzvot* at the proper time for each commandment... **he is also obligated to educate his daughter in what is appropriate for her** [aside from laws such as those pertaining to Nazirites]". So too ruled the author of *Petaḥ Hadevir* (to OH 225, subparagraph 4) **that from the words of all the *poskim* it is proven that a father is obligated to educate his daughter in the *mitzvot* which she is obligated to do**. (And see *Responsa Yabi'a Omer* for additional *poskim* who ruled similarly.) Rabbi Yosef concludes:

> And especially in light of what I wrote, that the main thing is to recite this blessing without God's name and Kingship,

15a. See above, pp. 5-6, and *ibid.*, note 10.

> there is no fear of saying it also for a daughter who has reached the age of *mitzvot*, and this requires no more relish [i.e., elaboration].[16]

Therefore, according to most *poskim*, the blessing *Barukh Shepetarani* refers to the obligation of a father to educate his son. Since, according to most *poskim*, this obligation also applies to a daughter, and since this blessing in any case does not include God's name and Kingship, there is no reason to prevent a father from reciting *Barukh Shepetarani* for his daughter.[17]

IV. A Mother Reciting *Barukh Shepetarani*

We have already seen that *Barukh Shepetarani* is a function of the obligation to educate. Therefore, the question of whether a mother is permitted to recite this blessing depends upon whether a mother is obligated to educate her children. This too is a subject of controversy,[18] but there is no doubt that in our day we should give preference to the approach of Rabbi Avraham Min Hahar (of Montpelier, Provence, died 1315) in his commentary to *Nazir* 29b (ed. Blau, p. 216):

> And **the *halakhah* follows Rabbi Yoḥanan**... and it stands to reason that Rabbi Yoḥanan thought that **both a father and a mother** are obligated to educate **both a son and a daughter** in the *mitzvot*, and only according to Resh Lakish

16. For other *poskim* who discussed the obligation of a father to educate his daughter, see ET, Vol. 16, cols. 164-165 and Shmuel Glick, *Haḥinukh Bire'i Haḥok Vehalakhah*, Vol. 1, Jerusalem 5759, pp. 94-97.
17. As for Rabbi David Luria's view that the father is exempt from teaching his daughter Torah, I have already proved in my responsum about the ordination of women as rabbis (see below, pp. 358-366) that in our day "a person is **obligated** to teach his daughter Torah", like the view of Ben Azzai in Mishnah *Sotah* 3:4.
18. See *Magen Avraham* to OH 343, subparagraph 1; *Mishnah Berurah* to OH 616, subparagraph 5 and OH 640, subparagraph 5; ET, Vol. 16, cols. 165-166; Rabbi Yeḥiel Mikhal Ḥarlap, "*Ha'av Veha'em Beḥinukh Habanim Vehabanot*", *Or Hamizraḥ* 18 (Tevet 5729), pp. 71-79; and Shmuel Glick (above, note 16), pp. 98-102.

> is it necessary to say that he thought [that a mother is not obligated to educate her daughter].[19]

In other words, in his opinion, a mother is obligated to educate her sons and daughters, and we may therefore conclude that she may recite *Barukh Shepetarani* both for a son and for a daughter.

V. Practical *Halakhah*

The blessing *Barukh Shepetarani* is not mentioned in the Talmud or by the major *poskim* such as the Rif, Rambam, Rosh, *Tur* and Rabbi Yosef Karo in the *Shulḥan Arukh*. It is based on the words of Rabbi Eleazar b"r Shimon in *Bereishit Rabbah,* and it is first mentioned in eleventh-century Ashkenaz as a blessing recited with God's name and Kingship when the son goes up to the Torah for the first time at age thirteen. Rabbi Yisrael Isserlein and the Rema omitted God's name and Kingship from the blessing, since it is not mentioned in the Talmud, but the Vilna Gaon and others continued to recite it with God's name and Kingship. After the Rema, this blessing also spread to Sefardic Jewry.

Originally, the *midrash* and the blessing reflected the belief that the father is punished for the sins of his son. Most *Aḥaronim,* however, explained that the blessing came to emphasize that until the age of thirteen a father is obligated to educate his son in the Torah and the *mitzvot;* from then on the son is obligated to apply what he has learned from his father. This explanation applies in our day as well, and therefore there is good reason to recite this blessing.[20]

In the past, this blessing was not recited for a daughter since, in any case, they did not note her coming of age. But in our day,

19. This was also the opinion of Rabbeinu Peretz of Corbeil (d. 1298) in his *Ḥiddushim* to *Nazir* 29b and Rabbi Yitzḥak b"r Aharon of Karlin in *Keren Orah* to *Nazir, ibid.*
20. It should be emphasized that according to the ancient Ashkenazic custom and according to the Gaon of Vilna's commentary to OH 225:2, one should

since every girl has a *Bat Mitzvah,*[21] it is fitting and desirable that both parents recite *Barukh Shepetarani,* for we adopt the position of Rabbi Avraham Min Hahar that "both a father and a mother are obligated to educate both a son and a daughter in the *mitzvot*".

David Golinkin
Jerusalem
23 Kislev 5754

recite the blessing of *Barukh Shepetarani* with God's name and Kingship. On the other hand, whoever is not comfortable reciting this blessing may recite the blessing *Sheheḥeyanu* (on condition that he is wearing a new item of clothing or will eat a new fruit – see Adler, p. 73). Rabbi Michael Graetz of Magen Avraham congregation in Omer proposed a new blessing, without God's name and Kingship: "*Barukh hamezakeh et beni* (or: *biti*) *bekiyyum hamitzvot*" — "Blessed is He who grants my son (or: daughter) the merit of fulfilling the commandments". For another proposal, see Frymer-Kensky.

21. There are many responsa about this as well. For a good summary of the various opinions, see the responsum of Rabbi Ovadiah Yosef listed in the Bibliography below; his *Responsa Yeḥaveh Da'at*, Part 2, No. 29; and above, pp. 4-6.

BIBLIOGRAPHY

I. GENERAL

Adler — Rabbi Binyamin Adler, *Hilkhot Vehalikhot Bar Mitzvah*, Jerusalem, 5743, pp. 77-81

Cohen — Rabbi J. Simcha Cohen, *Timely Jewish Questions, Timeless Rabbinic Answers*, Northvale, N.J., 1991, pp. 253-258

Ellinson — Rabbi Elyakim Ellinson, *Ha'ishah Vehamitzvot, Sefer Rishon, Bein Ha'ishah Leyotzrah*, Jerusalem, 1977^2, pp. 172-175

Frymer-Kensky — Tikva Frymer-Kensky, *Moment*, August 1998, pp. 32-33, 63

Gilat — Yitzḥak Gilat, *"Barukh Shepetarani Mei'onsho Shel Zeh"*, *Sinai* 118 (5756), pp. 176-186

Glatt — Rabbi Aaron Glatt, " 'Thank God, I'm Exempt': When a Son Becomes Bar Mitzvah", *Journal of Halacha and Contemporary Society* 51 (Spring 2005), pp. 107-120

Kasher — Rabbi Menaḥem Mendel Kasher, *Ḥumash Torah Sheleimah,* Vol. 4, Jerusalem, 5694, pp. 1024-1025; Vol. 6, Jerusalem, 5698, p. 1438

Rifkind — Yitzḥak Rifkind, *Le'ot Ulezikaron*, New York, 5702, pp. 37-38 and 16

Schlesinger — Rabbi Eliyahu Schlesinger, *"Be'iniyan Birkat Barukh Shepetarani"*, *Barkai* 5 (5749), pp. 59-63

Sherwin — Rabbi Byron Sherwin, *In Partnership with God*, Syracuse, New York, 1990, pp. 159-163

II. RECITING *BARUKH SHEPETARANI* FOR A DAUGHTER

A. Justifying the custom not to recite the blessing for a daughter

Eliyahu — Rabbi Mordechai Eliyahu, quoted by Aharon Cohen, *Zeved Bat*, Jerusalem, 5750, p. 12

Halevi — Rabbi Ḥayyim David Halevi, *Aseh Lekha Rav*, Part 1, No. 31

Leiter — Rabbi Nattan Neta Leiter, *Responsa Tziyun Lenefesh Ḥayah*, Jerusalem, 5724, No. 55

Luria — Rabbi David Luria in *Ḥiddushei Radal* to *Bereishit Rabbah, parashah* 63, note 13

Roth — Rabbi Meshulam Roth, *Responsa Kol Mevasser*, Part 2, Jerusalem, 5733, No. 44

Sapir — Rabbi Sinai Sapir, *Responsa Minḥat Ani*, Warsaw, 5607 (1847), No. 3

Sofer — Rabbi Ya'akov Ḥayyim Sofer, *Kaf Haḥayyim* to OH 225:15

Teomim	Rabbi Yosef Te'omim, *Peri Megadim* in *Eshel Avraham* to OH 225, subparagraph 5
Tzirelson	Rabbi Yehudah Leib Tzirelson, *Lev Yehudah*, Kishinev, 5636 (1936), No. 2
Volk	Rabbi Eliezer Lipman Hacohen Volk, *Ein Eliezer*, Jerusalem, 5688 (1928), No. 14

B. PERMITTING RECITING THE BLESSING FOR A DAUGHTER

Aburbia	Rabbi Amram Aburbia, *Netivei Am*, second edition, Petaḥ Tikvah, 5729, p. 130
Epstein	Rabbi Barukh Halevi Epstein, *Barukh She'amar Lekhol Tefillot Hashanah*, Tel Aviv, 5739, pp. 189-190 (but according to him, the boy or girl recites the blessing!)
Nissim	Rabbi Yitzḥak Nissim, *Noam* 7 (1964), pp. 1-5 = *Responsa Yein Hatov*, Part II, Jerusalem, 5739, No, 6
Yosef	Rabbi Ovadiah Yosef, *Responsa Yabi'a Omer*, Part 6, OH, No. 29

III. A MOTHER'S RECITATION OF THE BLESSING *BARUKH SHEPETARANI*

A mother is not obligated to recite the blessing for her daughter

Luria	Rabbi Shlomo Tzvi Luria, *Meishiv Halakhah*, Lodz, 5683 (1923), No. 350
Te'omim	Rabbi Yosef Te'omim, *loc. cit.*

A mother does not pronounce the blessing for her son or daughter

Adler	Rabbi Binyamin Adler, *op. cit.*, p. 81

A mother pronounces the blessing for her son or daughter

Ellinson	Rabbi Elyakim Ellinson, *op. cit.* pp. 181-184

6. *ALIYOT* FOR WOMEN

Oraḥ Ḥayyim 282:3

Question from Congregation *Adat Yisrael*, Nahariya: *May women read from the Torah and/or have an aliyah when the Torah is read in public?*

Responsum: In 1955, the Committee on Jewish Law and Standards of the Rabbinical Assembly was asked this question and two responsa were written on the subject (see the Bibliography at the end of this responsum). Rabbi Aaron Blumenthal permitted *aliyot* for women with no restrictions and five Committee members supported his responsum. Rabbi Sanders Tofield permitted *aliyot* for women on special occasions such as a *Bat Mitzvah* ceremony and ten Committee members supported his responsum. One member voted against both responsa and supported the accepted practice whereby women are not called up to the Torah (Rabbi Gershon Weiner, Discussion, pp. 34-36).

In 1986, Rabbi David Novak wrote a new responsum on this matter and ruled that women are not permitted to read from the Torah in public nor recite the blessings. However, where it was already customary for women to be called up, the prohibition should be limited, following the approach of the author of *Ḥasdei David* i.e., women may go up to the Torah, but should not be called up or they should be called up for a *hosafah* [additional *aliyah*] after the seven prescribed *aliyot*. In the responsum below,

* In 1994, my friend Rabbi Rivon Krygier of Kehillat Adath Shalom in Paris translated this responsum into French and, in the process, caught a number of errors. I thank him for his corrections which have been incorporated into this version of the responsum.

we will, generally speaking, support Rabbi Blumenthal's approach, but we will also cite numerous *poskim* not cited by him and we shall disagree with him on certain points.

I. The Talmudic Sources

1. Our Rabbis taught: All go up among the count of seven, **even a woman** and even a minor;[1] but the Sages said: a woman should not read from the Torah *mipnei kevod hatzibbur* – out of respect for the congregation. (Bavli *Megillah* 23a)

2. And all go up among the count of seven, **even a woman** and even a minor; a woman should not be brought to read in public. A synagogue that has only one person capable of reading, he stands and reads and sits, stands and reads and sits, stands and reads and sits, even seven times. (*Tosefta Megillah*, 3:11-12, ed. Lieberman, p. 356)

3a. Rabi Zeora in the name of Rav Yirmiyah: the slave goes up among the count of seven. (Yerushalmi *Megillah* 4:3, fol. 75a)

3b. Did not Rabi Zeira say in the name of Rav Yirmiyah: the slave goes up among the seven called up to read? (Yerushalmi *Ketubot* 2:10, fol. 26d)

4. A minor reads from the Torah and translates. (Mishnah *Megillah* 4:6)

5. And he translates [the scroll of *Eikhah* on the Ninth of

1. The printed editions of the Bavli read: "And even a minor and even a woman", but the reading cited here appears in several manuscripts of Bavli *Megillah* (see R.N.N. Rabinowitz, *Dikdukei Soferim Lemassekhet Megillah*, Munich, 1877, p. 121, letter *yod*), in many *Rishonim* cited below, as well as in all versions of the *Tosefta*.

> Av] so that the rest of the people, the women and children should understand it, **since women are obligated to hear the reading of the Book like men,** and how much the more so men... **and it is appropriate to translate for the people, the women** and the children every *seder* [Torah portion] and Prophet for Shabbat after the reading of the Torah... (*Massekhet Soferim* 18:5-6, ed. Higger, pp. 316-317)

II. The Simple Meaning of the *Beraita* in the Bavli

Before we discuss the approaches of the *poskim,* three comments must be made about the *beraita* in the Bavli.

1. "All go up": A number of *Rishonim* (Ra'avan on *Berakhot,* paragraph 185, fol. 97a; Maharam, *Teshuvot, Pesakim Uminhagim,* ed. Kahana, Vol. I, Jerusalem, 5717, *Teshuvot* section, paragraph 47; *Piskei Rid Limegillah,* Jerusalem, 5731, column 267; Ran on the Rif to *Megillah,* ed. Vilna, fol. 13a, s.v. *hakol;* and others) led by the Ribash (*Responsa of the Ribash,* No. 326 at length) interpreted "go up" as "go up to complete" or "completes" or "joins", but Rabbi Yosef Faur has already proved (pp. 123 ff.) that this interpretation is not the simple meaning. They were compelled to interpret it thus in order to explain why it is permissible for women, slaves and minors who are "exempt" from reading the Torah – see below – to go up and read.

2. "Among the count of seven": Similarly, some rabbis explained that women and minors go up to read "among the count of seven", but not among the count of three (or four or five or six – *Piskei Rid loc. cit.; Magen Avraham* to OH 282, subparagraph 5; and more). However, it seems more likely that the *beraitot* were simply giving an example, because it is known that "the Sages speak of the ordinary custom" (i.e., give concrete examples that were common in their time, see Mishnah *Shabbat,* 6:9 and more) and the Mishnah in *Megillah* (source No. 4) proves this. There it states "a minor reads from the Torah and translates" in a simple fashion, without any restrictions. Had there been a contradiction

between the Mishnah and the *beraitot* regarding minors, the *Gemara* would certainly have commented on it.

3. "But the Sages said: a woman should not read from the Torah *mipnei kevod hatzibbur*": Prof. Saul Lieberman has already noted (*Tosefta Kifshuta*, p. 1177): "and from 'but the Sages said' etc. is the Bavli's interpretation of the first clause", and this is also proven by a comparison of the *beraita* in the Bavli and the *beraita* in the *Tosefta*. Both *beraitot* contain an ancient *halakhah* with a later addition. Indeed, the concordances reveal that the phrase "*kevod tzibbur*" mentioned in the Bavli here, appears nowhere in the Mishnah, *Tosefta,* halakhic *midrashim* or the Yerushalmi. In all the sources we shall cite below from the Bavli, the phrase is used by *Amoraim* or by the anonymous editors of the Tamud. If so, then the second sentence in the Bavli was added in the period of the *Amoraim* or of the editors of the Talmud. Similarly, the second sentence in the *Tosefta* was apparently added at the end of the Tannaitic period (and so explained Elbogen, p. 128.)

III. Various interpretations of the *beraita* in the Bavli

Many *poskim* cited the *beraita* verbatim, without explaining it or dealing with its cryptic language.[2] Other *poskim* paraphrased the *beraita,* following Maimonides (*Hilkhot Tefilah* 12:17): "A woman shall not read in public because of *kevod hatzibbur*. A

2. *Seder Rav Amram Gaon*, ed. Goldschmidt, p. 75 and from there in *Maḥzor Vitry*, p. 93 and *Siddur Rashi*, p. 250 (with omissions); Rabbeinu Ḥananel *ad loc.*; the Rif to *Megillah*, ed. Vilna, fol. 13a; Rabbi Yehudah Albarceloni, *Sefer Ha'itim*, Cracow, 1903, pp. 269-270 and again on p. 271; Rabbi Avraham b"r Nattan Hayarḥi, *Sefer Hamanhig*, ed. Rafael, Jerusalem, 5738, p. 160; *Tur* OH 182; Rabbi David Abudraham, *Abudraham Hashalem*, Jerusalem, 5723, p. 130; Rabbi Meir b"r Shimon Hameili, *Sefer Hame'orot Lemegillah*, New York, 5727, pp. 332-333; Rabbi Avraham Min Hahar to *Megillah*, New York, 5735, p. 161 (there is a gap in the manuscript, but it is clear that he quoted from the *beraita*); Ra'avan, *Even Ha'ezer Lemegillah*, ed. Ehrereich, fol. 176c; Rabbi Yitzḥak of Vienna, *Or Zaru'a, Hilkhot Keri'at Hatorah*, paragraph 383, Part 2, fol. 79a at the bottom; *Piskei Harosh Lemegillah*, Chapter *Hakorei Omed*, paragraph 5; Rabbi Alexander Zuslin Hacohen, *Sefer Ha'aguda Lemegillah*,

minor who knows how to read and understands to whom the blessing is made[3] goes up among the number of readers".[4] Finally, many *poskim* dealt only with minors and dropped women from the discussion entirely.[5]

On the other hand, the *poskim* who truly **explained** the *beraita* can be divided into two groups:

A. One group thinks that even without the addition of *kevod tzibbur*, women do not go up to the Torah or go up just for some of the *aliyot* or go up if they want to obligate themselves **because women** — and minors too, according to some — **are exempt from reading the Torah in public**.

B. On the other hand, a second group thinks that according to the essence of the law as stated in the first clause of the *beraita*, women go up to the Torah for all the *aliyot* **because women are obligated to read the Torah in public,** and if they do not go up, the only reason for this is *kevod tzibbur* mentioned in the second clause of the *beraita*. We shall now present both schools of thought:

Chapter *Hakorei Omed*, paragraph 28; Rabbi Menaḥem Azaria of Fano, *Alfasi Zuta Lemegillah*, second edition, Jerusalem, 1979, p. 220; and Rabbi Yosef Karo, OH 282:3.

3. Look carefully at Yerushalmi *Berakhot* 7:2, fol. 11b; *Hagahot Maimoniyot* and *Kesef Mishneh* to the Rambam cited in the text; and Rabbi Faur, pp. 121-123.
4. Rabbi Aharon Hacohen of Lunel, *Orḥot Ḥayyim, Hilkhot Keri'at Sefer Torah*, paragraph 4; *Kol Bo, Hilkhot Keri'at Hatorah*, ed. Lvov, 1860, fol. 10c at the bottom; Rabbi Ya'akov Hazzan of London, *Eitz Ḥayyim*, ed. Brody, Part 1, Jerusalem, 5722, p. 50.
5. *Sefer Ha'orah*, ed. Buber, Lvov, 1905, p. 43; Rabbi Menaḥem ibn Zeraḥ, *Tzeidah Laderekh*, 1, 2, 6, ed. Warsaw, 1880, fol. 28b; *Siddur Ra'avan* which was published as *Siddur Rabbi Shlomo Migermeiza*, ed. Hirschler, Jerusalem, 5732, p. 171; Rabbi Eleazar of Germeiza, *Harokeaḥ*, paragraph 56, ed. Jerusalem, 5727, p. 43; Rabbi Moshe of Coucy, *Semag, Assin*, No. 19, ed. Venice, 1547, fol. 102d; Rabbi Mordechai ben Hillel Ashkenazi, *Hamordechai Lemegillah*, paragraph 809; Rabbi Avraham Danzig, *Ḥayei Adam* 31:39; Rabbi Shlomo Ganzfried, *Kitzur Shulḥan Arukh* 23:24; Rabbi Ḥayyim David Halevi, *Mekor Ḥayyim Hashalem* 122:13-14.

A. Women Are Exempt from Reading the Torah in Public

1. One of Rashi's teachers (Rabbi Yitzhak b"r Yehudah **OR** Rabbi Yitzḥak Halevi)[6] and Rabbi Shmuel of Falaise (*Or Zaru'a*, Part 2, fol. 59c in the middle) think that women are exempt from reading the Torah, but may fulfill the *mitzvah* and recite the blessing as we learned in source No. 1 "All go up", were it not for the matter of *kevod tzibbur*. They even use the same *beraita* to prove that women may fulfill **all** PTBC and recite a blessing over them.

2. Rabbi Yitzḥak of Vienna (*Or Zaru'a*, Part 2, fol. 62a at the bottom; and briefly in *Tosafot* to *Rosh Hashana* 33a, s.v. *ha*) thinks that women are exempt from reading the Torah, but one who is exempt may fulfill the obligation of one who is obligated by Rabbinic law: "... for a person who is voluntarily fulfilling a commandment may fulfill the obligation of one obligated to do so by Rabbinic law". He then cites three examples: a son recites the Grace after Meals for his father if his father ate a Rabbinically prescribed amount of food (*Berakhot* 20b); Rabbi Yehudah permits a minor to read the *Megillah* in public (*Megillah* 19b); and our *beraita*. Rabbi Yitzḥak of Vienna does not discuss the issue of whether women go up for some or all of the *aliyot*, but in his opinion, women are permitted to go up to the Torah even though they are exempt from reading the Torah.

3. Rabbi Nissim of Gerona (Ran on the Rif cited above) thinks that women and minors are exempt from reading the Torah. Therefore, he interprets "go up" as meaning "go up to complete" or "to join", on condition that the women and minors do not go up for **all** the aliyot "**because they are not obligated, they do not totally fulfill the public's obligation**." According to the original law in the Mishnah (*Megillah* 4:1), whereby only the first and last to go up recited the blessing, women and minors did not go up

6. This responsum appears in at least nine places in the name of Rabbi Yitzḥak b"r Yehudah **OR** in the name of Rabbi Yitzḥak Halevy **OR** in the name of Rashi and once, erroneously, in the name of Rabbi Yitzḥak ibn Giyyat (*sic!*). See the sources cited above, p. 60, note 37.

first or last "because of the blessing, since the other readers could not not **fulfill** their obligation through their blessing." But now that the Sages established that each person who goes up recites the blessing (*Megillah* 21b at the bottom), a woman and a minor may even read the first and last sections and certainly recite the blessings, just as a minor who gets the *maftir aliyah* recites the blessing over the *haftarah*.

A similar opinion was mentioned before him briefly in *Orḥot Ḥayyim* (*Hilkhot Keriat Sefer Torah*, paragraph 4) and afterwards at length in the *Responsa of the Ribash* (Nos. 35, 321, 326). The opinion of the Ran and the Ribash was accepted by the Rema in OH 282:3 and was then cited in the *Levush ibid., Shulḥan Arukh Harav* 282:5 and the *Arukh Hashulḥan* 282:9.

4. Rabbi Menaḥem Hameiri cites a similar opinion in two of his books (*Beit Habeḥira Limegillah*, ed. Hershler, pp. 73-74 = *Kiryat Sefer*, ed. Hershler, p. 85) in the name of "there is someone who says." According to this interpretation, one adult is obligated to fulfill Moshe Rabbeinu's *takkanah* [enactment] (Yerushalmi *Megillah* 4:1, fol. 75a – "Moshe enacted for Israel to read from the Torah on Shabbat and holidays") and the rest of the *aliyot* were enacted by Ezra (Yerushalmi *ibid*. and Bavli *Bava Kama* 82a – "Ezra enacted to read Torah on Monday and Thursday and Shabbat *Minḥah*") and may be **completed** by a woman or a minor. Undoubtedly, this commentator also thinks that women and minors are exempt from reading the Torah in public. (This opinion was accepted by Rabbi Saul Lieberman, p. 1177).

5. The Meiri cites another interpretation (in the two books mentioned above) as does Rabbi David b"r Shmuel Kokhavi (*Sefer Habatim*, ed. Blau, New York, 5735, p. 265 and cf. Rabbeinu Tam in *Tosafot* to *Rosh Hashana* 33a, s.v. *ha*, at the end). This approach differs in one aspect from the Ran's approach mentioned above, but it too assumes that women are exempt from reading the Torah. According to this approach, a woman could have completed **one of the middle *aliyot*** specifically during the period of the Mishnah when only the first and last

readers made a blessing, but now that all who are called up recite a blessing, a woman is **forbidden** to recite it. The Meiri concludes (in the two books mentioned above):

> and so logic dictates, for how can she recite the blessing **when she is exempt**! But a minor recites the blessing because he is included in [the commandment of] Torah study and others are commanded to teach him.

6. Rabbi Avraham Ḥayyim Rodríguez (*Responsa Oraḥ Letzaddik*, Leghorn, 1780, No. 3) deals among other things with the question of whether women may be included in a ***minyan*** for reading the Torah. And he writes (fol. 7a):

> and furthermore who said to him that she can join the ten for Torah reading as she can for the *Megillah* reading? The law is different there, since they are obligated to in the *Megillah* reading and **this is not the case with the Torah reading**. As the author of the *Beit Yosef* wrote in the name of the Ran that they are not obligated to do so.

7. Rabbi Yehudah Ayyash (in his commentary on OH, *Mateh Yehudah*, Leghorn, 1783, paragraph 282, subparagraph 7; he is cited by Rabbi Ovadiah Yosef, p. 130) wrote that women are not obligated to hear the Torah read **because they are exempt from Torah study,** and the terminology "are obligated" in *Massekhet Soferim* [source No. 5] is to be understood as a "general caution".

8. Rabbi Ḥayyim Yosef David Azulay says (in his *Kisei Raḥamim* on *Massekhet Soferim* 18:4 [source No. 5], Leghorn, 1803, in *Tosafot* s.v. *shehanashim*, based on the *Tosafot* to *Rosh Hashanah* 33a and the Meiri cited above) that **women are exempt from hearing the Torah reading**. They are obligated only to observe the *mitzvah* of *Hakhel*, listening to the Torah being read once every seven years (Deut. 31:1-13), because, as is well-known, women are exempt from Torah study and from PTBC. Therefore, it seems that "women are obligated" in *Massekhet Soferim* means that "it is a

good custom, and therefore the ruling has become common in our areas that women do not go to the synagogue of women [i.e., the women's section]... rather some old women and not regularly".

9. Rabbi Yosef Te'omim (in his *ḥiddushim* to *Megillah, Rosh Yosef,* Lemberg, 1863, fol. 80d at bottom, s.v. *leima Rabbi Akiva,* at the end) seeks reasons why a woman is not counted in the *minyan* for reading the Torah. He says among other things "**that women are not obligated to read the Torah** so how can they be counted?"

10. Rabbi Yeḥiel Michel Epstein (*Arukh Hashulḥan,* OH 282:11) quotes from *Massekhet Soferim* [source No. 5] and explains that it is not referring to an absolute obligation, but rather, like the obligation of children, **because women are exempt from Torah study** "and, furthermore, there is no greater PTBC than this [i.e., public Torah reading]". He even quotes the words of Rabbeinu Tam cited above. He also explains that reading the Torah is unlike *Hakhel* which is a special commandment to be carried out once in seven years. "But that we should say that they are obligated to hear the Torah read every Shabbat, this is certainly an astonishing thing and everyday practice will prove it". Rather, *Massekhet Soferim,* meant it as a "morally recommended practice".

B. Women are obligated to hear the Torah reading and, were it not for *kevod tzibbur,* they would read from it.

1. Rabbeinu Manoaḥ of Narbonne (*Sefer Hamenuḥah al Hamishneh Torah, Hilkhot Tefilah* 12:17, ed. Horowitz, Jerusalem, 5730, p. 186) explains as follows: **"If it were not for *kevod tzibbur,* [a woman] would read and bless**, for just as the Torah was given to male Israelites it was given also to females...". Furthermore, "Scripture equated a man to a woman regarding all the punishments in the Torah" (*Pesaḥim* 43a). And so it is written: "thus shall you say to the house of Jacob" (Exodus 19:3) and the *Mekhilta* (*Beshalaḥ, Massekhta debaḥodesh, Parashah* 2, p. 207) explains: "this refers to women". In other words, if women are included in all the

punishments in the Torah, then they are obligated to **read** the Torah, and furthermore, God chose them and gave the Torah as well. And if you should say that women are exempt from Torah study based on the *derashah* "And you shall teach it to your sons – your sons and not your daughters" (*Kiddushin* 29b), one can reply that they should not recite the blessing of "who has sanctified us with His commandments and commanded us to engage in Torah study" (and contrary to the *Shulḥan Arukh*, OH 47:14). "But, in any event, they were commanded to observe the commandments written in the Torah, and therefore **they can bless "who has chosen us" and "who has given us" [=the blessings before and after the Torah reading] and read the Torah the same as men, if it were not for the issue of *kevod tzibbur***". In other words, whoever has been given the Torah and is obligated by its punishments must read it in public and this has nothing to do with the *mitzvah* of Torah study and therefore, were it not for the matter of *kevod tzibbur*, women would go up to the Torah exactly like men.

2. Rabbi David b"r Shmuel Kokhavi (*Sefer Habatim*, *op. cit.*, p. 265) writes:

> One of the great scholars wrote that those who pray in their homes with a *minyan*, **a woman may read there from the Torah**, because it is not considered a *tzibbur* [a congregation] except in the synagogue.

In other words, when there is no "congregation", a woman may go up and read from the Torah like a man because there is no fear of *kevod hatzibbur*.

3. Rabbi Avraham Gumbiner (*Magen Avraham* to OH 282, end of subparagraph 6) explains as follows:

> We learn from here [source No. 1] **that a woman has an obligation to hear the Torah reading even though it was enacted because of Torah study** and women are not obligated to study Torah. **In any case, they are com-**

> **manded to hear like the commandment of *hakhel*,** to which women and children are obligated... and nevertheless one can say that even though they are not obligated, they go up as part of the count, and this is what the Tosafists wrote at the end of *Rosh Hashanah* (fol. 33a, s.v. *ha* in the middle).

Later on, he cites *Massekhet Soferim* [source No. 5] whereby women are obligated to hear the Torah reading and concludes "and here it is customary for the women to go outside" or, in other words, they do not view it as an obligation. In any case, he seems to think that women are obligated **to hear** the Torah reading, similar to the *mitzvah* of *Hakhel*, even though they are exempt from Torah study. In his opinion, apparently, were it not for the issue of *kevod tzibbur*, women would be called up to the Torah.

4. Rabbi David Pardo discusses our subject in his commentary on *Tosefta Megillah* [source No. 2] (*Ḥasdei David* on the *Tosefta*, ed. Vilna of the Bavli, fols. 6b-c):

> ... and it seems in any case that if she has gone up she should not come down **since, according to the law, she goes up as part of the count** and, moreover, according to what the author of the *Magen Avraham* wrote in paragraph 282 [=the quotation from *Massekhet Soferim*] "that women are obligated to hear the Book just like men", it stands to reason that since an obligation applies to her, if she went up, she should not go down.

He adds that this is proven from the language of the *Tosefta* before us that: "'women are not **brought** to read', **but if a woman went up on her own, then she went up, since [the prohibition] is only a matter of *kevod tzibbur*".** In other words, a woman is obligated to read the Torah as stated in *Massekhet Soferim* and this was only prevented due to *kevod tzibbur* and therefore if she goes up on her own and is not called up, she may read. (This opinion was accepted by Rabbi Yosef Faur, note 18).

5. Rabbi Ya'akov Emden (*Hagahot Yavetz* on *Megillah* 23a) explains: It seems that a woman does not read according to the end of the *beraita* in the Bavli, wherever this is possible, but in a place where there are not seven men present who are able to read and there is a woman who is able and it cannot be done without her, "all go up" according to the beginning of the *beraita*. In other words, he too thinks that women are obligated to read the Torah and are not called up solely because of *kevod tzibbur*, but in situations where there is no alternative, the original law is upheld and women go up as part of the seven.

Indeed, this understanding of Rabbi Emden is proven from his book *Sefer Birat Migdal Oz* (*Shoket* 2, paragraph 10, Zhitomir, 1874, p. 24):

> It would seem that when ten people pray and read Torah in a small group in the home of a woman who has given birth, and her husband is not present, **we should set up the matter according to the law that a woman goes up and reads from the Torah** in such a case. Even though the Sages said that she should not read because of *kevod tzibbur*, they only meant it when there was a large congregation and that it should not be done regularly. But in such a case which is rare and for her sake, one should say that they did not decree it [to forbid women's *aliyot* due to *kevod tzibbur*]. In any case, they said explicitly that she goes up among the count of seven – and if not now, when? This is my opinion if my colleagues will agree with me.

6. Despite what Rabbi Ḥayyim Yosef David Azulay wrote in his commentary on *Massekhet Soferim* (see above), in his commentary on the *Shulḥan Arukh* (*Birkhei Yosef* to OH 282:7), he supports the approach of Rabbi Avraham Gumbiner cited above. We have learned in a *beraita* in *Megillah* 22b that there are four *aliyot* on *Rosh Ḥodesh* because one does not work on *Rosh Ḥodesh* and therefore it is possible to add another *aliyah*. The *Tur* explains in OH 417 (based on the *Tosafot* to *Megillah* 22b, s.v. *she'ein*) that this

refers to women who do not work on *Rosh Ḥodesh* and come to synagogue to hear the Torah read. "We deduce from this that they are connected to **listening** to the Torah reading." In other words, they are obligated to **hear** the Torah reading, similar to their obligation in the *mitzvah* of *Hakhel*. His comments also seem to indicate that were it not for the issue of *kevod tzibbur*, women would go up to read the Torah.

7. Rabbi Shmuel Avigdor of Karlin (*Minḥat Bikurim* on the *Tosefta*, in ed. Vilna of Bavli *Megillah*, fol. 6b) explains the *Tosefta* [source No. 2] as follows: " 'A woman is not brought': **even though she goes up as one of the seven being called,** in any case she should not read in public to begin with due to *kevod tzibbur*". In other words, a woman is obligated to read the Torah and may go up after the fact, but before the fact she does not go up due to *kevod tzibbur*.

8. Rabbi Ḥanokh Hendel Friedland (*Divrei Ḥanokh*, Lemberg, 1884, No. 21) writes that women are obligated to read the Torah as it is written in *Massekhet Soferim* and he offers three proofs for this: This is what emerges from *Tosafot* (on *Rosh Hashana* 33a, s.v. *ha*, at the end). This is what emerges from Rashi to *Megillah* (21b, s.v. *ubanavi*): "that the sole purpose of the translation is for the women and the ignorami who do not understand the Holy Tongue... and in the translation of the Torah we must make an effort so that they understand the commandments". This is what seems to be indicated by the *Gemara* in its reference to loss of work on *Rosh Ḥodesh* on folio 22b (which we cited above in paragraph 6). In his opinion, the blessing is recited over the reading of the Torah in public and not over the positive commandment of Torah study. "If this is so, since they go up for the count of seven and exempt men from their obligation, **it proves that women too are obligated**".

IV. Women "are obligated" to hear the public Torah reading to the same extent as men.

The *poskim* in the first group above assumed that women are exempt from reading the Torah because it is part of Torah study and women are exempt from Torah study. However, there is not a shadow of a doubt that the second approach should is preferable. In other words, women "are obligated" to hear the Torah read in public to the same extent as men (see below), but the Sages decreed that they do not go up only because of *kevod tzibbur*. There are five proofs for this assertion:

1. This is proven by the language of the *beraita* in the Bavli and the *Tosefta* [sources 1 and 2]. Were women exempt from reading the Torah because of Torah study or because it is a PTBC, the *Tanna* would have said so explicitly in the first clause, just as the *Tannaim* do in other places. If a late *Tanna* or *Amora* (see section II, 3 above) took the trouble to add a restrictive sentence to the last clause of the *Tosefta* and the Bavli, this means that according to the first clause, a woman and a minor go up to read Torah exactly like men.

2. If this is a case of Torah study, then why would a "slave go up for the count of seven" (source No. 3 above; and that is how Rabbeinu Ḥananel and numerous other *Rishonim* ruled – see Rabbi Faur, note 24 and the Rema in OH 282:3) when everyone knows that a slave is exempt from Torah study (see source No. 3 in both passages in the Yerushalmi and also Bavli *Ketubot* 28a)!?

3. If this is a case of Torah study, why does "a minor read from the Torah and translate" [source no. 4] when everyone knows that minors are exempt in general from all the commandments!?

4. "And *Rabbeinu* Tam says... the blessings recited before and after reading the Torah are not recited over the commandment of Torah study, because if one has already recited the blessing of *'veha'arev na'* or exempted oneself by reciting the passage of *'ahavah rabah'* [the second blessing before the *Shema* in the

morning], he still repeats the blessings [over the reading of the Torah]" (*Tosafot* to *Rosh Hashana* 33a, s.v. *ha* at the end).

In other words, whoever has recited the Torah blessings in the early morning blessings or "*ahavah rabah*" and then goes up to read from the Torah is not exempt from reciting the blessings for reading the Torah. This means that there is a totally different commandment involved here.

5. *Massekhet Soferim* [source No. 5] proves that "women are obligated to read from the Book just like men", and even though *Massekhet Soferim* sometimes disagrees with our Talmud, this *halakhah* meshes well with the other proofs cited here.

V. What kind of obligation is involved in reading from the Torah in public?

If women, minors and slaves may, by virtue of the original law, read from the Torah in public, what kind of obligation is involved here? If there is no requirement of Torah study here as claimed by the Meiri, the Ran and the Ribash, what obligation is there? We have already seen two other possibilities (cf. Rabbi Feldman, pp. 296-297):

1. According to Rabbeinu Manoaḥ cited above, women may recite the blessings "who has chosen us" and "who has given us" because the Torah was given to them as well and they, too, are obligated by its punishments. In other words, reading the Torah in public is a kind of fixed public declaration to remind the nation that God chose us from among all the nations and gave us His Torah. However, if that is the case, it is difficult to understand why a **slave** is also included among the seven who are called up.

2. According to Rabbi Avraham Gumbiner cited above, women are obligated **to hear** the Torah reading and similar to the commandment of *Hakhel* (Deuteronomy 31:10-13; Neḥemiah 8:1-8; *Ḥagigah* 3a "Women come **to hear**"; Maimonides, *Hilkhot Ḥagigah* 3:1). However, this explanation does not hold up to

careful scrutiny. If women are obligated to **hear** the Torah reading, why do they go up as part of the seven to **read**? If the commandment is to **hear**, why is this not reflected in the blessings' formulae? Moreover, this explanation has no basis in the sources and it is insufficient to explain why a minor and a Canaanite slave can be counted among the seven who read (cf. *Ḥagigah*, ibid: "Why do the children come [to *Hakhel*]? To give a reward to those who bring them up" – and not in order to hear or read!).

3. The most convincing approach was already stated by some *Rishonim* and *Aḥaronim* and was very nicely summarized by Rabbi Faur (pp. 125-126) in his discussion of minors going up to read from the Torah. This approach was already hinted at in the *Mekhilta* (*Beshalaḥ, Massekhta Devayasa, Parashah* 1, p. 154):

> "And they went three days in the wilderness and found no water" [Exodus 15:22]... It was because they had left words of Torah for three days that they became rebellious. It is for this reason that the Prophets and the Elders enacted that they should read from the Torah on Shabbat, Monday and Thursday. How so? They read on Shabbat and interrupt on Sunday, and they read on Monday and interrupt on Tuesday and Wednesday, and they read on Thursday and interrupt on the eve of Shabbat.

The parallel *baraita* in the Bavli (*Bava Kama* 82a) adds: "**so that they should not sleep for three days without Torah**". Based on the *Mekhilta* and Yerushalmi *Megillah* 4:1, fol. 75a, Maimonides writes (*Hilkhot Tefilah* 12:1): "Moses, our teacher, enacted for Israel that they read from the Torah in public on Shabbat, Monday and Thursday at *Shaharit*, so that they should not tarry for three days without **hearing** Torah". "Regarding the Torah reading, **hearing** is not merely the means to fulfill the obligation to read, it is rather the **purpose** of the enactment" (Faur, p. 125). In other words, the **public** has an obligation **to enable the Torah to be heard in public** so "that they should not tarry for three days without hearing Torah", but an **individual** has no obligation to **hear** the Torah recited or to **read** the Torah in public. Therefore, it does not matter who actually reads the Torah in public – a woman, a minor and a slave are all qualified to read the Torah in public. And this is how five of the *Rishonim* understood our topic:

1. Rabbeinu Tam wrote (he is quoted in *Tosfot Rabbi Yehudah Sirlion* to *Berakhot* 47b, ed. Sachs, Jerusalem, 5732, p. 521, and cf. *Or Zaru'a,* Vol. 1, paragraph 196; *Piskei HaRosh* to *Berakhot,* Chapter 7, paragraph 20; and *Tosafot HaRosh* to *Berakhot, ibid.*):

> And the reason a minor, a slave and a woman who are not commanded to study Torah go up in the quorum of seven **is because the Torah scroll is there to be heard.** And their blessings are not in vain, since they do not pronounce a blessing "Who has sanctified us with His commandments and commanded us on the [study of] Torah", but rather "who has chosen us" and "who has given us".

2. Rabbeinu Yehonattan Hacohen of Lunel (in his commentary on the Rif to *Megillah,* ed. Mirsky, Jerusalem-New York, 5716, p. 79) states in his commentary to source No. 4:

> "A minor reads from the Torah" – **since Torah reading is only to enable the public to hear, what does it matter if the person who accomplishes this is an adult or a minor?** "But he does not recite [the *Shema* in public responsively]", since he is not obligated to perform this religious duty, he cannot perform it on behalf of a congregation.

3. The Meiri (in *Beit Habeḥira* to *Megillah,* p. 79, and it requires further study as to why he contradicts his position cited above) in his commentary on that same Mishnah states:

> "A minor reads from the Torah", **since the intention is only to enable the public to hear,** and this is not an absolute commandment like other commandments so that we

> should say about it: "Whoever is not himself under obligation [to perform a religious duty cannot perform it on behalf of a congregation] (Mishnah *Rosh Hashanah* 3:8).

4. Rabbi Yosef Ḥaviva (*Nimukei Yosef* to *Megillah*, ed. Blau, New York, 5720, p. 88, but it appears that the editor did not understand his comments):

> "A minor reads from the Torah", **since Torah reading is only to enable the public to hear**, what difference does it make if [the reader] is an adult or a minor?

5. Naḥmanides dealt with our issue in another context. The Mishnah in *Megillah* (23b) enumerates *devarim shebikdushah*, matters of holiness, that require a *minyan*. Rabbi Zeraḥiah Halevi asks (*Hama'or Hakattan* to *Megillah* 5a, ed. Vilna, fol. 3a): why does the Mishnah not count the *Megillah* reading among those things that require a *minyan* as is implied by fol. 5a? Naḥmanides replies (*Milḥamot Hashem, ibid.*), that all those things "enumerated in our Mishnah (on fol. 23b) **are all public obligations**... but [in the case of] *Megillah*, just as the public is obligated, so too is every individual...". Thus, reading the Torah is a public obligation, not a private one.

A similar explanation is repeated by quite a few *Aḥaronim* such as Rabbi Menaḥem Mendel Schne'erson (1789-1866).[7] And this is how Rabbi Yosef Rafael Ḥazan (*Tur*key and Israel, 1741-1820) explained it:

> ... it seems to me **that the Prophets' enactment was not for each and every individual to read or hear the Torah recited on Shabbat and Festivals,** rather that the *seder* [portion] of the the day be read on Shabbat and Festivals in

7. *Responsa Tzemaḥ Tzedek*, OH, No. 35 cited by Rabbi Ovadiah Yosef, p. 132. For other *Aḥaronim* who held this opinion, see *ibid.* and also *idem, Sefer Halikhot Olam*, Vol. 1, Jerusalem, 5758, pp. 242-244 and Rabbi Yitzḥak Yosef, *Yalkut Yosef*, Vol. 2, p. 191.

> public. And as long as the *seder* of the day was read in public, even if the individuals did not hear it, the Prophets' enactment was fulfilled (cited by Rabbi Faur, p. 127).

This explanation not only explains the sources cited above, but also explains five surprising facts or laws related to the reading of the Torah in public:

1. Reading of the Torah is not included in the list of commandments or even in the list of Rabbinic commandments (such as the *Semag*, end of Positive Commandments, fol. 242c):

> For whoever did not hear the Torah reading has not transgressed, for this is Ezra's enactment **so that Israel should not remain without Torah**, and it is not even a Rabbinic commandment (Rabbi Eliyahu Halevy, 16th century, cited by Rabbi Faur, p. 126).

2. We do not recite a blessing "who has sanctified us with his commandments and commanded us" as in the case of reading the *Megillah*, because this is not an individual obligation of every person going up to the Torah, but rather a public obligation (Rabbeinu Tam cited above; Rabbi Ya'akov Yitzḥak Neiman quoted by Rabbi Shraga Feivish Schneebalg, *Responsa Shraga Hameir*, Part 4, London, 5743, No. 45).

3. Rabbi Abahu used to leave the synagogue between *aliyot* and this is still the accepted *halakhah* (*Berakhot* 8a; Maimonides *Hilkhot Tefillah* 12:9; *Shulḥan Arukh*, OH 146:1). Would it be conceivable that it is permissible to leave if there were an individual obligation to hear the reading?!

4. Rav Sheshet used to turn his head away and recite Mishnah by heart during the Torah reading and say: "we are occupied with ours and they with theirs" (*Berakhot, ibid.*) and therefore it was codified that a scholar may engage in Torah study while the Torah is being read (Maimonides, *ibid.; Shulḥan Arukh, ibid.*, paragraph 2). If there is a individual obligation to hear the Torah

read or some other individual obligation, is a scholar exempt from fulfilling individual *mitzvot*?!

5. Several Ashkenazic scholars maintain that an individual may study "the Torah text twice and the translation once" during the reading of the Torah (see *Beit Yosef* to OH 146, s.v. *katuv bamordechai* and to OH 285, s.v. *aval meesham va'elakh*) and that is how Rabbi Yosef Karo ruled in the *Shulḥan Arukh* (OH 146:2 and 285:5). Would such a custom be allowed had there been a personal obligation to hear the Torah reading?!

There is, therefore, no doubt that according to the basic law in the first clause of both *beraitot* [sources 1-2], it is permissible for women and minors to read the Torah in public exactly like men. The **only** reason to prevent women from reading is *kevod tzibbur*, as many of the above-mentioned *poskim* have stressed.

VI. What is the meaning of the Amoraic phrase *kevod tzibbur* in our *beraita*?

1. Rabbi Feldman writes (p. 295) that the Talmud, the *poskim* and the commentators do not explain the phrase *kevod tzibbur* in Bavli *Megillah* [source No. 1].

2. Rabbi Novak (Novak 1, p. 18 at the bottom) determines that it is not respectful for a woman to present herself before a congregation of men because *kevod tzibbur* in our passage means an "erotic distraction" (Novak 2, pp. 144-145). However, in his responsum he explains that "this is contrary to the sensibilities of a Torah observant congregation" (Novak 3, p. 24 in the English summary and cf. p. 28 in the Hebrew responsum).

3. Rabbi Meiselman also gives two totally different explanations (pp. 142-144). His first explanation – "due to sexual distraction" – is similar to Rabbi Novak's first explanation. His second explanation is based on a *halakhic* reason. Since women are exempt from reading the Torah in public (see the *poskim* above

who held this view), if we allow them to go up instead of men, this will offend the public's sensitivities.

4. Finally, Rabbi Tofield (pp. 1103-1104) maintains that the meaning changes from place to place in the Talmud and that its meaning here is: "contrary to public interest, not in keeping with public policy", so that Jewish men do not neglect the study of Hebrew and rely on women to read the Torah.

However, all of the above explanations do not stand up to careful scrutiny. Biale (pp. 26-27) already stressed that the "erotic" interpretation has no basis whatsoever. When our Sages want to discuss sexual distraction, they use phrases such as "*maḥshavot zarot*/foreign thoughts", "*yeitzer hara*/evil inclination", "*pritzut*/ licentiousness" or "*ervah*/lewdness" – not the phrase "*kevod tzibbur*/respect for the congregation". (Cf. Rabbi Uziel's remarks cited below.) The other explanations cited above are also unfounded assumptions with no factual basis. **The truth is that *kevod tzibbur* here means "a disgrace to the congregation"** and there are three proofs of this assertion: so explained one of the *Rishonim* (who was published after Rabbi Feldman's article!),[8] this is proven by **all** of the sources in the Bavli which use this phrase, and this is proven by the parallel *beraita* in the *Tosefta* [source No. 2]. Let us begin with the five sources in the Bavli:

1. According to Abaye (Babylonian *Amora*, fourth generation), a naked person may not read from the Torah due to *kevod tzibbur* and from this he concludes that a half-naked minor, dressed in rags may not read from the Torah **due to *kevod tzibbur*** (*Megillah* 24b). There is no doubt that *kevod tzibbur* there means "a disgrace to the congregation".

2. According to the Mishnah (*Yoma* 7:1), the High Priest would recite the third passage from the Torah by heart on Yom Kippur

8. Rashi does not explain the phrase in *Megillah* 23a, but it can be assumed that he interpreted *kevod tzibbur* as synonymous to "disgrace to the congregation" – see his commentary to *Megillah* 24a, s.v. *shelo yifsok*, s.v. *ve'eino nosei et kapav*, and s.v. *aval eino korei batorah*.

and not roll the Torah scroll to the end of Numbers. The Bavli comments (*Yoma* 70a, and cf. *Sotah* 41a): "Why?... Rav Sheshet (Babylonian *Amora,* third generation) said: Since we do not roll a Torah scroll in public". The Talmudic editors add: "**because of *kevod tzibbur***"[9] and Rashi explains: that they "will be waiting in silence for this". In other words, it is a disgrace to the congregation to have to sit and wait until the High Priest rolls the Torah scroll.

3. "And Rabbi Tanḥum (*Eretz Yisrael,* third generation *Amora*) said in the name of Rabbi Yehoshua ben Levi (*Eretz Yisrael,* first generation): the *shliaḥ tzibbur* is not allowed to undress the Ark in the presence of the congregation **because of *kevod tzibbur*** (*Sotah* 39b).

Rashi explains that they would bring the Torah scroll from another house and drape pretty clothes over the Ark and place the Torah scroll inside. When they finished the Torah reading, they would take out the Torah scroll in order to carry it to its place and Rabbi Joshua ben Levi ruled that the Torah should not be undressed in the presence of the congregation "since it is an imposition upon the congregation to wait there with the Torah scroll." In other words, in Rashi's opinion, *kevod tzibbur* means an imposition upon the congregation that they must wait. But it is preferable to interpret that there is a disgrace to the congregation in that they see the Ark "naked", like the laws cited above regarding a nude or semi-nude person.

4. "Rabbi Yitzḥak (*Eretz Yisrael,* third generation *Amora*) said: let the fear of the public always be upon you... the Rabbis said: it is derived from here: 'that the Kohanim are not permitted to ascend the platform while wearing their sandals'... what is the reason? Is it not **because of *kevod tzibbur*?...**" (*Sotah* 40a at the bottom).

9. The addition by the anonymous editors of the Talmud is missing in *Sotah* and in three manuscripts of tractate *Yoma* – see *Dikdukei Soferim* to *Yoma*, p. 203, letter *hei* and *Dikdukei Soferim Hashalem* to *Sotah*, Vol. 2, pp. 192-193, notes 25-26.

Contrary to all other versions (see *Dikdukei Soferim Hashalem, ibid.*, p. 186), Rashi's **reading** in the last line of the Gemara is "because of the fear of the public," but his **explanation** is similar to *kevod tzibbur* in the above sources: "because his clothes ride up... and his sandals are visible to the public and they are not appropriate to be seen because of the mud on them". In other words, **it is a disgrace for the congregation** to see the mud that is on the *kohanim's* sandals.

5. "Rabba and Rav Yosef (Babylonia, third generation *Amoraim*) both said: *ḥumashin* should not be read from in the synagogue **because of *kevod tzibbur*** (*Gittin* 60a).[10] The Mordechai explains there (paragraph 406): "and it concludes here that one does not read from it [i.e., a *ḥumash*] because of *kevod tzibbur*, **that it is a disgrace for them because they do not have more than one *ḥumash*** [and not a complete Torah scroll]".

Therefore, we have proved that *kevod tzibbur* in the Babylonian Talmud always means "a disgrace to the congregation" and as concluded by Rabbi Blumenthal (p. 1088). Indeed, this is how the Rivevan, Rabbi Yehudah b"r Binyamin (Italy, 13th century) understood our *beraita* (in his commentary to tractate *Megillah*, ed. Blau, New York, 5735, p. 296): "Because of *kevod tzibbur*. **It is a disgrace to the congregation** that a woman **should come** and read". However, what "disgrace" would there be if a woman goes up among the count of seven? The phrase "***shetavoh*/should come**" mentioned by Rabbi Yehudah undoubtedly refers to the parallel sentence in the *Tosefta* [source No. 2]: "A woman should not ***mevi'in*/be brought** to read in public" and therein lies the solution to our question. It says there in the second clause:

> **A synagogue that has only one person capable of reading,** he stands and reads and sits, stands and reads and sits, stands and reads and sits, even seven times.

10. For a **different** version of this *halakhah*, see Yerushalmi *Megillah* 3:1, fol. 74a at the top. The Bavli, however, should not be interpreted according to the Yerushalmi as Rabbi Tofield did on page 1103 because it is a case of two completely **different** traditions.

In other words, in that particular synagogue, there is "only one person capable of reading" (quite a common occurence in the Talmudic era[11]) and it is a disgrace for the congregation of men to have to bring a woman to read in public (because at that time, whoever went up to the Torah, read from the Torah himself). Therefore, it is preferable for one man to read all the *aliyot*.

Indeed, three twentieth-century rabbis independently reached the same explanation of this passage. Rabbi Ben-Tzion Meir Ḥai Uziel, Sephardic Chief Rabbi of Israel, explained the expression *kevod tzibbur* in a responsum written circa 1921 on women participating in elections:

> And *kevod tzibbur* means that they should not say that there is no one among the men who knows how to read, but it is not a question of *peritzut*/licentiousness.

And so explained Rabbi Samuel Gerstenfeld (p. 169) in 1959:

> ... the Sages would permit a woman to read before the *minyan*; but because of the shame of ignorance that would accrue to the congregation, they forbade such reading.

Rabbi Blumenthal also understood it this way (p. 1088) in 1955:

> ...it is an offense to the dignity of the congregation. What makes it offensive? The implication that there is no man present who can read from the Torah.

Finally, Biale stressed that this *halakhah* reminds us of a well-known *beraita* (*Berakhot* 20b = *Sukkah* 38a = *Tosefta Berakhot* 5:17, ed. Lieberman, pp. 27-28 just the first sentence; and cf. the parallel Yerushalmi passages cited there):

> Truly they said: a son may bless [the Grace after Meals] for

11. See Meir Bar–Ilan, *Proceedings of the American Academy for Jewish Research* 54 (1987), Hebrew section, pp. 1-12. There is a lot of literature on this topic, but this is not the place to elaborate.

> his father and a slave blesses for his master and a woman blesses for her husband, **but the Sages said**: let a curse strike the man whose wife and sons bless for him.

That is to say, a woman is obligated to recite the Grace after Meals (Mishnah *Berakhot* 3:3) and can fulfill her husband's obligation to do so, but it is a disgrace that a Jewish man is unable to bless the Grace after Meals by himself and needs the help of his wife or sons. We might add that the **structure** of the *beraita* is also similar! In *Tosefta Berakhot,* there is only the first sentence. At a later period, opponents of the original *halakhah* arose and added the second sentence which begins with the phrase **"but the Sages said". This is exactly what happened to our *beraita*** in ***Megillah*** 23a [source No. 1]. (Cf. a similar *halakhah* in Mishnah *Sukah* 3:10 and Brooten's remarks, pp. 94-95).

VII. May a congregation forgo its honor?

If a woman does not read from the Torah solely because of *kevod tzibbur,* we must clarify whether the congregation may forgo its honor. Rabbi Tchorsh (pp. 186-187) and Rabbi Novak (Novak 3, pp. 28-29) respond in the negative (and cf. *Tiferet Yisrael* to *Megillah* 4:6, note 45), whereas Rabbi Freehof (Freehof 1, pp. 68-69) responds affirmatively. Indeed, both opinions have support:

1. The Maharam of Rothenburg ruled (*Teshuvot Pesakim Uminhagim,* ed. Kahana, Vol. 1, Jerusalem, 5717, *Teshuvot,* No. 47; see Feldman, note 9; Lieberman, p. 1177, note 43; and Mack, p. 719 for parallel sources) that in a city where everyone is a *Kohen,* a *Kohen* shall go up twice "and women may read [the rest of the *aliyot*]... if there is no other alternative, **the honor of the congregation may be pushed aside** because of the blemish of the *Kohanim*".[12] In other words, in a city of *Kohanim,* the honor of the

12. For the historical reality in Germany that is reflected in the question, see Ḥaym Soloveitchik, *She'elot Uteshuvot Kemakor Histori,* Jerusalem, 5751, pp. 29-30, and also see Rabbi Blumenthal, pp. 1094-1095.

congregation is pushed aside and women read five *aliyot* in order to preserve the honor of the *Kohanim*.

2. Likewise, we have seen that in the opinion of Rabbi Ya'akov Emden (above, p. 165), if there are not enough men capable of reading, **the honor of the congregation is pushed aside** and women read from the Torah in accordance with the basic law.

3. According to a *beraita* in *Ḥullin* 24b "a person whose beard has grown full is eligible to become a *sheliaḥ tzibbur*, to go down before the Ark, and to raise his hands [to recite the Priestly Blessing]" and Rabbi Yosef Karo rules (OH 53:6): "only one whose beard has grown full may be appointed to lead services because of *kevod hatzibbur*". Some *poskim* (the *Baḥ* on the *Tur*; the *Taz*, subparagraph 2; *Ba'er Heitev*, subparagraph 9; the Mishnah *Berurah*, subparagraph 23; *Kaf Haḥayim*, paragraph 37) ruled **that the congregation may not forgo its honor**. However, there too, there is a *posek* who rules **that the congregation may to forgo its honor** (this opinion is cited in *Magen Avraham*, subparagraph 9).

4. The *Beit Yosef* (OH 53, s. v. *umidivrei Rabbeinu*) mentions "the custom of a minor leading the evening service on Saturday nights" and tries to justify the custom. He says, among other things, "and for this reason there is room for the custom, to say that the **congregation forgoes its honor**".

5. We saw above that, according to the *Gemara* in *Gittin* 60a, one does not read from *ḥumashim* in the synagogue because of *kevod tzibbur*, and so rules Rabbi Yosef Karo (OH 143:2). However, Rabbi Meir of Rothenburg ruled that "**if they forgo their honor, it is permissible**", provided that the *ḥumash* is written as a scroll like a Torah scroll (*Teshuvot Pesakim Uminhagim* cited above, *Pesakim*, p. 163, No. 115) and so ruled many other *poskim* (*Kaf Haḥayyim* to OH 143, paragraph 10).

6. We saw above that, according to the *Gemara* in *Yoma* and *Sotah*, it is forbidden to roll the Torah scroll in public because of *kevod tzibbur*, and so ruled Rabbi Yosef Karo in OH 144:3. But he adds

(according to the Mordechai and the Ritva): "but if they have only one Torah scroll and they need to read two different passages, they may roll it **and the honor of the congregation is pushed aside**".

Therefore, even though there is support for both opinions, in most cases that we have found, most of the *poskim* determined **that the congregation may forgo its honor**. There is no doubt that this is the correct ruling in emergency situations when there are not enough men who know how to read from the Torah (as Rabbi Ya'akov Emden stated in paragraph 2). However, Rabbi Yosef Karo ruled that the congregation may forgo its honor even in a situation where it is not necessary in order to conduct services (paragraph 4). **Therefore, it is permissible to rule that a congregation can forgo its honor and call women up to the Torah according to the basic law in the two *beraitot* [sources 1-2].**

VIII. The congregation need not forgo its honor because the original reason has disappeared.

However, even if we rule that the congregation is not permitted to forgo its honor in general, in our case there is no need for this. We have proven that *kevod tzibbur* in our *beraita* means disgrace or insult to the congregation of men who are unable to read. This concern only existed in an era when men learned to read from the Torah and women did not.[13] However, today, even among the ultra-Orthodox, women learn to read Hebrew and they study the Torah. Therefore, there is no reason why a man should be insulted by a woman reading from the Torah. In other words, the original reason for the rabbinic decree against women reading Torah has disappeared because the times have changed and now we can return to the basic law in the first clause of the two *beraitot*. It is permissible for a woman to **read**

13. See, for example, *Kiddushin* 29b and *Sotah* 20a and additional sources cited by Nattan Morris, *Toledot Haḥinukh Shel Am Yisrael*, Vol. 1, Jerusalem, 1977, p. 110. For my opinion on the issue of women studying Torah, see below, pp. 358-366.

from the Torah in public and how much the moreso to go up and only **recite the blessings,** because no man should be offended by the fact that she knows how to read or bless.

But how can we ignore the well-known principle that "no court can set aside a decision of another court until it is greater than it in wisdom and in number" (Mishnah *Eduyot* 1:5)? Furthermore, Maimonides ruled that this applies even if the original reason for the prohibition has disappeared (*Hilkhot Mamrim* 2:2)! The answer is that this issue is in dispute among the *poskim*, but Rashi, Ra'avad, the Meiri and the author of *Shita Mekubetzet* ruled that if the original reason and explanation for the rabbinic decree are no longer relevant, it is **permissible** for another court to cancel the prohibition, even if it does not exceed its predecessor in wisdom and numbers.[14] Therefore, we rule that the original reason for the rabbinic decree of *kevod tzibbur* no longer exists and we should return to the basic law.

Lastly, we must deal with two side issues which touch upon our topic.

IX. "Words of Torah are not susceptible to impurity."

There is a common belief that it is forbidden for women to go up to the Torah due to their menstrual impurity. Therefore, we must stress, following Rabbi Blumenthal (pp. 1097-1098) and Rabbi Feldman (p. 295), that this opinion is **contrary** to Talmudic law and to most *poskim*. In *Berakhot* (22a), the *Tanna* Rabbi Yehudah ben Beteira rules that **"words of Torah are not susceptible to ritual impurity",** whereas the widespread view is primarily based on a sectarian *beraita* known as "*Beraita*

14. The Ra'avad in his strictures on Maimonides, *ibid*; Rashi to *Beitzah* 5a, s.v. *mina amina la; Hameiri, ibid.*, ed. Lange–Schlesinger, Jerusalem, 5716, pp. 31-32; and *Shita Mekubetzet* to *Beitzah* 5b at the end. Also see ET, Vol. 6, columns 700-701 and Menaḥem Elon, *Hamishpat Ha'ivri*, third edition, Jerusalem, 5748, p. 445 and note 201.

Demassekhet Niddah."[15] Indeed, the major *poskim* such as the Rif, Maimonides, the *Semag*, the Rosh, the *Tur* and Rabbi Yosef Karo ruled according to the Talmud. The Rema and others tried to prevent women from entering the synagogue and praying during their menstrual period **as a custom**, but they were unsuccessful. And finally, not one of the dozens of *poskim* who dealt with our topic mentioned menstrual impurity as a reason to prevent women from going up to the Torah.

X. *Kol B'isha Ervah* [a woman's voice is lewdness] is unrelated to public Torah reading.

Likewise, there is a prevalant opinion today, that it is forbidden for a man to hear a woman singing, based on Samuel's statement: "a woman's voice is *ervah*/lewdness" (*Berakhot* 24a and *Kiddushin* 70a-b). However, we have shown elsewhere[16] that this opinion is based on a suggestion by Rabbi Joshua Falk (d. 1614) that the Ḥatam Sofer turned into *halakhah* in the early nineteenth century. However, this opinion is contrary to the simple meaning of Samuel's statement and to all of the opinions of the *Rishonim*: the Rif ignored Samuel's statement in both *Berakhot* and *Kiddushin*. One group of *Rishonim* ruled according to the passage in *Kiddushin* – and this is undoubtedly the original passage – that Samuel was referring to the **speaking** voice of a woman to the extent that this would lead to illicit sexual relations. This is also indicated by the third parallel to Samuel's statement in the Yerushalmi (*Ḥallah* 2:4, fol. 58c). On the other

15. See a thorough explanation in Yedidya Dinari, *Te'udah* 3 (5743), pp. 17-37. Also see Shmuel Safrai, *Tarbitz* 32 (5723), p. 335 = *Biyemei Habayit U'biyemei Hamishnah*, Jerusalem, 5756, p. 165; Mordechai Akiva Friedman, *Maimonidean Studies* 1 (1990), pp. 1-21; Rabbi Ovadiah Yosef, *Responsa Yeḥaveh Da'at*, Vol. 3, No. 8; Rabbi David Novak, *Law and Theology in Judaism*, Vol. II, New York, 1976, pp. 138-140; Shaye Cohen in: Susan Grossman and Rivka Haut, eds., *Daughters of the King*, Philadelphia, 1992, pp. 103-115; and Rabbis Diana Villa and Monique Susskind Goldberg, *To Learn and To Teach*, Number 5, Jerusalem, January 2008. For a new theory about the origin of these customs, see Elisheva Baumgarten, above p. 68, note 64.
16. See above, Chapter 2 and all of the Bibliography listed there.

hand, Rav Hai Gaon and most of the *Rishonim* in Germany explained Samuel's words according to the passage in *Berakhot* and ruled that it is forbidden to recite the ***Shema*** when a woman is singing nearby. Lastly, the Sages of Provence accepted both the above explanations. Only the *Aḥaronim,* especially the Ḥatam Sofer, established a general prohibition against hearing a woman singing, but their interpretation does not concur with the Talmud and the *Rishonim*. Furthermore, Emily Teitz has proved that **in practice** Jewish women always sang at home, at celebrations, as performers, as well as in the synagogue throughout the Middle Ages.[17] If so, there is no reason to prevent women from reading Torah in public because of *Kol B'isha Ervah.*

XI. Practical *Halakhah*

Women are "obligated" to hear the Torah read in public to the same extent as men, minors and slaves, because the purpose is to read the Torah to the congregation so that the congregation should not tarry three days without hearing the Torah. The only reason to prevent women from reading the Torah in public is *kevod tzibbur*. We have seen that this late phrase always means "a disgrace to the congegation" and in our case, the concern was that the men would be offended by the fact that a woman was reading because there were not enough men able to do so. Likewise, we have seen that every congregation can forgo its honor and allow women to read from the Torah or have an *aliyah*. Furthermore, we have seen that today there is essentially no need for such forgoing of honor because the original reason for the rabbinic decree has disappeared as a result of changing times and we now return to rule according to the basic law: "All go up among the count of seven, **even a woman** and even a

17. Emily Teitz, "*Kol Isha* – The Voice of Woman: Where Was It Heard in Medieval Europe?", *Conservative Judaism* 38 (Spring 1986), pp. 46-61. Despite certain errors in that article, there are enough proofs in it to justify what I wrote above.

minor". Finally, we have seen that women cannot be prevented from having *aliyot* for fear of menstrual impurity or because of "*kol b'ishah ervah*".[18]

David Golinkin
Jerusalem
12 *Shevat* 5748

18. It is worth adding that in most Conservative synagogues around the world, women are called up to and read from the Torah. A survey of 750 synagogues – Edya Arzt, *Women's League Outlook*, Fall 1988, pp. 17-18 – revealed that 460 synagogues call women up to the Torah without any restrictions and 61 do so on special occasions or together with their husbands. For previous surveys, see Jack Wertheimer in: *The American Synagogue: A Sanctuary Transformed*, Cambridge, 1987, pp. 137, 149. According to a 1995 survey, women go up to the Torah in 88% of Conservative synagogues in the United States – see Jack Wertheimer, ed., *Jews in the Center: Conservative Synagogues and their Members*, New Brunswick and London, 2000, p. 250.

BIBLIOGRAPHY

Biale — Rachel Biale, *Women and Jewish Law*, New York, 1984, pp. 24-29, 268

Blumenthal — Rabbi Aaron Blumenthal, "An *Aliyah* for Women," *Proceedings of the Rabbinical Assembly* 19 (1955), pp. 168-181 = Seymour Siegel and Elliot Gertel, eds., *Conservative Judaism and Jewish Law*, New York, 1977, pp. 266-280 = David Blumenthal, ed., *And Bring Them Closer to Torah: The Life and Work of Rabbi Aaron Blumenthal*, Hoboken, New Jersey, 1986, pp. 11-24 = David Golinkin, ed. *Proceedings of the Committee on Jewish Law and Standards of the Conservative Movement 1927-1970*, Jerusalem, 1997, pp. 1086-1099 (pages number here refer to the latter book)

Brooten — Bernadette Brooten, *Women Leaders in the Ancient Synagogue*, Chico, California, 1982, pp. 94-95, 249

Discussion — *Proceedings of the Rabbinical Assembly* 19 (1955), pp. 33-41 = David Golinkin, ed. *Proceedings of the Committee on Jewish Law and Standards of the Conservative Movement 1927-1970*, Jerusalem, 1997, pp. 382–390

Elbogen — Yitzḥak Moshe Elbogen, *Hatefillah Beyisrael Behitpatḥuta Hahistorit*, Tel Aviv, 1972, pp. 128, 429

Ellinson — Rabbi Elyakim Ellinson, *Ha'ishah Vehamitzvot – Sefer Rishon: Bein Ha'ishah Leyotzrah*, Jerusalem, 1977[2], p. 70

Faur — Rabbi Yosef Faur, "*Aliyat Kattan Likro Batora*", *Sefer Zikaron Leharav Yitzḥak Nissim, Seder Rishon*, Jerusalem, 5745, pp. 113-133

Feldman — Rabbi David M. Feldman, "Woman's Role and Jewish Law", *Conservative Judaism* 26/4 (Summer 1972) pp. 30-33 = Seymour Siegel and Elliot Gertel, eds., *Conservative Judaism and Jewish Law*, New

York, 1977, pp. 295-297, 302-303 (page numbers here refer to the latter book).

Friedmann — Rabbi Meir Friedmann, "Mitwirkung Von Frauen Beim Gottesdienste", *HUCA* 8-9 (1931-1932), pp. 518-521.

Freehof 1 — Rabbi Solomon Freehof, *Reform Jewish Practice and Its Rabbinic Background*, Vol. 1, New York, 1963, pp. 68-69

Freehof 2 — Rabbi Solomon Freehof, *Reform Responsa*, Cincinatti, 1960, pp. 40-42

Frimer — Rabbi Aryeh Frimer, "*Ma'amad Ha'ishah Bahalakhah – Nashim Uminyan*", *Or Hamizraḥ* 34 (5746), pp. 76-77 and with changes in his English article: "Women and Minyan", *Tradition* 23/4 (Summer 1988), pp. 57, 71-72

Gerstenfeld — Rabbi Samuel Gerstenfeld in: Baruch Litvin, ed., *The Sanctity of the Synagogue*, New York, 1959, p. 169

Golinkin — Rabbi David Golinkin, "*Hakol Olin Leminyan Shivah*", *Tarbitz* 68 (5759), pp. 429-433 (that article is based on this responsum, beginning with paragraph VI)

Ḥazan — Rabbi Eliyahu Ḥazan, *Responsa Ta'alumot Lev*, Vol. 3, No. 20

Levine — Rabbi Lee Levine, *The Ancient Synagogue*, New Haven, 2000, pp. 478-479

Lieberman — Rabbi Saul Lieberman, *Tosefta Kifshuta*, Part 5, *Seder Mo'ed*, New York, 5722, pp. 1176-1179

Lubitch — Rivka Lubitch, *Teḥumin* 17 (5757), p. 166

Mack — Ḥananel Mack in: Yosef Aḥituv and others, eds. *Ayin Tova*, 5759, pp. 715-720

Meiselman — Rabbi Moshe Meiselman, *Jewish Woman in Jewish Law*, New York, 1978, pp. 140-145, 196-197

Novak 1	Rabbi David Novak, *Law and Theology in Judaism*, New York, 1974, p. 18.
Novak 2	Rabbi David Novak, *Law and Theology in Judaism*, second series, New York, 1976, pp. 144-145, 211.
Novak 3	Rabbi David Novak, "May a Woman Be Called Up to the Torah in the Synagogue?", *Tomeikh Kehalakhah: Responsa of the Panel of Halakhic Inquiry*, Mt. Vernon, New York, 1986, pp. 23-31 (Hebrew responsum with an English summary)
Rosenak	Avinoam Rosenak, "Dignity of the Congregation... a Halakhic Ruling of Rabbi Joseph Messas", *Nashim* 13 (2007), pp. 183-206 = *Akdaumut* 20 (5768), pp. 55-70 (Hebrew)
Safrai	Dina Safrai, "*Minhag Ḥadash ba Lakevutsa*", *Amudim* 43/2 (581) (Marḥeshvan 5755), pp. 46-47
Safrai	Chana and Shmuel Safrai, "*Hakol Olin Leminyan Shivah*", *Tarbitz* 66 (5757), pp. 395-401
Shargel	Baila Shargel, *Lost Love: The Untold Story of Henrietta Szold*, Philadelphia, 1997, p. 333
Shilo	Shmuel Shilo, *Teḥumin* 17 (5757), p. 161
Shoḥat	Raphael Shoḥat, "*Al Devar Keriyat Habanot LaTorah*", *Shevilei Haḥinukh* 5/1 (Tishrei 5691/1931), pp. 35-36
Schochetman	Eliav Shochetman, *Teḥumin* 15 (5755), pp. 166-167
Sperber	Rabbi Daniel Sperber, *Darkah Shel Halakhah*, Jerusalem, 2007
Sperber	Rabbis Daniel Sperber, Mendel Shapiro, Shlomo Riskin and Prof. Eliav Shochetman, *Women and Men in Communal Prayer*, New York and Jersey City, 2010
Tchorsch	Rabbi Katriel Fischel Tchorsch, *Noam* 15 (5732) pp. 185-187
Tibber	Anthony Tibber, "*Halakhah* on *Aliyot* for Women", *Masorti: The Masorti Journal* 1 (1987), pp. 37-39

Tofield	Rabbi Sanders Tofield, "Women's Place in the Rites of the Synagogue: With Special Reference to the *Aliyah*", *Proceedings of the Rabbinical Assembly* 19 (1955), pp. 182-190 = David Golinkin, ed. *Proceedings of the Committee on Jewish Law and Standards of the Conservative Movement 1927-1970*, Jerusalem, 1997, pp. 1100-1108 (page numbers here refer to the latter book)
Uziel	Rabbi Ben-Tzion Meir Ḥai Uziel, *Responsa Mishpetei Uziel*, Part 3, *Ḥoshen Mishpat*, Tel Aviv, 1940, No. 6, p. 35
Weiss	Rabbi Avi Weiss, *Women at Prayer*, Hoboken, New Jersey, 1990, pp. 67-83
Yosef	Rabbi Ovadiah Yosef, *Responsa Yeḥaveh Da'at*, Vol. 4, Jerusalem, 5741, pp. 130-131 in a note
Yosef	Rabbi Yitzḥak Yosef, *Yalkut Yosef*, Vol. 2, Jerusalem, 5750, pp. 65-66

7. WOMEN AND THE MEGILLAH READING

Oraḥ Ḥayyim 689:1-2

In memory of my Mother and Teacher
Blume Devorah bat Esther z"l
On her shloshim, 28 Shevat 5772

Question: *Is it permissible for women to read Megillat Esther in public on Purim?*

Responsum: There are three basic approaches to this question in Talmudic and halakhic sources:

I. Women are obligated to read the Megillah and may therefore do so in public and fulfill the obligation of the congregation, including the men.

This approach is based on two Talmudic sources. The first is Mishnah *Megillah* 2:4 = Bavli *Megillah* 19b:

> All are fit to read the Megillah except for a deaf mute, an insane person and a minor.

On this, the Talmud comments (*Arakhin* 2b-3a):

> "All are fit to read the Megillah" to include what? To include women.

The Talmud in *Arakhin* then brings an Amoraic statement which also appears in *Megillah* 4a:

> For Rabbi Yehoshua ben Levi said: Women are obligated to

> read the Megillah because they too were included in that miracle.

Rashi comments in *Arakhin*:

> For they are obligated to read the Megillah and fit to read it and to fulfill the obligation of men to hear it.

Rashi is following here the well-known halakhic principle that whoever is obligated to do a *mitzvah* can fulfill the obligation of all those who are obligated to do that *mitzvah* (see Mishnah *Rosh Hashanah* 3:8).

Rashi's opinion is not an isolated one. The following halakhic authorities all rule according to the Talmud in *Arakhin* and/or according to the dual statement of Rabbi Yehoshua ben Levi that women are obligated to read the Megillah and can therefore read in public and fulfill the obligation of the entire congregation, including men.

THE BABYLONIAN GEONIM

Rav Yehudai Gaon, *Halakhot Pesukot*, ed. Sasson, p. 38 = the Hebrew version of that work, *Hilkhot Re'u*, ed. Schlossberg, p. 11 which quotes Rabbi Yehoshua ben Levi.

Halakhot Ketzuvot, ed. Margaliot, p. 87, which is an Italian version of part of *Halakhot Gedolot;* it quotes Mishnah *Megillah*.

SPAIN AND NORTH AFRICA

The Rif to *Megillah* 4a, ed. Vilna, fol. 2b who quotes Rabbi Yehoshua ben Levi.

Maimonides, *Hilkhot Megillah* 1:1-2, as stressed by the *Maggid Mishneh* and *Hagahot Maimoniot ad loc.*

Rabbi Avraham of Lunel, *Sefer Hamanhig*, ed. Refael, p. 249, who quotes Rabbi Yehoshua ben Levi with additional comments.

Ḥidushei HaRitva to *Megillah* 4a, fol. 5d.

Ran on the Rif to *Megillah* 19b, ed. Vilna, fol. 6b (but cf. below paragraph II for the Ran's **other** opinion).

Rabbi Yosef Karo, OH 689:1-2, according to *Yalkut Yosef*, note 21.

PROVENCE

Meiri to *Megillah* 4a, ed. Hirschler, pp. 20-21 and to *Berakhot* 47b, ed. Dickman, p. 179.

ASHKENAZ

Rabbi Yitzḥak ben Moshe of Vienna, *Or Zarua*, Part II, paragraph 368, fols. 77d-78a, who rules like Rashi and rejects *Halakhot Gedolot*.

MODERN RABBIS

Rabbi Yosef Kafiḥ in his commentary to Maimonides *loc cit.*, *Zemanim*, Part II, p. 824.

Rabbi Daniel Landes, "The Reading of the Megillah on Purim Night", March 1997 (unpublished).

Furthermore, the Ritva and the Ran in Spain and the Meiri in Provence (in his commentary to *Berakhot*) rule that since a woman is obligated to read the Megillah, she may also be counted in the *minyan* for the Megillah reading.

II. Women are exempt from *reading* the Megillah but are obligated to *hear* the Megillah.

This opinion is based on the *Tosefta* (*Megillah* 2:7, ed. Lieberman, p. 350) and the Yerushalmi (*Megillah* 2:4, ed. Venice, fol. 73b = ed. Vilna 2:5, fol. 21a).

The Tosefta states:

> Women and slaves and minors are exempt, And cannot fulfill the obligation of the public.

The Yerushalmi relates that

> Bar Kapara said: he must read it before women and minors because they too were in a state of doubt [as to whether they would live].
>
> Rabbi Yehoshua ben Levi did so. He would gather his children and the members of his household and read it before them.

Halakhot Gedolot (ed. Warsaw, fol. 40c = ed. Jerusalem, Vol. I, p. 406; cf. *Otzar Hageonim* to *Megillah*, p. 7) rules that

> women, slaves and minors are exempt from **reading** the Megillah but are obligated to **hear** it since all were in doubt [regarding] "to destroy, to kill, to exterminate" (Esther 3:13), and since all were in doubt, all are obligated to **hear**.

He then quotes Rabbi Yehoshua ben Levi from the Yerushalmi (along with an additional sentence which is not in our Yerushalmi).

Many attribute to *Halakhot Gedolot* the opinion that since women are only obligated to **hear** the Megillah, they can only fulfill the obligation of other women.

This approach of *Halakhot Gedolot* was followed by the following authorities:

NORTH AFRICA

Rabbeinu Ḥananel to *Megillah* 4a, who quotes Rabbi Yehoshua ben Levi with the reading "to hear".

SPAIN

Zohar Ḥadash, Vol. II, Ruth, fol. 47b

Ran on the Rif to *Megillah* 4a, ed. Vilna, fol. 2b (but cf. above in section I).

PROVENCE

Rabbi Yitzḥak ben Abba Mari, *Sefer Ha'ittur*, Part II, fols. 113c-d.

FRANCE AND ASHKENAZ

Tosafot to *Arakhin* 3a, s.v. *la'atoyei*.

Rabbi Eliezer ben Yoel Halevi, *Sefer Ra'aviyah*, ed. Aptowitzer, paragraph 569, pp. 292-293 and paragraph 843, p. 580.

Rabbi Eleazar of Worms, *Sefer Harokeaḥ*, paragraph 236.

Rabbi Simḥah of Speyer quoted by *Hagahot Maimoniot* to Maimonides *loc. cit.*

III. Women are obligated to *read* the Megillah, but can only fulfill the obligation of other women.

This opinion is not based on a Talmudic source but rather on another version of *Halakhot Gedolot*. It is quoted or mentioned by *Tosafot* to *Sukkah* 38a, s.v. *be'emet amru*; the Meiri to *Megillah* 4a, pp. 20-21; *Tur* OH 689; *Menorat Hama'or* by Rabbi Yisrael Al-nakawa, ed. Enelow, Part II, p. 212.

IV. Practical *Halakhah*

It is clear from the above that a rabbi who wants to rule leniently can rely on approach No. I, while a rabbi who wants to rule strictly can rely on approach Nos. II or III. Indeed, many if not most Orthodox rabbis do not allow women to read the Megillah in public or only allow them to read the Megillah for other women. However, if one follows the general rules of Jewish law it is clear that the Babylonian Talmud takes precedence over the *Tosefta* and the Yerushalmi (see ET, s.v *Halakhah*, Vol. 9, col. 247, note 108 and col. 250, note 147).

Indeed, this is exactly what the *Or Zarua* and the Meiri state explicitly regarding our topic. The *Or Zarua* (Part II, paragraph 368, fol. 77d) says that

> since the *beraita* in the *Tosefta* is not mentioned in our Talmud, we do not rely on it, and it seems to me that the

> main thing is as Rashi explained: to include women who are obligated to read the Megillah and fit to fulfill the obligation of men.

The Meiri states (in his commentary to *Megillah*, p. 21):

> And the main thing is not to push aside an explicit Talmudic passage in our hands by a *beraita* (i.e., the *Tosefta*) or by the Western Talmud (i.e., the Yerushalmi) and how much the more so by logic, but let us rely on the well-known principle that "all who are obligated in something fulfill the obligation of the public".

Therefore, it is clear that according to the Babylonian Talmud and a large number of early authorities, women are obligated to read the Megillah and can therefore read the Megillah in public for a congregation which includes men. This is not some modern innovation but the most authoritative halakhic opinion on this topic. Furthermore, it also stands to reason, as three of the *Rishonim* state, that women may be counted in the *minyan* for the Megillah reading.

David Golinkin
Jerusalem
28 Shevat 5772

BIBLIOGRAPHY

Berkovits	Rabbi Eliezer Berkovits, *Jewish Women in Time and Torah*, Hoboken, New Jersey, 1990, pp. 92-100
Cohen	Rabbi Aaron Cohen, *The Torah U-Madda Journal* 9 (2000), pp. 248-263 (a rejoinder to Rabbi Weiss)
Cohen	Rabbi Alfred Cohen, *Journal of Halacha and Contemporary Society* 30 (Fall 1995), pp. 25-41
Dimitrovsky	Rabbi H. Z. Dimitrovsky, *Ḥiddushei Harashba* to *Megillah*, Jerusalem, 1981, cols. 46-48
Ehrenreich	Rabbi Ḥ. Y. Ehrenreich, *Otzar Haḥayyim* 6/5-6 (5690), pp. 145-149
Feldman	Rabbi David M. Feldman in: Seymour Siegel and Elliot Gertel, eds. *Conservative Judaism and Jewish Law*, New York, 1977, pp. 300-301
Ginzberg	Rabbi Levi Ginzberg, *Peirushim V'ḥiddushim Bayerushalmi*, Part II, New York, 1941, pp. 175-176
Kuk	Rabbi Sh. Ḥ. Kuk, *Iyunim Umeḥkarim*, Vol. 2, Jerusalem, 1963, pp. 46-49
Kuk	*idem., Otzar Hahayyim* 6/4 (5690), pp. 106-108
Lieberman	Rabbi Saul Lieberman, *Tosefta Kifshutah* to *Megillah*, pp. 1147-1148
Ta-Shema	Yisrael Ta-Shema, *Hatefillah Ha'ashkenazit Hakedumah*, Jerusalem, 2003, pp. 223-226
Weiss	Rabbi Avraham Weiss, *The Torah U-Madda Journal* 8 (1998-1999), pp. 295-317
Yalon	Shevaḥ Yalon, *Kol Mitzvot Aseh Shehazman Garma Nashim Peturot*, M.A. Thesis, Bar Ilan University, Ramat Gan, 1990, pp. 107-113
Yosef	Rabbi Yitzḥak Yosef, *Yalkut Yosef*, Vol. 5, Jerusalem, 5748, pp. 287-289

8. RECITING VERSES HONORING ESTHER ALOUD DURING THE MEGILLAH READING

Oraḥ Ḥayyim 690:17

Question From Rabbi Einat Ramon: *When the Megillah is read in public on Purim, it is customary for the congregation to recite aloud four verses of redemption (2:5, 8:15, 8:16, 10:3), which are then repeated by the reader. What are the sources for this custom? May we institute a new custom of reciting aloud four* **additional** *verses of redemption related to Esther?*

Responsum:

I. The Primary Sources

The custom of reciting certain verses of redemption aloud during the Megillah reading is first mentioned in three medieval sources, which were then quoted or paraphrased by many other sources:

1. RAV SA'ADIA GAON (BABYLON, 882-942) IN HIS *SIDDUR*

In his *siddur*, Rav Sa'adia Gaon states that:

> In the Torah, there are ten verses that the congregation reads aloud, they and their Aramaic translation... And in the Prophets three... and in the writings two: "The Jews enjoyed light and gladness, happiness and honor" (8:16); "For Mordekhai the Jew ranked next to King Aḥashverosh... and interceded for the welfare of his kindred" (10:3, the last verse in the Megillah) (*Siddur Rav Sa'adia Gaon*, Jerusalem, 1940, p. 369).

This passage was quoted in *Teshuvot Hageonim* (ed. Harkavy, No. 208, pp. 97 and 310); *Sefer Ha'eshkol* (Provence, 12th century, ed. Albeck, Vol. 1, p. 172; ed. Auerbach, Vol. 2, p. 65); and in *Sefer Abudraham* (Spain, 14th century, ed. Jerusalem, p. 207). *Sefer Ha'eshkol,* ed. Auerbach says that "some add Esther 2:5 and 8:15 which are verses of redemption". This is clearly a later addition influenced by source No. 3 below.[1] *Sefer Abudraham* adds regarding the two verses quoted by Rav Sa'adia: "And this is the custom in most places in Spain".

2. RAV SA'ADIA GAON IN A RESPONSUM

In a responsum quoted in one version of *Seder Rav Amram Gaon* (Babylon, d. 875), Rav Sa'adia Gaon states that **three** verses are recited aloud: 8:15, 8:16 and 10:3 and he explains in great detail just how the reader and the congregation carry out this responsive reading (*Seder Rav Amram Hashalem,* Vol. 2, p. 178 = *Seder Rav Amram Gaon,* ed. Goldschmidt, pp. 101-102). It is clear from the difference in style and substance that Rav Sa'adia could not have stated these two different customs. It can be assumed that the second custom was stated by one of the Geonim and that the attribution is incorrect, as frequently occurs in geonic responsa.[2]

3. RAV KALONYMUS THE ELDER (SPEYER, 12TH CENTURY) OR RASHI (FRANCE, 1040-1104)[3]

This brief ruling is quoted by **many** medieval *poskim*. *Ma'aseh Hageonim* (ed. Epstein, p. 46) and *Sefer Hapardess* (ed. Ehrenreich,

1. See B. M. Lewin, *Otzar Hageonim* to *Megillah,* Jerusalem, 1933, p. 32, who should have stressed this point. Indeed, many scholars doubt the validity and accuracy of the Auerbach edition of *Sefer Ha'eshkol* – see *Encyclopaedia Judaica,* Vol. 2, col. 147 and the Introduction to the Albeck edition of *Sefer Ha'eshkol,* p. III.
2. See Robert Brody, *The Geonim of Babylonia and the Shaping of Medieval Jewish Culture,* New Haven and London, 1998, pp. 197-201.
3. See *Teshuvot Rashi,* ed. Elfenbein, New York, 1943, No. 130, pp. 157-158. His list of sources is very helpful, but it is difficult to understand which version of the *teshuvah* he actually copied.

p. 254) attribute it to Rabbi Kalonymus. *Maḥzor Vitry* (p. 210); *Siddur Rashi* (pp. 167-168); and *Shibboley Haleket* (p. 157) = *Tanya Rabbati* (ed. Horowitz, pp. 83-84 = ed. Baron, Jeruslaem, 2011, p. 150) attribute it to Rashi. It is later quoted as the "custom of France and Provence" by *Sefer Hamanhig* (Toledo, 1204, ed. Rafael, Vol. 1, p. 243) which is later quoted by *Sefer Abudraham*. It is also quoted without attribution by *Haggahot Maimoniot* (Germany, ca. 1290) to Maimonides, *Hilkhot Megillah,* Chapter 1, end of paragraph 7 and again at the end of Chapter 2, from whence it is quoted by Rabbi Moshe Isserles (Cracow, 1525-1572) in his *Darkey Moshe* to *Tur* OH 690 and in his glosses to *Shulḥan Arukh* OH 690:17 (and cf. 690:4). It is also quoted without attribution by *Orḥot Ḥayyim* (Provence, 14th century, Vol. 1, *Hilkhot Purim*, paragraph 30).

This is the Rabbi Kalonymus version of the custom:

> What the congregation is accustomed to recite in unison – "A Jewish man" (Esther 2:5), "And Mordekhai went out" (Esther 8:15), "For Mordekhai the Jew" (Esther 10:3) during the recitation of the Megillah – it is not a requirement or a custom but it is a rejoicing of the children (i.e., it is intended to make the children rejoice).

II. The Flexibility of the Verses Recited Aloud

As can be seen from the sources above, the list of verses recited aloud is not fixed; it even varies from version to version of the same source. This is hinted at in *Sefer Ha'ittur* (Provence, 12th century, Vol. 2, p. 224) which states that the congregation says aloud "some verses". The confusion is especially obvious in *Sefer Hamanhig*. Manuscript A in the Refael edition states that there are **three** verses and then proceeds to list **four**; the other manuscripts do not mention the number **three**; while *Sefer Abudraham* which quotes *Sefer Hamanhig,* explicitly mentions the number **four**! Indeed, *Orḥot Ḥayyim* mentions the custom of reciting four verses aloud and adds: "And there are places where they do not say 'A Jewish man' (2:5) and they say other verses **and everything**

follows the custom". The chart below summarizes many of the customs:

The Source	**2:4**	**2:5**	**6:1**	**7:9**	**7:10**	**8:15**	**8:16**	**9:32**	**10:3**
Rav Sa'adia's Siddur	-	-	-	-	-	-	x	-	x
Custom in Spain (Abudraham)	-	-	-	-	-	-	x	-	x
Rav Sa'adia's Responsum	-	-	-	-	-	x	x	-	x
Kalonymus, *Ma'aseh Hageonim*	-	x	-	-	-	x	-	-	x
Kalonymus – *Sefer Hapardess*	-	x	-	-	-	x	-	-	x
Rashi in *Maḥzor Vitry*	-	x	-	-	-	x	-	-	x
Rashi in *Siddur Rashi*	-	x	-	-	-	x	x	-	x
Rashi in *Shibolei Haleket*	-	x	-	-	x	-	x	-	x
Rashi in *Tanya Rabbati*	-	x	-	-	x	-	x	-	x
Sefer Hamanhig	-	x	-	-	-	x	x	-	x
Sefer Abudraham	-	x	-	-	-	x	x	-	x
Orḥot Ḥayyim	-	x	-	-	-	x	x	-	x
Haggahot Maimoniot	-	x	-	-	-	x	x	-	x
Rabbi Moshe Isserles	-	x	-	-	-	x	x	-	x
Iraq[4]	-	x	x	-	-	x	x	-	-
Gruzia (Georgia)	-	x	x	-	-	x	x	x	10:1-3
Sefaradim in Jerusalem	-	x	x	-	-	-	x	-	x
Kurdistan	x	x	x	-	-	8:14-16		x	10:1-3
Libya	-	x	x	x	-	x	x	-	x
Cochin	2:3-5, 22-23		5:14-6:1			8:14-16			9:31-10:3
Djerba	-	x	x	x	-	x	x	9:6-10	10:1-3
Rabbi Shemtob Gaguine (Israel, Syria, Turkey, Egypt)	-	x	x	-	-	x	x	-	x
Rabbi Ḥayyim David Halevi	-	x	x	-	-	x	x	-	x
Rabbi Yitzḥak Yosef	-	x	x	-	-	x	x	-	x

4. This section of this chart is based on the following sources: Asher Wassertil, editor, *Yalkut Minhagim*, third expanded edition, Jerusalem, 1996, pp. 174, 254, 325, 352, 381, 487, 526; Rabbi Shemtob Gaguine, *Keter Shem Tov*, Vols. I-II, Kaidan, 1934, pp. 540-541; Rabbi Ḥayyim David Halevi, *Mekor Ḥayyim Hashalem*, Vol. 4, no date, pp. 354-355; Rabbi Yitzḥak Yosef, *Sefer Yalkut Yoseph*, Vol. 5, Jerusalem, 1988, p. 299.

III. Explanations for the Custom

Both versions of Rav Sa'adia Gaon offer no reason for this custom. The other early sources quoted, offer a number of different reasons:

1. Rabbi Kalonymus = Rashi: To cause the children to rejoice.

2. *Shibbolei Haleket* = *Tanya Rabbati* adds an additional sentence to Rashi's words, which may be part of the original teaching:

> ... but it is a rejoicing of the children and noises before them so that they should rejoice, and also when they see a change in behavior like this, they ask: "What is this?" and, as a result, you come to tell the miracles of the Creator so that they will hear and learn to fear Him all the days [of their lives].

This explanation is reminiscent of the requirement "to teach your child" (Exodus 13:8) on Pesaḥ, but there is no such requirement on Purim. In any case, it really comes to explain the custom of blotting out Haman's name which was mentioned earlier in Rashi's teaching.

3. *Sefer Abudraham* quotes the author of *Mishmeret Hamo'adot* who gives three reasons for reciting verses aloud:

a. to wake a person up, that he should not fall asleep;

b. "we recite these verses because they are written regarding Mordekhai and in his honor because the miracle was through him";

c. "and even the last verse [of the Book of Esther] must waken us to have *kavanah* [=intent] for the last blessing and in honor of Mordekhai".

The explanation regarding staying awake is once again borrowed from Pesaḥ (*Pesaḥim* 109a), but makes no sense in the context of a very noisy Megillah reading.

4. *Orḥot Ḥayyim* says that we read aloud four verses of *Ge'ulah* [=redemption] in order to do *pirsum haness* – to publicize the miracle.

Thus, we remain with two convincing explanations of the early versions of this custom:

a. Verses 2:15, 8:15 and 10:3 – the three verses in the Rabbi Kalonymus/Rashi version – honor Mordekhai because the miracle was achieved through him.

b. Verse 7:10 in the *Shibboley Haleket* = *Tanya Rabbati* version and 8:16, which appears in most of the early sources, are verses of redemption which talk about the hanging of Haman and about the rejoicing of the Jews.

IV. The Role of Esther in the Purim Story

Needless to say, Mordekhai did not act alone. The Megillah itself repeatedly stresses the pivotal role of Esther. See, for example, verses 2:4, 7, 10, 15-17, 22; 4:15-17; 5:1-8; 7:1-8; 8:3-6; 9:12-13, 29-32.

Indeed, the Sages repeatedly stressed the pivotal role of Esther: she was one of seven prophetesses of the Jewish people (*Megillah* 14a). She "wore" the holy spirit (*ibid.*, 14b). She ate only kosher food in the king's house (*Yalkut Esther*, paragraph 1053). She prayed to God before going to see Aḥashverosh (*Esther Rabbah* 8:7). When Mordekhai told her that her three-day fast falls on Pesaḥ, she replied: "Wise one of Israel, if the Jewish people is destroyed, who will observe Pesaḥ!?" (*ibid.*, 8:6). Esther gave light to the Jewish people like the light of dawn (*Midrash Shoḥar Tov* 22:3, 6). "Esther is the end of all miracles" (*Yoma* 29a).

V. Reciting Verses Aloud in Honor of Esther

In light of the above, it is perfectly permissible to recite aloud four verses of redemption related to Esther:

a. Reciting verses aloud is a custom, not a Talmudic law.

b. The list of verses was in constant flux from the 10th to the 20th centuries.

c. *Orḥot Ḥayyim* stressed in the early 14th century that they recite different verses in different places "and everything follows the custom".

d. The original verses were selected to honor Mordekhai for his pivotal role in the miracle of Purim and to stress the redemption of the Jewish people. Esther played an equally pivotal role as emphasized by the Book of Esther and by the Sages; it is certainly appropriate to honor her in a similar fashion.

e. Finally, the Jews of Georgia, Kurdistan and Cochin recited verse 9:32 aloud in honor of Esther, and the Jews of Kurdistan and Cochin added verse 2:4 as well. It should be added that there is also an Ashkenazic custom of reciting verses 2:4 and 2:17 with a special tune, so someone realized their importance hundreds of years ago.

Therefore, I would suggest the following four verses:

1. Esther 2:4 "And let the maiden who pleases Your Majesty be queen instead of Vashti. The proposal pleased the king and he acted upon it".

2. Esther 2:7 "He was foster father for Hadassah – that is, Esther – his uncle's daughter, for she had neither father nor mother. The maiden was shapely and beautiful; and when her father and mother died, Mordekhai adopted her as his own daughter".

3. Esther 2:17 "The king loved Esther more than all the other women, and she won his grace and favor more than all the virgins. So he set a royal diadem on her head and made her queen instead of Vashti".

4. Esther 9:32 "And Esther's ordinance validating these observances of Purim was recorded in a scroll".

VI. Conclusion

In light of the countless rocket attacks on innocent civilians in Sderot and Ashkelon since June 2007 and of the horrific murder of eight children at the Merkaz Harav Yeshivah a week ago, we are reminded that we are still very far from *Ge'ulah* [=Redemption]. As we recite the four traditional verses of *Ge'ulah* connected to Mordekhai or four additional verses connected to Esther, we hope and pray to God for the realization of one of the verses of redemption (Esther 8:16): "The Jews enjoyed light and gladness, happiness and honor" – so may it be with us!"

David Golinkin
Jerusalem
9 *Adar* II 5768

9. WOMEN AS *MOHALOT*[1]

Yoreh De'ah 264

Question: *May women serve as Mohalot?*

Responsum:

I. The Biblical Period

Circumcision is one of the first *mitzvot* mentioned in the Torah (Genesis, Chapter 17). Interestingly enough, the second mention of this *mitzvah* (Exodus 4:24-26) relates how Tzipporah circumcised her son in the encampment on the road from Midyan to Egypt:

> At a night encampment on the way, the Lord encountered him [=Moses] and sought to kill him. So Tzipporah took a flint and cut off her son's foreskin, and touched his legs with it, saying, "You are truly a bridegroom of blood to me!" And when the Lord let him alone, she added, "A bridegroom of blood because of the circumcision".[1a]

The Sages viewed Tzipporah's act with favor. In the midrash (*Shemot Rabbah* 5:8, ed. Shinan, pp. 157-158) Tzipporah says: "for behold I have performed the *mitzvah*". One could derive from this biblical story that women may **always** perform a *brit* **or** that a woman can do so *bedi'avad,* after the fact, when there is no choice, e.g. in order to save Moses's life.

1. Brief references below refer to the Bibliography which follows.
1a. For a 14th century illustration of Tzipporah circumcising her son, see *The Rylands Haggadah*, Tel Aviv, 1988, fol. 14a. My thanks to David Oberman for pointing this out to me.

II. The Second Temple Period

The Book of Maccabees contains a story about women being killed for circumcising their sons. II Maccabees 6:12 relates that two women were murdered by the Greek-Syrians "for circumcising their sons". The parallel verse in I Maccabees 1:60-61 says that the women "who circumcised their sons" were murdered "along with those who circumcised them". This makes it sound like the women told **others** to circumcise their children. Finally, the Aramaic work *Megillat Antiochus,* which seems to have been written in *Eretz Yisrael* sometime between the 2nd-5th centuries, says (v. 35-36) that a woman "circumcised her son on the eighth day" and then jumped from the city wall together with her baby and they both died.[2] Thus, two out of these three sources relate that women circumcised their sons during the Maccabean revolt against the Greek-Syrians. This might indicate that women may **always** perform a *brit milah* **or** this might indicate that women performed circumcision only in times of persecution.

III. The Rabbinic Period

1. A *baraita* which appears in *Tosefta Shabbat* (6:8, ed. Lieberman, p. 70 and parallel sources[3]) talks about a woman who gave birth to male children and they were circumcised and died. "**She** circumcised one and he died, **she** circumcised the second and he died" etc. "A story is told of four sisters in Tzippori – **the first one** circumcised and he died, **the second [sister]** circumcised and he died, **the third [sister]** circumcised and he died", etc. The third story is told by the *Tanna* Rabbi Nattan about when he was in Cappadocia (*Tur*key). "**[She]** circumcised the first son and he died, the second one and he died", etc.

In all of these cases, it sounds like the mother **herself** performed the circumcision. Furthermore, these are all cases of

2. See Ziv, p. 40 and notes 5-7.
3. The parallel sources are *Shabbat* 134a; *Ḥullin* 47b; *Yerushalmi Yevamot* Chapter 6, fol. 7d and cf. *Shir Hashirim Rabbah* 7:3 quoted by Ziv, pp. 41-42.

lekhatḥilah, before the fact, and not *bedi'avad,* after the fact, as might have been the case in Exodus or in Maccabees.

2. The primary talmudic source about women serving as *Mohalot* is found in *Avodah Zarah* 27a:

> It has been stated: Whence could it be deduced that circumcision performed by a non-Jew is invalid? Daru bar Pappa said in the name of Rav: [From the words,] "And as for thee, thou shall keep my covenant" [Genesis 17:9]; while Rabbi Yoḥanan [deduces it from the words] *"himol yimol"* [*ibid.* v. 13, as if it says *hamol yimol*] – "he who is circumcised shall circumcise". What is the difference between them?...
> We must therefore say that the case wherein they differ is that of a woman. According to the one who relies on "Thou shall keep my covenant" [i.e., Rav], the qualification is not there, since a woman cannot be circumcised, while according to the one who relies on "he who is circumcised shall circumcise" [i.e., Rabbi Yoḥanan], the qualification is there, for a woman is like one who is circumcised. But does anyone hold that a woman is not [qualified to perform circumcision]? Does not scripture say, "So Tzipporah took a flint" [Exodus 4:25]? Read it as if it says "she caused to be taken". But it also says "And [she] cut off"? Read it as if it says "and she caused it to be cut off", by asking a man to do it. Or you may say it means that she only began and Moses came and completed it.

According to this passage, Rav, a first generation Babylonian *amora,* would **forbid** women to perform a *brit milah,* while Rabbi Yoḥanan, a second generation Israeli *amora,* would **allow** women to perform a *brit milah.*

Most of those who permit a woman to perform a *brit milah* base themselves on the well-known talmudic principle (*Beitzah* 4a) that when Rav and Rabbi Yoḥanan disagree, the *halakhah* follows Rabbi Yoḥanan. Some also rely on the biblical precedent of Tzipporah.

One of the few sources which prohibits women from performing a *brit milah* (*Tosafot* to *Avodah Zarah* 27a, s.v. *ishah*) says that Rav is correct because his verse is favored by the *Tanna* Rabbi Judah the Prince earlier in the *sugya* when he forbids **non-Jews** from performing *milah*.

IV. Medieval Authorities

Ya'akov Spiegel and Yossi Ziv have examined many medieval codes, midrashim and *piyyutim* written between the 8th-16th centuries and divided them into three groups.[4] We have added a few additional *poskim*:

A. Thirteen sources permit women to serve as *mohalot lekhatḥilah*, before the fact, without any conditions: Rav Aḥai Gaon, *She'iltot*, Babylon, ca. 750; *Sefer Basar Al Gabei Geiḥalim*, late Geonic Period; *Midrash Lekaḥ Tov; Midrash Sekhel Tov; Midrash Haḥefetz;* Rabbi Avraham ben Yitzḥak *Av Beit Din* of Narbonne as quoted in *Tamim De'im*, d. 1179; Rabbi Eleazar of Metz, *Sefer Yerei'im*, France, d. 1198; Rabbi Moshe of Coucy, *Sefer Mitzvot Gadol*, France, d. 1236; Rabbi Yitzḥak ben Moshe of Vienna, *Or Zaru'a*, Vienna, d. 1250; Rabbi Mordekhai ben Hillel Hakohen, the *Mordekhai*, Germany, d. 1298; Rabbi Meir Hakohen of Rothenburg, *Haggahot Maimoniot*, Germany, ca. 1300; Rabbi Menaḥem Recanati, Italy, late 13th century(?); Rabbi Isaiah di Trani the Elder, Italy, 13th century.

B. Twenty-six sources permit women to serve as *mohalot bedi'avad*, after the fact, if there is no man present who knows how to circumcise: Rabbi Shimon Kayara, *Halakhot Gedolot*, Babylon, ca. 825; Rav Amram Gaon, ca. 858 (quoted in *Siddur*

4. Spiegel, pp. 150-154; Ziv, pp. 43-46. Due to the large number of sources, I have not repeated the exact references which can be found in the footnotes of their articles.

Rabbeinu Shlomo b"r Nattan, Jerusalem, 1995, p. 142); Rabbi Tzemaḥ Gaon, ca. 872 (see Spiegel, note 17); Rabbi Yitzḥak Alfasi, Morocco and Spain, 1013-1103; Rabbi Avraham ben Yitzḥak *Av Beit Din* of Narbonne, *Sefer Ha'eshkol*, Provence, d. 1179; Rabbi Yitzḥak ben Abba Mari, *Sefer Ha'ittur*, Provence, d. 1190; Rabbi Aaron Hakohen of Lunel, *Orḥot Ḥayyim*, Provence, ca. 1300; *Kol Bo*, Provence, ca. 1300; Rambam, Egypt, d. 1204; Rabbi Eliezer ben Yoel Halevi, *Sefer Ra'aviyah*, Germany, d. 1225; Rabbi Avraham bar Yitzḥak Hakohen (see Spiegel, p. 152); Rabbi Ya'akov Hagozer; Rabbi Gershom b"r Ya'akov Hagozer; Rabbi Tzidkiyahu ben Avraham Anav, *Shibboley Haleket*, Italy, 13th century; Rabbi Ḥayyim ben Shmuel, *Tzror Haḥayyim*, Spain, 14th century; Rabbi Menaḥem Hame'iri, *Beit Habeḥirah*, Provence, d. 1315; Rabbi Eshtori Hafarḥi, *Kaftor Vaferaḥ*, Israel, ca. 1322; Rabbeinu Asher, Toledo, d. 1327; Ritva, Spain, d. 1330 (see Spiegel, note 11); Rabbi Ya'akov ben Asher, *Arba'ah Turim*, Toledo, d. 1343; Rabbeinu Yeruḥam, *Toledot Adam Veḥavah*, Toledo, d. 1350 (see Spiegel, *ibid.*); Rabbeinu Nissim Gerondi, Spain, d. 1380 (see Spiegel, *ibid.*); Rabbi Menaḥem ibn Zeraḥ, *Tzeidah Laderekh*, Spain, d. 1385 (see Spiegel, *ibid.*); Rabbi Yisrael Alnakawa, *Menorat Hama'or*, Toledo, d. 1391; Rabbi Yosef ibn Ḥaviva, *Nimukei Yosef*, Spain, early 15th century; Rabbi Yosef Karo, *Shulḥan Arukh*, Israel, d. 1575.

C. Six sources prohibit women from performing a *brit milah*: *Tosafot* to *Avodah Zarah* 27a; *Tosafot Rabbeinu Elḥanan, ibid.*; *Tosafot Shantz ibid.*; Rabbi Yitzḥak of Corbeil, *Sefer Mitzvot Katan*, France, d. 1280; Rabbi Isaiah di Trani the Younger, Riaz, Italy, d. 1280 (see Spiegel, note 9); and cf. Rabbi Moshe Isserles, *Shulḥan Arukh*, Cracow, d. 1572.

V. Why Did the Strict Approach Prevail?

If women in the Bible, Second Temple Period and Tannaitic Period performed *brit milah;* and if Rabbi Yoḥanan allowed it and the *halakhah* normally follows Rabbi Yoḥanan; and if so many medieval *poskim* allowed this before or after the fact – then why do we not hear about women actually performing *brit milah* in the medieval period?

Yossi Ziv (pp. 46-49) tried to clear up the mystery by examining the customs of Ethiopian Jewry which he culled from 38 interviews conducted in Israel in the years 1999-2003. After an Ethiopian Jewish woman gives birth, she is ritually impure for 40 days for a son and for 80 days for a daughter. She leaves her home with the baby and lives outside the village in "a house of a woman in confinement". Female relatives go with her to help her. Since she and her nursing baby are still impure on the eighth day, she or one of the other women performs the *brit milah*. It is never done by a man, because he would become ritually impure by touching the baby. On the 40th day for a boy or the 80th day for a girl, the mother and baby immerse in a river and become pure.

Ziv surmises that the Ethiopians preserved the original Palestinian customs of ritual purity, as reflected in the ruling of Rabbi Yoḥanan, that women may perform *milah*. In Babylon, the laws of purity had already disappeared, hence Rav ruled that a woman may **not** perform *brit milah*.

This is an interesting theory, but it does not hold up to careful scrutiny:

1. It is impossible to determine the origin of Ethiopian Jews, but many scholars agree that they were Ethiopians of Agau origin who adopted an Israelite identity at some point. Most of their beliefs and practices have parallels in the Ethiopian Orthodox Church. They usually follow biblical or apocryphal literature as opposed to talmudic or medieval Jewish custom.[5]

2. There is no hint in *Avodah Zarah* 27a that there is a connection between the laws of purity and women performing *brit milah*. Indeed, Rav and Rabbi Yoḥanan were actually discussing whether a **non-Jew** can perform *brit milah*; it is the *stam hatalmud*

5. See Steven Kaplan in: Michael Corinaldi, *Jewish Identity: The Case of Ethiopian Jewry*, Jerusalem, 1998, pp. 152-160.

or anonymous editor of the Talmud who transfers their argument to women and *brit milah*.

3. If the Ethiopian custom was related to Rabbi Yoḥanan, the latter would have **obligated** women to perform *brit milah*, not **allowed** it.

4. Rather, the reason that most rabbis limited the performance of *brit milah* to women *bedi'avad* or forbade it seems to be the general tendency by medieval rabbis to prevent women from performing *mitzvot* which the Talmud allows or even requires them to do. Good examples are *tefillin, tzitzit, Kiddush* on Friday night, and women as the *sandek* at the circumcision ceremony.[6]

VI. Practical *Halakhah*

There is no question that it is perfectly permissible for Jewish women to perform *brit milah lekhatḥilah*, before the fact. This is based on:

a. the precedents of Tzipporah, the Book of Maccabees, and the *beraita*;

b. the talmudic *sugya* in *Avodah Zarah* 27a – when Rav disagrees with Rabbi Yoḥanan, the *halakhah* follows Rabbi Yoḥanan;

c. thirteen medieval *poskim* who rule according to item b, before the fact;

6. Regarding *tefillin*, see above, Chapter 1. Regarding *tzitzit*, see *She'elot Uteshuvot Maharil Haḥadashot*, No. 7; Rabbi Moshe Feinstein, *Iggerot Moshe, Oraḥ Ḥayyim*, Part 4, No. 49; Aviva Cayam in: *Jewish Legal Writings by Women*, Jerusalem, 1998, pp. 119-142. Regarding *Kiddush*, see Rabbi Eliezer Berkovits, *Jewish Women in Time and Torah*, Hoboken, 1990, pp. 92-100. Regarding women as the *sandek*, see Daniel Sperber, *Minhagei Yisrael*, Vol. 1, Jerusalem, 1989, pp. 60-66 and Baumgarten, pp. 65-77.

d. there is **no** talmudic basis for permitting this only *bedi'avad*, after the fact, and the ultimate authority in Jewish law is the Babylonian Talmud.[7]

David Golinkin
Jerusalem
29 *Sivan* 5769

7. See above, pp. 112-114. Some of the *Rishonim* say that the idea of *bedi'avad* is based on the story of Tzipporah – but the Talmud makes no such claim.

BIBLIOGRAPHY

Baumgarten	Elisheva Baumgarten, *Mothers and Children: Jewish Family Life in Medieval Europe,* Princeton and Oxford, 2004, p. 65
Grossman	Avraham Grossman, *Ḥassidot Umordot,* Jerusalem, 2001, pp. 331-332
Rubin	Nisan Rubin, *Reishit Haḥayyim,* Tel Aviv, 1995, p. 91
Sperber	Rabbi Daniel Sperber, *Minhagei Yisrael,* Vol. 1, Jerusalem, 1989, p. 66, note 18 and Vol. 4, Jerusalem, 2001, pp. 8-9
Spiegel	Ya'akov Spiegel, "*Ha'ishah Kemohelet*", *Sidra* 5 (1989), pp. 149-157
Ziv	Yossi Ziv, "*Milah Beedey Ha'ishah*", *Netu'im* 11-12 (*Elul* 5764), pp. 39-54

10. THE PARTICIPATION OF WOMEN IN FUNERALS

Yoreh De'ah 359:1-2

Question from Rabbi Matthew Futterman of Congregation Netzaḥ Yisrael, Ashkelon: *In Ashkelon, Ashdod, Jerusalem and other places in Israel, there are various burial customs whose purpose is to separate men and women or to prevent the participation of women in the burial service. One custom uses a physical meḥitzah to separate men and women during the eulogy. According to another, men and women accompany the deceased from the "eulogy hall" to the grave in separate groups. According to a third custom, women attend the funeral service in the "eulogy hall", but the Ḥevrah Kaddisha prevents them – even immediate relatives of the deceased – from going near the grave and participating in the burial service. According to a fourth custom, women participate neither in the funeral nor in the burial. These customs, especially the latter ones, cause real anguish to the female relatives of the deceased – mothers, wives and daughters – and, in many cases, are contrary to the wishes of the deceased themselves. What is the source of these customs? Are they obligatory? Is it possible to rule otherwise?*

Responsum:

I. Separation Customs – Development and Reasons

1. In YD 359:1-2, Rabbi Yosef Karo rules as follows:

> 1) Where it is customary for woman to go out before the bier, they do so;
> where it is customary for them to go out behind the bier, they do so;

and now it is customary for them to go out only behind the bier, and this should not be changed.
2) One should prevent women from going out to the cemetery behind the bier.

Anyone studying these paragraphs immediately senses that "whoever taught one, did not teach the other". According to paragraph 1, women were accustomed to go out before or behind the bier, but "now" it is customary for them to go out behind the bier (and we shall see below that the original meaning was to go out to the cemetery), whereas according to paragraph 2, one "should prevent women from going out to the cemetery".

Indeed, in the *Beit Yosef* to *Tur* YD 359, Rabbi Yosef Karo cites three different sources: (1) *Sanhedrin* 20a: "Our Rabbis taught: where it is customary for women to go out before the bier, they do so; after the bier, they do so". (2) Yerushalmi *Sanhedrin* 2:4, fol. 20b: "Some *Tannaim* teach that the women go first and the men behind them, and some *Tannaim* teach that the men go first and the women behind them. The one who says the women go first, this is because they caused death in the world [due to Eve's sin]; the one who says that the men go first, this is because of the honor of the daughters of Israel, that the men should not gaze at the women. (3) And finally, Rabbi Yosef Karo adds:[1] "And in the *Zohar Parashat Vayakhel* it says **that one should prevent women from going out to the cemetery because if they go out they cause evil to the world, and therefore it is appropriate to prevent them**".

If so, according to Rabbi Yosef Karo, it is permissible according to both Talmuds for women to go to the cemetery, but it is appropriate to prevent this accepted custom because, according to the *Zohar*, this causes evil to the world.

1. It is, however, likely that both customs derive from Hellenistic culture – see William Smith, *Dictionary of Greek and Roman Antiquities*, second edition, London, 1865, pp. 555, 558-559; H. Blümner, *The Home Life of the Ancient Greeks*, London, Paris and Melbourne, 1893, p. 251; Oskar Seyffert, *A Dictionary of Classical Antiquities*, New York, 1956, p. 101.

2. Rabbi Yosef Karo's rulings were accepted as *halakhah* by many of the *Aḥaronim*,[2] but his rulings were understood in two different ways. In some communities, they apparently permitted women to go after the bier in a **funeral procession**, but prevented them from entering the **cemetery**.[3] However, in most communities, they prevented women from going after the bier **at all**. In other words, the women remained at home and attended neither the funeral service nor the burial service.[4]

2. Rabbi Mordechai Yaffe, *Halevush, Ateret Zahav, Hilkhot Kevurah*, paragraph 359; *Ḥiddushei Rabbi Akiva Eiger* to YD 359; Rabbi Avraham Danzig, *Ḥokhmat Adam* 155:25; Rabbi Yeḥiel Michel Epstein, *Arukh Hashulḥan* to YD 359; Rabbi Ḥayyim David Halevi, *Mekor Ḥayyim Hashalem*, 282:7, Part 5, p. 373.
3. This **may** have been the custom already in the time of the Maharil (d. 1427) in Ashkenaz – see *Minhagei Maharil*, ed. Spitzer, Jerusalem, 5749, pp. 606-607, on his daughter's participation in his wife's funeral. Rabbi Hillel ben Naftali Hertz (Lithuania, 1615-1690) in *Beit Hillel* to YD 359 testifes: "And so I saw the custom of the *Sefaradim* when I was *Av Beit Din* and *Rosh Metivta* in the holy community of Hamburg". He apparently meant that women go to the funeral, but not to the cemetery.
4. Rabbi Aharon Berakhya of Modena, *Ma'aver Yabok, Ma'amar Siftei Renanot*, Chapter 10, ed. Vilna, 1896, p. 210 testifies: "and there are some places where women do not go out after the bier at all". Rabbi Avraham Ḥayyim Adadi, *Vayikra Avraham*, Livorno, 1861, fol. 126c (who is then quoted by Rabbi Ḥayyim Sithon, *Eretz Ḥayyim*, Jerusalem, 1908, p. 228) testifies: "In the holy city of Safed, may it be rebuilt speedily, women do not go out at all, neither before the bier nor behind it, and even women in the market or outside their courtyards when the bier is carried past, enter a concealed place". A.M. Luncz, *Jerusalem* 1 (1882), p. 13, testifies that in Jerusalem "the sextons of the community supervise that... women do not go behind the bier". Rabbi David Sasson, *Massa Bavel*, ed. Benayahu, Jerusalem, 5715, p. 206, testifies that in Baghdad "they do not permit women to participate in a funeral unless it is the funeral of a great Rabbi". Rabbi Shem Tob Gaguine, *Keter Shem Tov*, Keidan, 1934, p. 662, paragraph 19, testifies that in Israel, Syria, Turkey, Egypt and London, women do not go behind the bier. Rabbi Amram Aburbia, *Netivei Am*, second edition, Tel Aviv, 5729, p. 350, testifies that "the custom in Jerusalem is not to allow women to go after the deceased, and they do not even permit them to look at the coffin from the balcony". Finally, Rabbi Yosef Kafiḥ, *Halikhot Teiman*, third edition, Jerusalem, 1982, p. 249 reports: "Women do not go out after the bier at

3. Rabbi Avraham Eliezer Hershowitz (*Sefer Otzar Kol Minhagei Yeshurun*, second edition, Lwow, 5690, 73:5, p. 313) mentions the *Shulḥan Arukh* and the *Zohar* and adds:

> the reason for this is that during the eulogy and the burial men and women mingle and push each other and one must worry about forbidden thoughts in a place appropriate to think about repentance... **and, in order to frighten the masses, they gave an explanation that they thought would be accepted.**

In other words, according to him, the real reason for keeping women away from the men is forbidden thoughts, and the *Zohar* only invented its explanation in order to frighten the simple folk.

4. Some *Aḥaronim* relate that there is a custom whereby women do not go to the cemetery during their menstrual period and they even support this custom.[5]

Thus, Rabbi Yosef Karo recommended to prevent women from going to the cemetery based on the *Zohar* "because if they go out, they cause evil to the world". Many *poskim* accepted his recommendation and many communities acted accordingly. One *posek* argued that the real reason for the custom is the fear of forbidden thoughts, and several *poskim* added a prohibition against menstruating women entering the cemetery.

However, if we carefully examine Talmudic literature and the *poskim*, we will find that most of the customs described in the question are contrary both to *halakhah* and to the actual practice

all, regardless of whether it is the bier of a man or a woman". Rabbi Refael Aharon ibn Shimon, *Nehar Mitzraim*, Na Amon, 1908, fol. 141a testifies: "How good, nice and pleasant is the Egyptian custom that no woman goes out after the bier at all, not in the city nor in the cemetery...". For other customs of Sefardic Jews, see Rabbi Herbert Dobrinsky, *A Treasury of Sephardic Laws and Customs*, Hoboken and New York, 1986, pp. 71, 90, 100.

5. Rabbi Yekutiel Greenwald, *Kol Bo Al Aveilut*, Part 1, Jerusalem and New York, 1973, pp. 167-168, refers to *Pitḥei Teshuvah* to YD 195, subparagraph 19 and *Ḥayyei Adam* 3:38. Yedidya Dinari, *Teudah* 3 (5743), pp. 35-36, cites another six *Aḥaronim* who hold the same view.

both in the Talmudic era and in the days of the *Rishonim* until the time of Rabbi Yosef Karo. We will see that there is no *posek* who demands separation during the eulogy.[6] We will see that the *Zohar* itself does not prohibit women from going to the cemetery, rather it **cautions** men **not to look** at the women during the funeral and burial. And even if we determine that there is a contradiction between the Bavli and the *Zohar*, the *halakhah* must be decided according to the Talmud. We will also see that there is no fear of forbidden thoughts in the cemetery and there is no halakhic source before the nineteenth century which prohibits menstruating women from entering a cemetery. Likewise, we will see that those who follow most of the customs described in the question force the daughters of Israel to violate the prohibition of *lo'eg larash* [mocking the unfortunate], they disregard *kevod haberiyot* [human dignity], and forget that during the eulogy and burial, we are obligated to respect the wishes of the deceased. And now we shall prove these assertions one by one.

II. Women always participated in funerals and burials from Biblical times until the time of Rabbi Yosef Karo.[7]

There is no shadow of a doubt that in ancient times women not only participated in funerals and burials, but also fulfilled a key role during these ceremonies. In the Biblical and Mishnaic periods, there were professional female lamenters.[8] Similarly, we

6. Regarding seperation of men and women in the Second Temple during *Simḥat Beit Hashoevah*, see *Zekhariah* 12:12-14 as explained in Yerushalmi *Sukkah* 5:2, fol. 55b and Bavli *Sukkah* 51b-52a and our discussion below, Chapter 14. However, I did not find any *posek* requiring separation during eulogies.
7. This paragraph is based on Ḥ. Y. Ehrenreich, *Otzar Haḥayyim* 7 (5691), pp. 125-126; *Ha'entziklopedia Hamikra'it*, s.v. אבל, קינה, קינות; Shmuel Safrai, *Beshilhei Habayit Hasheni Ubitekufat Hamishnah*, Jerusalem, 5743, pp. 82-85, 99. I thank my friend, Prof. Daniel Schwartz, who suggested that I look at Safrai's book.
8. Jeremiah 9:16-21; Ezekiel 32:16; II Chronicles 35:25; Mishnah *Ketubot* 4:4,

hear in the Talmudic period of women mourners – not professional lamenters – who clap hands as a sign of grief, sing dirges, and lament.[9] We have no explicit evidence about **where** the lamentations took place, but it is very difficult to assume that women fulfilled such a central role in the mourning rites but were not permitted to participate in the funeral or approach the burial site.

Indeed, there is much specific evidence showing that women participated in the funeral "before the bier" or "behind the bier". In addition to the *beraitot* from Bavli and Yerushalmi *Sanhedrin* cited by Rabbi Yosef Karo (above, p. 213), mention should be made of the words of the *Tanna* Rabbi Yehoshua in *Avot Derabi Nattan,* which are similar to one of the traditions in the Yerushalmi: **"For what reason do women go out in front of the bier?** What do they say? We caused all those who come into the world that they [will come] here".[10]

Moreover, women not only participated in every **funeral**, but also in the **burial ceremony**. We learn in a *beraita* which appears twice in the Bavli (*Mo'ed Kattan* 24a-b and *Kiddushin* 80b) and in an expanded version in Tractate *Semaḥot* 3:2 (ed. Higger, New York, 1931, pp. 109-110 and ed. Zlotnick, New Haven and London, 1966, p. 5 on the Hebrew side – I am quoting the latter edition):

> [A one-day-old child who dies] is buried without a coffin,

which is the source for *Semaḥot* 14:7, ed. Higger, p. 206; *Tosefta Nedarim* 2:7, ed. Lieberman, p. 105; *Tosefta Yevamot* 14:17, *ibid.*, p. 53; *Sanhedrin* 47a; *Nashei Deshekhnatziv* in *Moed Kattan,* 28b. Regarding women lamenters in fourteenth-century Saragossa, see the *Responsa of the Ribash,* No. 158. Regarding women lamenters among Oriental Jewish communities until today, see Yehudah Bergman, *Hafolklore Hayehudi,* Jerusalem, 5713, pp. 40-41 and Rabbi Yeḥiel Michel Tukachinsky, *Gesher Haḥayyim,* Part 1, p. 122, note 3. In Yiddish, the women lamenters were called ווייַנערן.

9. Mishnah *Moed Katan* 3:8; *Megillah* 3b; and cf. *Tosefta Kelim Bava Batra,* 2:8, ed. Zuckermandel, p. 592.
10. Version 2, Chapter 9, ed. Schechter, p. 25 – and from there mistakenly on p. 117 – and with changes in *Bereishit Rabbah* 17:8, ed. Theodor-Albeck, pp. 159-160.

> **he is buried by one woman** and two men. Abba Shaul says: by one man and **two women**. They said to him: one man is not left alone with two women [see Mishnah *Kiddushin* 4:12]... A thirty-day old [baby] that [dies] goes out [to be buried] with **men and women** in a small coffin carried in one's arms up to the age of twelve [months]. A twelve-[month]-old baby goes out [to be buried] with **men and women** in a small coffin carried on the shoulders up to the age of three years...

The participation of women in the **burial** is also proven from a source from the early Amoraic period in the Land of Israel:

> Rabbi Yehoshua ben Levi said: the Angel of Death told me three things... **and do not stand before the women when they return from the dead** because I am dancing before them and my sword is in my hand and I have permission to harm.

And the *Gemara* adds in Aramaic:

> and if he harmed, how can it be mended? He should jump four cubits from his place... and if there is another path, he should take it..." (*Berakhot* 51a).

Although *Ein Mishpat Ner Mitzvah* in *Berakhot* refers to the paragraph we are discussing in *Yoreh De'ah*, there is no doubt that Rabbi Yosef Karo and most *poskim* who ruled liked him **did not** base themselves on this source in the Bavli, but rather on the *Zohar*. However, this passage proves that despite the superstition that it is prohibited to **stand** "before the women when they return from the dead", women did indeed **participate** regularly in burial ceremonies during the Talmudic period.

Most *Rishonim* totally ignored Rabbi Yehoshua ben Levi's words. Most quote and explain the *beraita* in Bavli *Sanhedrin* – and some the Yerushalmi too – and rule like them.[11] Three

11. Rabbeinu Ḥananel to *Sanhedrin* 20a; Rabbeinu Yitzḥak ibn Giyyat, "*Sha'arei Simḥah*", Part 2, *Hilkhot Avel*, p. 41; Maimonides, *Hilkhot Avel* 12:1; *Yad*

Rishonim and three *Aḥaronim* even testify that in their day women did indeed go out to cemeteries:

1. The Maharam of Rothenburg tells us this indirectly in his *Hilkhot Semaḥot*.[12] He rules that a man may not give a *se'udat havra'ah* [first meal after the funeral] to a woman because he might get into a sinful habit (see more on this below) "and for this same reason **after the deceased has been buried**, because it is customary to escort the mourner to his home, **where there are no mourners other than women,** they should not be escorted." It is therefore clear that women mourners participated in the burial.

2. Two other *Rishonim* were concerned about Rabbi Yehoshua ben Levi's statement in *Berakhot*, but nonetheless testify that in their day women were accustomed to go to the cemetery. Rabbi Yitzḥak b"r Avraham, one of the Tosafists, is quoted by the Mordechai to *Sanhedrin*, paragraph 684, which is quoted in turn by the Rema in *Darkhei Moshe* to *Tur* YD 359:

> **and regarding our custom**, Rabbi Yitzḥak b"r Avraham was puzzled **that at the time of escorting the deceased to the cemetery, the women go out at the end, but upon returning they go out first.** And he explained that this custom is according to the opinion [in the *Gemara*] that they go out at the end, and since they are last when the deceased is escorted out, therefore they should be first when returning **so that no one should cross before them**.

3. Rabbi Shimshon bar Tzadok, a student of the Maharam of Rothenburg, openly expressed his concern for Rabbi Yehoshua

Ramah to *Sanhedrin* 20a; *Sefer Mitzvot Gadol, Assin Medivrei Soferim*, Paragraph 2, *Hilkhot Aveilut*, fol. 248a; *Hagahot Maimoniyot* to Maimonides *ad loc.*; Naḥmanides, *Torat Ha'adam*, ed. Chavel, p. 107; the Me'iri to *Sanhedrin* 20a; *Orḥot Ḥayim*, Part 2, pp. 572-573; *Tzeidah Laderekh*, 5, 2, 8; *Tur* YD 359.

12. ed. Kahana, Jerusalem, 5723, paragraphs 193-194, p. 168; ed. Landau, Jerusalem, 5736, paragraph 148, p. 143.

ben Levi's opinion (*Tashbetz*, ed. Warsaw, 1901, paragraph 457; ed. Lemberg, 1858, paragraph 449):

> **And when returning from the cemetery to their homes**, they say "he will destroy death" (Isaiah 25:8)... **the women go to their homes first** because the Angel of Death and Satan are dancing before them.

4. Rabbi Yoel Sirkis, the *Baḥ* (1561-1640) lived one generation **after** Rabbi Yosef Karo. In his commentary *Bayit Ḥadash* to *Tur* YD 359, he quotes the Yerushalmi "... women go after the men... **and that is the custom today**" and adds "**nevertheless,** the *Beit Yosef* wrote based on the *Zohar*". It is clear from his words that for him the *Beit Yosef's* approach is an innovation and that in his locale it was customary for women to go to the cemetery behind the men.

5. Finally, two *Aḥaronim* who were certainly familiar with the *Shulḥan Arukh*, relayed customs which permitted women to go to the cemetery while taking certain precautions to avoid the danger described in the *Zohar*. Rabbi Aharon Berakhyah of Modena (d. 1639) cites the *Zohar* in his book *Ma'avar Yabok* (ed. Vilna, 1896, p. 210) and adds:

> and therefore one should prevent the women from going to the cemetery **with** the men and all the more so upon returning, and under no circumstances should the men walk on the same path with the women then. I was informed by a worthy person that this is the widespread practice in the Land of Israel and in Babylonia and in the entire eastern kingdom, that the men walk first and there [in the cemetery] appointed sextons stand to separate the women so that they not start leaving until after all the men have left. And after the burial, the women stay there for about a quarter of an hour, until all the men have left...

6. Rabbi Yosef Yuzpe Hahn Nordlingen (d. 1637) of Frankfurt am Mein was also proficient in the *Shulḥan Arukh*. Nonetheless, in his book *Yosef Ometz* he testifies as follows (ed. Frankfurt am Main, 1928, p. 327):

> Much caution is needed to separate from the women **as they walk to and return from the burial**, and especially after the washing of the hands which chased away the spirits of impurity from him, so that they should not return and cling to him via them [the women]. And I have heard that in the holy congregation of Worms **it is the custom of the men to turn their faces toward the wall when the women come**.

It is apparent from all of the above that from ancient times until the 17th century, women were accustomed to go out to the cemetery with the men, except that they apparently walked separately before or behind the bier, according to the *beraitot* in Bavli and Yerushalmi *Sanhedrin*. Only two *Rishonim* added, according to Rabbi Yehoshua ben Levi in *Berakhot*, that it is forbidden to look at women's faces as they return from the cemetery. Even after the *Shulḥan Arukh*, the early custom continued to be practiced in Poland, Italy and Germany, except that two *Aḥaronim* added the condition that they should not look at women, based on the *Zohar*.

III. Rabbi Yosef Karo's Approach Compared to the *Zohar*

We have seen that Rabbi Yosef Karo's opinion is contrary to all the *poskim* who preceeded him. But that is not all. His opinion does not flow from the words of the *Zohar* itself! The *Zohar* does not demand to **prevent** women from going to the cemetery, rather that women not **look** at the men while going to and from the cemetery. The *Zohar*, following a detailed description of the danger, states:

> How is this corrected? When they take the deceased to the cemetery, a man should turn his face and leave the women

> behind. And if they are in front, he should walk behind so that he does not see them face to face. And when returning from the cemetery, he should not return on the same path where the women stand, nor look at them at all, but should take a different route.[13]

If so, the custom described by Rabbi Aaron Berakhyah and Rabbi Yosef Yuzpe Hahn is more in keeping with the *Zohar* than the ruling of Rabbi Yosef Karo! Indeed, in the 19th century, Rabbi Shlomo Ganzfried ruled in the *Kitzur Shulḥan Arukh* (198:10) like the *Zohar* itself and contrary to Rabbi Yosef Karo: "Great care should be taken so that the women **should not see** the men while walking to the cemetery, and how much the moreso when returning from the cemetery because there is, God forbid, danger in so doing".

IV. The *Zohar* Versus the Babylonian Talmud

Even if we were to say that Rabbi Yosef Karo's ruling is a direct result of the *Zohar*, it should be asked why he and most of the *Aḥaronim* preferred the *Zohar* over the explicit *beraita* in Bavli *Sanhedrin* and the other Talmudic sources. Indeed, many *Aḥaronim* sensed this contradiction and even attempted to resolve it.[14] Regarding Rabbi Yosef Karo, however, it is not surprising. He ruled according to the *Zohar* in dozens of places in the *Beit Yosef* and the *Shulḥan Arukh* and, according to Prof. Ya'akov Katz, Rabbi Yosef Karo "absorbed from the *Zohar* more than any other *posek* before him, and he also gave the *Zohar*'s rulings more far-reaching authority than his predecessors did".[15]

13. *Zohar, Parashat Vayakhel*, fol. 196a at the bottom.
14. *Beit Hillel* on YD 359; Rabbi Ya'akov ben Shmuel of Tzoizmer, *Responsa Beit Ya'akov*, Dierenfurth, 1696, No. 72 and from there in *Beit Leḥem Yehudah* to YD 359; the *Levush* (above, note 2): "and they said in the *Zohar* **according to his tradition**"; Moshe Kunitz, *Ben Yoḥai*, Vienna, 1815, p. 146; *Keter Shem Tov* (above, note 4); and *Gesher Haḥayyim* (above, note 8), Part 1, p. 130 and note 6.
15. Ya'akov Katz, *Halakhah Vekabbalah*, Jerusalem, 5744, p. 68. See also Moshe Ḥalamish, *Hakabbalah Batefillah, Bahalakhah Ubaminhag*, Ramat Gan, 5760,

However, this general approach of Rabbi Yosef Karo is not necessarily binding upon us. Many *poskim* discussed the contradictions between the Talmud and the *Zohar*[16] and they do not have a unified approach on the matter. Yet it is sufficient to note that *poskim* such as Rabbi Elya Halevi (a colleague of Rabbi Eliyahu Mizraḥi) and the Maharshal totally ruled out the halakhic authority of the *Zohar*. Others – such as the Radbaz, Rabbi Yitzḥak Karo, Rabbi Avraham Zakut and Rabbi Yehudah Obernik – determined that rulings and customs of the *Zohar* should be adopted to the extent possible, **but in the case of a contradiction between the Bavli and the *Zohar* or between the *poskim* and the *Zohar*, one must rule according to the Talmud and the *poskim*.** Furthermore, even *poskim* who supported the stringencies of the *Zohar* such as Rabbi Shneur Zalman of Liady stress that "we cannot force the public to be stringent" according to these stringencies (*Shulḥan Arukh Harav* OH 25:28 and cf. *Magen Avraham* to OH 25, subparagraph 20). We have proved above that, according to the Talmud, women participate both in the funeral and in the burial. Therefore, according to the above-mentioned principles, it is **prohibited** to "force **the public** to be stringent" and to prevent women from going to a funeral or a burial because of the "danger" described in the *Zohar*. At most, **an individual** who worries about this "danger" can refrain from looking at women according to *Ma'aver Yabok, Yosef Ometz* and *Kitzur Shulḥan Arukh*. However, the words of the *Zohar* cannot take precedence over Talmudic *halakhah* and over all the *poskim* who preceded Rabbi Yosef Karo.

V. There is no Evil Inclination in the Cemetery

Rabbi Avraham Eliezer Hershowitz suggested, as mentioned, that the real reason for prohibiting women from going to the

Chapter 7. For a list of *halakhot* in the *Shulḥan Arukh* which are based on the Zohar, see Moshe Kunitz (above, note 14), pp. 136-149.

16. *Sedei Ḥemed*, ed. Schneerson, Volume 9, *Kelalei Haposkim* 2:12-13, pp. 3616-3717; Boaz Cohen, *Kuntress Hateshuvot*, Budapest, 5690, pp. 22-23 and the literature in note 5; ET, s.v. *Halakhah*, Volume 9, columns 254-255; Ya'akov

cemetery is forbidden thoughts. Indeed, he could have based himself on the words of the *Amora*, Rabbi Yitzḥak who felt that "even when a man is between the death and burial of a loved one, his [evil] inclination gets the better of him" (*Kiddushin* 80b). But this suggestion is contrary to the opinion of the *Tanna* Abba Shaul (*ibid.*) and to that of the Tosafists. Abba Shaul ruled, as mentioned above, that a one-day-old child is buried "by one man and two women." The Bavli explains that, according to Abba Shaul, there is no need to be concerned about a man being left alone with two women because "when a mourner is in the period between death and burial, his [evil] inclination is broken" (*Kiddushin* 80b). Similarly, the Yerushalmi explains that "**the evil inclination is not found in the cemetery**" (Yerushalmi *Kiddushin* 4:11, fol. 66c).[17] The Tosafists dealt with this question in regard to the *beraita* in Bavli *Sanhedrin* 20a. They ask: Why is there no concern about looking at women, yet at the *Simḥat Beit Hashoevah*, they built *meḥitzot* in the Temple (*Sukkah* 51a)? They reply: "because in a time of anguish there is no concern for forbidden thoughts" and they then cite the words of the Yerushalmi.[18]

Therefore, according to many *poskim*, there is no reason to fear forbidden thoughts or the evil inclination at times of anguish and therefore these explanations do not justify separation between

Katz (above, note 15), pp. 52-69; Louis Jacobs, *A Tree of Life*, Oxford, 1984, pp. 13, 14, 73-76, 80-81; Moshe Ḥalamish (above, note 15), Chapter 5.

17. Cf. the Amoraic teachings cited in note 6 above and Rashi to *Sukkah* 52a, s.v. *she'assukin behesped*.
18. *Tosafot* to *Sanhedrin* 20a, s.v. *nashim*; there is a similar explanation in *Tosfot Harosh, ibid.* in: *Sanhedrei Gedolah*, Volume 3, Jerusalem, 5730, p. 81; *Tosfot Ḥakhmei Angliah, ibid.*, ed. Sofer, Jerusalem, 5728, p. 27; the Mordechai to *Sanhedrin*, paragraph 684; *Shita* on *Moed Kattan* by a student of Rabbeinu Yeḥiel of Paris, Part 2, Jerusalem, 5697, p. 96. Ostensibly, there is an internal contradiction in the *Tosafot*, because they also cite the Yerushalmi and, according to one opinion there, the women walked at the end "out of **respect** for the daughters of Israel, so that they [=the men] should not gaze at the women". However, one can reply that the Yerushalmi was concerned about a lack of **respect**, but not about sinful thoughts, and this is how Rabbi Ya'akov of Tzoizmer explained it (above, note 14).

men and women during the eulogy, funeral procession or burial ceremony.

VI. There is no halakhic basis for the custom of preventing women from entering a cemetery while menstruating.

This late custom is not mentioned in any *halakhic* source before the nineteenth century.[19] It undoubtedly stems from the widespread custom of preventing women from praying and from entering a synagogue during their menstrual period. Indeed, Rabbi Avraham Danzig includes both customs in the same paragraph in his book *Ḥayyei Adam*. However, the second custom is also contrary to Talmudic law whereby "words of Torah do not receive impurity" (*Berakhot* 22a) and is based primarily on a sectarian *beraita* entitled *Beraita Demassekhet Niddah*.[20] Indeed, the major *poskim* such as the Rif, Maimonides, *Sefer Mitzvot Gadol*, the Rosh, the *Tur* and Rabbi Yosef Karo ruled according to the *Gemara* that there is no prohibition in this matter. In any case, even those who justify distancing a menstruant from the synagogue, look for a leniency in the case of anguish. Here, for example, are the words of Rabbi Yisrael Isserlein (Austria, d. 1460):

> With regard to menstruating women, in truth, I allowed them [in the synagogue] on the High Holy days and the like when many women gather in the synagogue to hear the prayers and the Torah readings... and I relied on Rashi who allows [this]... for the **sake of women's peace of mind** because it made them sad and heartsick that all gathered to be in the congregation and they should have to stand outside...[21]

19. See above, note 5.
20. See Dinari quoted *ibid*. For additional literature, see above, p. 182, note 15.
21. *Terumat Hadeshen*, Part 2: *Pesakim Uketavim*, No. 132 and from there in an abbreviated form in *Responsa of the Rema*, No. 98 and in the Rema's glosses to OH 88:1.

If they allowed menstruating women to enter the synagogue in order to pray with the congregation on holidays – should they not all the more so be allowed to participate in the burial of their parents, brothers or husbands! And if they set aside an old custom due to anguish – should they not do so all the more for a late custom!

VII. "One who mocks the unfortunate insults his Maker."

Thus far we have shown that there is no halakhic justification for preventing a woman from participating in a funeral or burial. We shall now see that one who does so is violating a Rabbinic prohibition and is ignoring several basic concepts in *halakhah*. We have learned in the Bavli (*Berakhot* 18a):

> Raḥvah said in the name of Rav Yehudah: **all who see a deceased and do not escort him violate the principle of "One who mocks the unfortunate insults his Maker"** (Proverbs 17:5). And if he escorted him what is his reward? Rav Assi said: of him the Scripture says "he who gives graciously to the poor makes a loan to the Lord, and that which he has given, [God] will pay him back" (Proverbs 19:17).

Rav Yehudah's words are cited in YD 361:3. There is no doubt that Rabbi Yehudah was referring to women as well because he said "**all who see**" and we have seen above that during the Talmudic period women always participated in funerals and burials. And if unrelated people transgress the principle of "mocking the unfortunate", then daughters, wives and mothers, how much the more so![22]

22. Cf. Meir Benayahu, *Sefer Zikaron Larav Yitzḥak Nissim, Seder Shishi: Ma'amadot Umoshavot*, Jerusalem, 5745, p. 271.

VIII."Great is *Kevod Haberiyot* [human dignity] which sets aside a negative commandment in the Torah."

Several scholars have already dealt with this important concept.[23] Here we will only note that many rabbis set aside a *mitzvah* from the Torah or a rabbinic decree because of human dignity. In one *sugya* in the Bavli (*Berakhot* 19b-20a) four *Tannaim* ruled according to this principle: one *beraita* permits a *Kohen* to escort a mourner back from burying his departed even if the mourner passes through an impure place. Likewise, the *Tanna*, Rabbi Eleazar bar Tzadok permits a *Kohen* to become impure in order to honor the king. Another *beraita* rules that an elderly person may or even must refrain from returning a lost item if it is beneath his dignity. Finally, a fourth *beraita* determines that burying a *meit mitzvah,* a dead person who has no one to bury him, sets aside many other *mitzvot,* such as slaughtering the paschal sacrifice or circumcising one's son on time. Likewise, five Babylonian *Amoraim* used this concept to permit various prohibitions (Blidstein, pp. 140-141). In the Middle Ages, the *Rishonim* used this concept to be lenient regarding laws connected to *kevod hameit,* the honor of the dead (Blidstein, pp. 149-165). Even Rabbi Moshe Isserles used this concept in several of his responsa. Among others, he once performed a marriage for an orphan on **Shabbat** – despite the explicit prohibtion in Mishnah *Beitzah* 5:2 – in order to spare her insult and pain (Blidstein, pp. 168-170).

There is no doubt that some of the customs discussed here detract from human dignity, both that of the women themselves and of the other participants at the funeral. And if human dignity sets aside a negative commandment or a rabbinic decree, then all

23. Cf. above, p. 86 and see Y.D. Eisenstein, *Otzar Dinim Uminhagim,* New York, 1917, s.v. *kavod;* Ḥ.Z. Reines, "*Kevod Haberiyot Bahalakhah*", *Sinai* 27 (5710), pp. 157-167; Naḥum Rakover, *Hahaganah al Kevod Haberiyot,* Jerusalem, 1978; Eliezer Berkovits, *Hahalakhah: Koḥah Vetafkidah,* Jerusalem, 5741, pp. 105-113; Ya'akov Blidstein, "*'Gadol Kevod Haberiyot': Iyunim Begilgulehah Shel Halakhah*", *Shnaton Hamishpat Ha'ivri* 9-10 (5742-5743), pp. 127-185. My thanks to Rabbi Shlomo Fuchs for the last reference.

the more so is it able to set aside customs based on a superstition quoted in the *Zohar*!

IX. Does the eulogy come to honor living or the dead?

In *Sanhedrin* 46b-47a there are nine attempts to resolve the question as to whether the eulogy comes to honor the living or the dead. In the end, they decide that the eulogy comes to honor the dead, and so ruled Maimonides (*Hilkhot Eival* 12:1) and the *Shulḥan Arukh* (YD 344:9-10). If the eulogy is in honor of the dead, the funeral is also in honor of the dead, and there is no doubt that most deceased persons today would want **all** their relatives – both men and women – to attend their funeral and burial. Preventing the full participation of the female relatives of the deceased is not only an insult to the living, but also disrespectful to the dead.

X. Practical *Halakhah*

We have shown above that no *posek* requires separation between men and women during the eulogy. Since most *poskim* rule that there are no forbidden thoughts when in mourning, there is no point in upholding this custom. We have also seen that preventing women from participating in the funeral and burial is based solely on Rabbi Yosef Karo's interpretation of the *Zohar*. However, these customs contradict the custom of both Talmuds and of all the *Rishonim*. They are also not called for by the *Zohar* itself and, in any event, they prefer the *Zohar* over the Babylonian Talmud. Furthermore, we have proved that there is **no** fear of forbidden thoughts or ritual impurity due to menstruation at a cemetery. On the other hand, these customs force women to violate the prohibition of "mocking the unfortunate" and show disdain for "human dignity" and "the honor of the dead". **Therefore, it is forbidden for the *Ḥevrah Kaddisha* or the Rabbi to force the public to follow Rabbi Yosef Karo** and act contrary to all of the above. At the most, it is permissible for an individual or a family to be strict with themselves. But it is preferable to follow the Talmudic *halakhah* and to **encourage** women to pay respect to their loved ones and to participate in the eulogy, funeral procession and burial. The only custom which has any basis is the separation of the sexes during the funeral procession escorting the deceased to the cemetery. This is a custom based on the *beraitot* in Bavli and Yerushalmi *Sanhedrin* and *Avot Derabi Nattan*.[24] In any case, **it is a custom and not a *mitzvah*** or an obligation and, therefore, if it is contrary to the wishes of the family or the deceased, this custom should be set aside by the values of "human dignity" and "the honor of the dead".[25]

David Golinkin
Jerusalem
20 Iyar 5747

24. However, it is possible that it is based mainly on a Hellenistic–Roman custom – see above, note 1.
25. For two other Rabbis who objected to Rabbi Yosef Karo's approach to our topic, see Rabbi Eliezer Waldenberg, *Sefer Even Ya'akov*, Chapter 17, at the end of *Tzitz Eli'ezer*, Vol. 5, second edition, Jerusalem, 5745 and Rabbi Moshe Zemer, *Halakhah Shefuyah*, Tel Aviv, 5754, pp. 220-223 = *Evolving Halakhah*, Woodstock, Vermont, 1999, pp. 255-259.

11. WOMEN AND THE MOURNER'S *KADDISH*

Yoreh De'ah 376:4

In memory of Cecile Rotenberg z"l,
who passed away on the first day
of Rosh Ḥodesh Adar Bet 5749

Question from a woman in Jerusalem: *My mother passed away a short time ago and I had trouble finding a synagogue close to my home where I could recite mourner's kaddish every day. Some of the Orthodox synagogues say that this is prohibited or "not accepted". Some told me to recite kaddish quietly. Still others say it would be preferable for my husband to recite kaddish for my mother. Are they right? Is there a* ***halakhic*** *reason why a woman should not recite the mourner's kaddish for her parents or for other relatives?*

Responsum: This question was first asked in the seventeenth century and has since been dealt with by many *poskim* (see the Bibliography at the end of the responsum). In general, they can be divided into three groups: those who prohibit, those who permit under certain conditions, and those who permit women to recite the *kaddish*. However, we shall see below that the first two groups of *poskim* did not find any **inherent halakhic** reason to prohibit a woman from reciting the mourner's *kaddish* and therefore they based themselves on **external halakhic** or general sociological concerns. Indeed, the *halakhah* must contend with sociological factors, but these concerns do not have the power to overrule a simple *heter* [permissive ruling]. Moreover, those sociological concerns from the seventeenth century no longer exist today. On the other hand, there are many good reasons to support those who permit women to recite the mourner's *kaddish,* as will be explained below.

I. The Custom Until the Seventeenth Century

We did not find any explicit discussion of this issue before the seventeenth century, but we did find one hint that women in medieval Ashkenaz were **not** accustomed to recite the mourner's *kaddish.* Rabbi Ya'akov Weil (Germany, died before 1456) was asked if it was a *mitzvah* to notify someone whose mother or father had died within thirty days. He replied: according to the Mordechai at the end of *Hilkhot Semaḥot,* there is no need to notify him. "In any case, it was customary to notify the sons so **that they would pray** because the deceased has spiritual satisfaction from this, **but there is no custom about this for daughters**" (*Responsa Rabbi Ya'akov Weil,* No. 13). This responsum is cited by the Rema in *Darkhei Moshe Ha'arokh* to *Tur* YD 402:4; however in *Shulḥan Arukh* YD 402:12, the Rema changes the wording: "In any case, it was customary to notify sons so that they would recite the ***kaddish,*** but for daughters, there is no custom at all to notify them". It is not at all clear whether Rabbi Ya'akov Weil was even referring to the mourner's *kaddish,* but according to the wording in the Rema's glosses to the *Shulḥan Arukh,* it seems that in the Rema's time, women were **not accustomed** to recite the mourner's *kaddish.*

II. Those who Prohibit

A. It is forbidden to innovate or change customs.

1. The first authority dealing with this question was Rabbi Yair Ḥayyim Bachrach (Ashkenaz, 1638-1702) who discussed our topic in *Responsa Ḥavot Yair,* No. 222:

> This episode occurred in Amsterdam and is well-known there. A man passed away, leaving no son, and ordered before his death that ten [men] should be paid to study in

his house every day for twelve months and after the study, the daughter should recite *kaddish*. **And the scholars and the leaders of the community did not protest against this.** And even though there is no proof to prevent it because a woman is also commanded to observe the *mitzvah* of *kiddush hashem* [the sanctification of God's name], and there is a *minyan* of ten males who are called "the children of Israel" (*Megillah* 23b), and even though in the story about Rabbi Akiva, which is the source for orphans reciting *kaddish*, [the orphan] was a boy[1] – in any case, there is logic that a daughter also gives contentment to the soul [of a departed parent] because she is his offspring.

Nevertheless, one should be concerned that by doing this, the customs of the Jewish people which are also Torah will

1. This legend appears in at least 17 versions from the Middle Ages and many scholars have attempted to uncover the original version. For the most complete list of versions, see M.B. Lerner, "The Story of the *Tanna* and the Deceased – Halakhic and Literary Developments", *Asufot* 2 (5748), p. 67. For a discussion of the different versions, see Rabbi Levi Ginzberg, *Ginzei Schechter*, Book One, New York, 1928, pp. 235-236; Rabbi Michael Higger, *Masekhtot Kallah*, New York, 1936, pp. 68-72; A.N.Z. Roth, *Talpiyot* 7 (5721), pp. 369-381 and especially pp. 371-374; Yisrael Ta-Shma, *Tarbitz* 53 (5744), pp. 559-568 and an expanded version in his book *Minhag Ashkenaz Hakadmon*, third edition, Jerusalem, 5759, pp. 299-310; and especially Lerner cited above, pp. 29-70.
   The latter makes several new points: the original hero was Rabban Yoḥanan ben Zakai and not Rabbi Akiva; in an ancient version from the *Genizah*, the story refers to a historical event and not a legend; in that version, the father asks Rabban Yoḥanan ben Zakai: "For five years you will lead [my son] to the synagogue and teach him prayer, *Keriyat Shema*, three verses and he will go up and read from a Torah scroll, [and he will recite the blessing: *Barekhu et hashem hamevorakh*] and the congregation will answer him: *Barukh hashem hamevorakh le'olam va'ed* – and I am exempt from this judgement...". In other words, in the ancient version and in many other versions, there is no mention of the *kaddish*! In some later versions, they added *kaddish*, but the *kaddish* never appears in this legend as the sole way of saving the father from *Gehinom*! This means that this legend is not **the source** for the recitation of *kaddish* by an orphan; rather they added this to the legend after they were accustomed to recite the mourner's *kaddish*! For a recent study of this legend, see Yehudit Weiss, *Tarbitz* 78 (5769), pp. 521-554 and the literature in note 28 *ibid.*

be weakened and everyone will build an altar for himself [see *Ḥagigah* 22a] according to his own reasoning, and the words of the Rabbis will appear as derision and jest and they will end up treating them lightly.

Further on, the author of *Ḥavot Yair* cites several sources in order to prove that our Sages reinforced their own words more than they reinforced those of the Torah (*Berakhot* 34a, *Tosafot*, s. v. *melamdin; Yevamot* 36b). And he concludes: "therefore, in this matter which involves a gathering and publicity, we should protest".

There are several points in this responsum worth highlighting, because it serves as an important source for later *poskim*:

a. **There is no inherent halakhic reason to prohibit a wife or a daughter from reciting the mourner's *kaddish*.** On the contrary, reciting the *kaddish* is a way of sanctifying God's name, and women are obligated **by the Torah** to sanctify God's name. So we can deduce from the Yerushalmi (*Shevi'it* 4:2, fol. 34a = *Sanhedrin* 3:6, fol. 21b), the Bavli (*Sanhedrin* 74b) and the Rif (*ibid.*, fol. 17b); and this is also the ruling of Maimonides (*Sefer Hamitzvot*, Positive Commandments, No. 9; *Mishneh Torah, Hilkhot Yesodei Hatorah* 2:5 and 5:1) and *Sefer Haḥinukh* (No. 268 at the end, ed. Chavel, p. 354).[2]

b. Furthermore, there is no problem of including women in the *minyan*, because the father "ordered before his death that ten [men] should be paid to study in his house every day".

c. Finally, despite the fact that the famous legend about Rabbi Akiva and the orphan, which is the "basis" for reciting the

2. For *Aḥaronim* who held this opinion, see above, p. 110, note 29. It should be added that if this is the purpose of *kaddish*, then it is probably permissible to include women in a *minyan* to recite *kaddish* because several *Aḥaronim* ruled that women may be included in a *minyan* that is for the purpose of a public sanctification of God's name – see *ibid.*, note 30.

> mourner's *kaddish,* refers to a "son", "in any case, there is logic that a daughter also gives contentment to the soul [of a departed parent] because she is his offspring". If this is the case, why does the author of *Ḥavot Yair* prohibit it? For fear of weakening the power of customs, lest everyone will change them to his heart's content. Furthermore, he compares our topic to the things which our Sages enacted in order to strengthen their own words.

This is surprising. First of all, there is no connection between the two items being compared, because the mourner's *kaddish* was not enacted by our Sages, but rather began as a custom in medieval France and Germany.[3] Moreover, how can we take away from the Jewish people the right to change or innovate customs?! After all, **every** custom by definition springs from the people. A large part of our way of life was created by the people and the people has continued to develop and modify its customs continuously. Take, for example, the mourner's *kaddish* itself, *Simḥat Torah, Yizkor,* the *kippah, Kabbalat Shabbat,* the different prayer rites, and many other customs. Therefore, the author of *Ḥavot Yair* is rejecting an **internal** halakhic permission due to an **external,** sociological concern which is very questionable to begin with.

3. This is the conclusion of all the scholars who have dealt with this issue. The first to mention this custom were *Siddur Rashi,* paragraph 216, p. 101 (France, end of the 11th century); Rabbi Eleazar of Worms, *Sefer Harokeaḥ, Hilkhot Shabbat,* paragraph 53 and *Sefer Ḥassidim,* ed. Margaliot, paragraph 722, p. 443 (both from Ashkenaz, early 13th century); Rabbi Yitzḥak b"r Moshe of Vienna, *Or Zaru'a,* Part 2, *Hilkhot Shabbat,* paragraph 50, fols. 11c-11d (Ashkenaz, mid-13th century). The mourner's *kaddish* is also mentioned in tractate *Soferim* 19:9, ed. Higger, pp. 336-337, which was purported to have been written in Geonic times, but Dr. Debra Reed Blank has recently proved that the second part of tractate *Soferim* (chapters 10-21) was written in Europe in the 11th-14th centuries. See Debra Reed Blank, *Soferim: A Commentary to Chapters 10-12 and a Reconsideration of the Evidence,* Ph.D. Dissertation, Jewish Theological Seminary, New York, 1998 and her summary in *JQR* 90/1-2 (1999), pp. 1-26 and especially, pp. 4-5, note 10.

His responsum had a huge influence and many *poskim* quoted it as the law without adding anything at all.[4] Furthermore, two important *poskim* reiterated the same explanation for prohibiting this practice:

2. Rabbi Ḥayyim Ḥizkiah Medini (Crimea and Israel, 1832-1904) dealt with this topic in his monumental work, *Sedei Ḥemed*. After quoting the words of *Ḥavot Yair* and others, he concludes (*Asefat Dinim, Ma'arekhet Avelut*, Paragraph 160):

> And not along ago, I was asked by someone from a neighboring city that one of the Crimeans wanted a daughter to recite *kaddish* over her father who died without male offspring... **and I answered them that they may not change [things] and institute a new practice in the land, and even if this custom exists among Ashkenazim,** among the Sefaradim it is unheard of anywhere, and... this comes under the rule of "sit and do not do [anything] is preferable" and my response was accepted....

3. Rabbi Ben-Tzion Meir Ḥai Uziel (first Sefardic Chief Rabbi of Israel, 1880-1953) discussed this issue in *Responsa Mishpetei Uziel* (second edition, OH, No. 13). Among other things, he wrote:

> **... it seems clear that the whole matter of *kaddish* is a tradition from the words of ours Sages and, therefore, we should not add to their words and innovate logical deductions of our own accord** by explaining the reasons for the tradition... because its entire essence and sanctity is

4. *Pitḥei Teshuvah* to YD 376, subparagraph 3; *Eliyahu Rabbah* to OH 133, subparagraph 10; Rabbi Shlomo Hass, *Kerem Shlomo*, OH volume, Pressburg, 1843, to OH 131, paragraph 17 and *Yoreh De'ah* volume, Pressburg, 1840, in *Ketzat Dinei Kaddish*; Rabbi Yehudah ben Moshe Eli, *Kemaḥ Solet*, Salonika, 1798, *Hilkhot Aveilut*, paragraph 100, *Seder Kaddish*, fol. 169d in the name of *Leket Hakemaḥ* in the name of *Ḥavot Yair*; Rabbi Moshe Yekutiel Kaufman, *Leḥem Hapanim* to YD, *Kuntress Aḥaron* to paragraph 376, Henna, 1716, fol. 72c.

> the secrecy and mystery inherent therein and our intelligence cannot understand its reasons and secrets. Therefore, we should not add to or detract from their words of our own accord. Therefore, we should not innovate this custom of girls reciting *kaddish*.

Rabbi Uziel apparently thinks that mourner's *kaddish* was enacted by our Sages, but we have already seen that this custom was initiated in Germany and France in the Middle Ages. Moreover, he thinks that *kaddish* is connected to Jewish mysticism, but he does not quote any source to support this claim.

B. It is prohibited for various reasons.

Rabbi Shimon Frankfurter (died 1712) was a contemporary of Rabbi Yair Ḥayyim Bachrach in Amsterdam. In his book *Sefer Haḥayyim*, which discusses the laws of mourning, he apparently refers to the same case in Amsterdam described in the question sent to Rabbi Yair Ḥayyim Bachrach (this was suggested by Tuvia Preschel and seems to be the case). In paragraph 50, he comes up with various reasons in order to forbid girls from reciting *kaddish*, such as: *kevod hatzibbur*/respect for the congregation, *kol b'ishah ervah*/a woman's voice is lewdness, sinful thoughts, "one may not use women", and that the story of Rabbi Akiva dealt with a son. However, it is difficult to accept his reasons, especially in our times. *Kevod hatzibbur* is only connected to the reading of the Torah (see above, Chapter 6). *Kol b'ishah ervah*, according to its simple meaning, refers to a social conversation with a woman, not to times of prayer (see above, Chapter 2). In a modern, mixed society, there is no concern over sinful thoughts.[5] The concept "one may not use women" (*Kiddushin* 70a at the bottom) means that a woman should not serve men during a **meal,** and even the author of *Sefer Haḥayyim* knew that this concept and our topic are totally unrelated.

One sentence in his discussion is especially interesting: "How

5. See below, pp. 328-334.

much the moreso that a woman should not come among men and be worthy to fulfill their obligation to recite *kaddish* and *barekhu*". He is undoubtedly referring to the way *kaddish* was recited in his time. They did not recite *kaddish* in unison; rather one mourner would go before the congregation and recite the mourner's *kaddish* and *barekhu* at the end of the service. He was concerned that a woman mourner would appear to be a *sheliḥat tzibbur*. There is no such concern in our day, because each mourner stands in his place and recites the mourner's *kaddish* in unison with the other mourners. Rabbi Shimon Frankfurter concludes: "because a daughter has no obligation or requirement to recite *kaddish* and it is no more than foolish piety, because it is derision and jest...". This last sentence was quoted by two later *poskim*[6] but, as already mentioned, these arguments are not convincing.

C. It is prohibited without a reason.

Rabbi Yeḥezkel ben Avraham Katznellenbogen (Germany, 1670-1749) related to our topic incidentally in his *Responsa Knesset Yeḥezkel* (YD, fol. 53b). At the end of a discussion as to whether the son of a son or the son of a daughter may recite *kaddish*, the author writes:

> However, the son of a daughter **and all the more so a daughter** do not recite *kaddish* at all in the synagogue. And if they wish to make a [private] *minyan*, the daughter's son, or whoever wishes to recite *kaddish* for the deceased, may do so, **but a woman may not do so at all**.[7]

These words were quoted in brief by the *Ba'er Heitev* (to OH

6. *Leḥem Hapanim* cited above, note 4, and *Beit Leḥem Yehudah* on YD 376, paragraph 4 at the bottom of the page. In the second book, it says "בס"ח" and, as a result, later *poskim* such as Rabbi Ḥayyim David Halevi (p. 232), erred and thought this referred to *Sefer Ḥassidim*.
7. This responsum is quoted in full in *Sefer Kiryat Ḥannah* by Rabbi Gershon Koblenz, Metz, 1785, at the end of paragraph 35 and from there in *Pitḥei Teshuvah* to YD 376, subparagraph 7 and in *Sedei Ḥemed* cited above.

132, subparagraph 5) who seems to imply that it is **permissible** to convene a special *minyan* in order to enable a woman to recite the mourner's *kaddish,* but several *poskim* have already stressed that this is contrary to the opinion of the author of *Knesset Yeḥhezkel* (see, for example, *Sedei Ḥemed* mentioned above; Rabbi Shalom Rubin-Halberstam, p. 14, paragraph 2; and Rabbi Ḥayyim David Halevi, p. 232). However, he does not explain his opinion at all.

D. It is forbidden because of licentiousness.

Rabbi Ephraim Zalman Margaliot (Brody, 1760-1828) related to our question in the chapter on "The Laws of the Mourner's *Kaddish*" at the end of his book, *Mateh Ephraim,* which deals with the laws of the High Holy Days. In Gate 4, paragraph 8, he returns to the case cited above from *Ḥavot Yair*:

> He who had no sons, only a daughter, and commanded prior to his death that ten [men] should learn in his house for a payment and after their learning, his daughter should recite *kaddish* – he should not be obeyed and one must protest not to do so... How much the more so she should not be allowed to recite *kaddish* during the prayer service, and even if she is unmarried, it is forbidden. **How much the more so it is impossible, God forbid, for her to make her voice heard in public reciting *kaddish*,** whether in the synagogue whether in a *minyan* [at home]. Rather, if she wishes to earn merit for her father, she should be careful at all times during prayer, whether in the synagogue or whether in a *minyan* at home, **to pay attention during the recitals of *kaddish* to answer *Amen* with proper intention,** and He who knows thoughts [= God] will consider it as if she had recited *kaddish* and carried out her father's command.

Similar rulings are given by Rabbi Greenwald (p. 375, note 33), Rabbi Rabinowicz (pp. 87-88) and Rabbi Lamm (pp. 166-167), but they do not refer to the *Mateh Ephraim* nor do they explain their rulings. On the other hand, in *Elef Lamateh*, a commentary on *Mateh Ephraim*, Rabbi Margaliot himself explains his ruling at length. In his opinion, "in our times, where licentiousness is common", a daughter may not recite *kaddish* even in a *minyan* at home "**and even though there is no problem with *kol b'ishah ervah*,** as explained in OH 75 and EH 21. In any case, it is likely that she will try to make her voice pleasant and we say "for a women to sing and men respond is licentiousness" (see *Sotah* 48a).

However, this reason for forbidding is not convincing. After all, he himself acknowledges that "there is no problem with *kol b'ishah ervah*" (cf. above, Chapter 2 and Chapter 6, paragraph X) and the passage in *Sotah* deals with secular singing in a pub! Is there any connection between secular singing in a pub and reciting the mourner's *kaddish*!? And is it possible to imagine that a woman who is in mourning for her parent will try to make her voice pleasant!? Clearly this is a desparate attempt to prohibit the custom at any cost.

E. It is prohibited lest they make a mistake and count women in a *minyan*.

Rabbi Avraham Binyamin Zilberberg (Poland and the United States, twentieth century) discussed our topic in *Responsa Mishnat Binyamin*, No. 34. He prohibits the practice for four reasons:

1. "And how much the more so in these countries [=the United States] where people do not know how to make distinctions and they might mistakenly think that women can be counted in the *minyan* for *kedushah* and *barekhu*." (Cf. Rabbi Shalom Rubin–Halberstam, p. 14).

2. He never heard of such a custom in Poland.

3. All of the *Aḥaronim* quoted in *Sedei Ḥemed* agree that it is forbidden for a daughter to recite *kaddish* in the synagogue.

4. It seems clear from the Rabbi Akiva legend and other Talmudic sources that only "a son gives merit to his deceased father" (*Sanhedrin* 104a) and not a daughter.

And he concludes:

> Therefore, in my opinion, just as credit is received for asking, so will there be a double reward for refraining, **and the soul [of the mother of the daughters] will be in the Garden of Eden by virtue of the fact that they do not recite *kaddish* in the synagogue.** *(sic!)*

Once again, his reasons do not stand up to criticism:

1. This claim has already been rejected by the author of the *Ḥavot Yair* cited above. Furthermore, any child can distinguish between reciting *kaddish* and joining a *minyan*. Does a minor who recites the mourner's *kaddish* join the *minyan*? Does a minor who sings *Shir Hakavod* join the *minyan*?

2. This custom was indeed not common in Poland, but that is not a sufficient reason to reject it. On the contrary, we shall see below that the custom was **very** common in Lithuania.

3. Indeed, most of the *Aḥaronim* quoted in *Sedei Ḥemed* ruled that a daughter should not recite *kaddish*, but most of them are only **copying** from *Ḥavot Yair* without examining the question independently. In any case, this does not exempt us from reexamining the question.

4. Ostensibly, so it seems, but the author of *Ḥavot Yair* himself stressed that "there is logic that a daughter also gives contentment to the soul [of a departed parent] because she is his offspring" and Rabbi Ḥayyim David Halevi (see below) is of the opinion that "*bara*" in *Sanhedrin* means a son **or** a daughter.

To sum up, the above *poskim* forbid a wife or daughter to recite *kaddish* for various reasons, but they did not manage to find **an inherent halakhic** reason for doing so, and they therefore relied on **external** reasons or **sociological** concerns: "lest...", "for fear that..." and the like.

III. Those who are Lenient

A. It is forbidden in the synagogue; it is permissible in a *minyan* at home.

1. Rabbi Ya'akov Reisher (Germany, 1670-1733) discusses our topic incidentally in one of his responsa (*Responsa Shevut Ya'akov*, Part 2, YD, No. 93). He was asked by his student, Rabbi Ya'akov *Av Beit Din* of Greisnach:

> A man died here and he had only two young daughters and **the older one is four years old**, and during his illness he commanded me that I should give him a *heter* [permissive ruling] that his older daughter could recite *kaddish* for him and not in the synagogue at all, and now the father of the deceased is coming to recite *kaddish* for his son in the synagogue together with the others mourning a parent...

Rabbi Ya'akov Reisher discusses the matter and concludes that a father may recite *kaddish* for a son only where there is such an established custom in the city. However, his brother-in-law Rabbi Eliyahu Shapira, the author of *Elyah Zuta*, allows a father to recite *kaddish* even where there is no set custom

> in order to appease those who die, God forbid, without sons etc., but in the case before us, **where he already left a daughter who is reciting *kaddish* at home with a *minyan*** – because she certainly should not be permitted to do so in the synagogue at all – **there is already appeasement [of the deceased] in this**. And it seems that also with regard to prayer, the deceased's father should only lead the prayers at home in the *minyan* where the daughter is reciting

kaddish, but prayers and *kaddish* [in the synagogue], they have no [special] rights.

From this responsum, we can learn several important details about the subject under discussion:

a. Both Rabbi Ya'akov of Greisnach and Rabbi Ya'akov Reisher agreed without hesitation that the daughter may recite *kaddish* in a *minyan* at home.

b. This is a case involving a four-year-old girl. There is no telling how they might have ruled had it involved an adult woman.

c. According to Rabbi Ya'akov Reisher, "she certainly should not be permitted to [recite *kaddish*] in the synagogue at all". He does not explain himself, but the explanation is, apparently, similar to what we saw in *Sefer Haḥayyim*, that it is not proper for a daughter to go into the men's section to recite *kaddish*.

d. A daughter is preferable to the father of the deceased vis-à-vis reciting *kaddish* and appeases her father after his death.

2. Rabbi Avraham Yitzḥak Glick (Hungary, 1814-1909; *Responsa Yad Yitzḥak*, Part 3, YD, No. 340) was asked about a man who died without a son, just a daughter and a grandson. Who is preferable to recite *kaddish*? "If we follow the basic law, it seems to me preferable to have the daughter recite *kaddish*, rather than the daughter's son." He emphasizes the beginning of Rabbi Bachrach's responsum (although it is clear from his remarks that he never saw the original responsum!) and concludes that the daughter may recite *kaddish* in a special *minyan* in the privacy of her home and afterwards he refers to *Shevut Ya'akov* cited above.

3. Rabbi Ḥayyim David Halevi (1924-1998), who was the Chief Sephardic Rabbi of Tel Aviv, also ruled several years ago like Rabbi Ya'akov Reisher (*Aseh Lekha Rav*, Part 5, No. 33). He stressed three points:

1. Both the questioner and the respondent in *Shevut Ya'akov* ruled simply to allow the daughter to recite *kaddish;*
2. The "son" in the Rabbi Akiva legend is not necessarily a son, but also refers to a daughter who is his offspring.
3. He is surprised by the prohibition at the end of Rabbi Bachrach's responsum and writes, among other things:

> And why would the words of the Sages appear to be derision and jest if the daughter were to recite *kaddish* in a *minyan* at home, and why is it difficult to explain that a daughter is also his offspring, **and that when she sanctifies the name of God in a *minyan*** at home, she is causing contentment to the soul of her departed parents exactly like the recitation of ***kaddish*** by a son?

And if so, why is it forbidden for a daughter to recite *kaddish* in the synagogue?

> The reason is very simple, because it is not possible to engage in holy pursuits in a holy place in a manner and way that may cause **sinful thoughts**, even the slightest ones.

However, as mentioned above (note 5), in a modern, mixed society, there is no fear of sinful thoughts and, in any case, in our day, all the mourners recite *kaddish* together and usually the voice of one woman cannot be heard.

B. It is forbidden in the synagogue; it is permissible for a young daughter in the synagogue vestibule.

Rabbi Eleazar Fleckeles (Prague, 1754-1826) discussed our topic in his *Responsa Teshuvah Mei'ahavah* (Part 2, OH 229:10). After quoting *Ḥavot Yair* and *Knesset Yeḥezkel* who were opposed to a daughter reciting *kaddish,* he debated the issue: on the one hand, the Maharam Mintz (see below) said that reciting *kaddish* is part of the *mitzvah* to honor one's parents, and daughters are also obligated to observe this commandment (he quotes *Kiddushin* 34a). On the other hand, Rav said in *Berakhot* 17a that women merit a reward for three things: for bringing their sons to learn Torah in the synagogue, for bringing their husbands to learn Mishnah in the *Beit Midrash,* and for waiting for their husbands to return from the *Beit Midrash* in a faraway city. If that is the case, perhaps women can suffice with these activities. In the end, the *Knesset Yeḥezkel* decides that it is permissible for daughters to recite *kaddish* under certain conditions:

> But I saw in the holy congregation of Prague **a nice custom of our ancestors** in the vestibule of the Klausen synagogue where elderly men and women, the blind and the lame, sat from *Shaḥarit* until the afternoon and recited every day the entire book of Psalms. And it is the custom that all those who left no sons, **only daughters aged five and six, they recite *kaddish* there**, but inside a synagogue designated specifically for prayers, I have never seen this. And it is wrong for any woman, young or old, to come into the men's section of the synagogue, [since], according to the *Zohar* and the Sages of Truth z"l [Kabbalists], **a woman in the house of God is like placing an idol there** (*sic!*), and it makes no difference whether it is a young woman or an old woman. And those men who bring their little daughters into the synagogue – it is not proper what they do. [However,] just as it is a *mitzvah* to say something that will be heard, [it is also a *mitzvah* not to say something which will not be heard] (*Yevamot* 65b).

From this responsum we can also learn some important details about our topic:

1. In Prague, it was customary for young girls aged five and six to recite the mourner's *kaddish* in the vestibule of the synagogue and, in the opinion of Rabbi Eleazar Fleckeles, this is both a nice and an ancient custom.

2. According to him, a daughter or a woman is forbidden to recite *kaddish* in the men's section of a synagogue for mystical reasons and, indeed, he objects to bringing young daughters into the men's section for any reason. Similar to *Sefer Haḥayim*, he assumed that a woman could not to recite the mourner's *kaddish* in the women's gallery and would have to enter the men's section. However, it should be stressed **that there is no inherent prohibition against a daughter reciting *kaddish***; rather, it is only forbidden for a woman to enter the men's section of the synagogue in order to recite it.

C. It is forbidden in a synagogue for a daughter who has reached the age of bat mitzvah; it is permisible for a daughter under the age of 12.

Rabbi Yeḥiel Mikhel Tukechinsky (Israel, twentieth century) discusses this topic in his book, *Gesher Haḥayyim* (30:7, pp. 325-326). He cites various customs regarding a young daughter: Some allow her to recite even the *kaddish* after *Ein Keloheinu*, except that *Barekhu* is recited by a man. In some places they do not allow her to recite *kaddish* at all and in some places they allow her to recite *kaddish* in a *minyan* at home. "And an older daughter, they do not allow her in any case to recite *kaddish* in the synagogue." However, he gives no explanation for this distinction according to age.

In conclusion, even the above-mentioned *poskim* acknowledge that according to the basic law, there is no reason why a daughter or wife should not recite the mourner's *kaddish*. However, some of them prohibit this in a synagogue and others limit it to young daughters, apparently for reasons of modesty or sinful thoughts.

IV. Those Who Permit

A. Rabbi Eliezer Zalman Grayevsky (Eastern Europe, England, Israel, 1843-1899) discussed our subject at length in his book

Kaddish Le'olam (fols. 11a-12a). He gives many reasons why a daughter should be permitted to recite the mourner's *kaddish,* among them:

1. Even though the Rabbi Akiva legend deals with a son,[8] a daughter may also recite *kaddish* because she too is referred to as "offspring" for matters of inheritance and fertility, and therefore her reciting *kaddish* also provides contentment to the deceased.

2. The *kaddish* is not a prayer, but a great praise to God that His name should be sanctified and exalted, and the entire congregation responds *Amen;* it therefore makes no difference whether a son sanctifies God's name or a daughter.

3. "The source for the importance of *kaddish* is the verse 'And I will be sanctified among the children of Israel' (Leviticus 22:32) and women are also commanded regarding *kiddush hashem,*[9] and therefore, women may also recite *kaddish* over their fathers."

4. According to Rabbi Ya'akov Weil (d. 1456), in the name of Rabbi Yoḥanan ben Matityahu Treves (France and Italy, d. 1429),[10] someone who has no sons or daughters may pay someone to recite *kaddish* for him after his death. "And if so, a daughter can certainly recite *kaddish* for her father as she is preferable to hiring a stranger to recite *kaddish* because she is his offspring."

The truth speaks for itself and there is no need to add to his words.

8. See above, note 1.
9. See the sources quoted above in this responsum, p. 233.
10. I did not find this in his responsa, but this responsum is quoted in the *Beit Yosef* to *Tur* YD, end of paragraph 403 and cf. Rabbi Greenwald, *Kol Bo Al Aveilut*, p. 376.

2. Rabbi Yosef Eliyahu Henkin (Lithuania and New York, 1880-1973) discussed our topic in two places. In a short responsum from 1947, he allowed young women to recite *kaddish* on the basis of custom: "I remember from my childhood that a young woman recited *kaddish* in front of the men in a community of pious and God-fearing [Jews]". He added that in our day many sons grow closer to Judaism as a result of reciting *kaddish*. "For this very reason we should not push away the young women, since [reciting *kaddish*] causes people to grow closer to Judaism." Finally, he determined that it is appropriate for her to stand behind the *meḥitzah*, but "if she pushes her way in and enters inside the *meḥitzah*... we are not concerned", since in our day many mourners recite the *kaddish* in unison. However, we should not let her "come before the podium as the *sheliḥat tzibbur*", even if it is only for *kaddish*.

Rabbi Henkin returned to this topic in a short article in *Hapardess* in 1963. He dwells at length there on the philosophical aspect of the *kaddish* and emphasized that the *kaddish* by itself is worthless:

> and of course, merely reciting it without doing any good deeds, this is of no use to the deceased... and therefore the *kaddish* has to be connected to repentance, prayer and charity, and with the improvement in one's deeds comes... contentment to the deceased.

And it is forbidden for the *kaddish* to be for the mourners "a sort of incantation without any *kavanah* and understanding". And therefore

> if the daughter comes to pray in the women's gallery and improves her actions by observing the sanctity of Shabbat, *kashrut*, laws of family purity and modesty – all of which are essentials – and should then also desire to recite *kaddish* before the women at the same time that the men in the men's section are reciting *kaddish*, it is possible that there is no objection.

Later on, he prohibits women from reciting *kaddish* in the men's section.

Rabbi Henkin apparently changed his mind regarding the *meḥitzah* because of the fierce struggle surrounding this issue in the United States in the 1950s.[11] It is possible, however, to agree with everything else he says. It is permissible for a daughter to recite *kaddish* since this was the custom in Lithuania (see below) and since it brings daughters in mourning closer to Judaism. Similarly, we agree with him that the *kaddish* is not a magical incantation to bring contentment to the soul of the deceased parent, but rather a **symbol** of *mitzvah* observance in general, which has to be **one** of the *mitzvot* that the son/daughter observes in order to elevate their parents' souls. In any case, it is clear from both responsa that Rabbi Henkin thinks that it is permissible for a woman to recite the mourner's *kaddish* without any reservations, and that is how his grandson, Rabbi Yehudah Herzl Henkin, ruled in our days.

3. Rabbi Aaron Blumenthal (1907-1982), a Conservative Rabbi, allowed women to recite mourner's *kaddish* in 1977, and his opinion was accepted by the Committee on Jewish Law and Standards of the Rabbinical Assembly.

4. Rabbi Wayne Allen, in his role as a *posek* for the Union for Traditional Judaism, allowed women to recite mourner's *kaddish* in 1986, and the Union's Panel of Halakhic Inquiry agreed with him.

5. The Reform *poskim*, Rabbi Solomon Freehof of Pittsburgh (1892-1990) and Rabbi Moshe Zemer of Tel Aviv (1932-2011), allowed women to recite mourner's *kaddish* on the basis of some of the sources quoted above.

6. Besides the above-mentioned *poskim* who published lenient rulings on our topic, there is a long list of testimonies about

11. See below, Chapter 14.

poskim and communities who allowed women to recite the mourner's *kaddish*.

According to Nathaniel Deutsch, Hannah Rochel Verbermacher, The Maiden of Ludmir, recited *kaddish* for her father ca. 1826 when she was nineteen years old.

Rabbi Moshe Feinstein (1895-1986) – who was originally from Lithuania – testified in a responsum written in 1982 that "**in all generations they were accustomed that occasionally** a poor woman would enter the *Bet Midrash* to receive *tzedakah* **or a female mourner to recite kaddish".**

Rabbi Dr. Joel Wolowelsky proved in his writings that there was a common custom in Lithuania for girls and women to recite *kaddish* in order to elevate their relatives' souls: So ruled Rabbi Yosef Dov Halevi Soloveitchik (1903-1993) when he was asked by his students, and he added that that was the custom in the Vilna Gaon's *Kloiz* [synagogue] in Vilna before the Holocaust.[12] One of the elders of the Mir Yeshiva in Brooklyn, who was born and grew up in Vilna, attested that when his cousin died without sons, Rabbi Ḥayyim Ozer Grodzinski, the most important *posek* in Vilna before the Holocaust, ruled that his adult daughter should recite *kaddish* every day at the synagogue in Vilna. Another member of that same *minyan* in Brooklyn attested that his father studied with the *Ḥafetz Ḥayyim* (Rabbi Yisrael Meir Hakohen) and that he also ruled in the same way. This was also the custom in Eishishok, a well-known *shtetl* in Lithuania. The Rabbi of Bayit Vegan in Jerusalem wrote to Rabbi Wolowelsky that he also heard that years ago women would go into the synagogues of Meah She'arim in Jerusalem in order to recite *kaddish*.

Ya'akov Yehoshua (1905-1982), the father of noted Israeli author A.B. Yehoshua, attested to the custom in Jerusalem in the beginning of the twentieth century:

12. For the testimony of an Orthodox woman who recited *kaddish* in Rabbi Soloveitchik's Maimonides school in Boston, see Sarah Reguer's article. For various testimonies about Rabbi Soloveitchik's rulings, see Wolowelsky and Raḥel Berkovits, pp. 78-82.

> **It was the custom in some Ashkenazi synagogues that orphan girls were accustomed to recite *kaddish* after the death of parents who did not have male children.** Little girls used to recite *kaddish* with one of the relatives in the [men's section] and, when they got older, they would recite *kaddish* in the women's section or at the entrance to the synagogue. **It is told of Rabbi Shraga Feivel Frank,** the Rabbi of Yemin Moshe in Jerusalem, **that he requested in his will that his daughters recite *kaddish* for him...** this was not the custom in Jerusalem's Sephardic synagogues (Yehoshua, p. 138).

Indeed, I was informed by Yaffa Levine (December 20, 2004) that her mother-in-law Henia Liebe Levine (born 1924), was one of Rabbi Frank's daughters who had recited *kaddish* for her father many decades ago.

A similar story is told by Tikvah Sarig (1915-1997) who recited *kaddish* for her father Rabbi Dr. Yosef Zeliger at the age of four in Jerusalem in 1919. Since he had no sons, her father, a good friend of Rabbi Avraham Yitzḥak Hakohen Kuk, had left a written and oral testament that Tikvah should recite *kaddish* for him every day during the first year and on each *yahrzeit* until she turned seven. Despite her reluctance, her mother Leah woke her up early every morning to recite *kaddish*. After receiving a very moving blessing from Rabbi Kuk on *Erev Yom Kippur* 1919, Tikvah changed her attitude and went to synagogue by herself every morning to recite *kaddish*.

In 1992, Rabbi Eliyahu Abarg'il, who is the Rabbi of the Baka neighborhood in Jerusalem, allowed wives and daughters to recite *kaddish* in the women's section on the basis of the precedents of Jerusalem rabbis from decades ago.

Today it is also acceptable in Modern Orthodox synagogues in the United States for wives and daughters to recite mourner's *kaddish*,[13] and so ruled Rabbis Saul Berman and Moshe Tendler in

13. See *ibid*.

1989 when they were asked by Dr. Amnon Shapira (Shapira, p. 351-352).

Finally, Rabbi Isaac Klein (Russia and the United States, 1905-1979), one of the most important *poskim* in the Conservative movement, wrote that in our times, it is very accepted for daughters to recite *kaddish*, especially on Shabbat, even if there are male children. Indeed, today this is an accepted custom in all Conservative and Reform synagogues throughout the world.

It is known that the Jewish people have great power to decide halakhic matters that are under dispute, and this is in accordance with several *halakhic* concepts: *ma'aseh rav*/action is great (*Shabbat* 21a and parallels); "leave Israel alone; if they are not Prophets, they are the sons of Prophets" (*Pesaḥim* 66a); *Puk ḥazei mai ama devar*/Go out and see what the people do (*Berakhot* 45a and parallels); "Every *halakhah* that is weak in the rabbinic court and whose nature you do not know, go out and see what the public does and do it" (Yerushalmi *Peah* 7:6, fol. 20c = Yerushalmi *Ma'aser Sheni* 5:3, fol. 56b; Yerushalmi *Yevamot* 7:2, fol. 8a). Therefore, the common practice in Lithuania, the United States, and Israel before 1948 supports the other arguments listed above in favor of a permissive ruling.

V. Practical *Halakhah*

It is clear from all of the above that there is no inherent halakhic reason to prohibit women and daughters from reciting the mourner's *kaddish*. On the contrary, there are **six** reasons to permit this custom:

1. Rabbi Yair Ḥayyim Bachrach, Rabbi Eliezer Zalman Grayevsky and Rabbi Ḥayyim David Halevi already stressed that the main purpose of reciting *kaddish* is to sanctify God's name in public. Since women are obligated by the Torah to perform this *mitzvah*, how can one prevent them from reciting *kaddish*?!

2. A gloss to *Responsa Maharam Mintz* (Ashkenaz, 15th century; No. 80, ed. Domb, Jerusalem, 5751, p. 385 and cf. *Responsa Teshuvah Me'ahavah* quoted above) states that reciting the

mourner's *kaddish* is connected to the *mitzvah* of honoring one's parents, and that is why one must enable a guest to recite one *kaddish,* because at that time, every *kaddish* was recited by only one mourner:

> Furthermore, in order that a guest should not be totally pushed away from [fulfilling] a *mitzvah* that is obligated of him and to bring contentment to the soul of his father, and so that they should not, God forbid, say that this man is cannot be atoned for. **Therefore the Sages allowed him to observe the *mitzvah* of honoring [his parents]** to prove that their sins can be atoned for.

In other words, by reciting the mourner's *kaddish,* the son or daughter publically declare that the deceased parent merits forgiveness for his sins and, by so doing, honors his memory.

3. Rabbi Yosef Eliyahu Henkin already emphasized that the mourner's *kaddish* does not stand alone, but rather symbolizes the child's fulfillment of all the other *mitzvot.* Just as a son symbolizes his loyalty to the *mitzvot* by reciting *kaddish,* so does a daughter do the same (and cf. Henrietta Szold's words quoted below).

4. Rabbis Bachrach, Grayevsky and Halevi already emphasized – and the same can be deduced from Rabbi Ya'akov Reisher – that the legend of Rabbi Akiva and the orphan should not be taken too literally. That legend dealt with the **son** of the dead man, but it did not come to exclude his **daughter**. On the contrary, a daughter too is called the offspring of the deceased and she too gives contentment to the soul of her parents by reciting the *kaddish.*

5. Rabbi Grayevsky already emphasized: if it is permissible to hire a stranger who did not know the deceased to recite *kaddish,* how can we prevent a daughter from sanctifying God's name in order to elevate the soul of the deceased?!

6. In a large percentage of the synagogues in the world, women and daughters recite the mourner's *kaddish*. The custom reinforces all of the other arguments, based on the Talmudic principles of "action is great" and "go out and see what the people do".

VI. The Words of Henrietta Szold

Since we are discussing the reciting of mourner's *kaddish* by a woman, it is only fitting to conclude with the words of Henrietta Szold who voiced her opinion on the subject at the beginning of the twentieth century.[14] It is worth noting that she mentioned some of the same points made by the *poskim* cited above.

Henrietta Szold (United States and Israel, 1860-1945) is known as the founder of *Hadassah* and as the first director of Youth Aliyah. She was the oldest of eight daughters. Her mother died in 1916 and a friend named Ḥayyim Peretz offered to recite *kaddish* for her mother. Henrietta Szold refused in a touching letter (Szold, pp 92-93):

> I know well and appreciate what you say about the Jewish custom, and Jewish custom is very dear and sacred to me. And yet I cannot ask you to say *Kaddish* after my mother. The *Kaddish* means to me that the survivor publicly and markedly manifests his wish and intention to assume the relation to the Jewish community which his parent had, and that so the chain of tradition remains unbroken from generation to generation, each adding its own link. You can do that for the generations of your family, I must do that for the generations of my family...
>
> My mother had eight daughters and no son... When my father died, my mother would not permit others to take her daughters' place in saying the *Kaddish*, and so I am sure I am acting in her spirit when I am moved to decline your offer... You understand me, don't you?

14. And cf. the article by Sarah Reguer.

We certainly do. Henrietta Szold recited the mourner's *kaddish* for both her parents. We have now seen that this is the *halakhah* and the proper thing to do.[15]

David Golinkin
Jerusalem
II Adar 5749

15. For another effort by Henrietta Szold to increase women's roles in the synagogue, see above, p. 9, and note 18.

BIBLIOGRAPHY

I. *Poskim* and Responsa

A. THOSE WHO PROHIBIT

Bachrach — Rabbi Yair Ḥayyim Bachrach, *Responsa Ḥavot Yair*, Ramat Gan, 5757, No. 222.

Dobrinsky — Rabbi Herbert Dobrinsky, *A Treasury of Sephardic Laws and Customs*, New York and Hoboken, 1986, p. 94

Emden — Rabbi Ya'akov Emden, *Siddur Beit Ya'akov, Dinei Kaddish Yatom*, at the end of *Shaḥarit*, paragraph 46, Lemberg, 1904, fol. 92a

Felder — Rabbi Aaron Felder, *Yesodei Smochos*, New York, 1976, pp. 50, 119

Fink — Rabbi Reuven Fink, *Journal of Halacha and Contemporary Society* 31 (Spring 1996), pp. 23-37 with reactions *ibid.*, 32 (Fall 1996), pp. 97-111, by Rabbis Wolowelsky, Henkin and Fink

Frankfurter — Rabbi Shimon Frankfurter, *Sefer Haḥayyim*, Amsterdam, 1703, paragraph 50, fol. 49a

Fuks — Rabbi Yitzḥak Ya'akov Fuchs, *Halikhot Bat Israel*, Jerusalem, 5744, pp. 157-158

Goldberg — Rabbi Ḥayyim Binyamin Goldberg, *Penei Barukh*, Jerusalem, 5746, pp. 360-361

Greenwald — Rabbi Yekutiel Yehudah Greenwald, *Kol Bo Al Aveilut*, Jerusalem-New York, 5733, p. 375, note 33

Katznellenbogen — Rabbi Yeḥezkel Katznellenbogen, *Responsa Kenesset Yisrael*, Altona, 1732, end of YD, fol. 53a

Lamm — Rabbi Maurice Lamm, *The Jewish Way in Death and Mourning*, second edition, New York, 1975, pp. 164-167; but see a more lenient approach in the revised and expanded edition, New York, 2000, pp. 157-163

Lau — Rabbi Yisrael Meir Lau, *Responsa Yaḥel Israel*, Jerusalem, 5752, No. 90

Luria — Rabbi Ḥayyim Pinḥass Luria, *Meishiv Halakhah*, Part 1, Lodz, 1923, No. 469

Margaliot — Rabbi Ephraim Zalman Margaliot, *Mateh Ephraim*, Petrikov, 1906, *Dinei Kaddish Yatom* 4:8, pp. 297-298 and in *Elef Lamateh, ibid.*

Medini — Rabbi Ḥayyim Ḥizkiya Medini, *Sedei Ḥemed, Aseifat Dinim, Ma'arekhet Aveilut*, paragraph 160, ed. Schneerson, Vol. 4, p. 1417

Rabinowicz — Rabbi H. Rabinowicz, *A Guide to Life*, second edition, New York, 1967, pp. 87-88

Roth — Rabbi Meshulam Roth, *Responsa Kol Mevasser*, Part 2, Jerusalem, 5733, No. 44

Rubin-Halberstam — Rabbi Shalom Yeḥezkel Shraga Rubin-Halberstam, *Hapardess* 38/1 (Tishrei 5724), pp. 14-16

Uziel — Rabbi Ben-Tzion Meir Ḥai Uziel, *Mishpetei Uziel*, second edition, OH, Part 1, Jerusalem, 5707, No. 13 = *Piskei Uziel Beshe'elot Hazman*, Jerusalem, 5737, No. 3

Warman — Rabbi Shlomo Halevi Warman, *She'erit Yosef*, Part 2, New York, 5741, No. 60

Waldenberg — Rabbi Eliezer Waldenberg, *Tzitz Eliezer*, Vol. 14, second edition, Jerusalem, 5745, No. 7

Weiss — Rabbi Yitzḥak Ya'akov Weiss. *Minḥat Yitzḥak*, Part 4, Jerusalem, 5753, No. 30

Yosef — Rabbi Yitzḥak Yosef, *Yalkut Yosef*, Part 7, Jerusalem, 5749, pp. 221-222

Yosef Ḥayyim — Rabbi Yosef Ḥayyim of Baghdad (attributed to him), *Responsa Torah Lishmah*, Jerusalem, 5733, No. 27

Zilberberg — Rabbi Avraham Binyamin Zilberberg, *Responsa Mishnat Binyamin*, New York, 5708, No. 34

B. THOSE WHO ARE LENIENT

Flekeles — Rabbi Eleazar Flekeles, *Teshuvah Mei'ahavah*, Part 2, Prague, 1815, OH, No. 229:10

Glick — Rabbi Avraham Yitzḥak Glick, *Responsa Yad Yitzḥak*, Part 3, Satmar, 1909, *Yoreh De'ah*, No. 340.

Halevi — Rabbi Ḥayyim David Halevi, *Asei Lekha Rav*, Part 5, Tel Aviv, 5743, No. 33

Meizlish — Shaul Meizlish, *Zikaron Livrakhah, Minhagei Petirah Ve'aveilut Bemasoret Yisrael*, Tel Aviv. 1987, p. 65

Reisher — Rabbi Ya'akov Reisher, *Responsa Shevut Ya'akov*, Part 2, New York, 5721, YD, No. 93

Tukechinsky — Rabbi Yechiel Mikhel Tukechinsky, *Gesher Haḥayyim*, Part 1, second edition, Jerusalem, 5720, Chapter 30, Paragraph 7, pp. 325-326

C. THOSE WHO ALLOW IT

Abarg'il — Rabbi Eliyahu Abarg'il, quoted in *Yedi'ot Aharonot*, Nov. 19, 1992, p. 12

Allen — Rabbi Wayne Allen, *Tomeikh Kehalakhah*, Mt. Vernon, New York, 1986, p. 39

Berkovits — Raḥel Berkovits, *A Daughter's Recitation of Mourner's Kaddish*, New York, 2011, 93 pp.

Bleier — Rabbi Moshe Leib Bleier, a responsum from ca. 1955, cited by Millen (see below), pp. 190-194 and printed in Hebrew by Berkovits, pp. 88-89

Blumenthal — Rabbi Aaron Blumenthal, *Conservative Judaism* 31/3 (Spring 1977), pp. 31-32 = *And Bring them Closer to Torah*, edited by David Blumenthal, Hoboken, 1986, pp. 32-33

Donin — Rabbi Ḥayyim Halevy Donin, *To Pray as a Jew*, New York, 1980, p. 226

Feinstein — Rabbi Moshe Feinstein, *Igrot Moshe*, Vol. 8, Jerusalem, 5756, OH, Part 5, No. 12, p. 20

Freehof Rabbi Solomon Freehof, *Reform Jewish Practice*, Part 2, New York, 1979, p. 294

Grayevsky Rabbi Eliezer Zalman Grayevsky, *Sefer Kaddish Le'olam*, Jerusalem, 1891, fols 11a-12a

Henkin Rabbi Yehudah Herzl Henkin, *Hadarom* 54 (Sivan 5745), pp. 34-48 = *Responsa Benei Banim*, Part 2, Jerusalem, 5752, No. 7

Henkin Rabbi Yosef Eliyahu Henkin, *Kitvei Hagaon Rabbi Yosef Eliyahu Henkin*, Vol. 2: *Teshuvot Ivra*, New York, 1989, p. 6; *ibid.* pp. 3-5 = *Hapardess* 37/6 (Adar 5723), pp. 5-6

Klein Rabbi Isaac Klein, *A Guide to Jewish Religious Practice*, New York, 1979, p. 294

Soloveitchik

Rabbi Aaron Soloveitchik, *Od Yisrael Yosef Beni Ḥai*, Chicago, 5753, No. 32, p. 100

Wolowelsky

Rabbi Joel Wolowesky, *Tradition* 22/1 (Spring 1986), pp. 69-72; *Hadarom* 57 (Elul 5748), pp. 157-158; *Judaism* 44/3 (Summer 1995), pp. 282-290; *Women, Jewish Law and Modernity*, Hoboken, 1997, pp. 88-90

Zemer Rabbi Moshe Zemer, *Halakhah Shefuyah*, Tel-Aviv, 5754, pp. 227-233 = *Evolving Halakhah*, Woodstock, Vermont, 1999, pp. 265-273

II. General Bibliography

Auerbach Rabbi David Auerbach, *Halikhot Beitah*, Jerusalem, 5743, pp. 72-73

Brody Rabbi Shlomo Brody, "May women recite kaddish?", *The Jerusalem Post Magazine*, May 6, 2011, p. 43

Chernik Rabbi Sholom Shachne Chernik, *Ḥayim Uberakhah*, Part Two: *Lemishmeret Shalom*, New York, 5709, p. 94, paragraph 51

Deutsch Nathaniel Deutsch, *The Maiden of Ludmir*, Berkeley,

Los Angeles and London, 2003, p. 134

Ellinson — Elyakim Ellinson, *Ha'ishah Vehamitzvot, Sefer Rishon: Bein Ha'ishah Leyotzrah*, second edition, Jerusalem, 5737, p. 70 and note 17

Felder — Rabbi Gedalia Felder, *Yesodei Yeshurun*, Part 1, Toronto, 5714, pp. 227-228

Ganzfried — Rabbi Shlomo Ganzfried, *Kitzur Shulḥan Arukh* 26:20

Gorenberg — Gershom Gorenberg, *Ha'aretz*, June 5, 2009

Jakobovits — Rabbi Immanuel Jakobovits, *Jewish Law Faces Modern Problems*, New York, 1965, pp. 53-54

Kahana-Shapira — Rabbi Menaḥem Naḥum Kahana-Shapira, *Otzar She'elot Uteshuvot*, Vol. 2, Jerusalem, 5736, p. 71

Millen — Rochelle Millen, *Modern Judaism* 10/2 (1990), pp. 191-203; expanded in *Jewish Legal Writings by Women*, edited by Micah Halpern and Chana Safrai, Jerusalem, 1998, pp. 179-201 and expanded further in her book: *Women, Birth and Death in Jewish Law and Practice*, Hanover and London, 2004, Chapter 5 (pp. 133-136 contain a summary of the Hebrew version of this responsum)

Preschel — Tuvia Preschel, *Hapardess* 37/7 (Nisan 5723), p. 20

Reguer — Sara Reguer, "Kaddish from the Wrong Side of the Mechitzah" in: Susannah Heschel, ed., *On Being a Jewish Feminist: A Reader*, New York, 1983, pp. 177-181

Routtenberg — Max Routtenberg, *One in a Minyan and Other Stories*, New York, 1977, pp. 1–22

Sarig — Tikvah Sarig, *Imma Aggadah*, Tel Aviv, 5740, pp. 39-49

Sarig — Tikvah Sarig, "*Even Mekir Tiz'ak*", *Davar* June 2, 1984 (a poem from 1968)

Shapira	Dr. Amnon Shapira, *Amudim* 523 (Av 5749), pp. 351-352
Sofer	Barbara Sofer, "Eleven Months of Kaddish", *The Jerusalem Post Magazine,* July 9, 2010, p. 13
Steinberg	Rabbi Moshe Halevy Steinberg, *Hilkhot Nashim,* Jerusalem, 5743, Chapter 27, pp. 133-134
Szold	Marvin Lowenthal, *Henrietta Szold: Life and Letters,* New York, 1942, pp. 92-93
Tzuriel	Nava Tzuriel, *Maariv, Mosaf Hashabbat,* August 6, 2004, pp. 14-15, 28
Weil	Rabbi Ya'akov Weil, *Responsa Rabbi Ya'akov Weil,* Jerusalem, 5748, No. 13
Yehoshua	Ya'akov Yehoshua, *Yaldut Biyerushalayim Hayeshanah: Pirkei Havai Miyamim Avaru,* Vol. 5: *Shekhunot Biyerushalayim Hayeshanah Mesaperot,* Jerusalem, 1978, p. 138

I would like to thank Rabbi Theodore Friedman z"l, Rabbi Reuven Hammer, Professor Meir Benayahu z"l and Rabbi Paul Lederman who referred me to four of the books mentioned above.

12. THE ACTIVE PARTICIPATION OF WOMEN IN THE MARRIAGE CEREMONY AND *SHEVA BERAKHOT*

Even Ha'ezer 34:4; 62:4

Question from Rabbi Victor Hoffman: *It has been the custom for generations that bride and groom honor their male friends by inviting them to take an active part in the wedding ceremony and the ensuing seven days of celebration during which sheva berakhot or seven blessings are recited at the end of the Grace after Meals. Today, many couples wish to honor their female friends in a similar fashion both at the wedding ceremony and during the seven days of celebration. Is it permissible for women to actively participate in the wedding ceremony or the sheva berakhot recited during the seven days of celebration?*

Responsum: Let us open with the introduction to an article dealing with one of the topics discussed here:

> One of the most important phenomena of recent generations is the change in women's status in society and in their self-awareness within both general and [Jewish] society... the effects of this revolution are also apparent in the ultra-Orthodox world... gone is the era when *poskim* made their rulings based on the assumption that women, as a group, "do not understand". Today there are many women who are very concerned about Judaism, who fervently observe the *mitzvot*, who possess higher education in both Jewish and secular studies... Of course, these women understand and respect the view of the *halakhah*... but just as they understand that it is impossible to permit the forbidden, they feel insulted and deprived of their rights if we prohibit

> them from taking part in what it is possible to permit. Furthermore, in the last generation, the *Seridei Eish* emphasized (Part 2, No. 8) that this is obvious to anyone who is familiar with women's nature in these countries and that a prohibition can cause Jewish women to be alienated from religion... (Wolowelsky, *Amudim*, p. 86).

Our approach is very similar to this approach. It is very easy to prohibit all the things discussed in this responsum by arguing that "we follow the customs of our forefathers". However, this answer does not satisfy the women of our generation and does not bring them closer to the observance of the commandments. When asked about the participation of women in various Jewish ceremonies, it is imperative to delve deeply into the topic being discussed. Otherwise, the *halakhah*, which is derived from the root *halakh*, to go, will not be able to go with the times and to cope with the far-reaching changes of modern society.

We will now discuss various aspects of the wedding ceremony and of the seven days of celebration. Since many different topics are involved, we will present each one in the form of a question and respond to each one separately. The questions are presented according to the order of the ceremonies, and not in order of importance.

I. Is a woman permitted to hold the poles of the *ḥuppah* [wedding canopy]?

This is unquestionably permitted. As we explained elsewhere, we are accustomed today to a mixed society and there is no concern about sinful thoughts during a religious ceremony.[1]

1. See below, pp. 328-334. The author of the *Levush* cited there permits mixed seating at a wedding banquet "because now the women are very used to being among the men and there are not so many sinful thoughts". Regarding the custom of holding the *ḥuppah*, see Adler, p. 250.

II. Is a woman permitted to sing *piyyutim* [liturgical hymns] such as *Mee Adir Al Hakol*?

As we have proven elsewhere,[2] the concept of *kol b'ishah ervah* [a woman's voice is lewdness] originally referred to the **speaking** voice of a woman to the extent that this could lead to forbidden sexual relations and not to the **singing** voice of a woman during a religious ceremony. Regarding the *piyyutim* themselves, *Mee Adir* was first printed in the 17th century, but there is no requirement to recite it;[3] indeed, Sepharadim do not say it. Likewise, while the bride circles the groom, it is customary to sing the *piyyut Mi Ben Siaḥ Shoshan Ḥoḥim*, which was written in the 13th century at the latest, but this too is optional.[4] Therefore, it is permissible for a woman to sing these types of *piyyutim* at the beginning of the wedding ceremony.

III. Is a woman permitted to read the *ketubah* [marriage contract] aloud during the wedding ceremony?

This is a French-German custom dating from the Middle Ages.[5] According to most *poskim*, it was intended to separate

2. See above, Chapter 2.
3. This *piyyut* appears in *Seder Birkat Hamazon*, Dierenfurth, 1691 (according to Adler, p. 372, note 142) and in a manuscript published by David Kaufmann, *REJ* 24 (1892), pp. 289-291. Also see Aharon Ahrend, *Sidra* 7 (5751), p. 11. Rabbi Joseph Hertz, *The Authorised Daily Prayer Book*, New York, 1948, p. 1009, emphasizes that there is no requirement to recite it.
4. See Adler, p. 374, note 154 and Ahrend, *op. cit.*, p. 10 who adds that the original version was מבין שיחים.
5. This was Rashi's custom according to Rabbi Meshulam b"r Nattan in *Sefer Hayashar Lerabbeinu Tam*, No. 47, paragraph 7, p. 92 (and cf. *ibid.*, No. 45, paragraph 5, p. 82, for Rabbeinu Tam's remarks); *Tosafot* to *Pesaḥim* 102b, s.v. *she'ein*; *Hagahot Maimoniyot*, *Hilkhot Ishut*, Chapter 3, letter *samekh* and cf. Chapter 10, letter *gimmel*; Rabbi Ya'akov Ḥazan of London, *Eitz Ḥayyim*, Part 2, p. 240; the Mordechai to *Ketubot*, Chapter 1, paragraph 132, in the name of a responsum of Rashi; *Darkhei Moshe* to EH 62, paragraph 6, in the name of the Mordechai, *Tosafot* and *Asheri*; the Rema in EH 62:9; *Responsa Maharam Mintz*, No. 109, ed. Jerusalem, 5751, p. 538 with the glosses; Adler, p. 346.

between the *birkat erussin*/betrothal blessing and the *birkat ḥattanim*/marriage blessings so that the blessing recited over wine could be recited over two different cups of wine, because one does not perform two *mitzvot* with one cup of wine. If that is the case, the reading **itself** is of no halakhic significance and any woman capable of reading the Aramaic with comprehension may read the *ketubah* aloud during the wedding ceremony.[5a]

IV. Is a woman permitted to deliver a *derashah* [sermon] under the *ḥuppah*?

The *derashah* beneath the *ḥuppah* is meant to explain the importance of marriage in Judaism and to guide the young couple in their future together and it is permissible for a woman to explain these things just like a man.

V. Is it permissible for a woman be included in the *minyan* required for *birkat erussin* and *birkat ḥattanim*?

The betrothal ceremony consists of the blessing over wine, the *birkat erussin*, and the formula *harei at mekudeshet lee*/behold you are sanctified unto me. The marriage ceremony consists of the blessing over wine and another six blessings which together are referred to as *sheva berakhot* or *birkat ḥattanim* [the grooms' blessing].[6] During the Talmudic period, the betrothal ceremony and the marriage ceremony took place a year apart (Mishnah *Ketubot* 5:2) and therefore it comes as no surprise that the two ceremonies were different in nature. The betrothal ceremony required two witnesses (*Kiddushin* 65a-b) and there was no

For two other explanations for reading the *ketubah* aloud, see Efraim Kupfer, *Teshuvot Upesakim Mei'eit Ḥakhmei Ashkenaz*, Jerusalem, 5733, No. 129, pp. 199-200. However, these explanations were not reflected in later *halakhic* literature. For a custom of **not** reading the *ketubah* aloud, see Adler, p. 346.

5a. See Rabbi Kanefsky who allows a woman to read the *ketubah* aloud.

6. For a history of the *sheva berakhot*, see Glick, pp. 226-228, 241-246.

Talmudic requirement to betroth a woman in the presence of a *minyan*. The first to require a *minyan* for a betrothal was Rav Aḥa of Shabḥa (*She'iltot, Ḥayei Sarah,* No. 16, ed. Mirsky, pp. 107-108): "whereas whoever wants to marry a wife it is obligated of him to sanctify her first and recite the blessings of betrothal ***b'asarah*/ before ten** and the grooms' blessing **before ten**". Others who followed in his footsteps include Rav Sa'adia Gaon (*Sidur Rasag,* pp. 96-98 – but he permits betrothal with two witnesses after the fact); the Rosh (to *Ketubot,* Chapter 1, paragraph 12); *Ha'ittur* (Part 2, fol. 63a); the Meiri (to *Ketubot,* p. 34); *Responsa Binyamin Ze'ev* (end of No. 30); EH 34:4; and *Peri Ḥadash* (in *Likutei Even Ha'ezer,* paragraph 34).

On the other hand, Rabbi Shmuel Hanagid ruled (*Otzar Hageonim Leketubot,* pp. 13-14 and *Hilkhot Hanagid,* ed. Margaliot, paragraph 40) that there is no need for a *minyan* to recite the betrothal blessings. This approach was followed by *Sefer Ha'eshkol* (ed. Albeck, Vol. 2, p. 194); the students of Rabbeinu Yona (in *Shita Mekubetzet* to *Ketubot* 8a); *Tamim De'im,* No. 189; and the Ra'ah to *Ketubot* 8a. Contemporary Rabbis who agreed with them include Rabbi B.M. Levin (*Otzar Hageonim* to *Ketubot,* p. 14, note 2), Rabbi Uziel (in his responsum), Rabbi Margaliot (cited above), Rabbi Albeck (cited above), and Rabbi Rabinowitz (pp. 56-57).

There is no doubt that Rabbi Shmuel Hanagid is correct, for the following reasons (I have listed in parentheses who stated each reason):

1. Unlike *Birkat Ḥattanim,* there is no mention in the Talmud of the need for a *minyan* for the recitation of the *Birkat Erussin* (Rabbi Shmuel Hanagid, according to Naḥmanides and the Rosh).
2. If the betrothal **itself** is performed before two witnesses, why require ten people for the **blessing** over the betrothal? (Rabbi Shmuel Hanagid, *ibid.*).

3. Rabbi Shmuel Hanagid disagreed with the *She'iltot* "and said it was a scribal error" (according to Naḥmanides) and Rabbi Mordechai Margaliot agreed: "The Nagid's view is totally reasonable. And it is possible that the word ***'b'asarah***/before ten' is dittography". In other words, the word "*b'asarah*" may have been mistakenly written twice in the *She'iltot* because of the continuation of the sentence. Indeed, Rabbi Ḥanoch Albeck proved it was a scribal error by comparing the *She'iltot* to the parallel passages in *Halakhot Gedolot* and *Hilkhot Re'u* (in *Sefer Ha'eshkol, ibid.*; and cf. A.Ḥ. Freimann, *Seder Kiddushin Venissuin*, Jerusalem, 5705, pp. 16-17).

4. The Talmud (*Ketubot* 7b) compared the betrothal blessing to the blessings recited over fruit, before performing a *mitzvah* and *kiddush* – and these blessings do not require a *minyan* (*Shita Mekubetzet, ibid*).

If this is the case, according to the basic law, no *minyan* is required to recite the betrothal blessings. Indeed, the *Shulḥan Arukh* only demanded a *minyan* before the fact (EH 34:4; and also in the *Levush ibid.*) "and if there are not ten, this is not indespensable" (*Beit Shmuel, ibid*). Therefore, there is no **need** to determine whether a woman may be included in a *minyan* for reciting the betrothal blessings. If there is no *minyan* of ten men present, it is possible to rule according to the Talmud and Rabbi Shmuel Hanagid that no *minyan* is required or according to the *Shulḥan Arukh* that no *minyan* is required after the fact.

However, since the days of Rashi, it is customary to conduct the betrothal ceremony together with the marriage ceremony and therefore, **in practice**, a *minyan* is also required for the betrothal blessings, since *birkat ḥattanim* requires a *minyan*, as we learned in the Mishnah (*Megillah* 4:3 = fol. 23b): "and one does not recite... *birkat ḥattanim*... **with less than ten**". Similarly, a *beraita* (*Ketubot* 7b) states: "Our Sages taught: one blesses *birkat ḥattanim* **before ten** all of the seven days of celebration" and this is also proven from a midrash (*Vayikra Rabbah* 23:4, ed. Margaliot, p. 530 and parallels). This law was derived from various *asmakhtaot* [biblical prooftexts] given by different Sages.[7] Many derive this law from the verse (Ruth 4:2) "and [Boaz] took **ten men** of the elders of the city and said: sit here and they sat down",[8] whereas Rabbi Abahu learns it from the verse (*Psalms* 68:27) "Bless God in the congregations, the Lord from the fountain of Israel" (*Ketubot* 7b).

Based on the above-mentioned sources, the *poskim* ruled "that one does not bless *birkat ḥattanim* except before ten free adults" (Responsa of Rav Natronai in *Teshuvot Hageonim*, ed. Coronel, end of paragraph 55; Maimonides, *Hilkhot Ishut* 10:5; *Tur* EH 62; and *Shulḥan Arukh* EH 62:4). There are some who allow *birkat ḥattanim* to be recited after the fact with less than ten present (ET, s.v. *Ḥattanim*, note 49), but, generally speaking, all the *poskim* require a *minyan* for *birkat ḥattanim*.

Do the above sources allow a woman to be counted in a *minyan* for reciting *birkat ḥattanim*? The Ritba (*Ḥiddushim* to *Ketubot* 7b, ed. Goldstein, col. 44) derived from the verse in Ruth "ten **people**/*asarah* ***anashim***" that they should be "adult and males" or since it says [in Psalms] "**in the congregations**" that there is no **congregation** except for ten adult males (and cf. Novak, p. 41, who apparently agrees with his view).[9]

However, it is difficult to accept such a precise reading of the verses because the *Gemara* itself rejected such a precise reading when it stated: if we learn [that] ten men [are needed] from the verse "and [Boaz] took ten men **of the elders** of the city" "is it not

7. It should emphasized that both the betrothal blessing and *birkat ḥattanim* are rabbinic commandments and **all** the verses are simply an *asmakhta*. Indeed, this was emphasized by *Massekhet Kallah Rabbati* 1:2, ed. Higger, p. 173 and *Tosafot* to *Ketubot* 7b, s.v. *shene'emar*; cf. Rabbi Rabinowitz, p. 56. In contrast, Professor Halivni, pp. 3-5, apparently thinks that these blessings existed in Biblical times, but this approach is difficult to accept.
8. Huna bar Nattan in *Ketubot* 7a and again on 7b; Rabbi Eleazar b"r Yosi in Yerushalmi *Ketubot*, Chapter 1, fol. 25a = *Ruth Rabbah* 7:8, ed. Vilna, fol. 12a; *Pirkei Derabi Eliezer*, Chapter 19, fol. 44b = *Midrash Tehilim* 92:7, ed. Buber, pp. 406-407; *Kallah Rabbati* 1:1, ed. Higger, p. 174. For a later version of this *derashah*, see Rabbi Shimshon bar Zadok, *Sefer Tashbetz*, paragraph 467. On this subject, also see Glick, pp. 266-269.
9. Rabbi Uziel also forbids counting women in a *minyan* for *birkat ḥattanim*, but for other reasons – see his responsum.

possible for them not to be **elders** [=Sages]?" (*Ketubot* 7b). In other words, must the ten specifically be Sages? Indeed, if we derive laws from the precise wording of verses cited in the Talmud as *asmakhtaot*, it is possible to reach some strange conclusions. For example, the need for a *minyan* for a *davar shebikdushah*/a matter of holiness is learned in *Megillah* 23b from a double *gezeirah shavah* between *Koraḥ* and his **congregation** and the **congregation** of spies. Should we then derive from this that a *minyan* must be comprised of **ten wicked people**?! Therefore, it is preferable not make precise derivations from the *asmakhtaot* cited by the Sages.[10]

As for the phrase "ten free adults" which appears in the writings of the *poskim*, the *Maggid Mishneh* derives from it

> that a slave and a minor do not join [as] in *Berakhot* (47b)... and this is also the opinion [of Maimonides] z"l in Chapter 8 of *Hilkhot Tefillah* and the same applies to every event that requires ten, that they do not join (*Maggid Mishneh* to *Hilkhot Ishut* 10:5 and cf. *Kesef Mishneh* to *Hilkhot Berakhot* 2:10).

But we can read precisely in his footsteps that, in the opinion of Maimonides, a slave and and a minor are **not** included in the ten for reciting *birkat ḥattanim*, **whereas a woman may join** just as she apparently may join the ten for a *minyan* for prayer (look carefully at *Hilkhot Tefillah* 1:2-4; 8:4) and for reading the Torah (12:3 according to the reading of the *Kesef Mishneh ibid.* and the *Tur* in OH 143). On the other hand, when Maimonides wanted to exclude women, he did so explicitly with regard to *zimmun* (*Hilkhot Berakhot* 5:7) and *birkat kohanim* (*Hilkhot Nesiat Kapaim* 15:9).[11]

And if one were to say that Maimonides (and consequently

10. For similar precise readings of verses and their rejection regarding counting women in a minyan for prayer, see above, pp. 109-110.
11. See *ibid.*, p. 111, notes 33-34.

the *Tur* and the *Shulḥan Arukh*) wrote "ten free adults" to exclude women, then one could respond as follows:

1. There is no mention in the *Gemara* (*Ketubot* 7-8) of this and "*hamotizi meiḥavero alav hare'ayah*/the claimant must produce evidence".

2. The institution of ten or a *minyan* is a very ancient custom in Judaism and is not limited to matters listed in Mishnah *Megillah* 4:3 cited above. It is very clear that the Jewish people in ancient times believed that there is no congregation of less than ten, and therefore ten is the minimal number required for many different events: trials (Exodus 18:21 = Deuteronomy 1:15, Ruth 4:2 cited above, *The Damascus Covenant* 13:1-2); a city (Genesis 18:32; *Megillah* 1:3 "ten idlers"); courts (*The Damascus Covenant* 10:4 and Rabbi Yehoshua ben Levi in *Sanhedrin* 7b); declaring a leap year (*Pirkei Derabi Eliezer*, Chapter 8, fol. 20a; *Shemot Rabbah* 15:20); sanctifying the new month (Yerushalmi *Megillah* 4:4, ed. Vilna, fol. 30b); the feast of the leap month (*Sanhedrin* 70b); the *havurah* for eating the Passover sacrifice (Josephus, *Wars* 6, 9, 3; *Targum Pseudo-Yonatan* to Exodus 12:4 and cf. *Tosefta Pasḥa* 4:15, ed. Lieberman, p. 661); reading the *Megillah* (according to Rav Assi – *Megillah* 5a); and even for asking forgiveness from the dead (*Yoma* 87a).[11a]

If so, it can be assumed that one blesses *birkat ḥattanim* with ten people both at the marriage ceremony and during the seven days of celebration in order to give the marriage and the seven days a public and festive character and because "in the multitude of people is the king's glory" (Proverbs 14:28).[11b] And, apparently, a

11a. See Rabbi Ismar Schorsch, *JUDAISM* 55/3-4 (Fall-Winter 2006), pp. 73-83, for a recent discussion of the importance of the *minyan*.

11b. This approach finds ostensible support in *Pirkei Derabi Eliezer* = *Midrash Tehilim* (above, note 8): "All *edot ne'emanot* in Israel are in the presence of ten... *edot* of the marriage blessing is in the presence of ten, as it says (Ruth 4:2) 'And he took ten people' ". Rabbi Berzon, p. 112, note 5, thought that *edot* = **publicity** and therefore, according to *Pirkei Derabi Eliezer*, both a slave and a minor [and also a woman, according to our approach] may be woman is part of this public because *birkat ḥattanim* refers to both spouses in equal measure. Similarly, a woman is part of this public because, as we shall see below, she, too, is obligated to help the bride and groom rejoice.

All of the above, therefore, indicates that there is no essential or textual reason to prevent a woman from joining the *minyan* needed for *birkat ḥattanim*.[12]

VI. Is a woman permitted to recite the betrothal blessing?

In order to answer this question, it is necessary to clarify the purpose of the betrothal blessing, but there is no clear answer to this question.

1. The *Gemara* itself is in doubt about the nature of the blessing. Two amoraim relate in the name of Rav Yehudah:

> "Blessed are you O Lord... who has permitted us women married by *ḥuppah* and *kiddushin*" whereas "Rav Aḥa son of Rava concludes the blessing in the name of Rav Yehudah: "Blessed are you O Lord, who has sanctified Israel by *ḥuppah* and *kiddushin*". Whoever does not conclude the blessing, **it is similar to the blessing over fruit and blessings recited before performing *mitzvot***; and who-

included in the ten in order to publicize the matter. However, ***edot*** there is not **testimony** in Rabbinic Hebrew, but rather a ***mitzvah*** or a **law** in Biblical Hebrew (as in Psalms 119:14, 31, 36, 99, 111, 129, 144, 157 and many other verses). Indeed, Buber already stressed in his notes to *Midrash Tehillim* that the phrase *edot ne'emanot* in this midrash is based on the verse "*edotekha ne'emnu me'od*/Your *mitzvot* are very true" (Psalms 93:5), because the midrash is explaining Psalms 92-93 and it means that all the **true *mitzvot*** for Israel are in the presence of ten. Therefore, one cannot conclude from this midrash that *eidot* = **publicity** and this does not support what I wrote in the text.

12. See Rabbi Kahana who, with some hesitation, allowed a woman to be counted in the *minyan* for *sheva berakhot* under the *ḥuppah* in Lithuania in the year 1907!

> ever does conclude the blessing, **it is similar to the *kiddush*** (*Ketubot* 7b)

Indeed, the Ritba explains (in *Shita Mekubetzet* to *Ketubot* 7b, s.v. *vekhatav haritba*): "**this blessing is none other than a type of *kiddush*** [thanking God] for sanctifying us more than the other nations with regard to being fruitful and multiplying". And that is also how the the author of the *Itur* explained it (fol. 62d).

The *halakhah* was established that we conclude the betrothal blessing like the *kiddush* for Shabbat, and women are biblically obligated to observe the commandment of *kiddush* on Shabbat (*Berakhot* 20b). Therefore, according to this approach, it is permissible for women to recite the betrothal blessing, just as it is permissible for them to recite *kiddush* over wine on Shabbat.

2. Some say that this blessing is one of the blessings over *mitzvot,* similar to the blessings over circumcision and redeeming a first-born son (*Siddur Rav Sa'adia Gaon,* p. 96) "and the blessing should be recited before the *kiddushin* **either by [the groom] or by his emissary just as we recite blessings over all mitzvot** and afterwards [the groom] betrothes (Maimonides, *Hilkhot Ishut* 3:23; and cf. ET, s.v. *Erussin,* note 13, for other *Rishonim* who feel the same way; and this is also Rabbi Rabinowitz's opinion, pp. 57-58). According to this approach, the groom **himself** must recite the betrothal blessing and, if someone else recites it in his place, he is serving as the groom's **emissary**. Therefore, a woman is permitted to recite the blessing because she is permitted to serve as an emissary for *kiddushin* (EH 35:6 and Maimonides, *Hilkhot Ishut* 3:17 and this is derived from the laws of divorce – EH 141:31 and Maimonides, *Hilkhot Gerushin* 6:6).

3. Rabbi Efraim Zalman Shor thinks that the blessing was not enacted for the sake of the betrother [the groom], but rather for those gathered at the betrothal house, and in the words of the *Gemara* "the betrothal blessing is blessed in the betrothal house" (*Ketubot* 7b; *Tevuat Shor* to YD 1:59 = ET, s.v. *Erusin,* note 21). According to this view, there is no reason to prevent a woman from reciting this blessing.

4. According to Rabbi Mordechai Yaffe (*Levush Habotz Veha'argaman, Hilkhot Kiddushin* 34:1)

> just as *birkot hanehenin*/blessings of enjoyment are recited over every enjoyable thing that happens to come a person's way before he enjoys it... so too a blessing is recited first... a blessing of enjoyment for the woman who has been betrothed to him, whether he betrothed her himself or by an emissary, and if he betrothed her himself, he himself recites the blessing, and if his emissary betrothed her, then the emissary recites the blessing in his stead because he carried out the mission [of *kiddushin*] and it is our custom that another person blesses

This approach is surprising. Does a man marry to **enjoy** his wife? Furthermore, is there any similarity between the formula of the *birkot hanehenin*/blessings of enjoyment and the formula of the betrothal blessing? Therefore, it is difficult to accept this approach.

5. The Rosh determines (Rosh to *Ketubot,* Chapter 1, end of paragraph 12):

> **and this blessing was enacted to give praise to God** who has sanctified us with his commandments and distinguished us from the other nations and commanded us to sanctify a woman who is permitted to us and not one of the forbidden.

If it is a blessing of praise, there is no reason to prevent a woman from reciting the betrothal blessing.

Therefore, according to most of the approaches presented here (except for that of the *Levush* which we have rejected), it is permissible for a woman to recite the betrothal blessing.

VII. Is a woman permitted to recite *birkat ḥattanim,* the *sheva berakhot,* under the *ḥuppah* or at the end of the Grace after Meals during the seven days of celebration?

Here, too, we must clarify the purpose of *birkat ḥattanim,* and once again the answer is very unclear.

1. According to Maimonides, *birkat ḥattanim* is blessed **before** the marriage (*Hilkhot Ishut* 10:3). The *Beit Yosef* concludes from that (EH 62) "and the reason is clear, because all *mitzvot,* he blesses them prior to doing them". His words seem to indicate that this is **a blessing over *mitzvot*;** however Rabbi Berzon already questioned this approach (pp. 101-102): a) If this is a blessing over a *mitzvah,* why are the same blessings recited during the seven days of celebration? b) The formula of the blessings is the formula of blessings of praise and not the blessings before performing *mitzvot.* c) Maimonides indeed maintains that the **betrothal blessing** is a blessing over a *mitzvah* (see above) and, therefore, according to him, if he betrothed and did not recite the blessing, he should not recite the blessing; whereas with regard to ***birkat ḥattanim,*** Maimonides writes (*Hilkhot Ishut* 10:6) that he should go back and recite the blessing even after several days have elapsed. d) According to Maimonides, no *minyan* is necessary for the betrothal blessing, because it is a blessing over a commandment, whereas *birkat ḥattanim* requires a *minyan.* This seems to indicate that this is a different type of blessing.

2. According to Naḥmanides and the Ran, the *sheva berakhot* are **blessings of praise**. The Ran states (on the Rif to *Pesaḥim,* Chapter 1, ed. Vilna, fol. 4a, s.v. *ule'inyan*):

> and regarding the marriage blessings, it is customary not to recite them until after she enters the *ḥuppah* **because the blessings are none other than blessings of praise and glory,** and this is so because they are recited for the entire seven days... (and see the continuation for his rejection of the *Beit Yosef*'s approach mentioned above).

Rashi, on the other hand, stresses the matter only with regard to the last of the seven blessings: "**and in the last one, there is praise of God,** who created a wedding ceremony enabling a man and a woman to cling to each other with joy and gladness" (*Ketubot* 8a, s.v. *mesameaḥ* at the end; and cf. Rabbi Rabinowitz, p. 50 and note 20 for other *Rishonim* who concur).

3. Finally, there are *poskim* who stress that the purpose of the seven blessings is to **gladden the bride and groom**. Rashi explains: "it is a prayer that we pray and bless that **they should be happy in their success throughout their lives**" (*ibid.*). Rabbi David Abudraham gives a similar explanation (*Abudraham Hashalem*, p. 363):

> and know that the blessing *sameaḥ tesamaḥ* [may you gladden the beloved companions] is a way of asking for mercy for the bride and groom, **to gladden them in their union** and to wish them success in all their endeavors **like the joy** of the union of Adam [and Eve] in the Garden of Eden. (See the continuation; and cf. Rav Hai in *Otzar Hageonim* to *Ketubot*, p. 16, paragraph 55 and Rabbi Yisraeli, p. 165).

If we adopt one of the latter two approaches, we can rule that it is permissible for a woman to recite *birkat ḥattanim* both under the *ḥuppah* and during the seven days of celebration. For if the *sheva berakhot* are a matter of blessings in praise of God, is a man more obligated than a woman? And if it is a *mitzvah* to gladden a bride and groom, is a woman exempt from this *mitzvah*? (see below) However, since several *poskim* have recently discussed this question and reached different conclusions, we must discuss what they said.[13]

13. Rabbis Deblitzki and Felder forbid this practice without any explanation. Rabbi Steinberg is strict because of *kol b'ishah ervah*/"a woman's voice is lewdness", and lest allowing this will lead to other changes. Rabbis Halivni, Halevi, Yisraeli and Novak are strict about this after careful analysis. Rabbi Wolowelsky allows a woman to recite *sheva berakhot* during the seven days of celebration, but not under the *ḥuppah*. Rabbi Rabinowitz allows women to perform the entire marriage ceremony.

1. Rabbi Professor David Halivni has proved, as we did above, that *birkat ḥattanim* requires a *minyan*. And why is this so? Because it is a public event and the public wants to participate. It does so via the *sheliaḥ tzibbur* [literally, emissary of the congregation] who blesses *birkat ḥattanim* in the presence of a *minyan*. Unlike a regular *sheliaḥ tzibbur*, who only represents the worshippers of a particular synagogue, the person who recites *birkat ḥattanim* represents the **entire** public. He is **the** prayer leader and **the** cantor *par excellence*. As proof of this, he cites *Pirkei Derabi Eliezer*, Chapter 16, fol. 38a (and cf. the parallel in *Midrash Hagadol, Ḥayei Sarah*, ed. Margaliot, p. 408):

> **And like a cantor who stands and blesses the bride under her *ḥuppah*,** that is how they stood and blessed Rebecca as it says "And they blessed Rebecca and said to her..." (Genesis 24:60).

Indeed, he could have also cited an additional passage from *Pirkei Derabi Eliezer* (end of chapter 12, fol. 31a, which is abbreviated in the *Zohar*, *Tazria*, fol. 44b):

> As a cantor, **just as it is the cantor's way to stand and bless the bride under her *ḥuppah*,** so God stood and blessed Adam [and Eve], as it says (Genesis 1:28) "And God blessed them".[14]

Nevertheless, these sources only prove that in the eighth century, when *Pirkei Derabi Eliezer* was written,[15] it was customary for the cantor to recite *birkat ḥattanim*. **However, early sources from the Land of Israel prove the exact opposite – that any member of the congregation was allowed to recite these blessings.** In *Bereishit Rabbah* (end of Chapter 8, ed. Theodor-Albeck, pp. 66-67) – in a much earlier version of the

14. Rabbi Halivni, p. 6, also refers to Rav Sherira Gaon's responsum quoted in *Otzar Hageonim* to *Ketubot*, p. 16, paragraph 54, but that responsum deals with the betrothal blessing and not with *birkat ḥattanim*.
15. For the dating of *Pirkei Derabi Eliezer*, see Zunz-Albeck, *Haderashot Beyisrael Vehishtalshelutan Hahistorit*, Jerusalem, 5707, pp. 135-136.

second passage from *Pirkei Derabi Eliezer* – there is no reference to a cantor. It says there: "And God blessed them"... Rabbi Abahu said: **God took the cup of blessing and blessed them**... Rabbi Simlai said: we have found that God blesses grooms". In other words, any one of those present was allowed to take the cup of blessing and bless them and, in this case, God did so. This also clearly emerges from another early midrash (*Vayikra Rabbah* 23:4, ed. Margaliot, p. 530 and parallels):

> [This can be compared to] ten who entered to escort a bride [to her *ḥuppah*] and they did not know how to recite *birkat ḥattanim*, **and there was among them one who knew how to recite *birkat ḥattanim*, he is among them**, like "a rose among thorns" (Song of Songs 2:2).

And later on in the same passage (*ibid*. p. 532): **"Rabbi Yona taught his students even *birkat ḥattanim* and even the mourner's blessing, saying: be strong in everything".**

If so, the early sources prove that the *sheva berakhot* were recited by **any person who stands and represents the congregation present at the ceremony**. And perhaps this is the reason why it is customary to honor several **different** people with the *birkat ḥattanim* – to emphasize that the entire congregation present is participating in the celebration. And if so, the main question is: who belongs to this particular congregation? And since we have already proved that the congregation, for the purposes of *birkat ḥattanim*, includes women, there is no reason why the *shaliaḥ* [emissary] should not be a woman.

2. Rabbi Shaul Yisraeli maintains that the seven blessings were intended to gladden only the **groom** and not the bride (p. 165) and that *birkat ḥattanim* is a result of the dancing. This is proven, in his opinion, from the passage of *Keitzad Merakdin* (*Ketubot* 17a) which discusses the formula of praising the bride in order to endear her to her husband.

> And this *mitzvah* of gladdening the groom is not encumbent upon women, because it is not the way of

> modesty [for a woman] to go out before the groom to gladden him with song and dance and, as a result, the obligation of the blessings – which is, as mentioned, part of the act of rejoicing – is not encumbent upon the women.

And if you say that a woman can gladden the **bride** both by dancing and by reciting *sheva berakhot*, one can reply that "the entire *mitzvah* is to gladden the **groom**".

However, Rabbi Joel Wolowelsky has already proved, based on other sources, that every Jew – man and woman – is obligated to gladden a bride and groom. Maimonides derives this obligation, which is rabbinic, from the *mitzvah* of "you shall love your neighbor as yourself" (*Hilkhot Eivel* 14:1) and women are, of course, obligated to fulfill this *mitzvah* because it is a positive commandment without a set time (Mishnah *Kiddushin* 1:7).

The Radbaz (on Maimonides *ad loc.*), on the other hand, found the source for this obligation in *Berakhot* 6b:

> Rabbi Ḥelbo said in the name of Rav Huna: **Whoever** enjoys a wedding feast and does not gladden the groom violates five voices because it says "the voice of joy, the voice of gladness, the voice of the groom and the voice of the bride, a voice saying praise God in all his glory" (Jeremiah 33:11).

From the wording "**whoever** enjoys" one can learn that a woman is also obligated to fulfill this *mitzvah*. Furthermore, the Maharsha writes there: "Our Sages enacted these five voices in the seven blessings of the *ḥattanim*". In other words, the recitation of the seven blessings is actually how the *mitzvah* of gladdening the bride and groom is fulfilled, and if a woman is obligated to observe this *mitzvah*, then she may certainly recite *birkat ḥattanim*.

In other words, according to Rabbi Yisraeli *birkat ḥattanim* stems from the *mitzvah* to dance before a **groom**, and since a woman is exempt from the dancing, she is exempt from the blessings. But according to the above sources, ***birkat ḥattanim* is itself the basic and essential *mitzvah* which women are obligated to observe** and dancing is only **one** of the ways of gladdening a bride and groom. Furthermore, there is a hint in the midrash that women were also accustomed to dance before the bride and groom. And so we have learned in *Pirkei Derabi Eliezer* (Chapter 17, fol. 39b):

> Acts of loving kindness... from where do we learn [them]? From Jezebel, whose house was near the market, **and every groom who would pass by, she would come out of her house, clapping her hands and uttering words of praise, and escorting him for ten steps**.

In *Tur* EH 65, there is a slightly different version: "And there is in the midrash: 'why did the dogs not eat Jezebel's limbs? **Because she used them to dance before bride and groom**' ".

Of course, there is no obligation to learn *halakhah* from a midrash about Jezebel, but this is a hint that in the eighth century, when *Pirkei Derabi Eliezer* was written, it was customary for women to dance before the bride and groom. Therefore, it can be said that women are obligated to fulfill the *mitzvah* of gladdening the bride and groom both by reciting *birkat ḥattanim* and by dancing before them.

3. Rabbi Azaria Berzon tries to prove that, according to Maimonides, there is an inherent difference between *birkat ḥattanim* recited under the *ḥuppah* and *birkat ḥattanim* recited during the seven days of celebration (pp. 108-110). In his opinion, *birkat ḥattanim* during the marriage ceremony is the obligation of the **groom** (similar to Maimonides' approach to the blessing of betrothal cited above), whereas *birkat ḥattanim* during the seven days of celebration is the obligation of the **public**.

Rabbi Berzon came to this distinction by reading Maimonides in a precise fashion. In *Hilkhot Berakhot* 2:9-10, regarding the seven days of celebration, Maimonides uses the term *mevarkhin* [bless] in the **plural**, whereas in *Hilkhot Ishut* 10:3-6, he uses the singular form: "*vetsarikh levarekh*" [and he needs to bless], "and **he brings** a cup of wine and **he blesses**". Moreover, *Hilkhot Ishut* states (10:6): "**A person who betrothes** a woman and **blesses** *birkat ḥattanim* and is not alone with her in his home" and this undoubtedly refers to the groom himself; whereas in *Hilkhot Berakhot* he rules (2:9): "and this blessing is not **blessed** by slaves or minors", indicating that others recite it and not the groom himself.

With all due respect to Maimonides, it is difficult to accept this distinction. The *Gemara* (*Ketubot* 7b) does not differentiate at all between *birkat ḥattanim* under the *ḥuppah* and during the seven days of celebration. Furthermore, we have already seen that *birkhat ḥattanim* is not one of the blessings recited before fulfilling a *mitzvah*. And whether these are blessings of praise or blessings to gladden the bride and groom, the purpose is identical both under the *ḥuppah* and during the seven days of celebration. Finally, most *poskim* disagree with Maimonides and maintain that someone **other than the groom** should recite *birkat ḥattanim* (Adler, pp. 262–263; ET, s.v. *ḥattanim*, notes 51-52).

4. Rabbi Joel Wolowelsky, according to the above-mentioned viewpoint of Rabbi Berzon, only researched the issue of whether women may recite the *sheva berakhot* during the seven days of celebration and he permitted this. He relied primarily on the fact that Maimonides in *Hilkhot Berakhot* (2:9) writes: "and this blessing is not blessed by **slaves** or **minors**" and so ruled the *Shulḥan Arukh* (EH 62:4). And he explains (in *Teḥumin*, p. 119):

> The reason for this is, apparently, that slaves are not included in the laws of divorce and marriage (*Kiddushin* 41b) and therefore do not recite this blessing, as the *Sefer Hamenuḥah* explained, and minors, who have not yet reached marriagable age, are also exempt. But women, who are included in the laws of divorce and marriage, do bless this blessing (and cf. Wolowelsky, *Amudim*, pp. 86-87).

In summary, according to the essence of the law, the *sheva berakhot* are blessings of praise or they were meant to gladden the bride and groom both under the *ḥuppah* and during the seven days of celebration. On the one hand, there is no reason to prevent a woman from praising God at such an occasion and, on the other hand, a woman is obligated to gladden the bride and groom. Maimonides, apparently, differentiates between the *sheva berakhot* recited under the *ḥuppah* and the *sheva berakhot* recited during the seven days of celebration. For some reason, he thinks that the groom himself recites *birkat ḥattanim* under the *ḥuppah* and, if so, a woman is prohibited from reciting these blessings. On the other hand, during the seven days of celebration, he prohibits slaves and minors from reciting these blessings, but apparently permits women to do so. Ostensibly, therefore, whoever is concerned about Maimonides' approach will allow a woman to recite *birkat ḥattanim* only during the seven days of celebration. However, since in our time, it is not customary to follow Maimonides and require the groom to recite *birkat ḥattanim* himself, there is no longer any point in preventing a woman from reciting *birkat ḥattanim* under the *ḥuppah*.

VIII. During the seven days of celebration, *birkat ḥattanim* is only recited if "a new face" is present.[16] Is a woman considered "a new face"?

The source of this *halakhah* is *Tosefta Megillah* (3:14, ed. Lieberman, p. 357) and Rav Yehudah in the *Gemara* (*Ketubot* 7b). The Tosafot stated (in *Shita Mekubetzet to Ketubot* 7b, s.v. *v'zeh leshon haritba z"l = Ḥidushei Haritba, ibid.*):

> It is not called "a new face" unless an important person comes there who was not present originally for whom it is fitting to add joy for him, **and a woman is not fit for such a thing**, even though she may be important, **because a new face is only someone who could be included in the ten [needed to recite] *birkat ḥattanim*.**

16. For interesting medieval interpretations of "a new face", see Yisrael Ta-Shema, *Hatefillah Ha'ashkenazit Hakedumah*, Jerusalem, 5763, pp. 188-196.

On the other hand, the *Ḥatam Sofer* rules (in his *Ḥiddushim* to *Ketubot* 7a = Adler, p. 438, note 102) that a woman may be considered a new face if they increase rejoicing for her sake. There is no doubt that the approach of the *Ḥatam Sofer* is preferable. Even if the *Tosafists* are correct in saying that there is a connection between a new face and the *minyan*, we have already seen that it is possible to include women in the *minyan* for *birkat ḥattanim*. Furthermore, there is no hint in the *Gemara* that the two matters are linked. Finally, there are many explanations for "a new face" **but, other than the Tosafot above, there is no interpretation of this phrase which excludes women**. Below are some of the commonly accepted explanations for "a new face" (according to ET, s.v. *ḥattanim*, col. 639; and Adler, pp. 437 ff.):

1. Anyone who did not hear *birkat ḥattanim* during the marriage ceremony (Maimonides; one opinion in the *Shulḥan Arukh*).

2. Anyone who has not yet participated in any of the feasts that have been prepared (Rosh; *Tur*; a second opinion in the *Shulḥan Arukh*; *Ḥokhmat Adam*).

And there is also a dispute over whether only distinguished people are called "new faces":

1. Some say that a new face means a dignitary for whom one increases the rejoicing (*Tosafot*; the Rosh) or the amount of food served (the *Baḥ* based on the *Mordechai*).

2. Others say that even people for whom there is no extra rejoicing or larger amount of food served are considered new faces (*Shita Mekubetzet* according to Rashi; and others).

IX. Practical *Halakhah*

1. It is permissible for a woman to hold the poles of the *ḥuppah*.

2. It is permissible for a woman to sing *piyyutim* such as "*Mee Adir Al Hakol*".

3. It is permissible for a woman to read the *ketubah* out loud under the *ḥuppah*.

4. It is permissible for a woman to give a *derashah* under the *ḥuppah*.

5. There is no need for a *minyan* to recite the betrothal blessing. There is a Talmudic requirement to recite *birkat ḥattanim* in the presence of a *minyan* and a woman may be included in this *minyan*.

6. It is permissible for a woman to bless the betrothal blessing.

7. It is permissible for a woman to bless *birkat ḥattanim* both under the *ḥuppah* as well as during the seven days of celebration.

8. A woman may be considered "a new face" during the seven days of celebration.

X. "Love and Brotherhood, Peace and Friendship"

When something is **permitted**, it does not mean that it **must** be done. Every rabbi officiating at a wedding ceremony[17] must consider the people attending the celebration. One group may consider a woman holding one of the poles of the *ḥuppah* a significant innovation, whereas another group may be happy to allow a woman to recite *sheva berakhot*. In general, it is advisable to institute such changes gradually and not in one fell swoop. The wedding or festive meal intended to gladden the bride and groom should not be turned into an arena of conflict and controversy. And that is what Rabbi Joel Wolowelsky stressed with regard to *birkat ḥattanim* during the seven days of celebration:

17. On the need for a Rabbi to officiate at a wedding ceremony in our day, see Rabbis Shlomo Fuchs and David Levine, *Teshuvot Va'ad Hahalakhah Shel Knesset Harabbanim B'yisrael* 3 (5748-5749), pp. 93-98, which is also available at www.responsafortoday.com/vol3/8.pdf.

> Of course, if the fact that a woman is reciting the blessing will stir controversy and cause unpleasantness among the invited guests, then it is preferable that she not recite the blessing, so that we don't cause a situation where an action meant to express the joy of the wedding leads to controversy (*Amudim*, p. 87).

Any change or innovation should be done in a peaceful fashion so that during the ceremony or festive meal, "love and brotherhood, peace and friendship" prevail.

David Golinkin
Jerusalem
27 Tammuz 5751

BIBLIOGRAPHY

Adler	Rabbi Binyamin Adler, *Sefer Hanisu'in Kehilkhatam*, second edition, Jerusalem, 5745
Berzon	Rabbi Ovadiah Berzon, "*Birkat Ḥattanim*", *Teḥumin* 6 (5745), pp. 101-117
Deblitski	Rabbi Sraya Deblitzki, *Sova Semaḥot: Kol Dinei Sheva Berakhot*, Jerusalem, New York and Benei Berak, 5731, p. 78, note 70
ET, *Erusin*	ET, s.v. *Birkat Erusin*, Volume 4, columns 420-427
ET, *Ḥattanim*	ET, s.v. *Birkat Ḥattanim*, *ibid.*, columns 631-651
Felder	Rabbi Aaron Felder, *Oholei Yeshurun*, Vol. 1, New York, 1977, p. 30
Glick	Shmuel Glick, *Or Nagah Aleihem: Hazikah Shebein Minhagei Nisu'in Leminhagei Aveilut Bimasoret Yisrael*, Efrat, 5757
Grumet	Rabbi Zvi Grumet, *Tradition* 33/4 (Summer 1999), pp. 99-100
Halevi	Rabbi Ḥayyim David Halevi, *Aseh Lekha Rav*, Vol. 5, Tel Aviv, 5743, p. 388; and Vol. 7, Tel Aviv, 5746, pp, 344-345
Halivni	Rabbi David Weiss Halivni, "On Ordination of Women" in: *On the Ordination of Women as Rabbis*, New York, [1979], pp. 1-7
Kahana	Rabbi Ya'akov Ze'ev Kahana, *Sefer Toledot Ya'akov*, Vilna, 1907, EH, No. 5
Kanefsky	Rabbi Yosef Kanefsky, "When Will the Slander End?", August 18, 2009, www.JewishJournal.com
Levi	Rabbi Shlomo Levi, "May *Birkat Chatanim* (*Sheva Berakhot*) Be Recited by a Woman?", Yeshivat Har Etzion, April 16, 2007, www.vbm-torah.org
Novak	Rabbi David Novak, "Women in the Rabbinate?", *JUDAISM* 33/1 (Winter 1984), p. 41
Rabinowitz	Rabbi Mayer Rabinowitz, "An Advocate's *Halakhic* Response on the Ordination of Women", *JUDAISM*,

	ibid., pp. 55-58 and with minor changes in Simon Greenberg, ed., *The Ordination of Women as Rabbis: Studies and Responsa*, New York, 1988, pp. 108-112 (I refer to the first version)
Steinberg	Rabbi Moshe Halevi Steinberg, *Sefer Mishberei Yam*, Jerusalem, 5752, No. 85
Uziel	Rabbi Meir Ben-Tziyon Ḥai Uziel, *Piskei Uziel Beshe'elot Hazman*, Jerusalem, 5737, No. 74
Wolowelsky	Rabbi Joel Wolowelsky, *Amudim* 444 (Kislev 5743), pp. 86-88
Wolowelsky	Rabbi Joel Wolowelsky, *Teḥumin* 6 (5745), pp. 118-120
Wolowelsky	Rabbi Joel Wolowelsky, "Women's Participation in *Sheva Berakhot*", *Modern Judaism* 12 (1992), pp. 157-165
Wolowelsky	Rabbi Joel Wolowelsky, *Women, Jewish Law and Modernity*, Hoboken, 1997, pp. 56-69
Wolowelsy	Rabbi Joel Wolowelsky, *Akdamut* 13 (April 2003), pp. 203-204
Yisraeli	Rabbi Shaul Yisraeli, *Barkai* 1 (Summer 5743), pp. 163-166

13. WOMEN AS *POSKOT*

Ḥoshen Mishpat 7
(in *Birkei Yosef*, subparagraph 12)

Question: *May a woman serve on the Va'ad Halakhah [Law Committee] of the Rabbinical Assembly of Israel or, in other words, may a woman serve as a poseket and write responsa?*[1]

Responsum: Few *poskim* have dealt with this issue, and that is apparently because most women had not learned enough *halakhah* in the past in order to render halakhic decisions.[2] Even so, some *poskim* have related to this issue, both implicitly and explicitly.

I. Those who Permit

1. We have learned in the Mishnah (*Niddah* 6:4 = Bavli fol. 49b): "Whoever is eligible to judge is eligible to give testimony". The *Tosafot* raise an objection (*ibid.* 50a, s.v. *kol*): But Deborah judged Israel, even though, as a woman, she was inegible to testify! Among other replies, they answer: "If not, she was not judging **but rather teaching them laws**". And so we read in *Tosfot Harosh* (*ad loc.*, bottom of 49b): "**And Deborah is teaching the judges of Israel**". In other words, Deborah did not judge herself, but she was teaching laws to judges, and this indicates that it is permissible for a woman to render halakhic decisions.

1. We shall not discuss women as judges; for a brief discussion, see below, pp. 371-372.
2. The word *hora'ah* in many of the sources in this responsum means to render halakhic decisions, not to teach.

2. And so we can deduce from *Sefer Haḥinukh* (No. 158, ed. Chavel, p. 229), written in Spain in the 13th century. In a section which forbids one who is drunk from rendering halakhic decisions, he rules: "And the prevention of rendering halakhic decisions is [applicable] at any place and at any time in males **and also in a wise woman who is fit to render halakhic decisions**". In other words, a wise woman who is fit to render halakhic decisions is forbidden to do so when she is drunk; from this we deduce that it is permissible for a wise woman to render halakhic decisions.

3. And so ruled the Ḥida (Rabbi Ḥayyim Yosef David Azulai, 1724-1806) explicitly on the basis of the two *Rishonim* quoted above (*Birkei Yosef* to HM 7, subparagraph 12, which is then quoted in *Pitḥei Teshuvah, ibid.*, subparagraph 5).

> Even though a woman is ineligible to judge, **nevertheless, a wise woman may render halakhic decisions**, and this becomes clear from *Tosafot* according to one of his replies – that Deborah was teaching them laws. And so you shall see in *Sefer Haḥinukh*, for in No. 83 he agreed that a woman is ineligible to judge, but in No. 158 concerning those who are drunk, he wrote... "and also in a wise woman who is fit to render halakhic decisions" etc. – see *ibid.*

Five modern *poskim* have followed in their footsteps:

4. Rabbi Ya'akov Levinson ruled in 1920:

> The rendering of halakhic decisions regarding ritual law by a woman: **About this, no one disagrees that she is permitted to render halakhic decisions**, and an explicit proof is from *Tosafot Bava Kama* 15, *Gittin* 88, *Shevuot* 29 and *Niddah* 50 which replies that Deborah was not judging, but rather teaching them the laws. And this ruling was brought in *Sefer Birkei Yosef* and is mentioned in *Pitḥei Teshuvah* to HM 7.

5. Rabbi Yitzḥak Isaac Halevi Herzog, first Chief Rabbi of Israel, ruled in this way in one of his works, which was apparently written in 1948: "And it is established that a woman is fit to render halakhic decisions", and he refers to *Pitḥei Teshuvah* mentioned above.

6. Rabbi Eliyahu Bakshi-Doron – who later became Sephardic Chief Rabbi of Israel – ruled in 1979: "A woman and a proselyte may render halakhic decisions and teach Torah and halakhic decisions".

7. Rebbetzin Hannah Henkin concurred in an article published in 1998, though she was wary of calling women who render halakhic decisions *"poskot"*.

8. Rabbi Shlomo Riskin ruled in this way in an article published in 1999, on the basis of *Sefer Haḥinukh, Birkei Yosef* and Rabbi Bakshi-Doron.

II. Those who Forbid

We have seen thus far that the *Tosafot* and the *Sefer Haḥinukh* assumed that a woman may render halakhic decisions and the Ḥida and five *Aḥaronim* ruled so explicitly. However, there were several *Aḥaronim* who were opposed to women rendering halakhic decisions:

1. The first was Rabbi Avraham Gumbiner, the author of *Magen Avraham* (Poland, 1637-1683). In OH 263:5 the Rema ruled that on *Erev Shabbat* [Sabbath eve] women should light the candles, cover the candles with their hands, and bless, so that it will be considered *over le'asiyah,* as though they blessed the candles and then lit them. The author of *Magen Avraham* commented (subparagraph 12):

> And, if so, on *Yom Tov* she should bless [the candles] and then light [them] – **so is written at the end of *Sefer Haderishah* on *Even Ha'ezer* [in the introduction by the**

> **son of the author of the *Derishah*] in the name of his mother, "but there is no wisdom in a woman [except regarding the spindle]", since the Sages did not differentiate in this matter** [i.e., Shabbat and Yom Tov candles should be lit in the same fashion].

In other words, the wife of the author of the *Derishah* suggested that, since it is permitted to light fire on *Yom Tov*, there is no reason to cover the candles and then bless them, but one may bless the candles and then light them, as one generally does for other blessings. But Rabbi Avraham Gumbiner rejects her suggestion while relying on the words of Rabbi Eliezer in the *Gemara* (*Yoma* 66b):

> A wise woman asked Rabbi Eliezer: since [those who sinned with the Golden] Calf were all equal, why were their deaths unequal [Rashi: why did they die in three different ways]? He said to her: there is no wisdom in a woman except regarding the spindle, and so does Scripture say: "and all the women who were wise-hearted did spin with their hands (Exodus 35:25)".[3]

In other words, Rabbi Eliezer refused to answer because "there is no wisdom in a woman except regarding the spindle", and Rabbi Avraham Gumbiner rejected the halakhic approach of the wife of the author of the *Derishah* for the same reason. However, the approach of Rabbi Gumbiner is problematic, because Rabbi Eliezer was opposed to **all** Torah study by women (Mishnah *Sotah* 3:4) and it is, therefore, no wonder that he refused to answer a wise woman who had studied Torah.[4]

Moreover, two other *poskim* **agreed** with the opinion of the wife of the author of the *Derishah,*[5] and a third *posek* says explicitly: "And that which the *Magen Avraham* wrote 'there is no

3. For an even stronger version of this story, see the parallel in Yerushalmi *Sotah* 3:3, fol. 19a = *Bemidbar Rabbah* 9:48.
4. For an analysis of Rabbi Eliezer's approach, see below, pp. 358-366.
5. Her son Rabbi Yosef Yuzpa Falk as well as Rabbi Yeḥezkel Landau; they are quoted below, pp. 301-302.

wisdom in a woman' etc., that is the case with women generally, but not the case with wise women, as proved by the daughters of Tzlofḥad" (Rabbi Shem Tob Gaguine, *Keter Shem Tov*, Keidan, 1934, p. 177, in a note).

2. The second opponent was Rabbi Ephraim Zalman Margaliot (Brody, 1760-1828) in *Sha'arei Teshuvah* to *Oraḥ Ḥayyim*.[6] In *Hilkhot Pesaḥ* (OH 461:5 in the Rema) there is a law that a *matzah* which is inflated in the middle is forbidden. *Sha'arei Teshuvah*, subparagraph 17, says that in *Teshuvat Beit Ya'akov* it is related

> that the pupil of the Gaon, our teacher, Rabbi Heschel z"l said to him [=the author of *Beit Ya'akov*] that when a question concerning an inflated [*matzah*] occurred before him **he [i.e., Rabbi Heschel] would order his family members to render this halakhic decision** and to see if the inflation is not visible on both sides etc. [Gloss: It would seem that what he wrote that "**he would order his family members to to render this halakhic decision**", is an exaggeration and not precise, for God forbid to attribute nonsense to the Gaon z"l that **he gave the halakhic decision in this matter to his family members.** Rather, he was relying on their observation and discernment in this matter of halakhic decision-making according to the custom of women, who are accustomed to the activity of baking, and they know best how to distinguish and differentiate between an inflation caused by fire and an inflation caused by [the dough becoming] *ḥametz*. And as *poskim* do occasionally when there is a question concerning poultry... and it is necessary to know its nature, it is their habit to ask women who deal with this and are experts regarding chickens, **and they rely on women regarding this issue, but not to render halakhic decisions**.]

6. *Sha'arei Teshuvah* was written by Rabbi Ḥayyim Mordekhai Margaliot, but the glosses were culled from *Sefer Yad Ephraim* of his brother, Rabbi Ephraim Zalman Margaliot – see both their prefaces to *Shulḥan Arukh Oraḥ Ḥayyim*.

Apparently, the author of *Sha'arei Teshuvah* was correct, that in the case mentioned, the author of *Beit Ya'akov* did not mean the rendering of halakhic decisions. But his general surprise is not understood since, as we shall see below, women were relied upon not only to establish facts, but also to render halakhic decisions.

3. The third opponent was Rabbi Jacob Lauterbach (1873-1940), one of the foremost *poskim* of the Reform Movement in the United States. In a responsum from 1922 opposing the ordination of women as rabbis, he quotes from *Bemidbar Rabbah* 10:5:

> "And Mano'aḥ said: May your words soon come true!" (Judges 13:12) Mano'aḥ said to him: until now I heard from the woman, **and women are not *benot hora'ah*** and one should not rely on their words, but "May your words soon come true" – I want to hear from your mouth, because I do not believe her words, lest she changed the words or subtracted from them or added to them.

Rabbi Lauterbach understood *hora'ah* to mean rendering a halakhic decision and he concluded from this midrash that there is "a well-known and established principle that women may not have the authority to render decisions in religious or ritual matters". Rabbi Joel Roth, on the other hand, explained this midrash differently. He asks and answers: is there mention at all of a *halakhic* decision? Mano'aḥ's wife had conveyed the words of the angel to her husband, and nothing else! But "hora'ah" here means "instructions", as in our day, as is proven from verse 8: "And Mano'aḥ entreated the Lord and said... let him come again unto us and **instruct** us how the child to be born should be handled".[7] There is no doubt that Rabbi Roth is correct, and hence the proof that Rabbi Lauterbach quoted to forbid has disappeared.

7. Indeed, in the classic Soncino translation of *Midrash Rabbah*, Vol. 5, London, 1939, pp. 366, they translated: "and women are not qualified to give **directions**".

III. *Ma'aseh Rav* – Action is Great

Thus far we have seen eight *poskim* who permitted women to render halakhic decisions, but it may be argued that this is a case of "*halakhah ve'ein morin kein*" [i.e., a law which we do not follow in practice]. It is, therefore, necessary to check how they acted **in practice**, as we have written elsewhere:[8]

> It is known that the Jewish people have great power to decide halakhic matters that are under dispute, and this is in accordance with several *halakhic* concepts: *ma'aseh rav*/ action is great (*Shabbat* 21a and parallels); "leave Israel alone; if they are not Prophets, they are the sons of Prophets" (*Pesaḥim* 66a); *Puk ḥazei mai ama devar*/Go out and see what the people do (*Berakhot* 45a and parallels); "Every *halakhah* that is weak in the rabbinic court and whose nature you do not know, go out and see what the public does and do it" (Yerushalmi *Peah* 7:6, fol. 20c = Yerushalmi *Ma'aser Sheni* 5:3, fol. 56b; Yerushalmi *Yevamot* 7:2, fol. 8a).

Concerning our topic, it is possible to prove clearly and definitely, that women participated **in practice** in each and every stage of deciding *halakhah*, from the Tannaitic period until today. The following are the facts as they emerge from the sources, categorized according to subject, with each subject organized chronologically.[9]

A. Women studied practical *halakhah* and were proficient in it.

1. Rabbi Yoḥanan tells us that Beruriah, Rabbi Meir's wife, learned 300 teachings by heart per day from 300 rabbis (*Pesaḥim* 62b). The number 300 is a typical round number in Rabbinic

8. See above, p. 251.
9. It should be emphasized that we did not include in this survey women who primarily studied Bible and *aggadah*.

literature,[9a] but there is no doubt that Beruriah was indeed proficient in *halakhah* (cf. below, pp. 300-301).[10]

2. Fioretta, or Bathsheva – the wife of Rabbi Shlomo of Modena and the grandmother of Rabbi Aharon Berakhia of Modena, the author of *Ma'avar Yabok* (died 1639) – was a learned woman. Rabbi Aharon Berakhia tells us that "**Throughout her entire life, her mouth did not cease learning Bible, Mishnah, the literature of the *poskim*, and above all – Maimonides**... for all of them, she had a regular order of study every week...".[11] Elsewhere, he writes: "and I owe her fear and respect as towards a father and a mother **and also as a Rabbi,** for in the path of wisdom she instructed me...".[12]

B. Women taught practical *halakhah* to other women.

1. "And in the book of Rabbeinu Yitzhak b"r Menaḥem (France, 11th century) we do not have this reading. **And so his sister *Marat*** Beila (other readings: Bilit, Bellette) **instituted in his name that the women of her town should pick their teeth before immersing [in the *mikveh*].**"[13]

9a. See Naḥman Danzig, *Sinai* 83/3-4 (5738), pp. 153-158.

10. For a critical analysis of the Beruriah traditions, see David Goodblatt, *Journal of Jewish Studies* 26 (1975), pp. 68-75; Tal Ilan, *Jewish Women in Greco-Roman Palestine,* Tübingen, 1995, pp. 197-200; Brenda Bacon, *Nashim* 5 (2002), pp. 231-239.

11 From his preface to *Seder Ashmoret Haboker Meḥavurat Me'irei Shaḥar*, Mantua, 1524, as quoted by Simcha Assaf, *Mekorot Letoledot Haḥinukh Beyisrael*, Vol. 4, Jerusalem, 5703, p. 54, paragraph 54.

12 The preface to *Ma'avar Yabok*, ed. Vilna, 1896, fols. 7b-8a, and cf. also Rabbi Yehuda Aryeh of Modena, *Ḥayyei Yehudah*, ed. Karpi, Tel Aviv, 5745, p. 34 and note 9.

13. *Maḥzor Vitry*, p. 610 = the manuscript of *Sefer Assufot* quoted by Shmuel David Luzzatto in *Otzar Neḥmad* 2 (1853), p. 10 = *Sefer Ra'aviyah*, Vol. 1, p. 210 = *Or Zaru'a*, Part 1, paragraph 363, fol. 49c at the top; and cf. *Teshuvot Rashi*, ed. Elfenbein, No. 187, p. 205, and the parallel sources listed there.

2. **Ḥannah, the sister of Rabeinu Tam** (died 1171) used to teach the women not to bless the Shabbat candles until they completed lighting the second candle.[14]

C. Women taught Talmud and *halakhah* to men.

1. **So we are told of Miriam daughter of Rabbi Shlomo Shapira, a descendant of Rashi** (circa 1350): "The *Rabbanit Marat* Miriam, her resting place is in Eden, **ran a *Yeshivah* for a number of years** and she would sit in a tent, a curtain before her, **and taught *halakhah* before eminent young scholars**".[15]

2. **The *Rabbanit* Asenat Barazani**, wife of Rabbi Ya'akov ben Yehudah Mizraḥi of Mosul (Kurdistan) and daughter of Rabbi Shmuel bar Nattan'el Halevi Barazani (15th-16th **or** 17th centuries), stood at the head of their *Yeshivah* after they died. The rabbis in her generation called her "**Our Teacher Rabbi Asenat, may God protect her**", **"My mother my Rabbi**" and "the wife of a *ḥaver* [scholar] who is like a *ḥaver*". In a flowery letter asking for donations, she writes, among other things:

> **That I remained teaching Torah and chastising and preaching about ritual immersion, Shabbat, *niddah*** [laws of the menstruant], **prayer and the like**... at the feet of Sages I grew up, spoiled by my father z"l, no deed or skill did he teach me except for the work of Heaven, **to fulfill what is said "you shall recite it day and night"** [Joshua 1:8]. Because of many sins he did not have sons but rather daughters [cf. Numbers 26:33], and he had also made my husband z"l swear not to have me do any labor, and so he did as he was commanded. And, from the start, the Rabbi z"l was occupied with his own study and had no time to

14. The manuscript of *Sefer Assufot* quoted by Shmuel David Luzzatto, *ibid.*, and by Grossman, p. 339.
15. This passage was printed on the verso of the title page of *Responsa Maharshal*, Fiorda, 1768, as quoted by Ashkenazi, p. 131, and see there for many more references.

teach the students, **for I would teach the students in his stead, I was a help by his side [cf. Genesis 2:18]...**[16]

3. **Mazal-Tov Benvenida Ghirondi of Italy** (18th century) taught her son Tziyon: Bible, grammar, **Talmud with Rashi, and Maimonides** and "she raised many students for [the study of] Torah".[17]

D. *Poskim* relied on women who transmitted *halakhot* from their fathers or relatives.

1. "...Rabbi Shimon son of Rabbi Yannai (a second generation Israeli *Amora*) transmitted: I did not hear it from father, **my sister told me in his name**: An egg which had been laid on *Yom Tov*, one supports it with a vessel so that it should not roll" (Yerushalmi *Shabbat* 13:7, fol. 14b).

2. *Shemen sereifah*, "oil for burning", is oil which was intended for the Priestly gift of Terumah but was defiled and is waiting to be burned. "What about lighting *shemen sereifah* on *Ḥanukkah*?... Rabbi Nisa (a fourth generation Israeli *Amora*) said: Me, I did not learn this from father, **my mother told me: your father would say**: One who has no ordinary oil, lights *shemen sereifah* during *Ḥanukkah* (Yerushalmi *Terumot* 11:7, fol. 48b at bottom).

3. The father of Ravina bar Rav Huna (also called The Last Ravina, eighth generation Babylonian *Amora*, died 500 CE) passed away when Ravina was a child. As a result, **his mother taught him his father's customs** concerning the eating of bread (*Berakhot* 39b) and the eating of *ḥaddash* (*Menaḥot* 68b) and the

16. The quote is from Jacob Mann, *Texts and Studies*, Vol. 1, Cincinnati, 1931, pp 510-511. Cf. *ibid.*, p. 483; Ashkenazi, pp. 132-133; Uri Melammed and Renee Levin Melammed, *Pe'amim* 82 (Winter 5760), pp. 163-178 and all the literature listed there.
17. Ashkenazi, p. 125; Mordechai Shmuel Girondi, *Toledot Gedolei Yisrael Vege'onei Italia*, Trieste, 1853, p. 56.

second ruling was also accepted as *halakhah* (Maimonides, Laws of Forbidden Foods 10:12; OH 489:10).

4. One of the *Tosafists* was asked if it is permissible to place a pan on a meat pie and later bake a flat dairy cake under the pan or *vice versa* without kashering the pan by via *libun* [heating it until it is glowing hot]. At the end of the responsum it says:

> **And I asked the widow of my uncle R"Y** [Rabbi Isaac the Elder from Dampierre, 12th century] who said that her husband did not object, and they would bake under one pan a [meat] pie after a [dairy] flat cake... and so is the custom at the house of Rabbi Meir my grandfather **and at the house of Marat Miriam, granddaughter of Rabbeinu Shlomo [=Rashi]... but Marat Miriam, the wife of my uncle Rabeinu Tam** [died 1171] **is stricter and does *libun*...** and it is unknown to me if she did this in accordance with my uncle, or according to her first husband Rabbi Avraham who was [very strict], **and women are accustomed everywhere** that a woman lends her friend a flat [dairy] cake or [meat] pie, without inquiring as to what they had baked under it... and if I knew that Rabbeinu Tam was strict, I would have set aside my opinion for the sake of his, but as long as his opinion is unknown, then we rely on our own reasoning **and on the testimony of the daughters of the great [rabbis] of our generation** (*Teshuvot Maimoniot* to Maimonides, Laws of Forbidden Foods, No. 5).

5. The *Tosafot* to *Shabbat* 111b (s.v. *hai,* at the end) discuss the issue of wetting a garment on Shabbat:

> **And R"Y heard from the women that Rabbeinu Tam had permitted them to** [wash their hands] and wipe their hands on a garment, due to the dirt, so that they can pray and bless; but R"Y does not agree...

One must emphasize that Rabbeinu Yitzḥak does not question the right of women to transmit a legal ruling, but only opposes Rabbeinu Tam's reasoning.

6. The Ra'aviyah, Rabbi Eliezer ben Yoel Halevi (1140-1220) transmits in connection with the first meal after the burial:

> **And I heard from my aunt, the wife of Rabbeinu Shmuel Bar Natronai** [Ashkenaz, died 1175] **who had testified that her husband** would not let a mourner fast on [one of] the fast days preceding Rosh Hashanah if it was the day of burial [because the mourner is obligated to eat the first meal after the burial]..." (*Sefer Hara'aviyah, Hilkhot Avel,* paragaraph 841, p. 561).[17a]

7. Rabbi Shmuel of Falaise (France, 13th century) relates in his halakhic commentary to Rabbi Yosef Tov-Elem's *piyyut "Elohei Haruḥot Lekhol Bassar"*:

> ... in some countries it is customary to kneed the *matzot* very well in the vessel, **and my mother-in-law z"l told me in the name of my teacher my father-in-law Rabbi Avraham son of Rabbeinu Ḥayyim** that he was accustomed to prohibit this matter, because it is impossible to be careful that there will be no dough left between each kneading of the dough, and it becomes *hametz* due to delay... (*Or Zaru'a,* Part 2, paragraph 256, fol. 59a in the middle).

8. In one of his responsa, Rabbi Ḥayyim, the son of Rabbi Yitzḥak of Vienna, the author of *Or Zaru'a* (end of 13th century), discusses the question whether to recite the blessing *Asher Yatzar* only once in the morning, or each time a person goes to the bathroom.

17a. Ashkenazi Jews used to fast on the days when *Seliḥot* were recited before Rosh Hashanah. See David Golinkin, *Responsa in a Moment,* Vol. II, Jerusalem, 2011, p. 155.

> **And my mother-in-law z"l told me that *Rabbeinu*, my father my teacher ztz"l, used to**, when he got up at night to go the bathroom, wash his hands each time and recite the blessing (*Responsa Maharaḥ Or Zaru'a*, end of No. 101).

9. In another responsum, the Rabbi Ḥayyim tells us:

> And also concerning *dam tohar* [the blood of purity which flows after a birth, which should be pure but is considered impure], I have found responsa that this is part of the stringency of Rabbi Zeira [see *Berakhot* 31a]... **and my wife says that her great father, at the end of his days, had warned his family members** to observe *dam tohar* privately, because in France they would cling to *mitzvot*... (*Responsa Maharaḥ Or Zaru'a*, No. 146).[18]

10. Rabbi Gomprecht asked his brother, the Maharil (died 1427):

> **Our sister Bonlin, may she live long, told me that our father our teacher Rabbi Moshe of blessed memory instituted the custom** to use leeks for Pesach... for the first dipping and he dipped it in vinegar ... [Responsum:] That which our sister testified about our father our teacher z"l who used leeks for the first dipping, that is when he did not have *Karpass*... (*Responsa Maharil*, No. 58, ed. Satz, p. 63).

11. In *Minhagei Maharil* there is a discussion of the question whether it is permitted for a widow who remarries to immerse in the *mikveh* and have sexual relations on Shabbat eve.

And he told us a story that he was once asked about this,

18. On the controversy concerning *dam tohar*, see Maimonides, *Hilkhot Issurei Bi'ah* 11: 5-7 and *Tur* YD 194, s.v. *katav haramban* with the *Beit Yosef ad loc.* The concluding sentence in the responsum quoted requires further study, since they were actually more lenient about this in France.

> and he ruled that it is forbidden to immerse on those nights, as I already explained. **And the wife of Rabbi Zalman Ronkil** [=the Maharil's teacher] **was there, and she testified that it is permitted, since she had seen her husband permitting in such cases to immerse on Shabbat. And the couple listened to her and the widow immersed on Shabbat eve and her husband slept with her.**

Later on it is told that the husband died half a year later, and the Maharil told Rabbi Zalman "**the ruling of his wife in his name** and he showed him the law in *Tashbetz*" (*Minhagei Maharil, Hilkhot Shabbat*, paragraph 18, ed. Spitzer, Jerusalem, 5749, pp. 211-212). In other words, the Maharil disagreed with the ruling, but did not question the right of Rabbi Zalman's wife to render a halakhic decision in his name.

E. Women discussed halakhic issues with men.

1. "I heard from my father and teacher z"l, **who said in the name of the *Rabbanit*, the wife of Rabbi Yosef b"r Yoḥanan** (Treves, 14th century) – the father of Rabbi Matityahu (Paris, died 1385) [and] the grandfather of Rabbi Yosef in our generation (died 1429)... – **and a fine answer it is**" (Rabbi Shimon bar Tzemaḥ Duran, *Tashbetz*, Vol. 3, No. 78); cf. Levin, p. 47).

2. Ḥava Bachrach (1585-1652), grandmother of Rabbi Yair Ḥayyim Bachrach, had learned Bible, Talmud Bavli and Yerushalmi, Midrash, responsa and *poskim*. Many times she would sit with her father's students and, after the lecture, she would engage in complicated halakhic debates with them. Her grandson quotes some of her *ḥiddushim* in her name, and his book of responsa *Ḥavot Yair* is named after her (see Ashkenazi, p. 123 and the end of the introduction to *Responsa Ḥavot Yair*).

3. When Rabbi Ḥayyim Yosef David Azulai (the *Ḥida*) was in The Hague at the home of Rabbi Shaul Segal, he had a complicated halakhic discussion with him about a certain issue, and the *Rabbanit* Dina had participated.[19]

F. Women rendered halakhic decisions and the *poskim* agreed with their decisions.

1. Rabbi Yossi the Galilean was walking on the road when he met Beruriah. He said to her: "By which road to Lod?" "Foolish Galilean", she replied, "did not the Sages say: 'Engage not in much conversation with women'! [*Avot* 1:5]. You should have said: 'By which to Lod?'" Beruriah once discovered a student who was learning in an undertone... She exclaimed: "is it not written 'Ordered in all things, and sure'? (II Samuel 23:5) – If it is 'ordered' in your 248 limbs it will be 'sure', otherwise it will not be 'sure' "(*Eruvin* 53b-54a). In both cases the Sages did not reply, which implies that they accepted her words. Moreover, the major *poskim* ruled according to the second story (Maimonides, *Hilkhot Talmud Torah* 3:12; *Semag*, *Asin* 12; *Tur* and *Shulḥan Arukh* YD 246:22).

2. "If he plastered [an oven] when it was pure and it was defiled, when is it considered pure? Rabbi Ḥalafta of Kefar Ḥananya said: I asked Shimon ben Ḥananya who asked the son of Rabbi Ḥananya ben Teradyon, who said... **and his daughter [i.e., Beruriah] said**... When these words were recited before Rabbi Yehudah ben Bava, he said: **His daughter said it better than his son.**"[20]

19. Rabbi Avraham Itinga, *Siḥat Ḥulin Shel Talmidei Ḥakhamim Heḥadash*, Munkatch, 1909, quoted by S.Y. Agnon, *Sefer Sofer Vesipur*, Jerusalem and Tel Aviv, 5738, p. 333; cf. also Rabbi Ḥ.Y.D. Azulay, *Sefer Ma'agal Tov Hashalem*, Berlin, 1921, p. 153.

20. *Tosefta Kelim Bava Kamma* 4:17, ed. Zuckermandel, pp. 573-574. According to another version, she disagreed with her father – see Rabbi Saul Lieberman, *Tosefet Rishonim*, Vol. 3, Jerusalem, 1939, p. 17.

3. "*Klustra*" [a door bolt] – Rabbi Tarfon says it is impure, the Sages say it is pure, and Beruriah says: one detaches it from the [doorway] and hangs it on another on Shabbat. When this was told before Rabbi [Yehoshua], he said: **Beruriah spoke well!**[21]

4. Rabbi Samuel of Falaise (mid-13th century) and Rabbeinu Peretz (died 1295) transmit a custom of eating legumes on Pesaḥ only if they are boiled in hot water. They add:

> And so it appears, I believe, that I heard from Rabbi Yosef the Cantor of Troyes (13th century) **in the name of his mother** the daughter of Rabbeinu Barukh (end of 12th century), concerning beans, that they should not be cooked during Pesaḥ except in water which is boiling from the moment they are placed in the pot.[22]

5. As alluded to above (pp. 288-290), Beila, the wife of Rabbi Yehoshua Falk (1550-1614), decided two *halakhot* concerning the lighting of candles: a) On *Yom Tov* one should first recite the blessing and only afterwards light, in contrast to Shabbat; b) On *Yom Tov* one should light early as on Shabbat, and not wait until after *ma'ariv*. Her son Rabbi Yosef Yuzpa Falk quotes her words at length and concludes:

> And I looked this up in the *poskim* **and it seems in my humble opinion that she is right**, "and her counsel is blessed and her reason is excellent" and I decided to print this in a book in her name "and shouts of beautiful beautiful to her"! [see *Zekhariah* 4:7].[23]

21. *Tosefta Kelim Bava Metzi'a* 1:6, ed. Zuckermandel, pp. 578-579, with variant readings based on Lieberman, *ibid.*, pp. 34-35.
22. See the manuscripts which I quoted in the *Teshuvot Va'ad Halakhah Shel Knesset Harabbanim Beyisrael* 3 (5748-5749), p. 53, note 6.
23. In his preface to *Derishah* and *Perishah* on the *Tur Yoreh De'ah*, Lublin, 1596, which is printed in our day at the beginning *Tur* Oraḥ Ḥayyim. Rabbi Ḥ.Y.D. Azulay, *Maḥazik Berakhah* to OH 263:4, emphasized that the son agreed with his mother.

Rabbi Yeḥezkel Landa writes (in *Dagul Mirevava* to OH 263):

> And in my humble opinion, **his mother is right... and so it seems to me to rule according to the wife of the Gaon** ***Derishah*** and she is a woman who excelled in wisdom [cf. Exodus 35:26].[24]

6. Kreindel daughter of Rabbi Leib Mokhiaḥ (died 1742) was a learned woman. Her husband, author of *Sefer Zikhron Yosef,* quotes *ḥiddushim* in her name in his books (Ashkenazi, p. 125; Rabbi Ḥ.Y.D. Azulai, *Shem Hagedolim*, s.v. *rabbanit*; cf. Levin, p. 48).

G. Women wrote responsa in the name of their husbands.[25]

Marat Schundlein, wife of Rabbi Yisrael Isserlein (died 1460), wrote an entire responsum in Yiddish about the laws of *niddah* in her husband's name (*Leket Yosher,* Part 2, pp. 19-20).

H. Women asked learned halakhic questions.

1. Pamina or Pomona, the wife of Rabbi Daniel of Modena (end of 15th century) received a detailed responsum from Rabbi David

24. Regarding Beila, the wife of Rabbi Yehoshua Falk, see Ashkenazi, p. 122; Y.L. Hacohen Maimon, *Sinai* 50 (5722), pp. 371-372; and Batya Bromberg, *Sinai* 59 (5726), pp. 248-250.
25. In *Sefer Hapardess*, ed. Ehrenreich, pp. 160-161, there is a responsum of Rashi: "I am young... and lying on my sickbed... and since I am [weak] and my hand cannot hold the pen, **therefore [to] my daughter** [*velakhen biti*] I dictated these lines **and he wrote them** to my master [and] teacher". Many scholars thought that Rashi had dictated this responsum **to his daughter**. See, for example, L. Zunz, *Zur Geschichte und Literatur*, Berlin, 1845, p. 172; E. Carmoly, *Oholiba*, Rödelheim, 1863, p. 110; G. Karpeles, *Die Frauen der judischen Literatur*, Berlin, 1871, p. 10; Moshe Güdemann, p. 189, note 6; Ashkenazi, *Hamishor*, p. 18, and in his book *Ha'ishah*, p. 118.
However, this is actually a case of a scribal error, and it should say "**and to my daughter's son**" [*ul'ven biti*] – see Zunz, *ibid.*, p. 567; A. Berliner, *MGWJ*

Meir Imala concerning the kashering and roasting of meat (Ashkenazi, p. 121).

2. Flora Sassoon (1859-1936) was well-versed in Bible, Mishnah, Talmud and *poskim*. "She exchanged tens of halakhic responsa with famous Rabbis, especially the Rabbis of Baghdad."[26]

I. Women wrote responsa.

Tzertel, daughter of Rabbi Yehoshua Horwitz and wife of Rabbi Meir Schwartz, was learned in Talmud, *poskim*, midrashim and Bible. She wrote responsa and *ḥiddushim* in *Hacarmel*, *Hasharon* and other periodicals, and signed her name as צבי"ה – *Tzertel bat Yehoshua Horwitz* (Ashkenazi, p. 133).

IV. Practical *Halakhah*

In summary, the *Tosafists* and the author of *Sefer Haḥinukh* implied that a woman may render halakhic decisions, and the Ḥida and five modern rabbis have ruled so explicitly. Moreover, from the days of the *Tannaim* until today, women were accustomed to participate in all stages of studying and deciding *halakhah*: they studied *halakhah*, taught *halakhah* to other women, taught *halakhah* to men, conveyed halakhic rulings of their

12 (1872), pp. 287-288; M. Schwab, *REJ* 42 (1901), pp. 272-273; A. Berliner, *Ketavim Nivḥarim*, Vol. 2, Jerusalem, 5709, p. 184, note 11, and cf. *ibid.*, p. 288; Shlomo Buber, *Sefer Ha'orah*, Part 1, Lvov, 1905, p. 4; Ehrenreich, *ibid.*, note 56; A.M. Haberman, *Kiryat Sefer* 13 (1936-1937), p. 115, in a note; and Yisrael Elfenbein, *Teshuvot Rashi*, New York, 5703, p. 180, note 3.

26. Avraham Ben-Ya'akov, *Perakim Betoledot Yehudei Bavel*, Vol. 1, Jerusalem, 5749, p. 125 and see the entire chapter, pp. 123-135. For some of her halakhic questions, see Rabbi Yitzḥak Nissim, *Responsa Yayin Hatov*, Jerusalem, 5739, section OH in Part 1, Nos. 9, 13, 43. See also Carrie Davidson, *Out of Endless Yearnings: A Memoir of Israel Davidson*, New York, 1946, pp. 148-149 for an interesting vignette; Ashkenazi, p. 133; Stanley Jacobson, *The Sassoons*, London 1968, p. 208; and the speech which Flora Sassoon delivered at the annual meeting of the Rabbinical Seminary in London: *Sefat Peraḥ Shoshan*, Oxford, 1924. Cf. Levin, pp. 49-50, for a third woman who asked halakhic questions.

relatives, discussed halakhic matters, gave *halakhic* rulings, wrote responsa in the name of their husbands, asked learned questions, and wrote responsa themselves. And if they did so at a time when most women did not receive a Jewish education, all the more so in the present era! Therefore, it is perfectly permissible for women to give *halakhic* rulings and to write responsa.

David Golinkin
Jerusalem
22 Shevat 5752

BIBLIOGRAPHY

I. ON WOMEN AS *POSKOT*

Bakshi-Doron Rabbi Eliyahu Bakshi-Doron, *Torah Shebe'al Peh* 20 (5739), p. 72 = *Responsa Binyan Av*, Jerusalem, 5742, No. 65, p. 287

ET *Entziklopedia Talmudit*, s.v. *Hora'ah*, Vol. 8, col. 494, note 109

Halakhah Pesukah
Halakhah Pesukah Leḥoshen Mishpat, Vol. 1, Jerusalem, 5722, Paragraph 7, p. 95, notes 99-100

Henkin Chanah Henkin, "Women and the Issuing of Halakhic Rulings", in: Micah Halpern and Chana Safrai, eds., *Jewish Legal Writings by Women*, Jerusalem, 1998, pp. 278-287

Herzog Rabbi Yitzḥak Isaac Halevi Herzog, *Teḥukah Leyisrael Al Pi Hatorah*, Vol. 1, Jerusalem, 5749, p. 109

Lauterbach Rabbi Jacob Lauterbach in: Rabbi Walter Jacob, ed., *American Reform Responsa*, New York, 1983, p. 27

Levinson Rabbi Jacob Levinson, *Shivyon Hanashim Menekudat Hahalakhah: Leshe'elat Habeḥirot Be'eretz Yisrael*, New York, 1920, p. 10

Pyuterkovsky Malka Pyuterkovsky, "*Nashim Kedoverot Halakhah*", *De'ot* 55 (*Shevat* 5772), pp. 20-24

Riskin Rabbi Shlomo Riskin, "Women as Halakhic Decisors" (Hebrew), in: Naḥem Ilan, ed., *Ayin Tovah... Sefer Yovel Letovah Ilan*, Tel Aviv, 1999, pp. 698-704

Roth Rabbi Joel Roth in: Simon Greenberg, ed., *The Ordination of Women as Rabbis*, New York, 1988, pp. 163-164

II. ON LEARNED WOMEN THROUGHOUT THE GENERATIONS

Ashkenazi	Shlomo Ashkenazi, "Learned Women in the Family of Rashi" (Hebrew), *Bamishor* 1/27-28 (27 Tammuz 5700), pp. 18-19; *idem, Nashim Lamdaniot,* Tel Aviv, 5702; *idem, Ha'ishah Be'aspaklaryat Hayahadut,* Vol. 1, Tel Aviv, 5713, pp. 115-138; *idem, Dor Dor Uminhagav,* Tel Aviv, 1987, pp. 204-215 and elsewhere (the abbreviation Ashkenazi refers to his book *Ha'isha,* which is a reworking of *Nashim Lamdaniot*)
Azulai	Rabbi Ḥayyim Yosef David Azulai, *Shem Hagedolim,* Warsaw, 1876, p. 112, s.v. *Rabbanit*
Bat-Yehudah	Geulah Bat-Yehudah, "*Sh'tei Nashim Lamdaniot*", *Sinai* 141 (5768), pp. 194-202
Berliner	Rabbi Avraham Berliner, *Ḥayei Hayehudim Be'ashkenaz Bimei Habeinayim,* Warsaw, 1900, pp. 8-9
Epstein	Rabbi Barukh Halevi Epstein, *Mekor Barukh,* Vol. 4, Vilna, 1928, pp. 1953-1958
Felder	Rabbi Gedalia Felder, *Yesodei Yeshurun,* Part 1, Toronto, 5714, pp. 136-138
Güdemann	Rabbi Moshe Güdemann, *Sefer Hatorah Vehaḥayyim Be'artzot Hama'arav Bimei Habeinayim,* Vol. 1, Warsaw, 1897, pp. 189-190
Grossman	Avraham Grossman, *Ḥassidot Umordot,* Jerusalem, 5761, pp. 282-289, 337-339 [= *Pious and Rebellious: Jewish Women in Medieval Europe,* Waltham, Mass., 2004]
Landau	Bezalel Landau, *Maḥanayim* 98 (5725), pp. 144-149
Levin	Levin, Yael, *Akdamut* 13 (April 2003), pp. 46-50
Margaliot	Rabbi Reuven Margaliot, "*Nashim Shehuzkeru Batalmud*", *Leḥeker Sheimot Vekhinuyim Batalmud,* Jerusalem, 5720, pp. 39-42
Poznanski	Sh. A. Poznanski, "*Ḥayyei Ha'ishah Beyisrael Bimei Habeinayim*", *Knesset Hagedolah* 2 (1890), p. 95

Safrai	Shmuel Safrai "*Nashim Hakhmot Torah Betekufat Hamishnah Vehatalmud*", *Maḥanayim* 98 (5725) pp. 58-59
Zolty	Shoshana Pantel Zolty, *And All Your Children Shall Be Learned: Women and the Study of Torah in Jewish Law and History*, Northvale, New Jersey and London, 1993, pp. 140-146, 159-162, 177-188, 202-208, 215-218, 246-256

14. THE *MEḤITZAH* IN THE SYNAGOGUE

Question: *What are the sources for a meḥitzah/partition and ezrat nashim/women's gallery*[1] *in the synagogue? In Masorti/Conservative congregations in Israel and abroad it is customary to pray without a meḥitzah or women's gallery. Is this custom halakhically justified?*

Responsum: This question made the headlines in the 1950s when disputes arose in several congregations in the United States – one group demanded the institution of mixed seating, while the other demanded to continue separating men and women with a *meḥitzah,* a women's gallery or separate seating. The latter group enlisted the most important Orthodox Rabbis to write responsa and to warn against any change in synagogue seating arrangements (see numerous responsa in Litvin and CJ). One of these rabbis maintained that this is a "Pentateuchic injunction (*issur de'oraitha*) which can never be abandoned by any legislative act on the part of a rabbinic or lay body regardless of its numeric strength or social prominence. What was decreed by God can never be undone by human hand." (Rabbi J.B. Soloveitchik, cited in CJ, p. 50 and Litvin, pp. 139-140).

1. In this responsum, "*ezrat nashim*" usually means the women's gallery in a synagogue, unless it is an analysis of a Talmudic source referring to the "*ezrat nashim*" or Women's Court in the Temple. It should be added that in most of the medieval sources cited below in note 17, the women's area in the synagogue is not referred to as the "*ezrat hanashim*", but rather as "*beit haknesset shel nashim*/the women's synagogue". There is no doubt that the modern phrase *ezrat nashim* describing the women's area of the synagogue was derived from the ancient phrase for the Women's Court in the Temple. Yet, as we shall see below, this does not prove that there is any connection between them.

However, we still see below that this description is very far from reality. We will find that it is, indeed, an ancient custom to separate men and women during prayer, but it is not a Pentateuchal or even a Rabbinic law. There is no mention of any separation in the Temple in Jerusalem in the First Temple and early Second Temple periods. Towards the end of the Second Temple period, the Sages *hitkinu*/enacted that a balcony for women be constructed in the *Ezrat Nashim*/Women's Court of the Temple on Sukkot in order to avoid light-headedness which might occur during the Water-Drawing Celebration. However, that balcony was not in use the rest of the year and it is clear that they dismantled most or all of it every year at the end of Sukkot. On the contrary, it can be assumed that during the rest of the year, men and women circulated freely in the Women's Court and this may also have been the case even in the "*Shekhinah's* camp" near the altar. Similarly, there is no literary source or archaeological proof indicating the existence of a *meḥitzah* or women's gallery in the synagogue during the period of the Mishnah and Talmud. **They are first mentioned at the end of the Geonic period** and from then on are mentioned in various sources. However, even in those sources, the *meḥitzah* and women's gallery are only mentioned indirectly. **There a no halakhic source demanding or requiring a *meḥitzah* or a women's gallery in the synagogue until the end of the nineteenth century.** Such an explicit halakhic demand first appears among nineteenth- and twentieth-century Orthodox Rabbis as part of their struggle against the other streams in Judaism, but it has no halakhic basis in the Talmud and the literature of the *poskim*. Now we shall prove each of these claims one-by-one through a careful analysis of the sources.

I. Sources for Separation of the Sexes or for a Balcony for Women in the Temple

1. We have learned in Mishnah *Midot* 2:5:

> Originally [the walls of the Women's Court] were smooth. They surrounded it with a balcony so that the women look from above while the men are below so that they should not mingle.

At first glance, it is possible to explain that it is referring to a balcony built in the Women's Court for year-round use. However, Mishnah commentators such as Maimonides, Hameiri, Rosh, Bartenura, *Tiferet Yisrael* and others have already explained that this balcony was built solely because of the fear of "light-headedness" during the Sukkot Water-Drawing Celebration.[2] This is clearly apparent from the following sources:

2. *Mishnah Sukkah* 5:2:

> At the conclusion of the first festival day of Sukkot, they [the Priests and Levites] descended to the Women's Court **and they enact there a great enactment.**

3. *Tosefta Sukkah* 4:1, ed. Lieberman, p. 272:

> At first, when they saw the Water-Drawing Celebration, the men would see it from the inside and the women from the outside. **When the *Beit Din* saw that they were becoming light-headed, they made** three balconies in the Court, on the three sides, where the women sit and see the Water-Drawing Celebration, and they were not intermingled.

2. And perhaps there were permanent brackets and they added boards and a railing on *Sukkot* – see the commentators to Mishnah *Sukkah*; Prof. Saul Lieberman, *Tosefta Kifshuta* to *Sukkah*, p. 886; and Prof. Ḥanokh Albeck's supplements to Mishnah *Sukkah*, p. 477.

The two Talmuds explain "the great enactment" mentioned in the Mishnah:

4. Yerushalmi *Sukkah,* 5:2, fol. 55b:

> "And they enact there a great enactment". **What enactment were they making there?** That they would place the men alone and the women alone. As we have learned there [in *Mishnah Midot* quoted above]: "and smooth..." From whom did they learn it? **From the word of the Torah** "And the land shall mourn, each family by itself, [the family of the House of David by themselves, and their womenfolk by themselves]" (Zekhariah 12:12). Two *Amoraim*: one said this is the eulogy of the Messiah [the son of Joseph], and the other said – this is the eulogy of the evil inclination [for an explanation, see the following source]. The one who said this is the eulogy of the Messiah – if when they are mourning, the men and women are separated, when they are happy, how much the more so! The one who said this is the eulogy of the evil inclination – if at a time when the evil inclination does not exist, you say that men and women are separated, when the evil inclination exists, how much the more so!

5. Bavli *Sukkah* 51b-52a:

> **What was the "great enactment"?** Rabbi Eleazar said: As we have learned [above, source 1]: "were smooth...". Our Rabbis have taught: "Originally the women were inside and the men were outside, and this led to lightheadedness. **They enacted** that the women should sit outside and the men inside, and this still led to lightheadedness. **They enacted** that the women should sit above and the men below". [And the Talmud objects:] But how could they do so [i.e., modify any part of the Temple]?! Is it not written [when David instructed Solomon how to build the Temple] "All this that the Lord made me understand by His hand

on me, I give you in writing" (I Chronicles 28:19) [so the Temple plans came straight from God]! Rav said: **they found a verse and interpreted it**: "And the land shall mourn, each family by itself" etc. (Zekhariah 12:12). They said: Is it not a *kal vaḥomer* [an a fortiori argument]? If in the future ..., how much the more so [now]...

II. How did the Orthodox rabbis mentioned above understand these sources?

Below is a summary of their comments (see Rabbis Feinstein, Soloveitchik and Kotler in Litvin):

1. There was separation of men and women **in the Temple** via a women's balcony **all year long**.

2. The Temple plan is **Pentateuchal,** since the Babylonian Talmud quotes a verse from Chronicles. If so, Rav's *derashah* on the verse from Zekhariah, which comes to overturn that verse and justify separation beteween the sexes, is also **Pentateuchal**, as is implied by the expression "**from the word of the Torah**" in the Yerushalmi.

3. The synagogue is a *mikdash me'at*/"a little Temple" (Ezekiel 11:16 according to a midrash in *Megillah* 29a)[2a] and if the *meḥitzah* in the **Temple** is Pentateuchal, then the *meḥitzah* in the **synagogue** is also Pentateuchal.

4. Some of these Rabbis distinguish between **separation** and the **meḥitzah**. According to them, the **Torah** prohibited the mingling of the sexes – based on the verse in Zekhariah – while the Sages **enacted** the balcony/*meḥitzah*/*ezrat nashim*.

5. Some of them add another Pentateuchal prohibition: "let Him not find anything unseemly among you" (Deut. 23:15).

2a. On the synagogue as a *mikdash me'at*/little Temple, see Yosef (Jeffrey) Woolf, *Kenishta* 2 (5763), pp. 9-30 and the literature *ibid.*, in notes 12-14.

However these arguments do not flow from the above sources:

1. The balcony was built every year on Sukkot as "**a great enactment"** due to fear of light-headedness. This is how the *Rishonim* interpreted it and this is what emerges clearly from sources 2-5 above. During the rest of the year, there was no fear of light-headedness and therefore women and men circulated freely in the Women's Court as we shall prove below.

2. This separation in the Temple on Sukkot is not a Pentateuchal command, but rather a Rabbinic enactment. There are three proofs for this: the *Beraita* in the *Tosefta* [source 3] relates that "the **Beit Din... made** three balconies in the Court"; the *Beraita* in the Bavli [source 5] determines that "**they enacted**"; and the interpreted verse is taken from the book of Zekhariah and not from the Torah (cf. Yuter, p. 152; Aronson, CJ, p. 61; Ze'ev Safrai, *Moment*, p. 9). If so, how should one understand the words of Rav who determined that the Sages of the Second Temple period found a verse in Zekhariah and inferred the need for separation from it? There is no doubt that this is a late attempt by an **Amora** to justify a law of a **Tanna**, and this *sugya* is similar to most of the *sugyot* of this type. In these *sugyot*, there is a *Beraita*, a question on the *Beraita* from a verse, and an *Amora's* reply ("they found a verse and expounded it") justifying the *Beraita* with another verse (or even with the very same verse!).[3] In all of these cases, there is no Tannaitic source upholding the *Amora's* remarks. In other

3. Here is a list of the *sugyot* and the *Amoraim* which reply "they found a verse and interpreted it": *Ḥagigah* 15b (Resh Lakish); *Gittin* 48a = *Bava Batra* 72b = *Arakhin* 14b = *Arakhin* 27a (Rav Naḥman bar Yitzḥak); *Zevaḥim* 62a (Rav Yosef – there too they argue against the *beraita* with the verse from I Chronicles 28:19!); *Zevaḥim* 69b (Rabbi Yossi b"r Avin, and also the editor of the Talmud who followed Rabbi Yossi b"r Avin). On the other hand, in one *sugya* (*Bava Batra* 90a = *Menaḥot* 77a), Rav Ḥisda says "he found a verse and interpreted it" in order to a explain a *halakhah* of Shmuel and in another *sugya* (*Avodah Zarah* 52b), Rav Papa uses the same phrase to reject a "*leima mesaya lei*". In any case, our *sugya* is very similar to the first four cited above.

words, **the *Amora*** made up the *derashah* in order to defend the *Tanna.*

Similarly, the phrase "from the word of the Torah" in the Yerushalmi does not prove the reference is to Pentateuchal law. After all, we have seen that in the Tannaitic sources, the balcony is described as a Rabbinic enactment. In addition, this phrase is difficult in several other respects: it is a unique phrase in the Yerushalmi, because "from the word of the Torah" in the Yerushalmi is usually used in contrast to a law "from their words" [a rabbinic law] without reference to a specific verse (see Moshe Kosovsky, *Concordance to the Talmud Yerushalmi,* Vol. 2, Jerusalem, 1982, p. 796). Likewise, the phrase "From whom did they learn it? From the word of the Torah" is unique in the Yerushalmi (*ibid.*). Indeed, the author of the *Penei Moshe* commentary on the Yerushalmi noticed the strangeness of the expression and interpreted it as "from what is written in **Scripture**". This interpretation is confirmed by other sources in Rabbinic literature. Occasionally "Torah" means "Scripture" when it refers to a verse from the Prophets or the Writings.[4] Consequently, at the most, it may be said that the **Amoraim** found a scriptural hint for separation of men and women during the Water-Drawing Celebration, while the **Tannaim** viewed this as a Rabbinic enactment.

3. True, a **midrash** says that a synagogue is called "a little Temple", but we are dealing here with a **halakhic** issue. In other words, even if we admit that **in the Temple** there was a *meḥitzah* prescribed by Pentateuchal law – an argument which we contradicted above – this does not teach anything about the halakhic status of a *meḥitzah* in **the synagogue**. Indeed, there are hundreds of differences between the Temple and the synagogue,

4. See *Mekhilta Derabi Yishmael,* ed. Horowitz-Rabin, pp. 118, 139, 212 and parallels; *Bereishit Rabbah* 92:7, ed. Theodor-Albeck, pp. 1145-1146; *Bemidbar Rabbah* 13:2 and 18:22; *Sanhedrin* 91b-92a (four times); *Sanhedrin* 104b; and *Ketubot* 52b where a verse from Jeremiah is called "*de'oraita*". (My thanks to Prof. Judith Hauptman for the last example.)

both in terms of use and in terms of structure. If we want to know about the women's gallery/*meḥitzah* in the ancient **synagogue**, we must review Rabbinic sources and archaeological evidence about **ancient synagogues** and not draw analogies from **the Temple** to the synagogue. Morevoer, the balcony described in Tractate *Sukkah* was built for a special celebration. One cannot make analogies from a mass **celebration** in the Temple to communal **prayer** in the synagogue.[5]

4. There is, however, a certain difference between the descriptions of the separation in the above sources. From the *Tosefta* and the Bavli, it sounds like like a custom of the people, whereas, according to the Yerushalmi, the separation is also a Rabbinic enactment. In any case, as we have seen, both the separation and the balcony are not Pentateuchal, are not connected to the synagogue, and were not in force in the Temple the rest of the year.

5. According to its simple meaning, the verse "let Him not find anything unseemly among you" (Deut. 23:15) is referring to a man who had a seminal emission and to the requirement to relieve oneself outside the Israelite camp. In *Berakhot* 25b they derived from this verse that it is forbidden to recite the *Shema* while seeing nakedness through glass or an unclothed gentile. However, there is no attempt in either Talmud to draw a link between this verse and separate seating or a *meḥitzah* (see Aaronson, CJ, pp. 63-64). The modern rabbis who used this verse

5. This is implied by *Sefer Hama'asim Livnei Eretz Israel*, ed. B. M. Lewin, *Tarbitz* 1/1 (5690), p. 97 and by *Sefer Hapardess*, ed. Ehrenreich, Budapest, 1924, p. 72. Both authors use the above-quoted verse from *Zekhariah* 12 in order to deduce a *kal vaḥomer* from a time of mourning to a time of joy, hence women should not mingle with men during **a feast or a dance**. That is, like the Bavli and the Yerushalmi, they draw an analogy from the verse in *Zekhariah* to feasts and celebrations and not to the synagogue. This is a natural analogy, because the opposite of mourning is joy and not prayer. Cf. now Hillel Newman, *Hama'asim Livnei Eretz Yisrael*, Jerusalem, 2011, pp. 151-152 and his discussion on pp. 102-104 where he also refers to this responsum.

have therefore created a new *midrash halakhah* of their own accord.[6]

6. Finally, we may add a simple question: **if separate seating or a *meḥitzah* is a Pentateuchal or even a Rabbinic prohibition, why have we not heard of this prohibition in all of the *halakhic* literature dealing with the laws of prayer and synagogues from the time of the Talmud until the nineteenth century?!** All of the medieval *poskim* cited below refer to a *meḥitzah* incidentally; not one of them **requires** a *meḥitzah* or women's gallery or **prohibits** mixed seating. In other words, this "prohibition" was created by the above Rabbis in modern times.

Rather, if you wish to know the history of the *meḥitzah*, you must check the matter historically: was there separation of the sexes during prayer and in places of worship during the First and Second Temple periods? Was there separation or a *meḥitzah* in synagogues during the Mishnaic and Talmudic periods? In the Middle Ages? Only after such a thorough review will we be able to determine whether congregations that abolished the *meḥitzah* acted appropriately or not.

6. And according to Maimonides, doing so is prohibited – see Yuter, p. 151. Perhaps they arrived at this verse in Deuteronomy via Maimonides in *Hilkhot Keriyat Shema* 3:16, who juxtaposed the prohibition of seeing nakedness through glass, which is based on this verse, to the prohibition of "all of a woman's body is *ervah*/lewdness". On the other hand, perhaps these rabbis were influenced by *Yalkut Shimoni* on Deuteronomy, paragraph 934, ed. Mosad Harav Kuk, pp. 488-489. There is a passage there from *Shabbat* 150a which concludes with the verse in question and it is immediately followed by a passage from *Seder Eliahu Rabbah* which we will cite below, which prohibits a man from praying "amongst women". Perhaps these rabbis learned from *semikhut parshiot*,"the proximity of chapters", but it is clear from Tractate *Shabbat* and *Seder Eliyahu* that they refer to two completely separate matters.

III. There was no separation of the sexes during worship and in places of worship during the First and Second Temple periods.

There are several hints about this in the Bible and the Apocrypha:

1. Exodus 38:8 (and cf. I Samuel 2:22): "And he made the laver of copper, and its stand of copper, **from the mirrors of the women assembling**, who assembled at the door of the Tent of Meeting". The meaning of the verse is not clear, but according to the accepted interpretation (see Onkelos, Ibn Ezra and others), "the women assembling" were a group of women who "came every day to the door of the Tent of Meeting to pray and to listen to the commandments". One could claim that the women came to the Tent of Meeting as a separate group, but the Torah makes no mention of any attempt to separate between them and the men.

2. The commandment of *Hakhel*, gathering the people once every seven years to hear the Torah read aloud, is found in Deuteronomy 31:12: "Gather the people, **men and women** and children" and in Neḥemiah 8:1-2: "And Ezra the Priest brought the Torah before the congregation **both men and women**... and he read from it... before **the men and the women**." On the face of it, one could claim that the men and women gathered separately as defined groups in order to fulfill the *mitzvah* of *Hakhel*. But that is not so. Further investigation of the Bible teaches that a phrase such as "men, women and children" means **the entire people** (Genesis 14:16, Exodus 35:22, Deuteronomy 2:34, Judges 9:51, 16:27, Jeremiah 40:7 and primarily Ezra 10:1). These phrases teach something about the social ideology of the writer, but they do not teach us about any physical separation whatsoever. Therefore, men and women gathered together to hear the reading of the Torah in public. Furthermore, it stands to reason from the verse in Nehemiah, Chapter 8 that there was no *meḥitzah*, because verse 4 says: "And Ezra the Scribe stood upon **a wooden tower made for the purpose**". If the author took the trouble to report the construction of a tower, it is likely that had there been a

meḥitzah he would have reported on its construction. From this you may infer that there was no *meḥitzah* during the *Hakhel* ceremony.

3. I Samuel 1:9 ff.: Ḥannah prays next to or inside the sanctuary in Shilo. Eli the Priest does not protest this; he is only surprised that Ḥannah is praying quietly, contrary to the custom at that time. This is not an example of communal prayer, but there is proof here that it was permissible for a woman to pray near the sanctuary or inside it in ancient times.

4. Malakhi 2:13: "And this you do a second time: you cover the altar of the Lord with tears". According to the accepted interpretation (see Rashi and Radak), the Prophet is rebuking the Priests for taking gentile wives and their Hebrew wives are shedding tears on the altar. This implies that the women were able to approach the altar without restrictions.

5. Judith 4:11-12 (ed. Grintz, p. 106):

> **And every man of Israel and woman** and child dwelling in Jerusalem **fell [down] before the Temple** and they put ashes on their heads and spread out their sackloth before the Lord... **and they cried out in unison... to the God of Israel...**

The Book of Judith was apparently written in the 4th century BCE and there is explicit evidence here of a mixed prayer service inside the Temple.

IV. In the "Women's Court" of the Temple at the end of the Second Temple period, there was no separation of the sexes during the year.

Many mistakenly thought that the "Women's Court" of the Temple was meant for women only.[7] However, it is very clear

7. Safrai suggests (p. 332, and Brooten, p. 130, agrees) that the name Women's Court derives from the fact that women did not usually enter "the

from Tannaitic writings and from Josephus Flavius that women and men were present in the Women's Court all year round:[8]

1. There were four chambers in the four corners of the Women's Court – for wood, Nazirites, lepers, and wine and oil (*Midot* 2:5). These chambers were meant primarily for men's use and there is no doubt that men passed through the Women's Court to reach them.

2. "And there were chambers beneath the Court of the Israelites which opened into the Women's Court, and there the Levites played upon harps and lyres and cymbals and all instruments of music" (*Midot* 2:6).

3. According to Rav Ḥisda, Ezra the Scribe mentioned above read at *Hakhel* in the Women's Court, and the *Gemara* learns from this that the king also read from the Torah at *Hakhel* in the Women's Court (*Sotah* 40b-41a and parallels). As mentioned in the verses quoted above, women were also obligated to fufill this commandment. One can therefore assume that they were present in the Women's Court at *Hakhel* at the end of the Second Temple period just as they were present at *Hakhel* during the time of Ezra and Neḥemiah.

Shekhinah's camp" near the altar, even though by law this was permissible. (For another explanation, see Buchler, p. 698 ff.) In any case, there are contradictory sources regarding this. Josephus states in four places (*The Jewish Wars* 5, 5, 2, ed. Simḥoni, p. 302; *ibid*., 5, 5, 6, p. 305; and in *Antiquities of the Jews* and *Against Apion* which will be cited below) that it was forbidden for women to enter the "*Shekhinah's* camp", and so it appears from a *Tannaitic* source (a *beraita* in *Ḥagigah* 16b and parallels). On the other hand, there is one *Tannaitic* source that can be interpreted both ways (a *beraita* in *Kiddushin* 52b and Rashi and *Tosafot ad loc*.). Finally, there are many *Tannaitic* sources indicating that women did indeed enter the "*Shekhinah's* camp" – see *Tosefta Arakhin* 2:1, ed. Zuckermandel, p. 544; Mishnah *Bikurim* 1:5, 3:6; *Kiddushin* 1:8 and Bavli, *ibid*., 36b (=*Sotah* 3:1 and *Nazir* 6:9); *Zevaḥim* 3:1; and *Keilim* 1:8-9. For discussion, see Safrai, pp. 331-332 and Buchler pp. 697-706.

8. This is the view of Shmuel Safrai, *Ha'aliyah Laregel Bimei Bayit Sheni*, second edition, Jerusalem, 5745, p. 88 ff.

4. According to the Bavli, the High Priest read the Torah on *Yom Kippur* to the entire congregation in the Women's Court (*Yoma* 69a-b).

5. According to Mishnah *Sanhedrin* (11:2), there were three *Batei Din* [law courts] in the Temple: one at the gate of the Temple Mount, one at the gate of the *Azara* [Temple Court], and one in the *Lishkhat Hagazit* [Chamber of Hewn Stone]. The standard interpretation is that the second *Beit Din* was in the Women's Court near the entrance to the Court of the Israelites, and the third *Beit Din* was "half in the sanctified part and half in the profane part".

6. According to the *Tanna*, Rabbi Eliezer ben Ya'akov (*Tosefta Pesaḥim* 4:12, ed. Lieberman, p. 164, where he disagrees with the Mishnah *ibid.*, 5:10), when the "third group" waited to sacrifice the Paschal lamb on Passover eve, "it went and waited in the Women's Court".

7. One *Beraita* (*Ḥagigah* 16b and parallels) states: "Rabbi Yossi said: Abba Eleazar told me: once we had a calf for a peace-offering and we brought it to the Women's Court and women laid hands on it...". From here one learns of the presence of women in the Women's Court and that the men could mingle with them without any concern.

8. In two places Josephus Flavius relates that to the Women's Court "came all of the Jews, men and women, when they are purified of all impurity" (*Against Apion* 2: 8, paragraph 104, , ed. Kasher, p. 54 and cf. *Antiquities* 15, 11, 5, paragraphs 418-419, ed. Schalit, Volume 3, p. 201).

From all of the above sources, we learn that men were frequently present in the Women's Court during the course of the year, and we have seen clearly from sources 3, 7 and 8 that women also used to visit the Women's Court on various occasions. Nevertheless, we only hear of separation between them during the Water-Drawing Celebration due to fear of lightheadedness. As explained, all of this does not prove **anything** about the ancient **synagogue**, but it does come to contradict the opinion that it is possible to draw conclusions about synagogues from the supposed separation of the sexes in the Temple throughout the year.

V. There is no literary source or archaeological proof for the existence of a women's gallery in the ancient synagogue.

1. In *Antiquities of the Jews* (16, 6, 2, paragraph 164, ed. Schalit, Volume 3, p. 219), Josephus relates that the Emperor Augustus (who ruled from 27 BCE-14 CE) wrote in a decree on behalf of the Jews of Asia Minor and North Africa as follows:

> ... and if anyone is caught stealing their sacred books or their sacred monies from a sabbath-house or an *andron*, he shall be regarded as sacrilegious, and his property shall be confiscated to the public treasury of the Romans.

The word *andron* is problematic both in terms of the correct reading and in terms of its meaning. Among others, some scholars maintained that *andron* means "men's halls" (see references in Rosenthal pp. 654-655 and note 7) and this would then prove the existence of a women's gallery. However, this interpretation is no longer accepted today. Schalit translates it as a "synagogue or meeting place" and Shaye Cohen translates it as a "banquet hall" (for references and an explanation, see S. Cohen, 1987, and cf. Brooten, p. 260, note 160). If so, this source is not at all relevant to our discussion.

2. In *Antiquities of the Jews*, (14, 10, 24, paragraphs 259-261, ed. Schalit, Volume 3, p. 140) Josephus cites a decision by residents of Sardis in Asia Minor from the end of the first century BCE:

> The council and the people have decided... [that the Jews will be permitted] to congregate and conduct their communal life according to [their] traditional customs...

> **and that they will also be given a place where they will assemble with their wives and children and they will conduct the prayers handed down to them by their fathers** and they will make sacrifices to God....

This source teaches that women participated in prayer services and "sacrifices" in the synagogue at Sardis. And perhaps this proves that there was no separation of men, women and children during prayer services.

3. In his book, *On the Contemplative Life*, Philo writes of a Jewish sect, known as the *Therapeutae*, which existed in Egypt at the end of the Second Temple period. They left their families, secluded themselves in the desert, and gathered on Shabbat to hear a sermon from their leader and participate in a communal meal. In paragraphs 32–33 (ed. Daniel-Nataf, Jerusalem, 5746, pp. 189-190), he reports that the meeting hall was

> comprised of two galleries, one for men and one for women... the wall between the galleries, its bottom half was built to a height of three or four cubits, similar to a fence, while the upper part until the ceiling was left open. There were two reasons for this: to maintain the modesty appropriate for women's nature, and so that their ears can easily hear the words while sitting in hearing distance... without a barrier to the voice of the speaker.

Some perceived this source as proof of the existence of a *meḥitzah* in the synagogue of antiquity, but it cannot teach us anything about the structure of ancient synagogues. First of all, it refers to an ascetic sect which was completely different from Rabbinic Judaism. Moreover, Philo relates later on (paragraph 69, pp. 197-198) that in this sect, men and women also **ate** separately (but without a *meḥitzah*), and it is therefore difficult to draw analogies between them and Rabbinic Jews.[9] Finally, in

9. But it is possible that men and women belonging to the rabbinic circles of the Sages also ate separately in Mishnaic times – see below, p. 367, note 41.

several places Philo describes Shabbat observance in the synagogue in great detail (see Rosenthal, p. 654, note 5) and, in all of them, he makes no mention whatsoever of a *meḥitzah*.

4. Four places in Talmudic literature[10] describe the killing of Alexandria's Jews by the Emperor Trajan during the revolt against him in 117 CE. In the Yerushalmi, there is a long paragraph about the great synagogue of Alexandria and at the end it says: "And who destroyed it? Trogianus the wicked". Ten lines later there is a long story about his arrival in Alexandria and about his dialogue with the Jews. After killing the men,

> he said to their wives: if you listen to my legions [i.e., have sex with them], I will not kill you! They said to him: **what you did to the lower ones, do to the upper ones,** and he mixed their blood with the blood [of the men], and the blood flowed in the sea until Cyprus.

Commentators on the Yerushalmi, such as the authors of *Penei Moshe* and *Yefei Mar'eh*, had trouble understanding the highlighted sentence. In 1884, Rabbi Meir Ish-Shalom suggested (and cf. Sukenik in his English book and Prof. Saul Lieberman in *Tosefta Kifshutah* to *Sukkah*, p. 890) that the dialogue and the slaughter took place in that same great synagogue of Alexandria. There Trajan found the men learning, debated with them, killed them and then turned to the women who were sitting upstairs in the women's gallery and they answered: "**what you did to the lower ones, do to the upper ones**", and he killed them.[10a]

It is worth noting that Ross Kraemer, *Unreliable Witnesses*, Oxford, 2011, Chapter 3, now thinks that much if not all of this description of the Therapeutae may be Philo's own construction! For a summary of her thesis, see Renee Levine Melammed, *The Jerusalem Post Magazine*, December 9, 2011, p. 43. My thanks to Prof. Levine Melammed for her insights on this topic.

10. Yerushalmi *Sukkah* 5:1, fol. 55b; *Eikhah Rabbah*, ed. Vilna, 1:45, fol. 17c = ed. Buber, p. 83; *ibid.*, 4:22, fol. 29d = ed. Buber, p. 152; *Petiḥta* of *Esther Rabbah*, ed. Vilna, fols. 1b-c.

10a. Rabbi Meir Ish-Shalom was consistent. See above, pp. 6-7, re. the need for a women's gallery today.

However, Professor Safrai (and also Brooten, pp. 132-133) questions this interpretation, because the two parallel passages in *Eikhah Rabbah*, ed. Vilna, have the opposite reading in both places: "**do to the lower ones what you did to the upper ones**". Furthermore, there is a similar reading in one version of the Yerushalmi (in *Me'or Einayim*, Chapter 12, ed. Kassel, p. 181). If this is the correct version, it may referring to a wall. After Trajan killed the men on the wall, he killed the women below. If so, this story teaches us nothing about the women's gallery in the ancient synagogue.

5. A *sugya* in *Kiddushin* 81a deals with the laws of *yiḥud*, which forbid a man to be alone in a room with a woman. Among other things, it states: "Abaye used to encircle with clay jugs; Rava would use reeds". Many maintained that this was proof of a *meḥitzah* in the synagogue; however, this has not been proven at all. First of all, a synagogue is not mentioned at all in this passage and even Rashi is uncertain about what is being discussed. He explains: "a place where men and women gather, either for a *derashah* or a for a wedding ceremony". Moreover, if the reference here was to a synagogue, this source would prove that a women's gallery/*meḥitzah* did **not** exist in the Talmudic period and therefore Abaye and Rava had to build a temporary *meḥitzah* (cf. Brooten, pp. 134-135). Finally, the *Gemara* is relating individual actions and not *halakhah* for the masses and the *poskim* do not cite these actions as *halakhah*.

6. In a late midrash entitled *Sefer Eliyahu Upirkei Mashiaḥ Venistarot R. Shimon bar Yoḥai*, which was apparently written between the 8th-10th centuries, there is a description of God's House of Study in the World to Come:

> And all the serene women who would pay wages for their sons to teach them Torah, Bible [and] Mishnah, **stand at the reed partition made like a fence**, hear the voice of Zerubabel son of Shaltiel who translates in front of God, and they answer after him "Blessed be His holy name"

(Aharon Jellinek, *Beit Hamidrash,* Part 3, Leipzig, 1855, p. 75 = Yehuda Even Shmuel, *Midreshei Geulah,* Tel Aviv, 5703, p. 341).

Prof. Zeev Safrai suggested that we have proof here of the existence of a reed partition, made like a fence, in the *Beit Midrash*. However, an ancient Genizah fragment of this midrash was published in 1978 and it says there that the women "**stand on a reed mat built as a fence for the *bimah***".[11] Prof. Steven Fine explained that this refers to a fence or chancel screen which they would build around the Torah reading *bimah*. This type of fence or screen was common in ancient synagogues. According to the second reading of this passage – which is the older and more correct reading – they will honor the women in the World to Come by allowing them to stand next to the chancel screen which surrounds the *bimah* in order to hear the *derashah* and reply "Blessed be His holy name" etc. If so, this proves the **opposite**, that there was **no** women's gallery at the time this midrash was written.

7. John Chrysostom, a Church Father (ca. 347-407 CE), was an influential anti-Jewish preacher in Antioch, Syria. In his first speech *Against the Jews* (1, 2, 7), composed in 386 CE, he denigrates the synagogue as a place of abomination where "*gunaichon surpeton*", which means "men and women intermingled" according to Prof. Safrai (Safrai, p. 337). Ostensibly, this is convincing proof of mixed seating in the fourth century. However, it is difficult to rely on this source for two reasons. First of all, this is an anti-Jewish polemic and it contains many lies and a lot of nonsense. Moreover, Safrai's translation is apparently inaccurate. Meeks and Wilken translate it as: "But they gather rabble – **effeminate men** and prostitutes", and Harkins translates: "But these Jews are gathering choruses of **effeminates** and

11. This Genizah fragment was published by Simon Hopkins, *A Miscellany of Literary Pieces from the Cambridge Genizah Collections,* Cambridge, 1978, p. 12. Regarding this midrash, see Adiel Kadari, *Tarbitz* 73/2 (5764), p. 182 ff.

a great rubbish heap of harlots" and this is verified by Greek dictionaries. If so, this source teaches nothing about the setup of the ancient synagogue.

8. *Tosefta Megillah* (2:12 and ff.; 3:21 and ff.) and *Massekhet Soferim* deal with the structure and sections of the ancient synagogue and they do not mention a *meḥitzah* or a women's gallery.

9. Many modern rabbis have claimed that the *meḥitzah* is not mentioned in the sources because women in the Talmudic period simply did not go to synagogue. However, this argument is totally unfounded. Löw, Blau, Epstein, Brand, Levy, Safrai and Brooten have already proven, using twelve Talmudic sources and four external sources, that women attended synagogue on a regular basis. Here are two examples from the Bavli, one halakhic and one aggadic. A *beraita* in *Avodah Zarah* 38b rules that it is permissible for a gentile woman to stir the pot of a Jewess "**until she returns** from the bathhouse or the **synagogue** and she need not worry". *Sotah* 22a relates the story of a widow who used to pray every day in the *beit midrash* of Rabbi Yoḥanan, even though there was a synagogue in her neighborhood. Rabbi Yoḥanan asks her if there is a synagogue in her neighborhood, but he does ask her about the fact that she prays in public every day.[12]

10. At the beginning of the 20th century, several remnants of ancient synagogues were found in the Land of Israel. In some cases, archaeologists thought that they had discovered remnants of galleries, and some scholars decided without hesitation that these galleries were "certainly" used as women's galleries (see Krauss, Kohl and Watzinger, Sukenik, and Goodenough). However there is no basis for this determination. Thus far, **over one hundred synagogues** from the Talmudic period have been discovered in the Land of Israel, the Golan and trans-Jordan and about **ten** in the Diaspora. In the 1980s, Prof. Brooten reviewed all these findings again and found that in the Land of Israel, there

12. For an external source, see above, p. 321, paragraph 2. For other Talmudic sources, see above, pp. 96-99 and the literature *ibid.*, note 8.

is reasonable proof of a gallery in only **five** synagogues (pp. 104-123) and no proof at all of a gallery in the Diaspora (pp. 123-130)! Furthermore, there is no **archaeological** proof that the few galleries uncovered were used as women's galleries. Indeed, we know from rabbinic literature that synagogue galleries were used for different purposes (see Yerushalmi *Berakhot*, Chapter 2, fol. 5d = Yerushalmi *Shabbat*, Chapter 2, fol. 3a and especially Bavli *Ḥullin* 92a). Due to these doubts, archaeologists now refrain from claiming that these were women's galleries (see Levine in his various studies).

11. Finally, there is an important archaeological proof from silence that there were **no** women's galleries in the ancient synagogues. In the inscriptions which were uncovered in these synagogues, there are inscriptions in honor of those who donated a pillar, a row of pillars (*stoa*), steps, a door frame, a place of lodging, rooms, water installations, lamps, closets(?), mosaics and gates – **yet there is not a single inscription which mentions a women's gallery.**[13] This teaches us that there was no women's gallery during that period.

In summary, women use to visit ancient synagogues on a regular basis, yet there is not a single archaeological or literary proof of the existence of a *meḥitzah* or women's gallery during that period.

VI. Evidence of a *Meḥitzah* or a Women's Gallery in the Middle Ages

As mentioned above, there is no halakhic source before the nineteenth century which explicitly **requires** a *meḥitzah*/women's gallery. However, there are many medieval sources which indirectly prove its existence. The earliest source is, apparently, *Seder Eliyahu Rabbah*, which states: "And the Sages learned four things from him [= from King Hizkiya]... nor should a man stand

13. See Yosef Naveh, *Al Psifas Va'even*, Jerusalem, 5738 and Leah Roth-Gerson, *Haktovot Hayevaniot Mibatei Haknesset Be'eretz Yisrael*, Jerusalem, 5747.

among women and pray, ***mipnei da'at hanashim***".[14] The latter phrase apparently means "because of distraction caused by the presence of women".[15] This midrash, which was apparently written in the late Geonic period,[16] does not explicitly mention a *meḥitzah*, but such an attitude could have led to the construction of a *meḥitzah*. A women's gallery is first mentioned in several Genizah fragments from Fustat, Egypt, dating from the 11th century (see Goitein's studies), and Prof. Ze'ev Safrai conjectures that the women's gallery was a compromise between the Jewish custom of mixed seating and the Muslim custom in which women did not pray in a Mosque at all (Safrai, *Moment*, p. 8). From then on, the *meḥitzah* and "women's synagogue" are mentioned in Spain and especially in Ashkenaz.[17]

VII. Is it permitted to do away with the *meḥitzah*/ women's gallery?

We have thus far shown that these things are not a Pentateuchal or Rabbinic commandment, but rather ancient

14. Beginning of Chapter 9, ed. Ish-Shalom, p. 46 and from there in *Sefer Ra'aviyah*, Part 1, paragraph 77, p. 53 and in *Yalkut Shimoni* to Deuteronomy, paragraph 934, ed. Mossad Harav Kuk, pp. 488-489.
15. So it seems from the context, and that is how Braude and Kapstein translated in *Tana debe Eliyyahu*, Philadelphia, 1981, p. 147. For a different explanation, see Ze'ev Safrai in *Moment*, p. 6.
16. The number of guesses regarding the time and place of *Seder Eliyahu* is almost identical to the number of scholars who studied the subject – see good summaries in *Ha'entziklopedia Ha'ivrit*, s.v. "*Tanna debei Eliahu*" = EJ, under the same heading, and in Braude and Kapstein (above, note 15), pp. 3-12. I agree with those who date it at the end of the Geonic period.
17. **In Spain**: *Responsa Rashba*, Part 2, No. 182; Part 3, No. 155 (but the reading there is unreliable); and Part 6, No. 7. **In Ashkenaz**: the Mordechai to *Shabbat*, Chapter 3, paragraph 311, quoted by the *Tur*, Rema and Taz in OH 315 and in *Minhagei Maharil*, end of *Hilkhot Shabbat*, ed. Spitzer, Jerusalem, 5749, pp. 220-221 in the name of the the Aviya"h (but the Ra'aviyah, Part 1, paragraph 266, p. 342 **does not** mention a *meḥitzah* between men and women); *Hagahot Maimoniyot*, end of *Hilkhot Shevitat Assor*, s.v. *kol nidrei* (and from there in *Minhagim* of Rabbi Isaac Tirna for *Yom Hakippurim* and the *Beit Yosef* to OH 619); *Tosafot* to *Rosh Hashanah* 27b, s.v. *veshama; Sefer Ha'agudah* to *Kiddushin* 74a, ed. Cracow, fols. 106b-c = ed. Brizel, Volume 7,

customs which apparently emerged at the end of the Geonic period. Now we can ask: is it permissible to do away with an old custom such as this? Or perhaps an ancient custom accepted by *Kelal Yisrael* [the collective Jewish people] is unchangeable? Several Orthodox Rabbis who dealt with this issue, among them Rabbi Aharon Kotler, understood it as an ancient custom and nonetheless prohibited any change in the custom.

1. They pointed to sources such as *Pesaḥim* 50b; Yerushalmi *Pesaḥim* 4:1, fol. 30b = *Bereishit Rabbah* 94:4 (only in the printed editions!) and parallels; and *Beitzah* 4b. These sources stress that it is impossible to alter a custom of our forefathers, basing themselves on verses such as "My son, hear the discipline of your father, and do not forsake the Torah of your mother" (Proverbs, 1:8).[18]

2. They also pointed to Maimonides, *Hilkhot Mamrim* 1:1-2, that one must obey the Great Court in Jerusalem, as it says "You shall not deviate from everything that they tell you" (Deuteronomy 17:11), and he continues:

> ... and also things which they made as a fence around the Torah and what the hour demands – and they are decrees, enactments, and **customs** – it is a positive commandment to listen to them, and whoever transgresses, transgresses a negative command.

p. 245; *Minhagei Maharil* as cited above, *Hilkhot Shofar*, p. 287; *Responsa Maharil*, No. 53; Rabbi Yisrael Isserlein, *Trumat Hadeshen*, Part 1, No. 353; *The Memoirs of Gluckel of Hameln*, New York, 1932, pp. 49, 271ff..
For the physical evidence from European synagogues, see Krinsky, pp. 28-31, 112-113, but her remarks on Talmudic sources are based on Litvin and are in need of correction. Therese and Mendel Metzger report that in a 14th century manuscript from Aragon there is an illumination with three rows of women sitting behind the men, on the same floor, with no partition between them. Also see Cohen-Harris, pp. 6-9, who investigated other illustrations and *Image*, p. 15, for a picture of a women's gallery in Amsterdam in 1655 (which also seems to have been a gallery for men).

18. For other *derashot* along these lines, see Menaḥem Elon, *Hamishpat Ha'ivri*, third edition, Jerusalem, 5748, pp. 724-725.

However, these two arguments can be refuted:

1. Despite these *derashot*, thousands of ancient customs have been abolished throughout the generations, both by the people and by the *poskim*.[19] In order to prevent a change in a custom, it is not enough to merely cite these *derashot*.

2. Naḥmanides already questioned Maimonides's opinion on this issue (see *Leḥem Mishneh, ad loc.*), and, in any case, Maimonides was only dealing with customs of the Great Court in Jerusalem, and we have already proved that we are not discussing such a custom.

Many proponents of the *meḥitzah* denigrate rabbis who take into account contemporary sociological conditions. However, the fact of the matter is, that the *poskim* – including some of the very same Orthodox Rabbis, as we shall see below – always took into account the time and the place. Countless times in the history of the Jewish people, *halakhot*, and, all the more so, customs, were abolished because the original reason for the custom disappeared as a result of sociological changes.[20] There is no doubt we have such a case before us. In other words, in medieval society, where men and women were separated in many areas of life, a *meḥitzah* or women's gallery was necessary for "general modesty", as the Mordechai wrote (above, note 17). However, ***ha'idana***/now, in our day, when we live in a totally mixed society, a *meḥitzah* adds nothing to the synagogue because men are ***regilim***/used to sitting together with women at all times and in all places. On the contrary, in our day, separate seating detracts, because it cuts the synagogue off from reality and from life, divides families, and causes many women a feeling of alienation and inferiority which distances them from the synagogue (see Aaronson, in CJ, p. 59 and Adler in CJ 2, pp. 36-37).

However, this does not mean that **it is obligatory** to abolish

19. For several examples, see Elon, *ibid.*, pp. 760-764.
20. For many examples, see Louis Jacobs, *A Tree of Life*, Oxford, 1984, Chapters 9-10.

the *meḥitzah*. It all depends on the congregation praying in a given synagogue and, undoubtedly, in certain neighborhoods and cities, separation in the synagogue corresponds to the separation found in all areas of life. However, in most Jewish communities in the world today, the separation and the *meḥitzah* do not fit reality and do not add anything to the worship of God.

It should be stressed that the two concepts mentioned above – **ha'idana**/now and **regilut**/used to – are not new. They appear in the writings of many *poskim* throughout the generations and served as a basis for far-reaching changes in *halakhah*. **Ha'idana**/now appears in many Talmudic discussions as an explanation for changes in *halakhah*,[21] and even the Tosafists frequently used this halakhic concept (see, for example, *Tosafot* to *Kiddushin* 30a, s.v. *lo tzrikha*).[22] Even the Rema, who wrote in one place (OH 690:17) "and no custom should be abolished or mocked because not for naught were they established" wrote elsewhere: **"Nevertheless, if the matter changed from the way it was in the time of the *Rishonim*,** it is permissible to change the custom according to the times".[22a]

In our context, the concept **ha'idana**/now appears in the responsum of Rabbi Yechiel Ya'akov Weinberg, author of *Seridei Eish*, regarding the *meḥitzah*. He discusses, among other things, the dispute between Rabbi Moshe Feinstein and some Hungarian Rabbis over the height of a *meḥitzah* – the former was satisfied by

21. *Berakhot* 22a = *Ḥulin* 136b; *Shabbat* 95a; *Ta'anit* 17a; *Megillah* 21b and 31a; *Ketubot* 3a at the bottom; *Kiddushin* 71b at the top; *Bava Metzi'a* 42a (three times); *Avodah Zarah* 69b at the bottom.
22. In addition to *ha'iddana*/now, *poskim* frequently use phrases such as *akhshav*/now, *badorot halalu*/in these generations, *hashata*/now, and *nishtanu hateva'im*/natures have changed – to justify changes in *halakhah* and custom. For several examples, see Rabbi Louis Jacobs (above, note 20), pp. 157-158 and for dozens of examples from all periods, see Immanuel Löw, "*Ha-Iddana*", *HUCA* 11 (1936), pp. 193-206.

22a. *Responsa Rema*, ed. Ziv, No. 19 = other editions, No. 21, as paraphrased in the *Magen Avraham* and *Ba'er Heitev* to OH 690:17. Also see Asher Ziv, *Harema*, Jerusalem, 1957, pp. 100-106, and above, p. 144, note 9. My thanks to Rabbi Monique Süsskind Goldberg z"l who helped me clarify these references.

eighteen *tefaḥim* [handsbreadths], while the latter demanded a *meḥitzah* "above the heads". The latter even went so far as to rule that, in the absence of such a *meḥitzah,* "women are prohibited from coming to pray and it is better that they remain in their homes." Rabbi Weinberg responds:

> Their intention is certainly good, as they want to maintain the modesty of previous generations. **However, in our times, the situation and the nature of things have changed,** and if the women remain at home and do not come to the synagogue, they will forget Judaism entirely and it is certainly forbidden to push them away and to distance them due to a superfluous stringency with no solid basis in the Talmud or *poskim*. (*Seridei Eish,* Part 2, No. 14, pp. 29-30)

However, in light of all of the above, we may ask of Rabbi Weinberg what he asked of the Hungarian Rabbis: a) "In our times, the situation and the nature of things have changed"; in modern society, the *meḥitzah*/women's gallery are no longer needed and add nothing to Jewish prayer; b) The *meḥitzah* and women's gallery distance women from the synagogue, "and it is certainly forbidden to push them away and to distance them"; c) There is no obligation to follow this custom "due to a superfluous stringency with no solid basis in the Talmud or *poskim*".

The idea that **regilut**/being used to something prevents sinful thoughts is also not new.[23] It was suggested by various *poskim* throughout the generations in contexts similar to ours. The Ra'aviyah (Ashkenaz, d. 1220) raised the matter while dealing with the issue of *kol b'ishah erveh*/"a woman's voice is lewdness" (*Berakhot* 24a). He writes (Part 1, paragraph 76, p. 52; cf. above, p. 82):

> And all of these things [which we mentioned above] as

23. For an analysis of the term *regilut* [to be used to something], see Rabbi Yehudah Herzl Henkin, *De'ot* 3 (*Shevat* 5759), pp. 14-18 and also the debate between him and Rabbi Emanuel Feldman in *Tradition* 34/3 (Fall 2000), pp. 40-57.

> *ervah*/lewdness **are specifically so in something that is not usually revealed**, but a young woman who **is used to** uncovered hair, **we are not concerned because there are no sinful thoughts**, and so regarding her voice [to one who is **used to** hearing it].

In other words, sinful thoughts arise from not being used to something and a person who is used to seeing a young woman with uncovered hair or to hear her voice will not be adversely affected by these things.

This idea was developed extensively by Rabbi Mordechai Yaffe, author of the *Levush* (Poland, 16th century), regarding a topic very similar to ours. According to *Sefer Ḥassidim* (ed. Wistinetzki, paragraph 1176 = ed. Margaliot, paragraph 393 and again in paragraph 1120), if "women are sitting among men [at a wedding], where there are improper thoughts, then it is not possible to recite *'shehasimḥah beme'ono'* ", a phrase about joy added to the Grace after Meals at a wedding feast. Indeed, this view was accepted as *halakhah* by some *poskim* (see, for example, the *Baḥ* to *Tur* EH, end of paragraph 62, s.v. *ve'yeish omrim* at the end). The *Levush* (in the section on "customs" at the end of OH, paragraph 36) cites the above passage from *Sefer Ḥassidim* and writes:

> And people are not careful about this now, and perhaps because **now the women are very used to being among the men and there are not so many sinful thoughts, rather "they appear to us as white geese"** (*Berakhot* 20a) because of their habitual presence amongst us and therefore "since they are familiar to us, they are familiar to us".

And if, in the time of the Levush in the 16th century, the women were **used to** sitting among the men, how much the more so in our time! Therefore, the common practice today of mixed seating in the synagogue is justified, because in our times, we have gotten **used to** mixed seating and there are no sinful thoughts.

Finally, it should be noted that one of the most ardent supporters of the *meḥitzah* – Rabbi Moshe Feinstein – used the argument of being used to something when he wanted to cancel the prohibition of "a woman's hair is lewdness" (*Berakhot* 24a). He was compelled to do so in order to justify a *meḥitzah* of only eighteen *tefaḥim*. And here is what Rabbi Moshe Feinstein wrote, as quoted in the *Seridei Eish* mentioned above (Part 2, No. 14, pp. 19-20) :

> And regarding women who go with their heads uncovered, [Rabbi Feinstein] already wrote in *Igrot Moshe* that we can rely on the Rif and Maimonides that hair is not lewdness when reciting the *Shema* or the *Amidah*. **And how much the more so in our times, in which the vast majority of women go with their heads uncovered and people are already used to this, and hair is not in the category of places which are usually covered**...

Of course, in Rabbi Feinstein's opinion, being **used to** something cannot abolish the *meḥitzah* because it is a "Pentateuchal prohibition". However, according to our approach, the matter is simple. If being **used to** something can cancel "a woman's hair is lewdness" which is a Talmudic concept, then *kal vaḥomer* it can abolish the *meḥitzah* which is a custom not mentioned in any Talmudic source.

VIII. Practical *Halakhah*

In conclusion, we have discussed until now the historical and halakhic aspects of the *meḥitzah* in the synagogue. Historically, we have proven that the women's gallery/*meḥitzah* did not exist in the ancient synagogue. They are mentioned for the first time in Fustat, Egypt in the 11th century, and since then they are mentioned in Spain and Ashkenaz, but only incidentally. Halakhically, we have proven that it is permissible to abolish a custom on the basis of the principals of **"now"** and the fact that men are already **"used to"** sitting with women at all times and in all places.

Finally, we should mention three ideological reasons to abolish the *meḥitzah*/women's gallery in our time:

1. Judaism always adapted itself to the time and the place: our Sages or the major *poskim* permitted images in the synagogue when they stopped being afraid of idolatry; they allowed a non-Jew to light a fire on Shabbat because "everyone is considered like a sick person when it is cold"; they allowed teachers and rabbis to receive salaries despite the Talmud's objection; they allowed lighting Hanukkah candles inside the house "because it was dangerous" to light them outside; they transferred the early morning blessings to the synagogue because the uneducated did not know how to recite the blessings at home; and they let girls and women study both the Written and Oral Law.[24]

2. This custom hurts the feelings of many women and keeps them away from the synagogue. We may, therefore, abolish the custom in order to attract modern women to the synagogue.

3. There is enough alienation and loneliness in modern families. The synagogue should be a place that brings families together and not one that separates them.[25]

David Golinkin
Jerusalem
Sivan 5747

24. There is extensive literature about every one of these topics, but we will not expand upon them here.
25. Regarding this point, see Sarna, p. 366.

BIBLIOGRAPHY

Alonim	"*Al Ezrat Hanashim*", *Alonim* 31 (Nisan-Iyar 5707), pp. 34-35
Ben-Dov	Meir Ben-Dov, *Batei Knesset Bisefarad*, Tel Aviv, 1989, pp. 47 ff.
Blau	Ludwig Blau, *HUCA* 3 (1926), pp. 166-170
Brand	Yehoshua Brand, *Beḥinot* 6 (5714), p. 78
Brooten	Bernadette J. Brooten, *Women Leaders in the Ancient Synagogue*, Chico, California, 1982, pp. 103-141, 250-262; and in *Moment* 14/7 (December 1989), pp. 33-39
Büchler	A. Büchler, "The Fore-Court of the Women and the Brass Gate in the Temple of Jerusalem", *JQR* Old Series, X (1898), pp. 697–706
CJ	*Conservative Judaism* 11/1 (Fall 1956)
CJ 2	*Conservative Judaism* 11/2 (Winter 1957), pp. 33-37
Clark	Rabbi David Eli Clark, "Mixed Seating at Weddings", *The Journal of Halacha and* Contemporary Society X (Fall 1985), pp. 28-61; "*Yeshivah Me'urevet Bise'udat Nisu'in*", *Teḥumin* 20 (5760), pp. 160-170
Cohen B.	Rabbi Boaz Cohen, *Proceedings of the Rabbinical Assembly* 8 (1941-44), pp. 139-141 = David Golinkin, ed., *Proceedings of the Committee on Jewish Law and Standards of the Conservative Movement* 1927-1970, Jerusalem, 1997, pp. 1060-1062
Cohen O.	Orah Cohen, *Mishnei Evrei Hameḥitzah*, Beit El, 2007, Chapters 4-5
Cohen S.	Rabbi Shaye J. D. Cohen, "Women in the Synagogues of Antiquity", *Conservative Judaism* 34/2 (November-December 1980), pp. 23-29; *idem*, "Pagan and Christian Evidence on the Ancient Synagogue" in: Lee Levine, ed., *The Synagogue in*

Late Antiquity, New York, 1987, pp. 164-166, 176

Cohen-Harris — Elisheva Cohen-Harris, "Where did Medieval Jewish Women Stand?", *Conservative Judaism* 52/4 (Summer 2000), pp. 3-13

Deutsch — Gotthard Deutsch, *The Jewish Encyclopedia*, s.v. Frauenschul

Eibeschitz — Elḥanan Eibeschitz, "*Gezuztra Lesimḥat Beit Hashoevah...*", *Sinai* 104 (5749), pp. 1-9

Elbogen — Yitzḥak Moshe Elbogen, *Hatefilah Be'yisrael Behitpatḥutah Hahistorit*, Tel Aviv, 5732, pp. 350-352, 466

Ellinson — Rabbi Elyakim Ellinson, *Hatzne'a Lekhet: Ha'isha Vehamitzvot, Sefer Sheni*, third edition, Jerusalem, 5746, pp. 15-26

Epstein — Rabbi Louis M. Epstein, *Sex Laws and Customs in Judaism*, New York, 1948, pp. 78-83 = Aryeh Leib Epstein, *Darkei Ishut Uminhageha al Pi Torat Yisrael*, Tel Aviv, 5719, pp. 74-78

Fine — Steven Fine, "Chancel Screens...", in: Ḥayyim Lapin, ed., *Religious and Ethnic Communities in Later Roman Palestine*, Bethesda, Maryland, 1998, pp. 67-85, esp. pp. 82-84

Freehof — Rabbi Solomon Freehof, *Reform Jewish Practice*, New York, 1976, pp. 52-55

Goitein — Shlomo Dov Goitein, "*Yetziat Nashim Be'vinyan Beit Haknesset Bitkufat Hage'onim*", *Tarbitz* 33 (5724), p. 314; "*Beit Haknesset Vetsiyudo Lefi Kitvei Hagenizah*", *Eretz Israel* 7, Jerusalem, 5724, pp. 84, 86, 88, and the English summary on pp. 170-171; *A Mediterranean Society*, Vol. II, Berkeley, 1971, pp. 144-145, 152, 324

Goldman — Karla Goldman, *Beyond the Synagogue Gallery*, Cambridge, Mass. and London, 2000, pp. 93-99

Goodenough — E.R. Goodenough, *Jewish Symbols in the Graeco-Roman Period*, Vol. 1, New York, 1953, pp. 182,

193-194, 207, 226, 239

Gordis — Rabbi Robert Gordis, "Seating in the Synagogue: Minhag America", *JUDAISM* 36/1, (Winter 1987), pp. 47-53

Ginzberg — Rabbi Louis Ginzberg, *The Responsa of Professor Louis Ginzberg,* edited by David Golinkin, New York and Jerusalem, 1996, pp. 85-100

Greiver — Dorit Greiver, *De'ot* 22 (Tammuz 5765), pp. 18-21

Grossman and Haut — Susan Grossman and Rivka Haut, eds. *Daughters of the King: Women and the Synagogue,* Philadelphia, 1992, pp. 15-57, 117-134 (four articles)

Harkins — Paul Harkins, *Saint John Chrysostom: Discourses Against Judaizing Christians,* Washington, D.C., 1979, p. 9

Henkin — Rabbi Yehudah Herzl Henkin, *Responsa Benei Banim,* Jerusalem, 5741, Nos. 1-4, 35

Image — *Image and Impression,* New York, 2002, p. 15

Ish-Shalom — Rabbi Meir Ish-Shalom, "*Peirush Bema'amar Yerushalmi*", *Beit Talmud* 4 (5644), pp. 200-201; and cf. his remarks in *HUCA* 8-9 (1931-1932), p. 513 (in German)

Kerem — *Kerem* (Shevat 5718), pp. 1-7 (three responsa)

Kohl-Watzinger — H. Kohl and C. Watzinger, *Antike Synagogen in Galilaea,* Leipzig, 1916, p. 221

Krauss — Samuel Krauss, *Korot Batei Hatefillah Beyisrael,* New York, 5715, pp. 239-240; *Die Galilaischen Synagogenruinen,* Leipzig, 1911, pp. 15-16; *Synagogale Altertumer,* Belin-Wien, 1922, pp. 25, 355-357 (pp. 355-357 were translated into Hebrew in: Ze'ev Safrai, *Beit Haknesset Bitkufat Hamishnah Vehatalmud,* Jerusalem, 5746, pp. 57-58)

Krinsky — C. H. Krinsky, *Synagogues of Europe: Architecture,*

	History, Meaning, Cambridge, Mass. and London, 1985, pp. 28-31
Levy	Eliezer Levy, *Yesodot Hatefillah*, third edition, Tel Aviv, 5715, pp. 121-122
Levine L.	Lee Levine, *Ancient Synagogues Revealed*, Jerusalem, 1981, pp. 12, 34, 39, 65, 71, 119, 173, 174, 184; *idem*, *Cathedra* 60 (Nisan 5750), pp. 48-50; *idem*, *The Ancient Synagogue: The First Thausand Years*, New Haven and London, 2000, pp. 317-318, 471-477
Litvin	Baruch Litvin, ed., *The Sanctity of the Synagogue*, New York, 1959 (100 pages in Hebrew and Yiddish; 442 pages in English; includes responsa by Rabbis Feinstein, Soloveitchik, Kotler, Kasher and Kook)
Löw	Rabbi Leopold Löw, *Gesammelte Schriften*, IV, Szegedin, 1898, pp. 55-92
Meeks and Wilken	Wayne Meeks and Robert Wilken, *Jews and Christians in Antioch*, Missoula, Montana, 1978, p. 89
Metzger	Therese and Mendel Metzger, *Jewish Life in the Middle Ages*, Secaucus, New Jersey, 1982, p. 65
Minutes	Minutes of Meeting of Committee on Jewish Law, April 3, 1946
Raynor	Joyce Raynor, *Women's League Oulook* (Fall 1988), pp. 21-23
Rosenthal	Yehudah Rosenthal, "*Letoldot Hameḥitzah*", *Meḥkarim Umekorot*, Vol. 2, Jerusalem, 1966, pp. 652-656
Safrai S.	Shmuel Safrai, *Tarbitz* 32 (5723), pp. 329-338 = *Eretz Yisrael Veḥakhameha Bitkufat Hamishnah Vehatalmud*, Hakibbutz Hameuḥad, 1983, pp. 94-104 = *Bimei Habayit Ubimei Hamishnah*, Jerusalem, 5754, pp. 159-168 (we refer to the page numbers in the original version)

Safrai Z.	Ze'ev Safrai in: Rachel Hachlili, ed., *Ancient Synagogues in Israel*, Oxford, 1989, pp. 78-79; *idem*, *Moment* 14/9 (April 1990), pp. 6-9
Sarna	Jonathan Sarna, "The Debate over Mixed Seating in the American Synagogue" in: Jack Wertheimer, ed., *The American Synagogue: A Sanctuary Transformed*, Cambridge, 1987, pp. 363-394
Schechter	Solomon Schechter, *Studies in Judaism*, First Series, Philadelphia, 1915, p. 318
Schiffman	Rabbi Lawrence Schiffman, *Moment* 14/7 (December 1989), pp. 40-49
Stern	Rabbi Joseph Stern, *Journal of Halacha and Contemporary Society* X (Fall 1985), pp. 30-38
Sukenik	E.L. Sukenik, *Beit Haknesset Ha'atik Be'veit Alfa*, Jerusalem, 1932, p. 15; "*Beit Haknesset Ha'atik Beḥamat Gader*", *Kovetz Haḥevra Ha'ivrit Leḥakirat Eretz Yisrael Ve'atikoteha* 3 (1935), p. 50; *Ancient Synagogues in Palestine and Greece*, London, 1934, pp. 47-48
Weinberg	Rabbi Yeḥhiel Ya'akov Weinberg, *Seridei Eish*, Part 2, No. 14
Yadit	Meir Yadit, EJ, s.v. "*Meḥizah*"
Yuter	Alan Yuter, "*Meḥizah*, Midrash and Modernity: A Study in Religious Rhetoric", *JUDAISM* 28/2 (Spring 1979), pp. 147-159
Zeitlin	S. Zeitlin, *JQR* 38 (1947-1948), pp. 305-308

I wish to thank my teacher, Prof. Shama Friedman, and my colleagues, Rabbi Theodore Friedman *z"l*, Yisrael Ḥazani, Rabbi Baruch Feldstern and Prof. Daniel Schwartz for their good advice and several references. However, this responsum reflects my opinion and not theirs.

15. THE ORDINATION OF WOMEN AS RABBIS*

Question: *Is it permissible to ordain women as rabbis?*[1]

Responsum: Before discussing the halakhic aspects of this question, it is appropriate to discuss the philosophical, sociological and practical aspects. During the last few months, I have spoken with many people about this subject and I have participated in many public fora on this issue. Here is a summary of most of the arguments which I have heard:

The Philosophical Aspect

1. **In favor of the ordination of women as rabbis**:

> The Judaism represented by those who are deeply rooted in the world of Torah Study does not know, or does not want to know, that there has been a revolution... in human reality, that today's woman is a different creature than she was during 300 or 500 generations. The image of the woman who is a doctor, a lawyer, a professor at a university... did not exist at all... a woman who is a Bank Manager... The *halakhah* does not recognize this image, and this is what produces a big crisis from the Jewish perspective. This understanding – that the human creature

* All the abbreviations which follow refer to the Bibliography at the end of this responsum, which is organized according to the order of the paragraphs in this responsum.

1. The *Beit Midrash* referred to in this responsum is now called the Schechter Rabbinical Semnary. For a description of the process which took place in 1992 regarding the ordination of women as rabbis, see *Responsa of the Va'ad Halakhah*, Volume 5, pp. 7-8.

> whom we call today "woman" is not the same creature that Aristotle considered defective, but is indeed another creature whose world is another world – this understanding has not been absorbed in the consciousness of halakhic men. It is impossible to say that this has not penetrated their knowledge, since everyone sees it in everyday life. However, for halakhic men, it is still a strange thing, unnatural, something even worse than a halakhic prohibition. For them, it is against Nature that women should play a totally equal part with men in cultural life... And it is clear that a Judaism which intends today, in 1992, to set up a society whose image is set by the Torah, must make a radical change in the status of women in society. Otherwise, there is no future for Orthodox Judaism, since, from now on, a society cannot be a proper human society, if women are not an integral part of cultural, political and social life.[2]

Against the ordination of women as rabbis: There is no doubt that the status of women in society has radically changed in the twentieth century, especially in the last thirty years. However, when there is tension between modern change and Jewish tradition, it is the tradition that has the upper hand and "the burden of proof is on the claimant". We must not rush ahead. Let us wait several generations to see whether egalitarianism is a passing fad or a permanent phenomenon. And so did Prof. David Weiss Halivni stress in his responsum on this subject:

> No changes of far-reaching consequences ought to be made in haste. We are an ancient people. Our origin hearkens back to the dawn of history. Haste to us means a generation or two. We need that long (even longer) to convince ourselves that the change we are about to make is not the result of a fleeting urge. When the change is for

2. Prof. Yeshayahu Leibowitz, in an interview in *Mossaf Ha'aretz*, April 17, 1992, p. 66.

Kelal Yisrael, we need even more time. We have to make sure that we are not acting out of our narrow geographical and cultural backgrounds. That only time can tell. For time not only heals; it also enlightens.[3]

2. In favor: "Do what is right and good" (Deuteronomy 6:18) is an important principle in Judaism. Justice and morality dictate an equal status for women in our days. Similarly, it is immoral to prevent a woman from fulfilling her desire to become a Rabbi.

Against: "Right and Good" is not decided by a majority vote, but by eternal, divine morality. According to Jewish morality, accepted throughout the generations, there **is** a difference between man and woman and we may not blur that difference. On the other hand, human morality, established by the majority, is fickle and even dangerous.[4] Moreover, if not ordaining women is immoral, does this mean that our ancestors were immoral? It is arrogant to say this. Therefore, it is better to say that they were influenced by the society and norms of their times, just as we are influenced by the society and norms of ours. As for self-fulfillment, there is no such principle in Judaism. The commandments are not intended to lead to self-fulfillment, but to sanctify life and to bring us closer to God. Is it "moral" to prevent a Jewish man from marrying his non-Jewish girlfriend? Is it "moral" to prevent a Jewish pianist from playing a concert on Shabbat? Is it "moral" to oppose homosexuality? Is it "moral" to oppose premarital sex? The fact that someone, or even the majority, wants to do a specific action does not mean that it is moral.

3. In favor: Egalitarianism is a good and desirable thing and an absolute value.

3. Rabbi David Weiss Halivni, *Ordination* I, p. 19 of his responsum.
4. It is sufficient to point to the examples of slavery in the United States, the "Final Solution" in Nazi Germany, and the Apartheid regime in South Africa. In these three cases, the majority of the people – tens of millions of good citizens – decided that racism, discrimination and even mass murder are good things, both natural and moral. Was the majority correct?

Against: This has yet to be proven. Egalitarianism has led to good things: a woman may now study whatever interests her and work in many professions that were previously closed to her, while a man helps out more with the housework and is more involved in raising his children. But this has also led to destructive consequences, such as promiscuity, the rapid transmission of sexual diseases, a huge increase in the number of unwed mothers, an increase in abortions, a huge increase in the rate of divorce, and women who have purposely become pregnant outside the framework of marriage. Moreover, equal status does not have to lead to an identical way of life. It says in the Torah: "Male and female He created them" (Genesis 1:27). This means that both women and men have equal and complete rights **and** that women and men are not equal beings by their very nature and creation.[5] In other words, women and men are **equal** but not **identical** and it is not desirable to aspire to make them identical.

4. In favor:

> Women make up over half of the Jewish People. They are a precious treasure. Their opinions and abilities can come to the aid of our people in many ways in order to magnify and glorify the Torah... Our Jewish life today is poor and hard enough without forgoing this enormous resource.[6]

Against: There is nobody who disagrees that women are a precious treasure to the Jewish People and that we must not forgo their power. But they do not need to bear the title "Rabbi" in order to influence. Gifted women are already serving as teachers, principals and leaders, and they will continue to do so without taking the proposed step. Moreover, there is a

5. This last point was taken from a position paper by Prof. Avigdor Shinan, which was prepared for day of study held at the *Beit Midrash* in Iyar 5752 (May 1992).
6. Rabbi Reuven Hammer, *Responsa of the Va'ad Halakhah*, Volume 5, p. 15.

phenomenon outside Israel that when women take over leading the synagogue, men come less and participate less.

The Sociological Aspect

1. **In favor**: Most of the students at the *Beit Midrash*, the members of the Rabbinical Assembly of Israel and the members of the congregations support the ordination of women as rabbis. Israeli public opinion does not need to influence our decision; we have to take into account, first and foremost, the feelings of the members of the Masorti Movement.

Against: The *halakhah* is established by the *poskim* who are proficient in its methods, and not by lay people. Furthermore, we have to take into account Israeli public opinion as a whole and not just that of the members of the Movement; and the Israeli public is opposed (and see below).

2. In favor: Our target audience is the secular public in Israel, and this public will certainly support this step.

Against: Our target audience is the religious and traditionalist public in Israel, and this public will certainly oppose this step.

3. In favor: This step will renew the Movement. It will refresh the general atmosphere and bring new members into the Movement.

Against: This was what they said in the Conservative Movement in the States when they allowed driving to the synagogue on Shabbat, and we all know that that is not what happened. We cannot renew a halakhic movement by ignoring the *halakhah* or contradicting it.

4. Against: Jews from Mediteranean countries will oppose this step and will not accept the proposed change.

In favor: In any case, these Jews are not flocking to the Movement and, therefore, it is impossible to decide according to their reaction.

5. Against: The congregations or individuals who oppose this step will leave the Movement.

In Favor: There is no need to leave. A person who is opposed can join a congregation which does not appoint a woman as Rabbi, and a congregation that is opposed will not appoint a woman as Rabbi.

The Human and Practical Aspect

1. **In favor**: The Rabbinical Assembly of Israel decided several years ago to accept as a member anyone who was ordained by the Jewish Theological Seminary of America, including women. Indeed, two Israeli women were ordained as rabbis by the Jewish Theological Seminary of America and have been accepted as members of the Rabbinical Assembly of Israel. One of them is already serving as Rabbi at Congregation "Eshel Avraham" in Be'er Sheva. Therefore, there is no logical reason to prevent women from studying for ordination at our *Beit Midrash* in Israel.

Against: To this we respond: "We are sorry for the first; should we be sorry for these, too?" (*Mekhilta, Masekhta De'amalek, Parashah* 1, ed. Horowitz-Rabin, p. 191). The Rabbinical Assembly erred and there is no reason to add insult to injury. We must restrict this mistake to the small number of women who are ready to travel to the U.S.

2. In favor: Traveling to New York causes women financial loss and familial pain. It is cruel to make it difficult for dedicated, committed women who want to be ordained (and there are at least three such women).

Against: The same as in the preceding paragraph.

3. Against: Many congregations will not appoint a woman as Rabbi.

In favor: Women will go to the congregations interested in them. It is a fact that Congregation "Eshel Avraham" in Be'er Sheva has appointed a woman as Rabbi and the congregation is growing.

These are the arguments of those who are in favor and of those who are opposed.

In my opinion, many of the arguments on both sides are correct. On the one hand, the woman of our day is not the woman described for the most part in Talmudic literature. Similarly, there is not much sense in preventing women from studying to become rabbis in Israel, if they can do so abroad. Preventing this only causes them mental anguish and financial loss. Similarly, the arguments about the target audience are not decisive in either direction. In my opinion, we need to satisfy the needs of the public that already belongs to the Movement, and the majority of this public is in favor.

On the other hand, I do not think that gender equality is an absolute value, neither in society nor in Judaism. This phenomenon is too new to be judged. For the time being, it can only be stated that equality is an aspiration in the Western world, and *halakhah* and Judaism must struggle with this aspiration. Similarly, I do not think there is an ethical imperative to ordain women because ethics continually change with changes in time and place. For the time being, it can only be stated that, in the eyes of the majority of Jews in the Western world, this is a fair, logical and desirable step.

If so, it remains for us to determine if this step, which appears to us to be fair, logical and desirable, is also in keeping with the demands of Jewish law. For, in the final analysis, if we are a halakhic Movement, it is not enough to discuss the philosophical and sociological aspects of a topic, but we must deal in a sincere and direct fashion with its halakhic difficulties. In order to decide if it is permissible for a woman to be a Rabbi, we must define the functions of the Rabbi in our day.

The functions of the Rabbi in our day

Most of those in favor of the ordination of women as rabbis say: "Rabbinical ordination means to teach, to educate and to be a personal example; it does not require serving as a witness or as a judge or fulfilling the *halakhic* obligations of the congregation (*lehotzi yedei ḥovah*).[7]

On the other hand, one of the opponents wrote:

> Now let us clarify what is rabbinical ordination **in our day**. This is explained in *Sefer Hashetarot* by Rabbi Yehudah Barceloni... And they are appointed **judges**...[8]

With all due respect, both of these viewpoints do not hold up to careful scrutiny. The first point of view defines the Rabbinate in an abstract way, disconnected from reality, in order to evade the true halakhic difficulties. The second point of view stresses **one** of the functions of the Rabbi, according to an example from Spain in the 11th-12th centuries, in order to ban women's ordination today. This is not the way to deal with this issue.

Anyone who examines the history of the Rabbinate knows that the functions of the Rabbi have changed constantly throughout the generations.[9] The Rabbi fulfilled different functions in different times and places: judge, *posek*, preacher,

7. Thus spoke Prof. Ze'ev Falk at the study day mentioned above and cf. the responsum of Rabbi Reuven Hammer cited above and Rabbi Gordon Tucker, *Ordination* II, pp. 16 ff.
8. Rabbi Saul Lieberman listed in the Bibliography, below, p. 384. Emphasis added.
9. There is a vast literature on this subject. See, for example, Simḥah Assaf, *Be'oholei Ya'akov*, Jerusalem, 5703, pp. 27-65; *Ha'entziklopedia Ha'ivrit*, Vol. 30, cols. 475-491; Salo Baron, *The Jewish Community*, Vol. 2, Philadelphia, 1942, pp. 66-100 with notes in Vol. 3; EJ, Vol. 13, cols. 1445-1458; Rabbi Gilbert Rosenthal, *Proceedings of the Rabbinical Assembly* 49 (1987), pp. 100-115.
10. Here are examples of or bibliography about most of the functions listed above: **Judge** – Rav Yehudah Habartzeloni quoted by Prof. Lieberman (above, note 8). **Posek** – Assaf, p. 28. **Preacher** – Rabbi Meir in Yerushalmi *Sotah* 1:4, fol. 16d and parallels; Rav Yehudah Aryeh of Modena; Rav Moshe Alshekh; the Ḥida (Rabbi Ḥayyim Yosef David Azulai); Assaf, pp. 52-53; Baron, pp. 95-97; and Yom Tov Lippman Zunz, *Hadrashot Be'yisrael*

teacher and *Rosh Yeshivah*. He performed marriages, divorces, *ḥalitzah* and conversions; was the *sheliaḥ tzibbur* and the one who received the most honored *aliyah* on every Shabbat and Festival; read *Megillat Esther* and blew the *shofar*, and so on.[10] As Rabbi Gilbert Rosenthal stressed in his article on the subject: "In sum, the rabbi was truly the communal factotum and it would be an error to assume that only the modern rabbi functions on all levels".[11] The question, therefore, is not what a rabbi did **in the past** or in the Orthodox world, but rather what does a rabbi do in Conservative congregations **today.** The plain fact is that a Conservative congregational rabbi not only functions as a teacher or as a personal example, but also serves frequently as a *sheliaḥ tzibbur*, Torah reader, *haftarah* reader, and *mezamen* [the one who leads the Grace after Meals]. He also reads from *Megillat Esther*, blows the *shofar*, performs marriages, serves as a witness at marriages (and even divorces) and serves as a member of a *Beit Din* for conversions.[12] Therefore, we must deal with all of the above issues in order to reach a *halakhic* ruling on the subject.

Vehishtalshelutan Hahistorit, Jerusalem, 5707, and especially Chapters 20, 22, 23. **Teacher and Head of Yeshivah** – Assaf, pp. 30, 34, 51-52. **Performer of marriages, divorces and *ḥalitzah*** – Rabbis Shlomo Fuks and David Levine, *Responsa of the Va'ad Halakhah of the Rabbinical Assembly of Israel* 3 (5748-5749), pp. 93-98. **Performer of conversions** – Rabbi Theodore Friedman, *ibid.*, p. 67. ***Sheliaḥ Tzibbur*** – *Minhagei Maharil*, ed. Spitzer, p. 292; Assaf, p. 53. **Receiver of an honored *aliyah*** – Rabbeinu Tam, according to *Tur* YD 400; Assaf, p. 49. **Reader of *Megillat Esther*** – Rabbi Meir in *Tosefta Megillah* 2:5, ed. Lieberman, p. 349 and parallels. ***Shofar* blower** – the Maharil, *loc. cit.*

11. Rosenthal (above, note 9), p. 107, and contrary to the opinion presented in EJ, Vol. 13, col. 1446, that the Rabbi began fulfilling cantorial functions and performing marriages in the 19th century under the influence of the Reform Movement.
12. And if you say that in Israel a Conservative Rabbi has no right to perform marriages, divorces or conversions, we would reply as follows: a) the Masorti Movement already has a *Beit Din* for conversions; b) the rabbis of the Movement already perform marriages (beginning in 1994); c) there is a constant judicial struggle on these issues and the situation may change in the near future; d) *Beit Midrash* graduates do not only serve in Israel. Three

"You Shall Not Place a Stumbling Block Before the Blind" (Leviticus 19:14).

Some of the proponents of the ordination of women as rabbis say: Let us ordain women as rabbis and **they** will decide, according to their halakhic knowledge, whether it is permitted for a woman to serve as a *sheliḥat tzibbur*, a witness, a judge and the like.[13] To this we reply that, if these actions are forbidden, then the *Beit Midrash* would be transgressing the prohibition of "You shall not place a stumbling block before the blind" (Leviticus 19:14). There are many opinions and *halakhot* related to this commandment,[14] but there is one *sugya* in the Bavli that is very similar to our case:

> ...The maidservant of the house of Rabi [=Rabbi Judah the Prince] saw a certain man thrashing his elder son. She said: "May this man be put into excommunication, for he has transgressed the commandment of 'you shall not place a stumbling block before the blind' – for thus we have learned in a *beraita*: "You shall not place a stumbling block before the blind" refers to striking one's grown son [i.e., who is past the age of *Bar Mitzvah*] (*Mo'ed Kattan* 17a).

Rashi explains: "Since he is grown, **lest** he kicks his father and thus he [=the father] commits a sin". In other words, according to the Bible and our Sages, a father is permitted to hit his child in order to educate him,[15] but he is forbidden to strike his **grown** son, because there is a reasonable possibility that the son will hit

graduates are now serving in France, England, and the U.S., and there is no doubt that they perform most of the functions stated above.

13. See Rabbi Gilah Dror, *Responsa of the Va'ad Halakhah*, Vol. 5, p. 29.
14. See, among others, Rabbi M.M. Kasher, *Torah Sheleimah* on that verse; Rabbi Yitzḥak Adler, *Lifnei Iver*, Ofakim, 5749; Rabbi Naḥum Rabinowitz, *Teḥumin* 11 (5750), pp. 41-72; *Journal of Halakhah and Contemporary Society* 11 (Spring 1986), pp. 5-18 and 19 (Spring 1990), pp. 7-32.
15. Proverbs 13:24 and 23:13-14; Mishnah *Makkot* 2:2; *Mekhilta Denezikin*, Parashah 4, p. 263; *Sifrei Zuta* to Numbers 35:22, pp. 333-334; *Tanḥuma Shemot*, paragraph 1 = *Shemot Rabbah* 1:1, ed. Shinan, pp. 35 ff..

him back, which is a Pentateuchal prohibition (Exodus 21:15). Indeed, this was accepted as the *halakhah* (YD 240:20).

We are faced with a similar situation. Perhaps according to the essence of the law it is permitted to ordain women as rabbis. But it is almost certain that a woman serving as rabbi will serve as a *sheliaḥ tzibbur* and the like, will perform marriages, will be member of a *Beit Din* for conversions and will sign a *ketubah*. Therefore, we must deal with these questions because, if they are forbidden for a woman, not only will she sin, but the *Beit Midrash* will transgress the commandment of "You shall not place a stumbling block before the blind".

But if you say that it is forbidden for a *kohen* to become defiled by the dead, and yet the *Beit Midrash* ordains *kohanim* as rabbis, we may reply that there are four differences between a rabbi who is a *kohen* and a rabbi who is a woman:

1. In the case of the *kohen* who is a rabbi, we are speaking of only one problematic task: the burial ceremony. In the case of the woman rabbi, we are speaking of most of her tasks, as we explained above.

2. The impurity of the *kohen* in our day is a rabbinical prohibition; testimony by women is a Pentateuchal prohibition, as we shall see below.

3. There is a lenient opinion that allows a rabbi who is a *kohen* to perform a burial ceremony;[16] we must check if it is permissible for a woman to perform the aforementioned tasks.

4. If a rabbi who is a *kohen* takes part in a burial ceremony, this does not invalidate the burial. However, if a woman rabbi participates in a *Beit Din* for conversion or signs a *ketubah*, it may

16. Rabbi Louis Epstein, *Proceedings of the Rabbinical Assembly* 3 (1929), pp. 155-167 = David Golinkin, ed., *Proceedings of the Committee on Jewish Law and Standards of the Conservative Movement 1927-1970*, Jerusalem, 1997, pp. 1433-1446.
17. Cf. Rabbi Joel Roth, *Ordination* II, p. 172.

be that the convert is not a convert and the couple is not married.[17]

Therefore, the *Va'ad Halakhah* decided, on the 21st of *Iyar* 5752 (May 24, 1992), by a majority vote, that we must deal with **all** the following questions:

I. Is it permissible for a woman to hold public office?

II. Is it permissible for a woman to study and teach Torah?

III. Is it permissible for a woman to render halakhic decisions?

IV. Women and public prayer and the PTBC: may a woman be counted in a *minyan*, serve as a *sheliḥat tzibbur*, read the Torah, read the *Megillah*, blow the *Shofar*, and perform the rest of the PTBC?

V. Is it permissible for a woman to perform marriages?

VI. Is it permissible for a woman to serve on a *Beit Din*, especially for conversions?

VII. Is it permissible for a woman to serve as a witness, especially to sign *ketubot* and *gittin* [writs of divorce]?

And now, let us deal carefully with each question.

I. Is it permissible for a woman to hold public office?

This question became a bone of contention for the first time in 1918, when they began to debate the right to vote within the *Yishuv* (see the book by Menaḥem Friedman on the history of this struggle). They asked at that time: Is it permissible for a woman to vote or be elected? There were *poskim* who forbade both things, whereas others (such as Rabbi David Tzvi Hoffmann) permitted women to vote but not to be elected. However, most of the *poskim* permitted women both to vote and to be elected. This question arose again seventy years later, in 1986, when Leah Shakdiel was appointed to the Religious Council in Yeruḥam (see Don-Yeḥia and Cohen for the history of the struggle). At that time there was also a conflict among the *poskim*, some forbidding and some permitting. Following are the principal arguments of those forbidding, together with the responses of those permitting.

Those who forbid rely on two types of arguments – general social concerns and specific halakhic sources. The first type of argument finds expression in an open letter written by Rabbi Avraham Yitzḥah Hacohen Kook in 1920:

> And regarding the Law, I have nothing to add to the words of the rabbis that preceded me. In the Torah, the Prophets and the Writings, as well as in the *Halakhah* and the *Aggadah*, we hear one voice: the obligation of the permanent public work falls on men, because "it is the way of men to conquer, but it is not the way of women to conquer" [*Yevamot* 65b]. The tasks of dominion, justice, and testimony do not belong to her and "all her glory is within" [cf. Psalms 45:14]. The effort to avoid mingling the sexes in meetings is like a thread which runs through the entire Torah. In any case, it is surely against the law any renewal of public leadership which will lead willy-nilly to the mingling of the sexes in one crowd and group in the course of the regular life of the community (Rabbi Kook, p. 189).

With all due respect to Rabbi Kook, it is possible to refute every one of these arguments, both on the basis of sources and on the basis of today's reality.[18] Here is one example. Rabbi Kook is concerned that the mingling of the sexes will lead to promiscuity, while Rabbi Uziel responds:

> It is logical to say that in any serious meeting and fruitful discussion there is no promiscuity. Every day, men meet women in commercial transactions, they negotiate, and there is no breach and no outcry [cf. Psalms 144:14]... When

18. Regarding the weakness of the argument that "all the glory of the daughter of the King is within", see Rabbi Raphael Harris, in *Responsa of the Va'ad Halakhah of the Rabbinical Assembly of Israel* 2 (5747), pp. 63-65.

> our Sages said, "do not converse excessively with a woman" (*Pirkei Avot* 1:5) they referred only to needless, unnecessary conversation, because it is this kind of conversation that leads to transgression. Not so a conversation which includes discussion of important and public issues. A meeting together for the purpose of public work, which is a sacred work, does not lead to sin or to frivolity. And all Jews, men and women, are sacred and are not suspected of breaching the limits of modesty and morality (*Mishpetei Uziel*, pp. 34-35).

The second type of argument relies primarily on two sources:

A. *Sifrei* to Deuteronomy, paragraph 157, ed. Finkelstein, pp. 208-209:

> "You shall set [a king over yourself]" [Deut. 17:15]... "king" and not queen... "A foreign man" – from here they concluded that a man can be appointed a leader over the public, **but you don't appoint a woman as a leader over the public**.

B. Maimonides, *Mishneh Torah, Hilkhot Melakhim* 1:4-5

> One may not set up a king from a group of converts... as it is stated: "You must not set a foreign man over you, one who is not your brother" (Deuteronomy 17:15). And not only kingship, but any ruling position in Israel, neither general, nor chief of fifties or chief of tens... Needless to say, a judge or a prince has to be from Israel, as it is stated: "From your own brethren set a king over yourself" (*ibid*.). **Every office you appoint has to be from your own brethren.**
> One may not set up a woman as king, since it is stated: "a **king** over yourself" (*ibid*.) and not a **queen**. **The same rule applies with every office in the Jewish People; only men may be appointed.**

Those forbidding rely mainly on the words of Maimonides

and reinforce them with the words of *Sifrei*. According to Maimonides, women are forbidden to occupy every Jewish office, so it is forbidden for them to be elected to any public office whether secular or religious, including a synagogue board and a religious council or to serve as a *gabbai*. One can assume that Maimonides and those ruling according to his view would have forbidden a woman to serve as rabbi as a consequence of the prohibitions mentioned above.

Nevertheless, there are at least seven good reasons to reject this ruling of Maimonides:

1. First of all,

> since this law is not mentioned in the Talmud, neither in the Mishnah nor in the *Gemara*; and since this law, which forbids to appoint a woman as a public leader, is not mentioned... in the words of the *poskim*, it is therefore a rejected ruling (Rabbi Uziel, and cf. Rav Tzair for a similar opinion).

2. It seems, from Maimonides' style, that he derived the law regarding women and public office by analogy to the law of a convert. Indeed, the Bavli banned a convert from "any office you appoint" (*Kiddushin* 76b = *Yevamot* 45b). However, we are not forced to make such an analogy – a convert and a woman have to be dealt with separately.

3. It is possible that Maimonides was influenced by his general attitude towards women (as Rabbi Roth suggested). For example, Maimonides ruled strictly regarding women studying Torah (see below, paragraph II). He also ruled that a married woman is forbidden to go out from her house more than once or twice a month (*Hilkhot Ishut* 13:11); no other *posek* gave such a ruling and Maimonides was, no doubt, influenced by Islam in this regard.[19]

19. For an exhaustive treatment of this topic, see Mordechai Friedman, "The Ethics of Medieval Jewish Marriage", in: S.D. Goitein, ed., *Religion in a Religious Age*, Cambridge, Mass., 1974, pp. 88-95, as well as a short summary of Friedman's approach in: S.D. Goitein, *A Mediterranean Society*, Vol. III, Berkeley, 1978, p. 153.

4. Furthermore, Maimonides' opinion is a *da'at yaḥid,* a lone opinion, opposed to the opinions of other *Rishonim*. The Rashba and the Ran were of the opinion (in their *Ḥiddushim* to *Shevuot,* beginning of Chapter 4) that women are generally unfit to judge. However, the Ran continues and says: "But if you argue that it is written about Deborah 'And she judged Israel' (Judges 4:4), **one can reply that she was not exactly judging, but rather leading**". The Rashba goes even further: **"She was a leader, everyone behaved according to her opinion, as if she were a queen"**. If it is permitted for a woman to lead the **entire** Jewish People like a queen, how much the more so other types of public office! (For other *Rishonim* who disagreed with Maimonides, see Rabbis Uziel, Twirk, Ginzberg and Rav Tzair).

And if you say that Maimonides relied on *Sifrei,* there are three ways to reply:

5. It is difficult to prohibit according to the *Sifrei,* since the correct reading there is in doubt. In the printed versions of the *Sifrei* and in some of the manuscripts, instead of "from here they concluded **that a man** [*ha'ish*] can be appointed a leader over the public" it says: "from here they concluded **that you should not** [*ein*] appoint a leader over the public". This refers apparently to **a non-Jew** since this *derashah* explains the words "a foreign man" (see the variant readings in Finkelstein, and also in Hoffman, Rav Tzair and Ginzberg). If so, the end of this passage in *Sifrei* is not related to our topic at all.

6. Even if the reading is definite, Maimonides should have rejected the opinion of the *Sifrei,* since this is what he did in a similar case. Regarding the case of a father annulling the vow of his minor daughter, Maimonides ruled:

> I said that this opinion is certainly the lone opinion of Rabbi Shimon, since an anonymous opinion in the *Sifrei* is that of Rabbi Shimon, for if this opinion were *halakhah,* the [*Gemara*] would certainly not have remained silent about this, for you will never find an analogy in one of the

> Talmuds which is not in the *Tosefta*... According to this I understand this topic, and I have not departed from the simple meaning of the verse. Therefore, I said that this analogy of Rabbi Shimon is his opinion alone.[20]

In our case, since the *derashah* does not appear in the Talmuds nor in the *Tosefta*, and since it contradicts the simple meaning of the verse about Deborah the Prophetess and what we know about other women who served in public office, we must reject the *Sifrei* as the lone opinion of Rabbi Shimon.

7. Finally, it is possible that the *Sifrei* dealt with an appointment by the *Sanhedrin*, and therefore we cannot compare it with our topic, since, in our days, appointments are made via democratic elections by the entire public. And so writes the Ran in the continuation of the above-mentioned passage: "Although the *Sifrei* states 'You shall set [a king over yourself] – king and not queen', there [in the case of Deborah], they did not appoint her but they conducted themselves according to her words". As a result, many *poskim* in the 20th century determined that it is permissible for the public to accept a woman upon them as their leader by elections or the like. Since the rabbinate is also an acceptance for a fixed period (se YD 245:22 in the Rema), the appointment of a woman as rabbi does not contradict the *Sifrei*.

Up to this point, we have refuted the opinion of those who forbid. Moreover, *ma'aseh rav*, action is great, and we know that in practice women served in public offices both in ancient and modern times. In Biblical times, we hear of Deborah the Prophetess (Judges 5-6), Ḥuldah the Prophetess (II Kings 22:14

20. *Responsa of the Rambam*, ed. Blau, No. 326, pp. 594-595. This responsum is cited by *Migdal Oz* to *Hilkhot Nedarim*, beginning of Chapter 12 and by *Tosfot Yom Tov* to Mishnah *Nedarim*, Chapter 1, whence it is quoted by Rav Tza'ir, p. 180.

ff.) and Atalia the Queen (II Kings 11). In the Second Temple period, we hear of Judith (Book of Judith 8:9 ff.) and, particularly, of Queen Salome or Shlomtzion Alexandra (141-67 BCE). In modern times, we know of at least fifteen women who served as a Ḥassidic *Admorim*, among them Odel, the daughter of the Ba'al Shem Tov; Mirosh, the daughter of Rabbi Elimelekh of Lyzhensk; Ḥannah Ḥava Twersky; Malka Twersky; Rachel, the daughter of the Apter Rebbe; Yente the Prophetess, and Ḥannah Rachel Verbermacher, the "Maid of Ludomir".[21] Therefore, since the opinion of Maimonides is a lone opinion, and since the opinion of the *Sifrei* is neither clear nor accepted, and since women in practice held public offices in the past – we return then to the simple meaning of the Bible, that it is permissible for a woman to serve in public office, including as congregational president, *gabbai* and rabbi.

II. Is it permissible for a woman to study and teach Torah?

We have learned in Mishnah *Sotah* (3:4 = Bavli *Sotah*, fol. 20a): "Rabbi Eliezer says: Whoever teaches his daughter Torah is considered as if he had taught her lechery".[22] The *Geonim*, for some reason, did not deal with this issue (there is no discussion in *Halakhot Pesukot, Halakhot Gedolot, She'iltot* or *Otzar Hageonim*). Maimonides (*Hilkhot Talmud Torah* 1:13) distinguished between teaching the Oral Torah, which if he taught her it is as if he taught her lechery, and the Written Torah, which he should not

21. Shlomo Ashkenazi, *Ha'isha Be'aspaklariat Hayahadut*, Part 1, second edition, Tel Aviv, 1979. pp. 55-60; Menachem Brayer, *The Jewish Woman in Rabbinic Literature*, Vol. 1, Hoboken, New Jersey, 1986, pp. 37-48. For a thorough bibliography on the Maid of Ludomir, see above, p. 71, note 82.
22. Rabbi Eliezer was very consistent in this matter. Cf. Yerushalmi *Sotah* 3:4, fol. 19a = Bavli *Yoma* 66b = *Bemidbar Rabbah* 9:48 and also *Massekhet Kallah* 1:3, ed. Higger, p. 126.
23. For an interesting contradiction in the words of Maimonides, see the article by Prof. Harvey, pp. 124 ff. For a novel interpretation of this ruling by Maimonides, see Aviad Hacohen, *Shenaton Hamishpat Ha'ivri* 14-15 (5748), pp. 119-120 and the entire article.

teach her in the first place, but if he did, it is not like lechery.[23] The *Tur* and the *Shulḥan Arukh* copied his words (YD 246, but there is a scribal error in the *Tur*'s version – cf. *Beit Yosef*). Most of the *poskim* followed Rabbi Eliezer and Maimonides, although they tried to limit their strict position:

1. Many *poskim* ruled that one may not teach them Talmud in depth, but one should teach them practical commandments pertaining to women.[24]

2. Others permitted Torah study by outstanding women such as Beruriah (Rabbi Ḥayyim Yosef David Azulai, *Responsa Tov Ayin*, No. 4), or claimed that Rabbi Eliezer was referring to a daughter who is a minor, but it is permissible to teach an adult daughter who wants to draw closer to God (Rabbi Shmuel Arkivolti quoted in *Torah Temimah* to Deuteronomy 11, note 48).[25]

3. Many modern *poskim* continued to forbid girls from studying the Oral Torah, but maintained that it is an **obligation** in our day to teach them the Written Torah, *Pirkei Avot*, books of *Mussar* and/or laws that pertain to women. This is because today every girl receives a secular

24. *Sefer Ḥassidim*, ed. Margaliot, paragraph 313 = ed. Wistinetzki, paragraph 835; and also ed. Wistinetzki, paragraph 1502; the introduction to *Sefer Mitzvot Katan*; Rabbeinu Yonah Gerondi in *Sefer Hayirah*; Rema in YD 246:6; *Shulḥan Arukh Harav, Hilkhot Talmud Torah* 1:16; Rabbi Yosef Karo in OH 47:14, where he rules that women bless the Torah blessing because they are obligated to study the laws pertinent to them.
25. It is worth noting that Rabbi Barukh Halevy Epstein, the author of *Torah Temimah*, heard of this source from his aunt, the learned Rayna Batya, who complained about the opposition of the *poskim* to Torah study by women! See Rabbi Barukh Halevy Epstein, *Mekor Barukh*, Part IV, Vilna, 1928, pp. 1961 ff. My thanks to Dr. Debbie Weissman, who brought my attention to this interesting chapter, and see *Tradition* 35/3 (Fall 2001), pp. 89-94 regarding the sources which he quotes. On Rayna Batya, see *The Torah U-Madda Journal* 6 (1996), pp. 91-128; *Nashim* 2 (1999), pp. 52-94; *Nashim* 3 (2000), pp. 249-256.
26. The *Ḥafetz Ḥayyim*; Rabbi Samson Raphael Hirsch in many places – see Ellinson, p. 158 and Breuer; the Ḥatam Sofer and Rabbi Yosef Ḥayyim

education and it would be an absurd and dangerous situation if the Daughters of Israel will receive a secular education without a parallel Jewish education.[26]

4. Other modern *poskim* go even further and – because of the needs of the hour – permit teaching girls both the Written and Oral Torah, despite the opinion of Rabbi Eliezer.[27]

However, as stated above, all of these *poskim* follow Rabbi Eliezer and Maimonides. But Rabbi Saul Berman has already emphasized that **the Talmudic Sages had three** different approaches to Torah study by women:

1. Rabbi Eliezer considered it **lechery**, as we saw above.
2. Issi ben Yehudah, Rabbi Eleazar ben Azaryah and others thought that women are **exempt** from Torah study.
3. Ben Azzai **obligates** women to study Torah.

The second opinion, the one that exempts, appears in *Sifrei* on Deuteronomy (paragraph 46, p. 104) and parallels (*Kiddushin* 29b, 30a and elsewhere): " 'And you shall teach them to your sons' (Deuteronomy 11:19) – your sons and not your daughters: this is the opinion of Rabbi Yosi ben Akiva [i.e., Issi ben Yehudah – see *Pesaḥim* 113b]".

The same can be deduced from *Tosefta Sotah* (9:7, ed. Lieberman, pp. 193-194 and parallels), where, according to the opinion of Rabbi Eleazar ben Azaryah: " 'Gather the people – the men, the women and the children' (Deuteronomy 31:12) – if men come to learn and **women come to hear**, children why are they

Sonnenfeld quoted in Ellinson, p. 156; Rabbi Zalman Sorotzkin; Rabbi Moshe Feinstein; and Rabbi Yosef Kafiḥ, who permits even Oral Torah under certain circumstances.

27. Rabbi Ben-Zion Firer; Rabbi Moshe Malka; Rabbi Eliezer Waldenberg; Rabbi Ḥayyim David Halevi; Rabbi Joseph Dov Soloveitchik cited by Rabbi Weiss, p. 63; Rabbi Aharon Lichtenstein; Rabbi Arthur Silver; and cf. Ellinson, pp. 160-162; Rabbi Joel Wolowelsky in *Tradition* 22/1 (Spring 1986), pp. 78-79 and in his book *Women, Jewish Law and Modernity*, Hoboken, New Jersey, 1997, pp. 113-118.

coming?...". In other words, women are exempt from **learning** Torah, but are obligated to **hear** the public reading of the Torah.

This exemption can also be deduced from a *beraita* found in *Shabbat* 150a: "... You may negotiate on *Shabbat* about **girls to be betrothed** and about a **boy to teach him the Book** or a trade...". This source says indirectly that, generally speaking, boys learned Torah while girls were betrothed at a young age and were exempt from the *mitzvah* of learning Torah.

The third opinion is that of Ben Azzai, which appears in Mishnah *Sotah* (3:4) mentioned above:

> If she [i.e., the *sotah* who drinks the bitter water] has any merit, it will suspend her punishment... Because of this, Ben Azzai says: **A man is obligated to teach his daughter Torah**, so that if she drinks – she will know that the merit suspends the punishment.

Rashi to *Sotah* 21b and others thought, for some reason, that Rabbi Yehoshua in that Mishnah agreed with Rabbi Eliezer, and the result, therefore, is that Ben Azzai is a *da'at yaḥid*, a lone opinion. However, Rabbi Ḥ. Y. Ehrenreich proved the opposite on the basis of the *Gemara* to that Mishnah. After the explanation of the words of Rabbi Eliezer, it says: "**And our Sages?** What do they do with the words 'I, Wisdom' (Proverbs 8:12)?...". In other words, the *Gemara* calls Ben Azzai "our Sages"! This means that, according to the Bavli, the opinion of Rabbi Eliezer is considered a *da'at yaḥid*, a lone opinion, while Ben Azzai agrees with the Sages! Furthermore, as we shall see below, there are many sources which prove that most of the Sages disagreed with Rabbi Eliezer and thought that women were either **exempt** from Torah study or even **obligated** to do so.

28. There are other sources which, it became clear after careful study, do **not** prove that women learned Torah in Talmudic times. See *Massekhet Soferim* 18:5, ed. Higger, pp. 316–317, together with what I wrote above, p. 161-162; *Mishnah Nedarim* 4:3, together with *Dikdukei Soferim Hashalem* to *Nedarim*, p. 300, note 20; *Tosefta Pisḥa* 10:7, ed. Lieberman, p. 197. For other possible sources, see Yalon, pp. 19-21 and Rabbi Halivni.

Halakhic Sources Which Show That Women Studied Torah[28]

1. *Mishnah Kiddushin* 4:13:

> A single man should not be a *sofer* [a Torah teacher to little children, because of the mothers and sisters who bring them to school] and **a woman should not be a *sofer*** [because of the fathers and brothers of the children].

It other words, it is not forbidden for women to learn Torah. It is only forbidden for them to learn the profession of teaching little children, lest they fraternize with the fathers or brothers of the children.

2. *Tosefta Berakhot* 2:12, ed. Lieberman p. 8 (= Yerushalmi *Berakhot* 3:4, fol. 6c):

> **Men and women with gonorrhea, menstruating women and those who gave birth are permitted to read from the Torah, the Prophets and the Writings and to learn by heart *Mishnah*, Midrash, *Halakhot* and *Aggadot*** [despite their impurity, because words of Torah do not receive impurity].

In the Bavli (*Berakhot* 22a = *Mo'ed Kattan* 15a), "menstruating women" was changed into "those who have sexual relations with menstruating women", while the terms "women with gonorrhea" and "those who gave birth" were omitted entirely, because they could not imagine that women read the Bible or learn Mishnah, Midrash, *Halakhot* and *Aggadot* by heart.[29] But, according to the simple meaning of the *beraita*, women did indeed learn Written

29. This was the conclusion of Rabbi Saul Lieberman, *Tosefet Rishonim*, Part 1, Jerusalem, 5697, p. 15, and again in *Tosefta Kifshuta* to *Berakhot*, New York, 5715, p. 20, as opposed to Rabbi Levi Ginzberg, *Peirushim Veḥiddushim Bayerushalmi*, Part 2, New York, 5701, p. 248.

and Oral Torah, either as an optional activity, according to Issi ben Yehudah, or as an obligation, according to Ben Azzai.

3. *Mishnah Sukkah* 3:10:

> If a slave **or a woman** or a child read aloud for him [the Hallel], he repeats after them what they say and it shall be for him a curse [because he did not learn to read and depends on their reading].

It other words, in the period of the Mishnah, there were women who knew how to read Hebrew, and we can assume that they learned from their fathers, or even with a teacher.

4. *Tosefta Megillah* 3:11, ed. Lieberman, p. 356 (cf. Bavli *Megillah* 23a):

> Everyone goes up among the count of seven, **even a woman**, even a child. A woman should not be brought to **read for the public**.

In the Tannaitic period, everyone who went up to the Torah read his own portion. Therefore, we can also deduce from here that women learned how to read. Otherwise, how could they imagine bringing them to read for the public?[30]

Aggadic Sources Which Show That Women Studied Torah

Other sources praise learned women from Biblical times, which gives the impression that the Sages had a positive attitude towards contemporary women who were involved in the study of the Torah:

1. *Bava Batra* 119b:

30. For a detailed discussion of women and *aliyot* to the Torah, see above, Chapter 6.

"It was taught [in a *beraita*]: The daughters of Zelopheḥad were wise, were exegetes, were righteous". This is followed by examples of their halakhic wisdom.

2. *Sifrei Zuta* to *Beha'alotekha,* paragraph 12, p. 277 = *Yalkut Shimoni* to *Beha'alotekha,* paragraph 741, p. 230:

   "With half his flesh eaten away" (Numbers 12:12). It means that she [Miriam the Prophetess] was half of us, **because she used to teach the women** while we teach the men.

3. *Seder Eliyahu Rabbah,* Chapter 10, p. 50:

   "Another explanation: 'And she used to sit' (Judges 4:5)... So Devorah goes and sits under the palm tree and **teaches Torah in public**..."

4. *Sanhedrin* 94b:

   "The yoke shall be destroyed because of oil" (Isaiah 10:27). Said Rabbi Yitzḥak Napaḥa: "The yoke" of Sennacherib "shall be destroyed because of the oil" of Hezekiah, which was burning in the synagogues and *Batei Midrash*... They searched from Dan to Be'er Sheva and they did not find an *Am Ha'aretz* [illiterate person] from Gabbat to Antipatris, and they did not find a boy or **girl**, a man or a **woman** who were not proficient in the laws of purity and impurity...

Historical Sources Which Show That Women Studied Torah

Finally, there are many testimonies about girls and women who studied and taught Bible, Talmud, *Halakhah* and *Aggadah* from the days of Beruriah, in the second century, until Mrs. Flora

31. See approximately thirty examples collected above, Chapter 13, pp. 289-300, and the bibliography listed at the end of that responsum. For a historical survey of the education of girls, see Brayer, pp. 90-125.

Sassoon, in the twentieth.[31] Furthermore, this phenomenon was not limited to exceptional women. In Egypt, for example, girls learned in the "Talmud Torah" together with their brothers and women even served as teachers in those schools (Goitein). In France too, we find testimony by a pupil of the Christian scholastic Abelard in the 12th century:

> The Christians who teach their sons do not do so for the sake of Heaven... Not so the Jews. Out of their zeal for God and love of His Torah, they send all their sons to learn so they can understand the Torah of God... **and not only the sons, but also the daughters**.[32]

In conclusion, there is no reason to engage in precise readings regarding the strict approach of Rabbi Eliezer and Maimonides. We must return to the approach of Ben Azzai and rule: **"A man is obligated to teach his daughter Torah"**, and this for five reasons:

A. This was the opinion of *Rabbanan*/"our Sages", according to Bavli *Sotah* 21b.

B. Ben Azzai's approach is supported both by Talmudic sources and the historical precedents cited above.

C. According to Rabbi Avraham de Boton – the author of *Leḥem Mishneh* – when there is a controversy between Rabbi Eliezer and Ben Azzai, the *halakhah* is according to Ben Azzai, since Rabbi Eliezer "is a Shammaite".[33]

32. E.E. Urbach, *Ba'alei Hatosafot*, fourth edition, Jerusalem, 5740, p. 18. Also see Avraham Grossman, *Ḥassidot U'Moredot: Nashim Yehudiot Be'eiropa Biyemei Habeinayim*, Jerusalem, 5761, p. 296, as well as all of Chapter 7, *ibid*. But cf. *Hagahot Rabbeinu Peretz* to the Semak, No. 221 – it is not clear whether the men there recited *Kiddush* for widows because the latter could not read Hebrew or because they thought that it must be recited by a man.
33. *Leḥem Mishneh* to *Hilkhot De'ot* 6:7, according to Rabbi Kafiḥ, p. 103. Cf. *Sefer Halikhot Olam* by Rabbi Yeshuah Halevi, 5730, p. 102: "The *halakhah* does not follow Rabbi Eliezer, because he is a Shammaite (see *Niddah* 7b)... Therefore, the *halakhah* does not follow him in every place, except in a place where the *Gemara* explicitly says that the *halakhah* is according to him".

D. The Committee on Jewish Laws and Standards of the Rabbinical Assembly arrived at a similar decision in 1974: "We declare that for the Conservative Movement the *mitzvah* to study Torah devolves equally upon women as upon men" (Blumenthal, p. 33).

E. The times and the nature of things have changed and *ha'idana*/now it would be absurd for girls to receive a limited Jewish education, while receiving, at the same time, an excellent secular education, which is equal in all respects to that of boys.[34]

Therefore, women in our day are obligated to study Torah exactly like men and it is permissible for women to study and teach any and all subjects related to the Torah without any doubt.

III. Is it permissible for a woman to render halakhic decisions?

The *Va'ad Halakhah* [Law Committee of the Rabbinical Assembly of Israel] ruled several months ago – in a majority decision – that a woman is permitted to render halakhic decisions, since that was the opinion of most *poskim* and since women did so in practice from Talmudic times until today. The discussion is lengthy so we will not repeat it here.[35]

IV. Women and public prayer and PTBC

There are two ways to deal with this question: according to specific topics or in a more general fashion. If we research the matter by topic, it can be proved that women are obligated to pray three times a day,[36] may join the *minyan* for *devarim shebikdushah* such as *Barekhu*, *Kaddish* and *Kedushah*,[37] may read

34. For the concept of *ha'idana*/now, see above, pp. 331-332.
35. The responsum appears above, Chapter 13. The vote in the *Va'ad Halakhah* was three in favor and one against.
36. See above, Chapter 3, paragraph I.
37. See *ibid.*, paragraph III.

from the Torah[38] and the Book of Esther in public,[39] and are Biblically obligated to recite *Kiddush,*[40] and to recite Grace after Meals according to the Yerushalmi and most of the *Rishonim.*[41]

However, even if we do so, this will not enable a woman rabbi to function in all the ritual areas demanded by her job since, as is well-known, women are exempt from PTBC such as blowing the shofar, counting the *omer, tefillin, tallit, sukkah* and *lulav.*[42] Indeed, according to many *poskim,* women are permitted to fulfill PTBC and even to recite a blessing upon them (see below), but they

38. See above, Chapter 6.
39. See above, Chapter 7.
40. *Berakhot* 20b; Maimonides, *Hilkhot Avodah Zarah* 12:3; *Tur* and *Shulḥan Arukh* OH 271; Yalon, pp. 114-117; and Rabbi Berkovits, pp. 92-100.
41. Mishnah *Berakhot* 3:3 and the Bavli *ibid.*, 20b; Mishnah *Berakhot* 6:1 and the Bavli *ibid.*, 45b; *Arakhin* 3a; and Yerushalmi *Berakhot* 3:3, fol. 6b. In *Berakhot* 20b there is a disagreement as to whether women are obligated to recite the Grace after Meals by the Torah or by the Sages. But the Yerushalmi and most of the *Geonim* and *Rishonim* (Rav Hai Gaon, the Rif, Ra'avad, Naḥmanides, Ran, Rashbatz and the *Or Zaru'a*) ruled that women are obligated **by the Torah** to recite the Grace after Meals. Furthermore, women are obligated to recite the *zimmun* for themselves. Therefore, why is it forbidden for them to recite the *zimmun* for men or to be counted in a *zimmun* of men? Some *Rishonim* say that it is because of licentiousness; others say that women don't sit regularly (*keva*) among men; while others say that the company of women is inappropriate. It appears that all of them were correct from the historical point of view, since it is clear that the Sages were opposed to counting women in the *zimmun* with men because in their day men and women dined separately and only prostitutes and professional "escort girls" (*Hetaerae*) reclined on couches and dined together with men. (This was suggested to me by Rabbi Theodore Friedman z"l; cf. a brief discussion in his book *Be'er Tuvia,* Jerusalem, 1991, English section, pp. 52, 54). However, *ha'idana*/now *nishtanu hateva'im*/nature has changed and it is possible to go back to the opinion of the Yerushalmi and of most of the *Rishonim* that women are obligated by the Torah to recite the Grace after Meals. And, as we know, everyone who is obligated to do something can fulfill the obligation of others – see below, note 43.
On women and the Grace after Meals, see Rabbi Novak, pp. 142-144; Rabbi Feldman, p. 302 and note 53; Rabbi Aaron Blumenthal, *Conservative Judaism* 31/3 (Spring 1977), pp. 34-35; and especially Berkovits, pp. 83-92.
42. *Mishnah Kiddushin* 1:7. This general principle, as we know, is not really a general principle – see *Kiddushin* 34a. Yalon proved in his dissertation that this principle was stated by Rabbi Shimon, but many *Tannaim* and early

cannot fulfill the obligation of the congregation.[43] Therefore, a woman rabbi would not be allowed to blow the shofar on *Rosh Hashanah* and it is doubtful whether she could count the *omer* in public[44] or recite the *sukkah* blessing in the synagogue *sukkah*,[45] as is the common practice among many rabbis. On the other hand, she could put on *tefillin*, wear a *tallit*, sit in the *sukkah* and hold the *lulav* as an optional activity, but not as an obligation. This situation will create some practical and educational problems:

a) Strange situations will arise. A women rabbi will serve as cantor on *Rosh Hashanah*, but will be unable to blow the shofar, or she will recite the *Kiddush* in the *sukkah*, but will be unable to recite the blessing "to sit in the *sukkah*" for the congregation.

b) It is desirable that a woman rabbi should be able to fulfill most ritual tasks, since she will frequently have to do so.[46]

c) Those who support the ordination of women as rabbis emphasize that a rabbi is an educational example. How could a woman rabbi be an example of observing practical commandments such as *tallit*, *tefillin*, *sukkah* and *lulav*, if she herself is **exempt** from those commandments, or does not even fulfill them at all?

Therefore, it is preferable to adopt the more inclusive method

Amoraim ignored it. It is only from the generation of Abaye and Rava onwards that this principle achieved prominence. For a shorter analysis, see Rabbi Berman, pp. 11-13.

43. Following the principle in Mishnah *Rosh Hashanah* 3:8 that "everyone who is not obligated to do something cannot fulfill the obligation of others".
44. Because those who cannot recite the blessing because they forgot to count for one day (OH 489:8) are obligated to fulfill their obligation by responding "Amen" after her blessing.
45. Because frequently the one who recites *Kiddush* also recites the blessing "to sit in the *sukkah*" and the congregation only responds "Amen" without reciting the blessing.
46. In Talmudic times they also thought that a rabbi must know how to fulfill ritual functions as needed – see above, p. 276.

of Rabbi Joel Roth regarding women and PTBC.[47] Here is his method in a very succinct fashion:

1) According to almost all the *poskim* (except Rabbi Avraham ben David of Posquières, Ra'avad), women are permitted to fulfill PTBC.[48]

2) According to many *poskim*, led by Rabbeinu Tam, women are permitted to recite the blessing over PTBC.

3) If women fulfill PTBC, all the requirements and specifications of those commandments apply to them.[49]

4) A woman may "obligate herself" to fulfill PTBC, just as a man may obligate himself regarding an optional matter.[50]

5) Once a woman obligates herself to fulfill all the commandments, her obligation has equal status to that of men, and she can fulfill their obligations for them.[51]

47. Rabbi Roth, pp. 127-148, and briefly in his article, pp. 70-74. However, it must be emphasized that I disagree with him on one central point. Time after time in his responsum (pp. 142, 146, 147, 169, and elsewhere), he stresses that were it not for his method, a woman is exempt from prayer and may not join a *minyan*, but he does not quote any source for this claim. However, we have demonstrated above, Chapter 3, that women are obligated to pray and may join a *minyan* even if we do **not** adopt his responsum.

48. On these issues, see above, pp. 58-63; Rabbi Chaim Listfield, *Conservative Judaism* 29/1 (Fall 1974), pp. 42-50; Rabbi Shlomo Yoseph Zevin, *Torah Sheba'al Peh* 12 (5730), pp. 19-25; Rabbi Shlomo Goren, *Torat Hashabbat Vehamo'ed*, Jerusalem, 5742, pp. 230-242; Rabbi Eliezer Berkovits, *Sinai* 100 (5747), pp. 187-194; and Rabbi Berkovits, pp. 70-74.

49. Rabbi Roth, pp. 134-135.

50. *Ibid.*, pp. 136-139, and we may add some other examples. About the "self-obligation" of men to recite the *Malkhuyiot*, *Zikhronot* and *Shofarot* verses, see OH 591, *Magen Avraham*, subparagraph 6 = *Ba'er Heiteiv*, subparagraph 3. About the "self-obligation" of women to recite *Havdalah*, see OH 296, *Mishnah Berurah*, subparagraph 35. About the "self-obligation" of women regarding the shofar, see *Minhagei Maharil*, *Hilkhot Shofar*, ed. Spitzer, p. 286, and also *Tiferet Yisrael* to Mishnah *Rosh Hashanah* 3:8, note 42.

51. Rabbi Roth, pp. 141-148. There is no doubt that Rabbi Roth was very innovative in his halakhic approach, but his opponents did not succeed in

Therefore, in order to enable a woman rabbi to participate in all aspects of public prayer and congregational life, we propose that in practice every woman accepted to study in the rabbinic track at the *Beit Midrash* will undertake in writing to accept upon herself all PTBC.

V. Is it permissible for a woman to perform marriages?

The *Va'ad Halakhah* decided unanimously in 1991 that it is permissible for women to participate in all parts of the marriage ceremony: the *piyyutim*, the *derashah*, the betrothal blessing and the seven blessings. The responsum is long, so we will not repeat it here.[52]

The individual, the public and *Kelal Yisrael*

Until now we have dealt with issues that affect the individual (a woman as a *poseket*) or a specific public (a woman as a cantor and the like). However, certain halakhic actions influence *Kelal Yisrael*, the collective Jewish People. Here is a telling example. In 1983, the CCAR (Central Conference of American Rabbis – the organization of American Reform rabbis) decided to change the definition of who is a Jew. They decided that from then on, there is a "presumption of Jewishness" if either the mother **or the father** is Jewish until he/she performs certain *mitzvot* or public actions that certify his/her Jewishness.[53] This step aroused the anger of many, including many Reform rabbis in Israel and the Diaspora. They said then: there are three circles in Judaism – the individual, the public and the *Kelal Yisrael*. If the individual decides either to change or ignore a specific *halakhah* – that is between him and God. If a certain congregation decides either to change or ignore

undermining his approach. See Rabbi Israel Francus, *Ordination* II, pp. 35-45, and Rabbi Roth's reaction in note 79 of his responsum. Also see Gideon Rothstein, *Tradition* 24/1 (Fall 1988), pp. 104-115 and Rabbi Roth's reaction, *ibid.* 24/4 (Summer 1989), pp. 112-114.

52. This responsum appears above, Chapter 12.
53. *American Reform Responsa*, New York, 1983, pp. 547-550.

a specific *halakhah* – that, too, remains between that specific congregation and God. However, if we change a *halakhah* related to conversion or to Jewish family law, that affects *Kelal Yisrael* and it is forbidden for a single movement in Judaism to act alone on such decisive issues.[54] Moreover, this will cause pain and shame for the child or the couple when they discover that many or most Jews do not recognize the conversion, marriage or divorce.

This issue must stand before anyone who deals with the question of the ordination of women. If a Jew asks a woman rabbi to rule on a halakhic issue, that is between him and God. If a specific congregation allows a woman rabbi to blow the shofar in public – that too is between them and God. However, if a woman rabbi signs a *Ketubah*, that couple is not married according to classical *halakhah* as accepted by *Kelal Yisrael* and if she signs a *get* [bill of divorce], that couple is not divorced, with everything that that implies. Finally, if a woman rabbi participates in a *Beit Din* for conversion, that convert is not a convert according to accepted *halakhic* opinion.

After this introduction, we may now deal with the two last issues.

VI. May a woman be part of a *Beit Din*, especially a *Beit Din* for conversion?

Most rabbis today do not serve as judges for *dinei mamonot* [civil law related to monetary cases]. On the other hand, most of them do participate in *Batei Din* for conversion, since conversion

54. This was the reaction of Rabbi Uri Regev in an interview in *The Jerusalem Post* (Friday, July 8, 1983, p. 15). For similar opinions about the importance of *kelal yisrael*, cf. Rabbi Moshe Zemer, *Halakhah Shefuyah*, Tel Aviv, 5754, pp. 54-55 = *Evolving Halakhah*, Woodstock, Vermont, 1999, pp. 53-55 and Rabbi Immanuel Jakobovits in *Ish Bigvurot*, edited by Moshe Ḥalamish, Jerusalem, 5750, English section, pp. 28-29. On the need for a joint *Beit Din* for family law of the three movements in Judaism, see Rabbi Ira Eisenstein, *Proceedings of the Rabbinical Assembly* 17 (1953), p. 53 = Golinkin (above, note 16), p. 788.

requires a court of three who are qualified to judge (*Yevamot* 46b; Maimonides, *Hilkhot Issurei Bi'ah* 13:6; *Tur* and *Shulḥan Arukh* YD 268). Indeed, our *Va'ad Halakhah* ruled some years ago that a *Beit Din* for conversion must be composed of three ordained rabbis (Rabbi Tuvia Friedman, *Responsa of the Va'ad Halakhah of the Rabbinical Assembly of Israel* 3 [5748-5749], p. 67, also at www.responsafortoday.com).

From a narrow halakhic point of view, there are sources, *Rishonim* and also modern *poskim*, who permit a woman to judge under certain circumstances.[55] However, the question still remains: "What have the Sages accomplished by this enactment?" If we permit women rabbis to take part in *Batei Din* for conversions, these converts will be invalidated not only by the Chief Rabbinate, but by a high percentage number of Conservative rabbis in the world as well as by Orthodox rabbis abroad who do recognize our conversions. Will this benefit the converts or *Kelal Yisrael*? A step like this will only increase disagreements within the Jewish People and will cause personal harm to the convert. Therefore, if women are going to be accepted into the rabbinic track in the *Beit Midrash*, they will need to undertake in writing not to participate in a *Beit Din* for conversion, until it is decided otherwise.

55. For modern *poskim*, see the Bibliography at the end of this responsum. The following sources forbid women to serve as judges: *Sifrei Devarim*, paragraph 13, ed. Finkelstein, p. 21; Yerushalmi *Shevuot* 4:1, fol. 35b = Yerushalmi *Sanhedrin* 4:10, fol. 21c = Yerushalmi *Yoma* 6:1, fol. 43b; Bavli *Gittin* 5b; *Tosafot* to *Niddah* 50a, s.v. *kol hakasher* and parallels (except for *Bava Kamma* 15a); *Sefer Haḥinukh*, No. 83 and elsewhere; *Tur* HM 7; *Shulḥan Arukh* HM 7:4.
The following sources permit women to serve as judges: *Kohelet Rabbah* to Chapter 2:8, ed. Vilna, fol. 7c = *Kohelet Zuta*, Chapter 1, p. 91 = *Yalkut Shimoni* to Kohelet, paragraph 968; *Bava Kamma* 15a = *Kiddushin* 35a; the Ritva to *Kiddushin* 35a; *Tosafot* to *Bava Kamma* 15a, according to the explanation of the Ḥida, *Birkei Yosef* to HM 7, subparagraph 11; "some of the commentators" in *Sefer Haḥinukh*, paragaraph 83; the Ran to *Shevuot*, beginning of Chapter 4, who permits her to judge if she is accepted by the parties.

VII. Is it permissible for a woman to serve as a witness, especially to sign *ketubot* and *gittin* [writs of divorce]?

There is no doubt that, in the eyes of our Sages, women are Biblically disqualified as witnesses. This is what they learn in *Sifrei* Deuteronomy (paragraph 190, ed. Finkelstein, p. 230) from a *gezeirah shavah*, and it is also hinted at or stated in many other sources (Mishnah *Rosh Hashanah* 1:8; Mishnah *Shevu'ot* 4:1; *Shevu'ot* 30a; *Bava Kamma* 88a; *Pirkei Derabbi Eliezer* fol. 34a). It was also codified by the major *poskim* (Maimonides, *Hilkhot Edut* 9:1–2; *Shulḥan Arukh* HM 35:14).

In his responsum on the ordination of women as rabbis, Rabbi Joel Roth proposed three possible ways to change or to circumvent this *halakhah*; but as of this writing, nothing has been done about this. Moreover, about a month ago (Iyar 5752, May 1992) this issue arose arisen again at the annual convention of the Rabbinical Assembly in the U.S. Fifty percent of the rabbis present voted in favor of a Resolution that urges the Committee on Jewish Law and Standards of the Rabbinical Assembly to accept the testimony of women (and their judging) and fifty percent were against (53 rabbis were in favor and 51 were against).[56] In other words, it is possible that there are halakhic methods to change this *halakhah*, but these two facts teach us that this is not yet the proper time to do so. If we permit women rabbis to serve as witnesses at marriages and divorces, we will produce people invalidated for marriage, who will be disqualified not only by the Chief Rabbinate of Israel, but by about half of the Conservative rabbis in the world, as well as by the Orthodox rabbis outside Israel who do recognize our marriages and divorces. Once again, we must ask: "What have the Sages

56. The Resolution is entitled "Gender Equality in Halacha" and was published in the *Proceedings of the Rabbinical Assembly* 54 (1992), pp. 316-317. I want to thank my father and teacher, Rabbi Noah Golinkin [z"l], who was present at the convention and told me the results of the vote. In 2001, some of the members of the Committee on Jewish Law and Standards wrote several new responsa on this issue – see below in the Bibliography and cf. above, pp. 21-22.

accomplished by this enactment?" Therefore, if women are accepted to the Rabbinic track in the *Beit Midrash*, they will need to undertake in writing not to serve as witnesses for *kiddushin* and *gittin* until it is decided otherwise.

Practical *Halakhah*

In light of all of the above, it is permissible for the *Beit Midrash* to ordain women as rabbis, on condition that the women in the rabbinic track will undertake in writing to accept upon themselves all PTBC and to refrain from participating in *Batei Din* for conversion or to serve as witnesses at marriages and divorces.[57]

The Golden Mean

We have learned in the Yerushalmi (*Hagigah* 2:1, fol. 77a):[58]

57. It is worth pointing out that this ruling is almost identical to the majority opinion of the *Va'ad Halakhah* in a letter I wrote on 4 Tammuz, 5747 (July 1, 1987). I wrote then (in Hebrew):
"...Nowadays, women are accepted into the Jewish Theological Seminary following the responsum of Rabbi Joel Roth... On the other hand, the problem of women as witnesses remains unresolved from a halakhic point of view, despite the different solutions proposed by Rabbi Roth. Therefore, there is a halakhic possibility of ordaining women as rabbis, on condition that they accept upon themselves PTBC and that they will not serve as witnesses...
We are convinced that in Israel it is not yet the proper time to ordain women as rabbis. In our opinion, such a step will bring irreparable harm to the future of our Movement in Israel and will also gravely damage the internal unity of the Movement. Of course, it is very possible that the social reality in Israel and in the Movement will change in the future, and it is well-known that "a change of times" leads, in many cases, to changes in *halakhah*.
Sincerely: David Golinkin, with the agreement of: Rabbi Theodore Friedman, Chair; Rabbi Joseph Heckelman; Rabbi Raphael Harris. (Rabbi Reuven Hammer was opposed and did not sign that letter.)"
In the meantime, the atmosphere in the Movement changed, as we explained in this responsum, but the halakhic problems remain. Therefore, we ruled as we did.
58. Cf. *Tosefta Ḥagigah* 2:5, ed. Lieberman, p. 381. That passage deals with *Ma'aseh Merkavah* [mystic speculations on the Divine Chariot], but this is

> This Torah is like two paths: one of fire and one of snow. If he takes the one, he dies by fire; if he takes the other, he dies by snow. What should he do? He should walk in the middle

The *halakhic* ruling we have suggested is a compromise – between tradition and change, between conservatism and revolution, between the accepted *halakhah* throughout the generations and the needs of the times. Like any other compromise, it will not satisfy the extremists who stand at both ends of the debate. Nevertheless, we hope that it will satisfy most Conservative Jews, who strive for the golden mean.

David Golinkin
Jerusalem
28 Sivan 5752

true for many issues in *halakhah*, in Judaism and in life. Also see Maimonides, *Hilkhot De'ot* 1:4.

BIBLIOGRAPHY

General Bibliography on the Ordination of Women as Rabbis

(For recent literature on this topic, see above, p. 11, note 22; p. 17, note 34; and pp. 22-23, notes 47-50.)

Brukstein	Arnon Brukstein, *Semikhat Nashim Lerabbanut Veḥazanut Batenuah Hakonservativit*, M.A. thesis, Hebrew University, Jerusalem, 1990
CJ	*Conservative Judaism* 48/1 (Fall 1995) (the entire issue)
Geller	Laura Geller in: T.M. Rudavsky, ed., *Gender and Judaism*, New York and London, 1995, pp. 243-353
Golinkin	David Golinkin, *An Index of Conservative Responsa and Prectical Halakhic Studies: 1917-1990*, New York, 1992, pp. 76-77
Jacob	Rabbi Walter Jacob, ed., *American Reform Responsa*, New York, 1983, pp. 25-43
Kellenbach	Katherina von Kellenbach, "The Life and Thought of Rabbi Regina Jonas", *Leo Baeck Institute Yearbook* 39 (1994), pp. 213-225
Kopelowitz	Ezra Kopelowitz, "Three Subcultures of Conservative Judaism and the Issue of Ordaining Women", *Nashim* 1 (1998), pp. 136-153
Nadell	Pamela Nadell, *Women Who Would be Rabbis: A History of Women's Ordination 1889-1985*, Boston, 1998
Ordination I	*On the Ordination of Women as Rabbis*, New York, 1979
Ordination II	Rabbi Simon Greenberg, ed., *The Ordination of Women as Rabbis: Studies and Responsa*, New York, 1988
Ordination III	*JUDAISM* 33/1 (Winter 1984) (the entire issue)
Shakdiel	Leah Shakdiel, *Amudim* 633 (Av 5759), pp. 22-23

Volume 5 — *Responsa of the Va'ad Halakhah of the Rabbinical Assembly of Israel* 5 (5752–5754), pp. 7-83 (five responsa in Hebrew with English summaries; also available at www.responsafortoday.com)

Wenger — Beth Wenger, "Politics of Women's Ordination" in: Jack Wertheimer, ed., *Tradition Renewed: A History of the Jewish Theological Seminary of America*, Vol. II, New York, 1997, pp. 483-523

Zola — Gary Zola, ed., *Women Rabbis: Exploration and Celebration*, Cincinnati, 1996

I. Women in Public Office

A. GENERAL STUDIES

Otzar — *Otzar Haposkim Leḥoshen Mishpat*, Vol. 1, Jerusalem, 5752, pp. 80-82

Safrai — Ze'ev Safrai, *Hakehillah Hayehudit Be'eretz Yisrael Bitkufat Hatalmud*, Jerusalem, 5755, pp. 282-284

THE 1918 AFFAIR

Cohen — Yeḥezkel Cohen, *Ha'ishah Bimkorot Hayahadut (Hagut: Me'asef Lemaḥshavah Yehudit)*, Jerusalem, 5743, pp. 83-95 = *Hapeninah: Sefer Zikaron LePeninah Rapel*, Jerusalem, 5749, pp. 51-62

Ellenson and Rosen — Rabbi David Ellenson and Michael Rosen, "Gender, Halakhah and Women's Suffrage" in: Rabbis Walter Jacob and Moshe Zemer, eds., *Gender Issues in Jewish Law: Essays and Responsa*, New York and Oxford, 2001, pp. 58-81

Friedman — Menaḥem Friedman, *Hevrah Vedat: Ha'ortodoksiah Halo-Tzionit Be'eretz Yisrael 1918-1936*, Jeusalem, 5738, pp. 146-184

Nehorai — Mikhael Tzvi Nehorai, *Tarbitz* 59 (5750), pp. 498-502

Zohar — Zvi Zohar, *Hei'iru Penei Mizraḥ*, Tel Aviv, 5761, Chapter 12

THE SHAKDIEL AFFAIR

Cohen — Yeḥezkel Cohen, ed., *Nashim Behanhagat Hatzibbur: Hamaḥloket al Ḥaverut Nashim Bemo'eitzah Datit*, Jerusalem, 5751

Don-Yehiya — Eliezer Don-Yehiya, *Mosdot Dati'im Bama'arekhet Hapolitit: Hamo'eitzot Hadatiot Beyisrael*, Jerusalem, 5749, Chapter 8

Elon and Barak — Menaḥem Elon and Aharon Barak, "*Pesak Hadin Be'atirat Leah Shakdiel*" in *Hapeninah, op.cit.*, pp. 63-126

Elon — Menaḥem Elon, *Ma'amad Ha'ishah*, Tel Aviv, 2005, Chapter 1

B. Responsa

1. STRICT RULINGS

Halevi — Rabbi Ḥayyim David Halevi, *Hatzofeh*, 24 II Adar 5749 = *Teḥumin* 10 (5749), pp. 118-123 = *Nashim Behanhagat Hatzibbur, op. cit.*, pp. 87-91 = *Responsa Mayim Ḥayyim*, Tel Aviv, 5751, No. 70 (he permits it according to Jewish law, but forbids it because the men will not agree to sit next to a woman in a Religious Council)

Hoffman — Rabbi David Tzvi Hoffmann, *Jeschurun* 6/5-6 (May-June 1919), pp. 262-266 (German) = Hebrew translation in: *Hakibbutz Bahalakhah*, second edition, Sha'alavim, 5748, pp. 286-290 (they may vote; they may not be elected); and a response to Ritter in: *Jeschurun* 6/11-12 (November-December 1919), pp. 515-521

Kuk	Rabbi Abraham Isaac Hacohen Kuk, *Ma'amarei Hare'iyah*, Jerusalem, 5744, pp. 189-194
Mintzberg	Rabbi Yisrael Ze'ev Mintzberg, *Sefer Zot Ḥukat Hatorah*, Jerusalem, 1920
Ritter	Dr. B.R. Ritter, *Jeschurun* 6/9-10 (September-October 1919), pp. 445-448
Spitzer	A. Sh. B. Spitzer, *Ya'akov Rosenheim Jubilee Volume*, Frankfurt, 1935, pp. 1-47
Tchorsh	Rabbi Katriel Fischel Tchorsh, *Hadarom* 42 (Tishrei 5736), pp. 23-28
Tukachinsky	Rabbi Yeḥiel Mikhel Tukachinsky, *Ha'ishah Al-pi Torat Yisrael*, Jerusalem, 1920; *Ma'amar Degel Yisrael*, Jerusalem, 1930
Weinberg	Rabbi Yeḥiel Ya'akov Weinberg, *Seridei Eish*, Part 2, No. 52; Part 3, No. 105 (it is legally permitted, but it should be forbidden because Rabbi D.Z. Hoffman so ruled and on the basis of custom and because "all the glory of the daughter of the King is within")
Zlotnik	Rabbi Y.M. Zlotnick, *"Ha'ishah Uzekhuyotehah"*, *Hamizraḥi*, Warsaw, 25 Av 5679 (1919)

2. LENIENT RULINGS

Bakshi-Doron	Rabbi Eliyahu Bakshi-Doron, *Torah Shebe'al Peh* 20 (5739), pp. 66-72 = *Responsa Binyan Av*, Jerusalem, 5742, No. 65
Eliyahu	Rabbi Mordechai Eliyahu, *Teḥumin* 7 (5746), pp. 518-519 (permitted for a community or organization; forbidden for the entire people)
Feinstein	Rabbi Moshe Feinstein, *Igrot Moshe, Yoreh De'ah*, Part 2, Nos. 44-45 (he allows a woman to serve as a *kashrut* supervisor)
Frank	Rabbi Tzvi Pesaḥ Frank, quoted by Rabbi Hirschensohn, p. 12

Frimer	Rabbi Avraham Aryeh Frimer, *Hatzofeh*, 12 Marḥeshvan 5747 (November 14, 1986) = *Nashim Behanhagat Hatzibbur, op. cit.*, pp. 92-93
Ginzberg	Rabbi Louis Ginzberg in: David Golinkin, ed., *The Responsa of Professor Louis Ginzberg*, New York and Jerusalem, 1996, pp. 270-271
Herzog	Rabbi Yitzḥak Isaac Halevi Herzog, *Teḥukah Leyisrael Al-pi Hatorah*, Vol. 1, Jerusalem, 5749, pp. 95-113
Hirschensohn	Rabbi Ḥayyim Hirschensohn, *Malki Bakodesh*, Part 2, Saint Louis, 1921, pp. 12-15, 192-209
Levinson	Rabbi Ya'akov Levinson, *Shivyon Hanashim Minekudat Hahalakhah: Leshe'elat Habeḥirot Be'eretz Yisrael*, New York, 1920, pp. 18-32 = *Hatorah Vehamada*, New York, 1932, pp. 22–56
Nisenboim	Rabbi Yitzḥak Nisenboim, "*Al Devar Zekhuyot Hanashim*", in: *Ha'ishah Bimkorot Hayahadut, op. cit.*, pp. 77-81
Rav Tza'ir	Rabbi Ḥayyim Tchernowitz (Rav Tza'ir), "*Leshe'elat Beḥirot Hanashim*", *Ha'olam* 9/23-24, 1920 = *Ha'ivri* 10/16-17, 1920 = *Besha'arei Tziyon*, New York, 1933, pp. 175-185
Roth	Rabbi Joel Roth, *Ordination* II, pp. 162-163
Rozen	Rabbi Yisrael Rozen, *Teḥumin* 19 (5799), pp. 17-27
Twirk	Rabbi Elimelech Twirk, *Hadarom* 41 (Nisan 5735), pp. 63-68
Uziel	Rabbi Meir Ben-Tzion Ḥai Uziel, *Responsa Mishpetei Uziel, Ḥoshen Mishpat*, No. 6 = *Piskei Uziel Beshe'elot Hazman*, Jerusalem, 5737, No. 44
Zemer	Rabbi Moshe Zemer, *Ha'aretz*, 11 Tishrei, 5746 (September 27, 1985); expanded in his book, *Halakhah Shefuyah*, Tel Aviv, 5754, pp. 211-215 = *Evolving Halakhah*, Woodstock, Vermont, 1999, pp. 241-247

II. Women and Torah Study

(This list has not been updated for the present book due to the wealth of new material.)

Ellinson	Rabbi Elyakim Ellinson, *Ha'ishah Vehamitzvot, Sefer Rishon: Bein Ha'ishah Leyotzrah*, second edition, Jerusalem, 5737, pp. 143-162
Bamberger	Rabbi Zekel Halevi Bamberger, *Otzar Haḥayyim* 4 (1928), pp. 146-148
Berman	Rabbi Saul Berman, *Tradition* 14/2 (Fall 1973), pp. 14-15
Blumenthal	Rabbi Aaron Blumenthal, *Conservative Judaism* 31/3 (Spring 1977), pp. 32-33 = *idem, And Bring Them Closer to Torah*, New York, 1988, pp. 153-154
Breuer	Mordechai Breuer, *Edah Udyoknah*, Jerusalem, 5751, pp. 115-118
Brayer	Rabbi Menachem Brayer, *The Jewish Woman in Rabbinic Literature*, Vol. 2, Hoboken, New Jersey, 1986, pp. 83-129
Cohen	Naomi Cohen, *Tradition* 24/1 (Fall 1988), pp. 28-37
Cohen	Rabbi J. Simcha Cohen, *Intermarriage and Conversion: a Halakhic Solution*, Hoboken, New Jersey, 1987, pp. 119-121
Ehrenreich	Rabbi Ḥ. Y. Ehrenreich, *Otzar Haḥayyim* 5 (1929), pp. 14-18
Feinstein	Rabbi Moshe Feinstein, *Igrot Moshe, Yoreh De'ah*, Part 3, No. 87 and Part 2, No. 109
Felder	Rabbi Gedalia Felder, *Yesodei Yeshurun*, Part 1, Toronto, 5714, pp. 136-138
Firer	Rabbi Ben-Tziyon Firer, *Noam* 3 (5720), pp. 131-134
Friedman	Simḥah Friedman, *Talmud Torah Lenashim Beyameinu*, Tel Aviv, 5740

Goitein	Shlomo Dov Goitein, *Sidrei Ḥinukh Bimei Hageonim Ubeit Harambam*, Jerusalem, 5722, pp. 63-74; and in his book, *A Mediterranean Society*, Vol. II, Berkeley, 1971, pp. 183-185
Hacohen	Mordekhai Hacohen, *Maḥanayyim* 98 (5725), pp. 28-43
Ḥafetz Ḥayyim	Rabbi Yisrael Meir Hacohen, *Likutei Halakhot Lemassekhet Sotah*, Pieterkow, 1918, pp. 21-22 in note
Halevi	Rabbi Ḥayyim David Halevi, *Aseh Lekha Rav*, Vol. 2, No. 52
Halivni	Rabbi David Halivni, *Mekorot Umesorot, Massekhet Shabbat*, Jerusalem, 5742, p. 302, note 2
Harvey	Waren Zev Harvey, *Tradition* 19/2 (Summer 1981), pp. 122-130
Kafiḥ	Rabbi Yoseph Kafiḥ, *Ketavim*, Vol. 1, Jerusalem, 5749, pp. 102-105 = *Ha'ishah Vehinukhah, op. cit.*, pp. 31-37
Kaufmann	David Kaufmann, *Bemah Narim et Ruaḥ Hadat Bekerev Nasheinu Ubenoteinu*, Zhitomir, 1909
Leibowitz	Yeshayahu Leibowitz, *Amudim* 449 (Iyar 5743), pp. 266-268
Lichtenstein	Rabbi Aharon Lichtenstein, in: Ben-Tziyon Rozenfeld, ed., *Ha'isha Veḥinukhah*, Kefar Saba, 5740, pp. 157-163
Malka	Rabbi Moshe Malka, *Responsa Mikveh Hamayyim*, Part 3, No. 21
Meiselman	Rabbi Moshe Meiselman, *Jewish Woman in Jewish Law*, New York, 1978, pp. 34-42
Novak	Rabbi David Novak, *Law and Theology in Judaism*, Vol. II, New York, 1976, pp. 53-55
Sharfstein	Tzvi Sharfstein, *Haḥeder Beḥayei Ameinu*, New York, 1943, pp. 120-122

Silver	Rabbi Arthur Silver, *Tradition* 17/3 (Summer 1978), pp. 74-85
Swidler	Leonard Swidler, "Women and Torah in Talmudic Judaism", *Conservative Judaism* 30/1 (Fall 1975), pp. 21-40
Sorotzkin	Rabbi Zalman Sorotzkin, *Moznayim Lamishpat*, Part 1, No. 42 (see *Nashim* 4 [2001], pp. 119-139 for a detailed analysis of this responsum)
Waldenberg	Rabbi Eliezer Waldenberg, *Responsa Tzitz Eliezer*, Vol. 9, No. 3
Wahrman	Rabbi Shlomo Wahrman, *Hadarom* 46 (Nisan 5738), pp. 55-62
Weinberger	Rabbi Moshe Weinberger, *Journal of Halacha and Contemporary Society* IX (Spring 1985), pp. 19-52
Weiss	Rabbi Avraham Weiss, *Women at Prayer*, Hoboken, New Jersey, 1990, pp. 57-66
Winkler	Rabbi Michael Shalom Winkler, *Otzar Haḥayyim* 5 (1929), pp. 14-15
Yalon	Shevaḥ Yalon, "*Kol Mitzvot Aseh Shehazeman Geraman Nashim Peturot*": *Iyun Bamekorot Hatanna'iyim Uvasugyot Ha'amora'iyot*, M.A. Thesis, Bar Ilan University, Ramat Gan, 5750, pp. 10-29

III. Women as *Poskot*

See above, p. 305.

IV. Women and Prayer

See above, pp. 119-123.

V. Women Officiating at Marriages

See above, pp. 284-285.

VI. Women as Judges

A. GENERAL

Riskin	Rabbi Shlomo Riskin, in: Naḥem Ilan, ed., *Ayin Tovah,* Hakibbutz. Hame'uḥad and Ne'emanei Torah Va'avodah, 5759, pp. 700-703

B. MODERN *POSKIM* WHO FORBID WOMEN TO SERVE AS JUDGES:

Lauterbach	Rabbi J. Z. Lauterbach, *American Reform Responsa,* New York, 1983, pp. 27-28
Lieberman	Rabbi Shaul Lieberman, in: *Tomekh Kehalakhah,* Mt. Vernon, New York, 1986, pp. 14-22
Novak	Rabbi David Novak, *Ordination* III, p. 42
Uziel	Rabbi Meir Ben-Tzion Ḥai Uziel, *Responsa Mishpetei Uziel, Ḥoshen Mishpat,* No. 5 = *Piskei Uziel Beshe'elot Hazman,* Jerusalem, 5737, No. 43

C. MODERN POSKIM WHO PERMIT WOMEN TO SERVE AS JUDGES (THOUGH SOME OF THEM LIMIT THEIR PERMISSION TO SPECIFIC CASES):

Bakshi-Doron	Rabbi Eliyahu Bakshi-Doron, *Torah Shebe'al Peh* 20 (5739), pp. 66-72 = *Responsa Binyan Av,* Jerusalem, 5742, No. 65
Falk	Ze'ev Falk, *Si'aḥ Meisharim* 24 (Sivan 5753), pp. 56-59
Halevi	Rabbi Ḥayyim David Halevi, *Aseh Lekha Rav,* Vol. 8, No. 79; *Nashim Behanhagat Hatzibbur, op. cit.* p. 90
Hirschensohn	Rabbi Ḥayyim Hirschensohn, *Malki Bakodesh,* Part 2, Saint Louis, 1921, pp. 182-192
Levinson	Rabbi Ya'akov Levinson, *Shivion Hanashim Menekudat Hahalakhah: Leshe'elat Habeḥirot Be'eretz Yisrael,* New York, 1920, pp. 10-17 = *Hatorah Vehamada,* New York, 1932, pp. 27-35

Rav Tza'ir	Rabbi Ḥayyim Tchernowitz (Rav Tza'ir), "*Le-she'elat Beḥirot Hanashim*", *Ha'olam* 9/23-24, 1920 = *Ha'ivri* 10/16-17, 1920 = *Besha'arei Tziyon*, New York, 1933, pp. 181-182
Roth	Rabbi Joel Roth, *Ordination* II, pp. 164-166

VII. Women as Witnesses

Blumenthal	Rabbi Aaron Blumenthal, *Conservative Judaism* 31/3 (Spring 1977), pp. 33-34 = *idem, And Bring Them Closer to Torah*, New York, 1988, pp. 34-35
Dror	Rabbi Gilah Dror, Vol. 5, pp. 30-31
Geller	Rabbi Myron Geller, "Woman is Believed", CJLS, February 15, 2001, 42 pp.
Gordis	Rabbi Robert Gordis, *The Dynamics of Judaism*, University of Indiana Press, 1990, pp. 182-183 = *Ordination* II, pp. 55-57
Graetz	Rabbi Michael Graetz, Vol. 5, pp. 20-24
Greenberg	Rabbi Simon Greenberg, *Ordination* II, pp. 75-76
Grossman	Rabbi Susan Grossman, "The Testimony of Women is as the Testimony of Men", CJLS, 2001, 20 pp. (with a concurring opinion by Rabbi Arnold Goodman, 5 pp.)
Hirschensohn	Rabbi Ḥayyim Hirschensohn, *Malki Bakodesh*, Part 2, Saint Louis, 1921, pp. 173-181
Holtzer	Rabbi Gershon Holtzer, *Sinai* 67 (5730), pp. 94-112
Kelman	Rabbi Na'ama Kelman, "*Ha'im nashim pesulot leha'id? Skirah hilkhatit mereishit haposkim ad yameinu*", unpublished.
Meiselman	Rabbi Moshe Meiselman, *Jewish Woman in Jewish Law*, New York, 1978, pp. 73-80
Mandl	Rabbi Herbert Mandl, in: *Tomeikh Kehalakhah*, Mt. Vernon, New York, 1986, pp. 68-69
Novak	Rabbi David Novak, *Ordination* III, p. 42

Rabinowitz	Rabbi Mayer Rabinowitz, *Ordination* II, pp. 117-119 = *Ordination* III, pp. 64-65
Rabinowitz	Rabbi Mayer Rabinowitz, *Conservative Judaism* 39/1 (Fall 1986), pp. 19-21
Roth	Rabbi Joel Roth, *Ordination* II, pp. 149-162
Rubinstein	Rabbi Shmuel Tanḥum Rubinstein, *Torah Shebe'al Peh* 10 (5728), pp. 99-108
Tucker	Rabbi Gordon Tucker, *Ordination* II, pp. 15-19, 28

Eulogies

"THIS IS YOUR LIFE MORAH DEVORAH"

A Eulogy for Devorah Golinkin z"l (1922–2012)

by David Golinkin

Delivered at Beth Shalom, Columbia, Maryland, January 23, 2012

A few weeks ago, we read the weekly portion of Vayeḥi in which Jacob blesses his children (Genesis 49:1-33):

ויקרא יעקב אל בניו ויאמר:
האספו ואגידה לכם את אשר יקרא אתכם באחרית הימים...
ויכל יעקב לצות את בניו,
ויאסף רגליו אל המטה ויגוע ויאסף אל עמיו.

> And Jacob sent for his children saying:
> Gather and I will tell you what will happen to you
> in the end of days...
> And Jacob finished instructing his children,
> and he gathered his legs into the bed, and he expired,
> and he was gathered unto his people.

Starting about a month ago, our mother and grandmother Devorah/Dolly Golinkin z"l followed in the footsteps of Jacob. On Hanukkah, Mordy and I came to spend time with Mom and Abe, and during the past few weeks, Abe and my wife Dory and Mordy and I said goodbye to Mom/Savta. This was very difficult, but we were blessed to talk to Mom up until January 12th. We told her how much we loved her and she did the same.

I would like to sketch the 89 years of Mom's life in broad strokes, emphasizing some of her unique qualities and contributions.

Childhood

Our mother was born in New York City on September 11, 1922. She was named Bluma Devorah (Blossom Doris) for her maternal grandmother, Bluma Devorah Leder, who had passed away at a young age in 1913 in Reishe, Galicia. For many decades Mom was called Dolly, until 1978 when people in Columbia started calling her Devorah. Her Hebrew school pupils always called her "Morah Devorah".

Mom's parents were immigrants from Lomze and Reishe respectively. Her father, Avraham Nattan (Avrum Nossen) Perlberg, was a Hebrew writer, poet and professor of Hebrew at the Mizraḥi Teachers' Seminary and Yeshivah College in New York.

When he passed away at the young age of 45 in 1934, Grandma Esther had to earn a living and raise two small children – Dolly age 11 and Sue age 8 – by herself. She managed to buy or rent a store in Laurelton, Queens, New York, which she called the "Pearl Kiddy Shop", in an excellent location next to Woolworth's. Grandma, Dolly and Sue lived at the back of the shop. The shop was open until 9 pm and the girls helped out in the store. The girls took piano lessons with Miss Bisby and ballet lessons with Miss Gazarian, but Grandma also made sure that they went to *shul* and Hebrew school.

I assume that life was tough growing up during the Depression without a father, but Mom never used to complain about her childhood.

I do know that from her father she inherited a love of Hebrew, Jewish Music and Judaism. From her mother she inherited a love of Judaism and a capacity for hard work. During all the years that Abe and I were growing up, our mother ran the house; taught Hebrew school; taught Spanish; was a devoted Rebbetzin; and was very active in Sisterhood and Hadassah.

Spanish

Many of you, who knew our mother in her later years, did not know that she was a Spanish Professor and teacher for 42 years from 1943 until 1985. She was inspired in high school by a Spanish teacher named Mrs. Lait to become a Spanish teacher.

Mom graduated from Queen's College "with distinction" in 1943 with a major in Spanish and a minor in education. She received an M.A. in Spanish from Columbia University in 1946, and finished all of the course credits towards a Ph.D. from Columbia University between 1948 and 1951.

Mom taught Spanish at many universities and high schools in Arlington, Knoxville and Maryland, including: Queens College, Syracuse University, Hunter College, George Mason University – where she was an Assistant Professor – and the University of Tennessee. She even published an academic article in *Hispania*, September 1971 on "Some Pedagogic Tools for Third Year College Spanish Classes".

She also helped me learn Spanish. In 1974-75, I needed to take a proficiency exam in Spanish at Hebrew University – in addition to Hebrew and English – since I was studying Medieval Jewish History. Mom was a devoted letter-writer, so I asked her to write to me that year in Spanish. She readily agreed and, as a result, I passed the exam.

Morah Devorah

In 1997, our mother was honored by The Council on Jewish Education Services at the Associated in Baltimore, for 34 years of teaching Hebrew school. All of her hundreds of pupils called her Morah Devorah. She began to teach at the Ar-Fax pre-school at our father's congregation in Arlington. I remember as a child attending that school and then helping our mother teach there from time to time.

She also taught at the Hebrew School in Knoxville. When she left in 1977, the kids put on a skit "This is Your Life – Dolly Golinkin". Here are a few excerpts which show their affection for Mom:

Listen and we shall see
A woman so kind, so wise, so true
A teacher for me and you
Morah Devorah is this teacher's name
Soon she will leave us and
We will not be the same.
She'll move to a new place and
We'll miss her so much
So let us show her our own
special show...

Finally, the Golinkins came to Knoxville
and that is where we met Dolly Golinkin.
For the last seven years she has been our teacher – Morah Devorah.
We were her first class in Knoxville. She taught us to love Judaism.
Mrs. Golinkin taught us Jewish arts and crafts.
She taught us Jewish dances.
Mrs. Golinkin taught us about the Jewish calendar and holidays.
Mrs. Golinkin taught us symbols of the synagogue.
Morah Devorah taught us Hebrew readiness.
She has taught us Jewish songs.
Mrs. Golinkin is our teacher now. She taught us about Chanukah.
We will miss her.

And so – Morah Devorah,
we wish to say:
we will miss you greatly.
We wish you much happiness
and joy in your new life.
You will always be in our thoughts.
This Is Your Life Morah Devorah.

Finally, here in Columbia, Mom taught at the Columbia Jewish Community School, where she was honored in 1987-88, **and** at the Consolidated Hebrew School, which included Beth Sholom. She taught 3rd, 4th and 6th grades – retiring in 1997.

Wife

In Genesis 2:18 it says that God created Eve as an "*eizer kinegdo*", which literally means as a "helper against him". There is a famous midrash (*Yevamot* 63a), which says "*zakhah – ozarto, lo zakhah – kinegdo*", "if a man merits it, she helps him, if not, she is against him".

Our father *zakhah* – merited it: There is no question that **everything** that our father accomplished from 1951–2002 was due to the love, help and support of our mother.

They met in the Romance Language department of Hunter College, where our mother taught Spanish, in the fall of 1950. Our Great Uncle George sang the praises of his niece to our father, but did not give him her phone number. So our father found "D. Perlberg" in the phone book – it turned out to be our mother's Aunt Dora. Our parents were married in June 1951 and they were full **partners** for fifty-one-and-a-half years, until our father passed away in February 2003.

This partnership is epitomized by one classic story. When our parents became engaged in 1951, our father did not buy our mother an engagement ring. Instead, they decided **together** to donate the money to UJA. It was as if they both were engaged to the State of Israel. It wasn't until 10 years later that our mother got her engagement ring.

Our father had three pulpits between 1950 and 1986: Arlington, Knoxville, and Columbia. There is no question that he succeeded in all three places because of our mother's help and support: beloved Rebbetzin; Morah Devorah; "Evenings with the Rabbi" in Arlington; Ḥavurot in Knoxville and Columbia; officer and Committee Chair in Sisterhood in all three places.

Similarly, Mom **enabled** Abba to teach 200,000 adults how to read Hebrew via the Hebrew Literacy Campaign beginning in

1978 and the Hebrew Reading Marathons from 1986-2002. Abe told me that beginning in 1986 when Abba "retired" from Beth Shalom, he would work on Hebrew Literacy every day from 8am to 2am. Mom supported him in every way: they ate supper every day **together**; they taught 150 Hebrew marathons from New York to Honolulu **together**; Mom drove Abba to all of his classes (he was a terrible driver); and Mom attended all of his classes. In short, Mom **enabled** Abba to do everything that he did.

There is a famous story in the Talmud about Rabbi Akiva and his wife Rachel (*Nedarim* 50a; *Ketubot* 62b–63a). Rachel sent Rabbi Akiba off to study in a Bet Midrash. He returned after 12 years with 12,000 students. Rabbi Akiba said to them: "*sheli vishelakhem – shelah hu*" – "what is mine and yours – is **hers**".

Mother, Grandmother, Great-Grandmother

Our mother's love for us was unconditional. It didn't matter where we were or what we did. During the past few years, whenever I called her, I would say "Mom, how are you?" and Mom would reply "Much better – now that I hear your voice". For the past few years, whenever I left Columbia to go back to Israel, Mom would say things like "Do you have to leave?" or "It's a shame you live so far". Our mother was a Zionist and was proud of the fact that I lived in Israel, but it was very difficult for her that we lived so far away – simply because she loved us.

There is no question that Abe and I became Jewish educators because of Mom. It is, of course, true that we had the incredible example of our father, but it was mostly Mom who drove us to school at the Hebrew Academy of Washington (now called the Berman Academy) from 1961-1970. It was 45-60 minutes each way through rush-hour traffic.

It was also Mom who in the late 1960s urged us to join USY. We resisted. We said: "we go to a day school; why do we need to join USY?!" I think that she replied that we should share some of the knowledge that we had acquired. So we began to give *divrei torah* and lead singing at USY *kinusim* and conventions – and the rest is history.

One more vignette: for many years every year Mom would bake *hamentashen* and send them to us by airmail to Israel. They arrived **before** Purim or **on** Purim or **after** Purim. They usually arrived in many small pieces, but that made no difference. Each package of *hamentashen* was a package of pure love.

Mom loved Chaya and Mordy and Yair very much, even though she did not see them often enough. She loved telling stories about Chaya as an infant because she saw Chaya a lot until age 3, when we lived in New Jersey for 3 years. Mom liked to recount: When Chaya wanted her Savta to cut something, she would say "Savta, make two pieces" and when she needed help going up the stairs, she would say "Savta, help Chaya".

Mom loved hearing stories about the kids and would "*kvell*" at their successes. She loved to talk to them on the phone. Her last phone calls were to Chaya and Mordy on Thursday, January 12th.

During the past three years, Mom doted on stories about her great-grandson Rei, whom she met two years ago. Whenever I told her stories about Rei, her eyes would light up and her face would break into a huge smile.

In conclusion, I want to thank the many people here in Columbia – they are too numerous to mention by name – who helped our mother since June 2002, when she had her hip operation, and especially since this past September, when her health began to decline. Their support and kindness were incredible and our entire family joins me in saying Todah Rabbah.

Finally, I want to thank my brother Abe, who took care of our mother since June 2002 with amazing devotion. We learn in the Talmud in the tractate of *Kiddushin* 31b:

תנו רבנן: איזהו מורא ואיזהו כיבוד?...
כיבוד -- מאכיל ומשקה, מלביש ומכסה, מכניס ומוציא.

Our Sages have taught:
What is **fear** of parents and what is **honor**?...
Honor – he gives food and gives drink,

he clothes and covers up,
he helps his parents go in and go out.

These days, many people hire **others** to do these tasks. Abe fulfilled the mitzvah of *kibbud av va'em* according to its simple meaning in the Talmud: he did it himself.

Our mother told us on many occasions that she did not want to live in a nursing home. Abe made it possible for her to live in her beloved home on Thunder Hill Road until just a few weeks ago.

Our mother Devorah/Dolly was beloved by her sons, grandchildren and great-grandson; by her sister Sue Cooper, brother-in-law Rabbi Baruch Goldstein, and by her extended family; by her thousands of Hebrew and Spanish pupils throughout North America; and by her hundreds of friends in Arlington, Knoxville and Columbia. *Yehi zikhra baruch!*

A EULOGY FOR RABBI MONIQUE SÜSSKIND GOLDBERG Z"L

(1947-2012)

by David Golinkin

Delivered in Jerusalem, the eve of 27 Adar 5772 – March 3, 2012

Before I eulogize Monique z"l, I want to thank her husband Gavriel. Reb Shlomo z"l made the *shiduch* between them approximately 42 years ago and also performed their wedding. There is no doubt that it was a good *shiduch*. If not for Gavriel's devotion, Monique z"l could not have lived in Jerusalem and could not have accomplished all that she accomplished.

We have learned in *Sanhedrin* 22a: "Rabbi Yoḥanan said: any man who lost his first wife, it is as if the Temple was destroyed in his day". Therefore, Gavriel, we cannot comfort you tonight, but we can thank you for everything you did for Monique for decades.

We have learned in *Yoreh Deah* (344:1) in the Laws of Mourning: "It is a great *mitzvah* to eulogize the deceased as is fitting... and it is forbidden to exaggerate... and a Sage and a *Ḥassid*, one mentions his wisdom and piety". Therefore, I want to stress that the things I will say about Rabbi Monique Süsskind Goldberg z"l are not an exaggeration but the simple truth.

We have learned in *Sanhedrin* 97b: "Abaye said: The world does not contain less than 36 *tzaddikim* who receive the *Shekhinah* in every generation".

There are only two people I have met in my life who, in my opinion, are among the *Lamedvovnikim*, the 36 *tzaddikim*, and Monique z"l was one of them. She was a rare blend of *yirat shamayim*, love of Torah, love of Eretz Yisrael, love of people and *joie de vivre* – despite the severe physical limitations from which she suffered most of her life.

Who is Wealthy?

We have learned in *Pirkei Avot* (4:1): "Ben Zoma said... who is wealthy? He who is happy with his portion, as it is written (Psalms 128:2) 'You shall enjoy the fruit of your labor, you shall be happy and it is good for you' – you shall be happy in this world, and it is good for you in the next".

Most commentators think that Ben Zoma meant a person who is happy with his **wealth**, but Rashi explains (*Mishnat Reuven*, p. 127): "Happy with his portion – and accepts everything favorably, everything which God gives".

Monique z"l had good reasons to be bitter – she contracted polio at the age of two-and-a-half, she spent most of her life in a wheelchair, and she suffered from asthma and other problems connected to her physical condition.

Nevertheless, Monique smiled constantly, loved to laugh, and received everyone with a cheerful countenance. In other words, she was very **wealthy** because she was happy with her lot and "accepted everything favorably, everything which God gives" and about her it is said "you shall be happy in this world and it is good for you in the next".

Love of Torah

I met Monique z"l in 1995 when she came to study at Schechter. She came with a B.A. and an M.A. in Bible from Hebrew University and with an excellent recommendation from Prof. Sara Yefet. But, if I'm not mistaken, she had no background in Talmud and *Halakhah*. But Monique **loved** to learn Torah and she was **very** smart. She was also a *masmid*. She had the *sitzfleisch* to study for many hours in a row. Within a few years, she became a *talmidat hakhamim,* well-versed in Talmud and *Halakhah*.

That is why I chose her in 1999 to become a Research Fellow in the Center for Women and Jewish Law at the Schechter Institute, and she was very successful in that task until she became ill in October 2010. She co-wrote or co-edited ten books or periodicals: seven *Za'akat Dalot* booklets; five *To Learn and to Teach* booklets; the book *Za'akat Dalot; Ask the Rabbi; Responsa and Halakhic Studies* by Rabbi Isaac Klein; *The High Holy Days* by Rabbi Hayyim Kieval; the Index to Prof. Levi Ginzberg's *Legends of the Jews* in Hebrew; *God Believes in Man* by Prof. A.J. Heschel; *Malki Bakodesh*, Vol. 2 by Rabbi Ḥayyim Hirschenson; and the English version of my book *The Status of Women in Jewish Law*.

Monique was a very thorough scholar who possessed the tremendous patience needed to check every source in a book with hundreds of sources.

We have learned in *Yevamot* 97a: "*Talmidei Hakhamim*, when we say a teaching in their name in this world, their lips move in the grave". Monique left a legacy of a shelf full of books and pamphlets. Every time we will learn from them and quote them "her lips move in the grave".

Love of *Eretz Yisrael* and the State of Israel

We have learned in Yerushalmi *Shabbat*, Chapter 1: "Whoever is established in *Eretz Yisrael* and... speaks Hebrew and reads the *Shema* in the morning and the evening, he is guaranteed a place in *Olam Haba*.

Monique loved *Eretz Yisrael*, the State of Israel and Hebrew with all her soul. It would probably have been easier for her to live in Belgium near her family, but she wanted to live in Jerusalem and speak Hebrew, and so she did for over forty years.

Love of People

Monique did not like to speak *Leshon Hara*. Sometimes she needed to tell me some negative information about someone, but she did not want to mention his name. Therefore, she would hint, so that I would take the hint, without mentioning any name.

She also knew how to correct a mistake in a very gentle

fashion. In my Hebrew volume *Ma'amad Ha'isha Bahalakhah* (p. 64, note 40 = above, p. 111, note 40) I quoted something which Rabbi Ḥayyim of Volozhin had said in name of the Gaon of Vilna. I relied on a secondary source, but Monique checked the primary source and discovered that the secondary source had added an entire sentence to the quotation. As usual, she called me on a Friday and said something like "I **think** there is a mistake in this source" and then we checked together and discovered what had transpired.

Yirat Shmayim – Fear of Heaven

We have learned in *Berakhot* 33b: "Rabbi Ḥanina said: Everything is in the hands of Heaven, except for the fear of Heaven".

And Rashi explained: "Everything which happens to a person is from God, such as tall or short, poor or rich, smart or foolish, white or black, everything is in the hands of God. But *tzadik* or *rasha* does not come from Heaven. This was given to a person and He placed before him two paths, and he should **choose** *yirat shamayim*."

Monique's physical state came from God, but **she** chose the path of *yirat shamayim*. Her fear of Heaven was expressed in different ways, such as *tefillah*, observing *mitzvot*, studying Torah and singing – and she particularly liked to sing the songs of her rabbi and teacher, Rabbi Shlomo Carlebach z"l.

Yehi zikhra baruch!

ORIGINAL PLACE OF PUBLICATION

The Participation of Jewish Women: *Nashim* 21 (Spring 2011), pp. 46-66.

***Nine Approaches:** Hebrew originally appeared in *Mada'ey Hayahadut* 40 (5760), pp. 91-102; revised in *Ma'amad*, Introduction. It also appeared in German in *Religionen in Israel* 5 (October 1999), pp. 64-74.

1. ***Tefillin***: Hebrew originally appeared in *Assufot* 11 (5758), pp. 183-196; revised in *Ma'amad*, Chapter 1; English originally appeared in *Conservative Judaism* 50/1 (Fall 1997), pp. 3-18.
2. ***Kol B'isha Ervah***: www.schechter.edu/responsa.aspx?ID=62.
3. ***Minyan* and *Sheliḥot Tzibbur:*** Hebrew originally appeared in *Va'ad Halakhah* 6, pp. 59-80; revised in *Ma'amad*, Chapter 2.
4. ***Imahot***: www.schechter.edu/responsa.aspx?ID=35 = *Responsa in a Moment* II, No. 6.
5. ***Barukh Shepetarani***: Hebrew originally appeared in *Va'ad Halakhah* 5, pp. 101-108; revised in *Ma'amad*, Chapter 3.
6. ***Aliyot***: Hebrew originally appeared in *Va'ad Halakhah* 3, pp. 13-29; revised in *Ma'amad*, Chapter 4.
7. **Reading the Megillah:** www.schechter.edu/responsa.aspx?ID=64
8. **Esther Verses:** www.schechter.edu/responsa.aspx?ID=19 = *Responsa in a Moment* II, No. 19.
9. ***Mohalot:*** www.schechter.edu/responsa.aspx?ID=44 = Responsa in a Moment II, No. 23.
10. ***Funerals**: Hebrew originally appeared in *Va'ad Halakhah* 2, pp. 31-40; revised in *Ma'amad*, Chapter 5.
11. ***Mourner's *Kaddish***: Hebrew originally appeared in *Va'ad Halakhah* 3, pp. 69-80; revised in *Ma'amad*, Chapter 6.

12. ***Marriage Ceremony:** Hebrew originally appeared in *Va'ad Halakhah* 4, pp. 91-103; revised in *Ma'amad*, Chapter 7.
13. ***Poskot**: Hebrew originally appeared in *Va'ad Halakhah* 4, pp. 107-117; revised in *Ma'amad*, Chapter 8.
14. ***Meḥitzah**: Hebrew originally appeared in *Va'ad Halakhah* 2, pp. 5-20; revised in *Ma'amad*, Chapter 9.
15. ***Ordination:** Hebrew originally appeared in *Va'ad Halakhah* 5, pp. 37-69; revised in *Ma'amad*, Chapter 10.

ABBREVIATIONS FOR THE ABOVE LIST

* = the first time this chapter has appeared in English.

Ma'amad = David Golinkin, *Ma'amad Ha'ishah Bahalakhah: She'eilot Uteshuvot*, Jerusalem, 2001.

Responsa in a Moment II = David Golinkin, *Responsa in a Moment*, Vol. II, Jerusalem, 2011.

Va'ad Halakhah = *Responsa of the Va'ad Halakhah of the Rabbinical Assembly of Israel*, Vols. 1-6, 5746-5758; also available online at www.responsafortoday.com

GLOSSARY OF ABBREVIATIONS AND HEBREW TERMS

admor/admorit: a ḥassidic *rebbe*/a female *rebbe.*

agunah/agunot: a chained woman who cannot remarry because her husband refuses to give her a *get.*

aggadah: the opposite of *halakhah,* non-legal portions of the Talmud and midrash.

Aḥaronim: rabbis from the time of the *Shulḥan Arukh* (ca. 1575) until today.

aliyah: the honor of being called to the Torah. In the Talmudic period, and until today among Oriental Jews, each person read his own portion. Since medieval times, most Jews rely on a *ba'al korei* who reads from the Torah while the person who goes up only recites the blessings before and after.

am ha'aretz: an ignorant person.

Amidah: the silent devotion, which is the main prayer in every service.

Amora/Amoraim: Rabbi of the Talmudic period (ca. 220-500 CE), who taught and studied in the academies in Israel and Babylonia.

Arvit: the evening service, also called *Ma'ariv.*

Ashkenaz: originally Germany. Later on came to include France and Eastern Europe as well.

Ashkenazim: the Jews who hail from *Ashkenaz.*

asmakhta: an attempt by the Sages to find scriptural support for an existing rabbinic law.

Barekhu: the call to prayer in the *Shaḥarit* and *Arvit services.*

Barukh Shepetarani; a blessing traditionally recited by a father at the Bar Mitzvah of a son.

Bavli: the Babylonian Talmud.

Beit Din/ Batei Din: court(s) of Jewish law.

Beit Midrash/Batei Midrash: house of study, Talmudic academy.

beraita/beraitot: a tannaitic (see *Tannaim*) dictum not included in the Mishnah.

Birkat Hagomel: a blessing recited upon recovering from a serious illness or after a dangerous journey.

Birkat Kohanim: the Priestly Blessing which is included in the *Amidah* of *Shaḥarit;* in Israel it is recited by the *Kohanim* every day.

CJLS: the Committee on Jewish Law and Standards, founded in 1927, which writes responsa for the Conservative movement.

da'at yaḥid; the lone opinion of one rabbi or *posek.*

Dayan: a judge in a *beit din.*

derashah, derashot; a homiletic explanation of a verse **or** an entitre sermon.

dam tohar: "the blood of purity" which flows after a birth; it should be pure but is considered impure.

davar/devarim shebikdushah: matters of holiness, parts of the liturgy which require a *minyan.*

din Torah: a case brought before a *Beit Din.*

dinei mamonot: Jewish civil law related to monetary cases.

EH : *Even Ha'ezer,* the section of the *Tur* and the *Shulḥan Arukh* dealing with marriage and divorce.

Ein Keloheinu: one of the concluding *piyyutim* which is usually sung together at the end of Shabbat and festival services.

EJ: *Encyclopaedia Judaica,* 16 vols., Jerusalem, 1972.

erev Shabbat: Sabbath eve.

ET: *Entziklopedia Talmudit,* 30 volumes , Jerusalem, 1947ff.

Ezrat Nashim: the Women's Court in the Second Temple; also the modern term for the women's section in Orthodox synagogues.

gabbai: a person who gives out the honors in a synagogue and/or stands next to the Torah reader and corrects the Torah reading. Also a person in charge of collecting and distributing *tzedakah.*

Gemara: the commentaries of the *Amoraim* on the Mishnah; frequently used as a synonym for Talmud.

Geonim: The rabbis who headed the Babylonian academies between the seventh and eleventh centuries. Their authority extended from Babylonia through North Africa and Spain. They wrote commentaries, codes and responsa.

get/gittin: a Jewish writ of divorce

gezeirah shavah: a method of deriving laws when the same word or words appear in two different verses in the Torah.

ḥaddash: the new grain which can only be eaten after the Omer is brought to the Temple on the 16th of Nisan (Leviticus 23:10-14).

haftarah: a portion from the Prophets which parallels the Torah reading; it is read on Shabbat and festivals after the Torah reading.

ḥagigah: a sacrifice offered by visitors to the Temple on the festivals (Exodus 23:14).

hakafot: a procession around the synagogue, with the *lulav* and *etrog* on *Sukkot* and with the Torah scrolls on *Simḥat Torah.*

hakhel: a ceremony of reading the Torah in the Temple once every seven years to the men, women and children – see Deuteronomy 31:10-13.

halakhah: Jewish law.

ḥalitzah: a ceremony which allows a brother's childless widow to remarry – see Deuteronomy 25:5-10.

ḥametz: leavened bread, cakes or crackers which may not be eaten on *Pesaḥ.*

ḥassidim: followers of the Ba'al Shem Tov, a movement of Jews which arose in the 18th century, who wanted to serve God in joy.

ḥazzarat hashatz: the loud repetition of the *Amidah.*

heter: a permissive ruling.

ḥevrah kaddisha: a group of Jews who purify the dead by performing *tohorah* and then bury them.

ḥiddushim; novellae on the Talmud written by *Rishonim* and *Aḥaronim*.

HM : *Ḥoshen Mishpat*, the section of the *Tur* and *Shulḥan Arukh* dealing with civil law.

ḥumash, ḥumashim: originally a scroll which contained one of the five books of Moses; today a printed book which contains the entire Pentateuch or five books of Moses.

ḥuppah: the wedding canopy or the wedding ceremony.

Kabbalat Shabbat: the Friday evening service before *Barekhu* or the entire Friday evening service.

Kaddish: an Aramaic prayer which separates the various parts of the service; the mourners' *Kaddish* is recited by mourners at the end of part of the service or of the entire service.

kal vaḥomer: an argument from minor to major.

kashrut: the Jewish dietary laws.

kavanah: intent.

Kedushah: a liturgical section which is recited during the loud repetition of the *Amidah*.

Kelal Yisrael: the collective Jewish people.

Keriyat Shema: the reading or recitation of the three paragraphs of the *Shema* during *Shaḥarit*, *Arvit*, and before going to sleep.

ketubah/ketubot: a Jewish marriage contract without which a couple may not be married.

kevod haberiyot: human dignity.

Kiddush: the prayer recited over wine on Shabbat and festivals.

kiddush hashem : the sanctification of God's name.

kiddushin: the act of betrothal after which the couple is considered legally married. Today it is the first half of a Jewish wedding ceremony.

kloiz: a synagogue in *Ashkenaz* and Eastern Europe.

kohen, kohanim: descendants of Aaron and the Priestly tribe.

lulav: the palm fronds, one of the four species of plants waved on *Sukkot* (Leviticus 23:40).

Ma'ariv: the evening service, also called *Arvit*.

maftir: the final *aliyah* on Shabbat and festivals; the person who has this *aliyah* reads the *haftarah*.

Marat: Mrs., Madam, an honorific title for a distinguished woman.

megillah: the Scroll or Book of Esther.

meḥitzah: partition separating men and women in a synagogue.

midrash/midrashim: rabbinic exegesis of a verse or an entire compilation of such exegesis such as *Midrash Rabbah*.

mikveh: ritual bath.

Minḥah: the afternoon service.

minyan: a quorum of ten required for specific rituals.

Mishnah: a collection of mostly legal sources, edited by Rabbi Yehudah Hanassi, circa 200 CE.

Mitnagdim: those opposed to the *Ḥassidim*.

mitzvah: commandment.

Mussaf: the additional service recited on *Rosh Ḥodesh,* Shabbat and Festivals.

Mussar: ethics.

Ne'ilah: the fifth and final service on Yom Kippur.

niddah: a menstruating woman.

Nishmat Kol Ḥai: a beautiful prayer recited at the end of the *Pesukei Dezimra* section of the service on Shabbat and festivals.

OH : *Oraḥ Ḥayyim*, the section of the *Tur* and the *Shulḥan Arukh* dealing with prayer, the synagogue, Shabbat and festivals.

Pesukei Dezimra: the preliminary section of Psalms in the *Shaḥarit* service.

perissat shema: the Talmudic practice whereby the leader recites the *Shema* aloud responsively with the congregation.

Pitum Haketoret: a passage from the Talmud describing the incense in the Temple, which is recited after *Ein Keloheinu* in the *Shaḥarit* service.

piyyut/piyyutim: a liturgical poem such as *Lekha Dodi.*

posek/poskim: a halakhic decisor.

poseket/poskot: a female halakhic decisor.

PTBC : positive time-bound commandments.

Rabbanit: the wife of a rabbi.

responsum/responsa: a rabbi's written reply to a halakhic question.

Rishon/Rishonim: Talmudic commentators and *poskim* from the 11th-16th centuries.

Rosh Yeshivah: head of a Talmudic academy.

Sefer Torah: a Torah scroll.

semaḥot : plural of *simḥah,* joyous occasion.

Sepharadim: Jews of Spain or descendants of the Jews expelled from Spain; also used to denote other non-Ashkenazic groups of Jews.

Shaḥarit: the morning service.

sheheḥeyanu: a blessing recited over new fruits and clothing and at the beginning of Jewish festivals.

sheliaḥ/sheliḥat tzibbur: the cantor who leads the congregation in prayer.

Shema: the reading or recitation of the three paragraphs of the *Shema* during *Shaḥarit, Arvit,* and before going to sleep.

sheḥitah: Jewish ritual slaughter.

Shekhinah: God's Divine Presence.

Shemoneh Esreh: the Eighteen Benedictions, a synonym for the weekday *Amidah.*

Sheva Berakhot: the seven wedding blessings, also called *Birkat Ḥattanim.*

Shir Hakavod: a *piyyut,* also called *Anim Zemirot.*

Shofar: the ram's horn blown on Rosh Hashanah.

shul: a Yiddish word for a synagogue.

Shulḥan Arukh: a law code written by Rabbi Yosef Caro (Spain and Israel 1488-1575), to which Rabbi Moshe Isserles, the Rema (Poland 1520-1572) added his glosses, which helped make it the most influential code to this day.

siddur: prayer book.

Simḥat Bat: a ceremony for naming a baby girl.

sugya: a passage of the Talmud which comes to explain one phrase or sentence in the Mishnah.

sukkah: a booth in which Jews eat and sleep during the festival of *Sukkot.*

takkanah: a rabbinic enactment.

tallit: a Jewish prayer shawl which contains four *tzitzit* or specially tied fringes on the four corners.

tallit kattan: a miniature *tallit* worn under the shirt.

Talmud: a series of tractates which include the Mishnah written by the *Tannaim* and the Gemara, the discussions of the Mishnah by the *Amoraim* and the editors of the Talmud. The Babylonian Talmud became the basis for all subsequent Jewish law. Also see Yerushalmi.

Tanna/Tannaim: rabbis of the Mishnah, the *Tosefta*, and the *beraitot* who studied and taught in the Land of Israel from the late Second Temple period until 220 CE.

Targum: an Aramaic translation of the Bible.

tefaḥ/tefaḥim: a handsbreadth used to measure height.

Tefillah: in the Mishnah – the *Amidah;* in later Hebrew – prayer in general.

Tefillin: phylacteries worn on the arm and head in keeping with Deuteronomy 6 and 11.

Tosefta: a collection of *beraitot* (see *beraita*) which was edited according to the order of the Mishnah during the following generation.

tzitzit/tzitiziyot: the special fringes tied on the four corners of a *tallit*.

vekhol ma'aminim: a *piyyut* recited during *Mussaf* on Rosh Hashanah and Yom Kippur.

YD : *Yoreh Deah,* the section of the *Tur* and the *Shulḥan Arukh* dealing with *kashrut, niddah, aveilut* and other rituals.

Yerushalmi : the Jerusalem Talmud, ed. Venice, 1523-1524.

yeshivah: a Talmudic academy.

yibum: levirate marriage – see Deuteronomy 25:5-10.

yiḥud: the prohibition for a man to be alone with a woman lest it lead to sexual impropriety.

yishuv: the Jewish community in Palestine before 1948.

Yom Tov: the three pilgrim festivals and Rosh Hashanah.

zimmun: invitation to begin the Grace after Meals when there are at least three adults who ate together.

Zohar: the classic work of Jewish mysticism attributed to Rabbi Shimon bar Yoḥai but actually written in 13th century Spain by Moshe de Leon.

SUBJECT INDEX

Pages in bold designate an entire chapter devoted to the subject.
A page number may refer to a note on that page.